WORLD POLITICS

Pol Theory 30
& Inter 90
Am FB - 30
I confer Res

ABOUT THE AUTHORS

Alfred de Grazia is Director of the Center for Applied Social Research, New York University, where he is also Professor of Government. He previously taught at the University of Minnesota, Brown University, and Stanford. He has written a dozen books on various phases of political science and many articles in administration, scientific method, and public opinion. He is the editor of the *American Behavioral Scientist*. His nonacademic experience includes positions as a consultant to a number of corporations and government agencies and as a member of the United States delegation to the General Conference of UNESCO.

Thomas H. Stevenson is co-author of two texts in the fields of history and politics, and co-editor and co-author of a third. He is the editor of a collection of essays on social welfare. He has written and translated numerous periodical and encyclopedia articles. He is the translator of a forthcoming new English-language edition of Frédéric Bastiat's *Sophismes Économiques*. He has been a member of the faculties of William Woods College, the University of Santa Clara, and Michigan College of Mining and Technology.

COLLEGE OUTLINE SERIES

WORLD POLITICS

A Study in International Relations

by
ALFRED DE GRAZIA
New York University

THOMAS H. STEVENSON
*Formerly, Michigan College
of Mining and Technology*

BARNES & NOBLE, INC., NEW YORK

PUBLISHERS • BOOKSELLERS • SINCE 1873

Thanks are owing to Mrs. Stephanie Neuman and Professor Robert Woetzel for their helpful readings of the manuscript, and to Mr. George B. de Huszar for his co-operation in the planning of the book.

This book is an original work (No. 76) in the original College Outline Series. It was written by distinguished educators, carefully edited, and produced in accordance with the highest standards of publishing. The text was set on the Linotype in Old Style No. 7 by the Plimpton Press (Norwood, Mass.). The paper for this edition was manufactured by the S. D. Warren Company (Boston, Mass.) and supplied by the Canfield Paper Company (New York, N.Y.). This edition was printed by the Hamilton Printing Company (Rensselaer, N.Y.) and bound by Sendor Bindery (New York, N.Y.). The cover was designed by Rod Lopez-Fabrega.

CONTENTS

PART 3   INSTRUMENTS OF
          WORLD POLITICS

CHARTS AND MAPS

Tabulated Bibliography of Standard Textbooks

This *College Outline* is keyed to standard textbooks in two ways.

1. If you are studying one of the following textbooks, consult the cross references here listed to find which pages of this *Outline* correspond to the appropriate chapter of your text. (Roman numerals refer to the textbook chapters or units, Arabic figures refer to the pages of this *Outline*.)*

2. If you are using this *Outline* as your basis for study and want another treatment of the subject, consult the pages of any of the standard textbooks as indicated in the Quick Reference Table on pp. x–xiii.

Haas, Ernst, and Whiting, Allen S. *Dynamics of International Relations.* New York: McGraw-Hill Book Company, Inc., 1956.

II (331–334); V–VI (123–132); VII (106–107, 285–288); VIII (110–111); IX (334–337); XI (109–111, 325–328); XII–XIII (141–143, 146–147); XIV (95–96, 107–109, 154–156, 158–160); XV (245–248); XVI (68–70, 74–78); XVII (279–280, 299–301); XVIII (288–294, 296–299); XIX (348–350, 356–360); XX (112–113, 307–310, 345–348, 351–353); XXI (162, 177, 197–198, 338–343); XXII (103–106, 114–115, 117–118).

Hartmann, Frederick H. *The Relations of Nations.* 2nd ed. New York: The Macmillan Company, 1962.

I (1–6); II (9–15, 18–21, 331–334); III (123–132); V (106–107, 285–288); VI (275–280, 296, 350); IX–X (20–21, 50–52, 345–351, 355–356); XI (294–296); XII (351–353); XIV (37, 63–64, 307–310); XVII (110–111, 158); XIX (61–62, 69–72, 74–78); XX (70–71); XXI (112–113); XXII (26–29, 94–96, 109–111); XXV (108, 115–116); XXVI (68–70, 100–101, 181–182); XXVII (61–63, 81–82, 175–177); XXVIII (165–166); XXIX (244–271); XXX (100, 221–222); XXXI (108–109, 216–217, 225, 227–234, 237).

Lerche, Charles O. *Principles of International Politics.* New York: Oxford University Press, 1956.

II (280–281, 331–334); III (285–287, 334–337); IV (123–135); V (112–113); VI (104–106, 110–111, 114–115, 145, 158); VII (106–107, 110, 286–288, 296–297); VIII (279–281, 282–284, 288–301, 350–353); IX (356–360); X (50–52, 345–351); XI (104, 115, 338–343); XII (315–318, 320–328); XIII (105, 327–334); XIV (302–305).

Mills, Lennox A., and McLaughlin, Charles H. *World Politics in Transition.* New York: Holt, Rinehart and Winston, Inc., 1956.

I (1–6, 112–113); II (9–15, 280–281); III (114–115, 331–334); IV (105); V (123–135, 307–310); VI (334–337); IX (125–128); X (124–125, 312–318, 320–325);

* This *Outline* is unique among books on its subject in that it devotes a section entirely to the history of world politics. Since tabulating this section would make the Tabulated Bibliography unnecessarily long and complicated, most cross references to Part I have been omitted. The student may find the appropriate discussion in the *Outline* by consulting the Index.

XI (106–107, 285–288); XII–XIII (142–143, 155–156, 164–165, 176, 181, 285–287); XIV (275–284, 288–296); XV (345–351, 356–360); XVI (112–113, 351–353); XVII (94–96, 104, 109–111, 145–147); XVIII (165–166); XIX (166–169, 227–234, 235–236, 258); XX (171–174, 175, 176–177); XXI (96, 100–101, 181–182, 198–199); XXII (70–73, 182, 184–185); XXIII (218–222); XXIV (95–96, 100, 101, 107–108, 115–116, 158–160, 197–198); XXV (108–109, 116–117, 211–213ff., 224–225); XXVI (104, 110–112, 145, 307–310); XXVII (110, 357, 358–359); XXVIII (114–115, 234–260, 325–328, 353–354); XXIX (302–305, 334–337, 340–343).

Morgenthau, Hans J. *Politics among Nations*. 3rd ed. New York: Alfred A. Knopf, 1960.

I–II (1–6); V (10–12, 15–16, 23–24, 27–29); VII (105); VIII–X (123–132); XV–XVII (114–115, 331–334); XVII (279–280, 296, 350); XIX (281); XX (104–106, 334–337); XXI (104, 115–116); XXIII (63–64, 307–310); XXIV (70–71, 112–113); XXVI (352–354); XXVII (21, 50–52, 58, 61); XXVIII (345–351); XXX (325–328, 340–343, 356–360); XXXI–XXXII (106–107, 285–288).

Organski, A. F. K. *World Politics*. New York: Alfred A. Knopf, 1958.

I (1–6); II–IV (12–13, 14–16, 18–19, 21–23, 114–115, 331–334); V–VIII (121–132); IX (257, 282); X (197–198); XII (20–23, 103–107, 132–135); XIII (106–107, 285–288); XIV–XVI (50–52, 68, 70–71, 345–351, 356–360).

Padelford, Norman J., and Lincoln, George A. *The Dynamics of International Politics*. New York: The Macmillan Company, 1962.

I–II (1–6); III–IV (123–132); V (105, 330–331); VI (18–19, 21–23, 114–115, 331–334); VII (10–12, 15–16, 23–24, 27–29, 32–39, 107–109, 116–117, 257); VIII (302–307); X (141–143); XI (164–165, 175–177); XII (154–156, 214–215); XIII (106–107, 285–288); XIV (334–337); XV (107, 118, 325–328); XVI (307–310); XVII (275–284, 291–296, 299–301); XVIII (50–52, 345–360); XIX (110–111, 145, 162, 177, 197–198, 338–343).

Palmer, Norman D., and Perkins, Howard C. *International Relations*. 2nd ed. Boston: Houghton Mifflin Company, 1957.

I (12–13ff., 114–115, 280–281, 331–334); II (125–128); III (125–126, 128–132, 312–316, 318–320); IV (106–107, 285–288); V (107, 118, 334–337); VI (66–67); VII (107–109, 116–117, 256–257, 282); VIII (37, 63–64, 307–310); X (294–296); XI (275–280); XII (50–52, 62–64, 96–99, 345–351, 356–360); XIII (112–113, 309–310, 351–353); XIV (328, 356–360); XV (99–101, 110, 340–341); XVI (108–109, 114–115, 216–217ff., 312–318); XVII (82–83, 111–112, 261–271); XVIII (114–115, 244–248, 252–260); XIX (325–328); XX (110–111, 338–343); XXI (100–101, 107–109, 115–118, 158–160, 197–198); XXII (25–33, 94–96, 100–101, 109–113, 117–118, 141–143, 145–147); XXIII (See index); XXIV (302–305); XXV (104–105, 280–281, 312–318, 331–334).

Rienow, Robert. *Contemporary International Politics*. New York: Thomas Y. Crowell Company, 1961.

I (10–15, 20–23, 275–277, 280–281, 331–334); II (123–132); III (136–137); IV (42–43, 48, 55–56, 148–160); V (162–170, 258); VI (110–111, 171–195, 340–343); VII (261–271); VIII (244–252); IX (114–115, 209–243); X (114–115, 252–260); XI (285–288); XII (197–203); XIII (276–277, 296–299, 302–305); XIV (334–337); XV (279–284, 288–294, 296–301); XVI (96–99, 345–351); XVII–XVIII (110–111, 117–118, 338–343); XIX (304–307); XXI (312–328, 357).

Schleicher, Charles P. *International Relations*. Englewood Cliffs, N.J.: Prentice-Hall, Inc., 1962.

I (1–6); II (9–93); III (12–13, 18–19, 21–22, 114–115, 331–334); IV (105); VII (106–107, 285–288); VIII (50–52, 96–99, 345–351); IX (110–112, 117–118, 338–343); X (294–296); XI (123–132); XIII (296–299, 302–305); XIV (115); XV (110–111, 117–118, 353–355); XVI (328, 349–350, 356–360); XVIII (275–

278, 299–301); XX (307–310); XXI (136–147); XXII (109–111, 162–164, 171–177, 178–182, 188–194, 205–208, 338–343); XXIII (103–109, 115–116, 118, 148–160, 327); XXIV (108–109, 112–113, 209–225); XXV (114–115, 227–243); XXVI (244–252, 352–354); XXVII (114–115, 252–260); XXVIII (29–32, 261–271, 338–340).

Schuman, Frederick L. *International Politics*. 6th ed. New York: McGraw-Hill Book Company, Inc., 1958.
Prologue (1–6); I (9–11); II (11–17, 276–277); III (18–118); IV (101–102, 275, 280–281ff.); V (294–296, 350); VI (83–84, 95–100, 285–288); VII (20–21, 50–52, 62–64, 67–68, 70–73, 97–99, 112–113, 307–310, 345–353, 355–360); IX (111–112, 114–115, 338–340, 343, 349–350); X (149, 227–260, 331–334); Addenda (353–354); XI (66–92, 99–100, 180–181, 183–185, 221–222); XII (103–109, 112–113, 115–118, 154–160, 197–198, 211–217); XIII (66–78, 81–84, 86–88, 103–107, 109–113, 117–118, 146–147, 165–166, 175–177); XIV (114–115, 227–232, 252–260, 261–271, 312–328); XV (302–310).

Van Dyke, Vernon. *International Politics*. New York: Appleton-Century-Crofts, 1957.
I (1–6); III (280–281); IV (331–334); V (105); VI (15–16, 23–24); VIII (330–331); X (123–132); XII (307–310); XIII (326, 340–341, 357–359); XIV (106–107, 282–288, 294–296); XV (279, 288–294, 296–301); XVI (302–307); XVII (118, 325–328, 334–337); XVIII (50–52, 67–68, 70–73, 96–99, 345–351); XIX (348–349, 356–360); XX (197–198, 256–257, 282, 349–350).

QUICK REFERENCE TABLE TO STANDARD TEXTBOOKS

(Roman type indicates pages. Italic type indicates chapters.)

Chapter in Outline	Topic	Haas & Whiting	Hart-mann	Lerche	Mills & McLaugh-lin	Morgen-thau	Organ-ski	Padelford & Lincoln	Palmer & Perkins	Rienow	Schlei-cher	Schu-man	Van Dyke
I	Introduction: The Study of World Politics		*1*		3-10	*1, 2*	*1*	*2*	xi-xxxvi		*1*	2-27	*1*
II	The Beginnings of the Modern State System		21-27 134-135 137-138		110-111 130-131				6-9 191-192 248-251		19-23	*1, 2*	
III	World Politics from 1789 to 1900		27-30 135-137 138-143 357-364		111 131-138	457-465			9-12 17-19 192-198 251-253		23-26 49-51 150-151	80-89	
IV	The Growth of the United States, 1789 to 1917	289-291			318-320				198-201 698-699				
V	The Background and Campaigns of World War I		364-373		414-419 460 493-496	290-291						89-93	
VI	The Peace Settlement after World War I	463-466	191-201 215-223	233-234 277-284	55-60 320-330 347-351 460-462	298-303 440-441 465-477	411-416		337-347			93-94 159-161 210-217 328-330	357-367

x

See pages vii–ix for complete list of titles.

QUICK REFERENCE TABLE TO STANDARD TEXTBOOKS (Continued)

(Roman type indicates pages. Italic type indicates chapters.)

Chapter in Outline	Topic	Haas & Whiting	Hart-mann	Lerche	Mills & McLaughlin	Morgen-thau	Organ-ski	Padelford & Lincoln	Palmer & Perkins	Rienow	Schlei-cher	Schu-man	Van Dyke
XV	The British Commonwealth of Nations		566-574		223-228 251-254 433-438 440-446			286-298 541-543	732-750	*5*	483-485	579-586	
XVI	Western Europe		541-556		*13* 20-22 228-236			298-304 543-545	750-758 764-766	*6*	485-490	462-467 483-495 563-574	
XVII	Eastern Europe						262-268		673-682				
XVIII	Communist China							320-331	758-761	160-163	518-526	537-541	
XIX	Japan, South Korea, and Nationalist China		599-606 612-615		554-556				764-766		526-542	448-454	
XX	South and Southeast Asia		615-624		448-453 679-698				761-763	158-160 163-174	*25*	380-391 633-637	
XXI	The Middle East and Africa South of the Sahara	*15*	576-586		446-448 646-672				*18*	*8, 10*	*26, 27*	371-380 637-640	
XXII	Latin America		586-590						*17*	*7*	*28*	629-633	

xii

See pages vii-ix for complete list of titles.

1   INTRODUCTION: THE STUDY OF WORLD POLITICS

This book deals with the facts that explain world events. It describes the interrelations of nations and peoples as shown by their political and military history, their power capabilities, and the instruments they use to carry out their foreign policies.

THE PRESENT GREAT INTEREST IN WORLD POLITICS

Since World War II the American people have had a greater interest in world politics than ever before. This heightened interest is the product of numerous factors. Probably the most important of these factors has been the shift in the seat of world power, in which predominance over world politics has moved from western Europe to the United States and the Soviet Union. Correspondingly, the United States government has assumed a vastly increased role in world affairs. As a consequence, the problems of distant lands may affect the life of every American citizen. This situation results from such developments as the two recent world wars, various technological advances, and changed attitudes among the leaders of the United States.

Shift in the Seat of World Power. Since about the year 1900 there has been a pronounced shift in the seat of world power, from the countries of Europe on or near the Atlantic seacoast to countries either partly or entirely non-European. During the period extending approximately from the year 1500 to 1900, the dominant states of the world were European, notably Spain, Portugal, France, Holland, Great Britain, Germany, and Italy. In the nineteenth century, however, certain other states became the seats of increasing concentrations of power; this process was accelerated in the twentieth century by such events as the two world wars and the diffusion of industrial techniques among previously "backward" peoples. Today, as a result, the United States and the Soviet Union—the "superpowers"—overshadow any individual country in western Europe; China and Japan are in many ways comparable to major European countries, and China is a potential superpower; and India, Pakistan, and Indonesia are all potential great powers.

The Present Status of World Power. The present status of world power has two main characteristics, which are distinctive but interrelated: *bipolarity* and the *"Cold War."* Bipolarity refers to the situation in which there are but two countries in the world that exercise controlling power over the world community—the United States and the Soviet Union—and these serve as poles attracting or repelling all other countries. This is a unique situation in world history. The "Cold War" is simply the present form of the war declared in 1918 by Soviet leaders against all non-Soviet states in the world. The "Cold War" phase of the Soviet struggle for world-wide hegemony began in the years 1944–45, when the Soviet Union by a series of steps installed a Soviet-dominated government in Poland. The "Cold War" is waged with every available instrument of attack and defense except organized, uniformed troops that wage battles openly. The "Cold War" is related to bipolarity in that the United States is the main target of Soviet aggression.

Increased Role of the United States in World Politics. Although by 1865 the population, territory, and agricultural output of the United States rivaled those of the European great powers, neither American leaders nor the American public seemed to want the United States to have a major role in world politics. Americans in general were far more concerned with the development of their own country and with the countries of Latin America. Moreover, they had a tradition, confirmed in the Monroe Doctrine, of noninterference in European problems. Since the 1890's, however, and particularly since 1939, most American leaders have sought to wield the power of the United States in the arena of world politics. Today the chief motives for the exercise of this power are the defense of American overseas strategic and commercial interests; the protection of many countries whose national independence and well-being are deemed essential to the security of the United States; and the upholding of principles, even overseas, that are believed fundamental to American political, economic, social, and cultural life.

The Role of the American Citizen in World Politics. Because of the increased power of the United States relative to other countries in the world, and because of the determination of most American leaders that this power be exercised in the realm of world politics, the individual American citizen has a major role in world politics. For instance, the

American citizen is taxed to support the armed forces necessary to back present-day American foreign policy and to finance the various programs of American monetary aid to other countries. Also, as a voter he is called on periodically to take some share in creating foreign policy by his choices in national elections. Moreover, under present law he may be obliged to pass a specified time in the armed forces. Finally, he may expect to be personally involved should the United States be the target of military attack. To understand what his role is, and to learn how he can act within this role in co-operation with other individuals who seek a peaceful world in which they can enjoy the maximum possible number of their traditional freedoms, the individual American citizen needs to study world politics.

THE RISE OF THE FIELD OF INTERNATIONAL RELATIONS

The field of international relations—that is, relations among governments and peoples—which is the principal subject of world politics, is one of the newest of the social studies.

Development of International Law. The development of international law—the body of rules that are often used to define relations among governments—was an important factor in the rise of the field of international relations. International law emerged because of practical needs, especially after the Treaty of Westphalia, which closed the Thirty Years' War (1618–48) and laid the basis for the modern state system. The most important aspect of international law in this connection is its implication that, at least to some extent, governments are sovereign and responsible legal entities. Because of its emphasis upon the sovereignty of states and the rights of neutrals, the study of international law was particularly suited to the feeling of aloofness toward other countries that Americans displayed in the nineteenth century.

Emergence of the Field of International Relations. The emergence of the field of international relations can be dated from, and largely ascribed to, the increasingly close relations among governments and peoples after 1648. By the nineteenth century these relations were continuous and virtually omnipresent. They involved mainly such questions as trade, imperialism, and colonization; however, they were concerned with the social and cultural realms of human behavior as well. Growing recognition of the significance of these relations promoted the study of international relations.

Recent Stimuli for the Study of International Relations. The principal recent stimuli for the study of international relations have been

the two world wars and the work of organizing the League of Nations
and the United Nations. The wars brought a heightened demand for information about world politics that led to a great employment of foreign correspondents by newspapers and that caused governments to discuss their foreign policies at length with the public. They also led to an
expanded study of international relations. Whereas before World War I
there was little academic attention given to this subject, today almost
all universities, and many colleges as well, offer courses in international
relations. This process was speeded by the wider recognition of the fact
that the study of international law, which is concerned with intergovernmental (and, only indirectly, private) relations in a narrow sense, is
insufficient to explain the ever-increasing variety of relations among nations. The League of Nations, and even more the United Nations, helped
to widen this recognition through their possession of agencies designed
to cope with international economic and social problems. Finally, the
very work of organizing the League and the United Nations led to a
more thorough scrutiny of international law, politics, and economics.

SCOPE AND METHOD OF INTERNATIONAL
RELATIONS

The field of international relations is in one sense as old as men's deliberations about how to control their tribe's relations with another
tribe. Certainly, too, Greek and Roman philosophers dealt with war and
peace, and with the disputes between Greeks and Persians, Romans and
barbarians. Later, writers of the sixteenth and seventeenth centuries, especially in Italy, Spain, and Holland, produced a voluminous literature,
first on what laws could and did control the relations among nations,
and second on what really were the ways in which nations conducted
their interrelations. At this point, and until the twentieth century, the
field embraced the study of international law, diplomatic practice, and
political history.

Present-Day Scope of the Field. Today the field includes these
three areas and much more.

THE SCOPE ACCORDING TO PROFESSOR WRIGHT. Professor Quincy
Wright in *The Study of International Relations* gives the field a broad
scope indeed. He declares that it should draw upon all materials relevant
to understanding decisions important to world affairs. World history, political geography, regional economic studies, psychology, and sociology
can all contribute to this goal. All of these, and more, help develop what
he calls the "root disciplines." These are international law, diplomatic
history, military science, international politics, international organiza-

tion, international trade, colonial government, and the conduct of foreign relations.

NEW DEVELOPMENTS. Within these areas there are many new developments. For instance, the subject "colonial government" must be revised so as to deal principally with "ex-colonial government relations with ex-colonies," in addition to which there must be a subtopic for the relations between the Soviet Union and its satellite "colonies" of Eastern Europe. "Space law" is a new branch of international law. Comparative psychology is taking a large place in the study of the conduct of foreign relations, as "wars of nerves," "psychological warfare," and "making friends through economic aid" become important.

The Method of Studying International Relations. The method of studying international relations involves many techniques, that is, the technique of each discipline that contributes to the study of world affairs. The techniques of these disciplines, such as geography, demography, and history, are to be applied to specific problems. Let us assume that a person undertakes to study the controversy between India and Communist China in the last decade over the national independence of Tibet. First, he assimilates all the background material he can relative to the interrelations of the two disputing countries, the similar and the distinctive traits of their governments, their political geography, their ways of life, their present-day policies, and their alliances and enmities with other countries and peoples. Then he studies what he can find about Tibet. If possible, he will next journey to India in order to interview Indians and Tibetans in India who were involved in the dispute. Since he may not be able to talk with the Chinese Communists, he will try to reach people who have talked with them about this subject. He may collect and analyze questionnaires. He will collect and analyze Chinese, Tibetan, and Indian materials such as proclamations, newspapers, and debates. If there is much material, he will use the quantitative techniques known as "content analysis." If he thinks it useful, he might put the whole problem in the framework called "the decision-making approach" in which he strives to discover how the Indian authorities reached certain decisions. Or he might choose the framework of "game-theory," viewing all the moves of the Chinese and the Indians as a playing-out of the possibilities of each contestant in the struggle to determine the fate of Tibet. Or he might engage in "elite analysis"; that is, by isolating the leaders involved in the actions of the three countries, he might seek to show, by psychological and sociological analysis, how the characters, backgrounds, and typical modes of behavior of the leaders influenced the actions they took. These are a few examples of the techniques and approaches that the researcher may choose in order to cope with his problem.

The Approaches of This Outline. This introductory outline of international relations approaches the field by the easiest routes. First, it analyzes world politics from a historical point of view. Such an analysis describes the emergence of great powers and their behavior toward one another and reveals the forces that work for peace as well as those that work for war. Second, it reviews the world power structure, indicating the various factors that make a country a great power and describing both the great powers and a number of other significant states and regions. Third, the book discusses the various instruments that governments and their leaders may use to carry out national foreign policy—international law, economic and psychological tools, war and disarmament, and the United Nations—and attempts to assess the extent of, and limits on, the capabilities of each instrument.

Review Questions

1. What factors in particular underlie the present great interest in world politics in the United States?

2. What role in world politics is being presented to the American citizen?

3. What is the connection between international law and the study of international relations?

4. What factors in recent years have stimulated the study of international relations?

5. What effect have certain occurrences since 1945 had upon the scope of international relations as it was defined by Professor Quincy Wright?

6. Considering the many techniques in the method for studying international relations, just how would one go about studying the dispute between the Netherlands and Indonesia over West New Guinea?

PART 1 THE HISTORY OF WORLD POLITICS

2 THE BEGINNINGS OF THE MODERN STATE SYSTEM

Although governments with some institutions similar to those of today existed in ancient and medieval times, the nation-state, which distinguishes world politics today, came into being about 1500. It arose out of a combination of a strong, centralized government and of a feeling of nationalism. Several large nations became prominent in Europe and fought for power during the sixteenth, seventeenth, and eighteenth centuries. Most powerful of these were France, England, and Spain in western Europe, and Sweden, Russia, and Turkey in eastern Europe. At the same time, the nations of Europe established colonies overseas. Thirteen English colonies in North America became the United States.

GOVERNMENTS IN ANCIENT AND MEDIEVAL TIMES

In ancient and medieval times, governments arose in many places. Some of these governments had institutions and practices not unlike those of governments today, and others provided the roots from which modern governments grew.

Primitive Governments. Primitive governments had little if any formal organization, for the state as it exists today is of comparatively recent origin. Among prehistoric men, the family was often the basis of the political order. Superior to the family were family systems and clans, which included a number of families stemming from a common ancestor. Still larger were the tribes, comprised usually of a number of clans or family systems. Tribes often warred against one another, in disputes over such matters as land, water, cattle, or women. Yet there were also long periods of peace, which contributed to the development of more advanced cultures. Today in many parts of Africa the real government is still at the tribal stage.

9

Early Empires. Empires, consisting of large areas ruled by a single government, developed in many parts of the ancient world, including China, India, Assyria, Persia, and Egypt. Ordinarily these empires were the results of conquests by one state of its weaker neighbors. Partly for this reason, the governments of these empires were almost invariably despotic. For technological reasons there were few political or military contacts between these empires save those that abutted on one another. Nevertheless, there is evidence of considerable economic and even cultural interchange between empires remote from one another.

The City-State. The type of political organization called the city-state was best known in Greece during the first millennium before Christ.

Origins of the Greek City-State. The city-state, a small political unit that in some areas, such as Egypt and Italy, was the forerunner of an empire, appeared in many parts of the world. In ancient times nowhere was it so successful a political body as in Greece. The origins of the city-state in Greece owed much to the configuration of the land, for Greece is cut up into many small, comparatively isolated valleys. In such a valley, one village would make itself supreme over all the others and over the neighboring countryside as well. Though the city-state, like the early empires, was often the product of conquest, in many cases the government was not despotic. Rather, the political leaders might give the citizens—a privileged group that was a minority of the population— a considerable voice in the government.

Relations among Greek City-States. Although these city-states were divided from one another by mountain ranges and arms of the sea, they nevertheless maintained fairly close relations with one another. These relations were sufficiently close that the city-states might compose their own rivalries to fight such non-Greek peoples as the Persians, whom they termed "barbarians."

Relations among the city-states had certain similarities to modern international relations. These governments exchanged representatives (modern ambassadors), negotiated treaties, and waged wars over such issues as colonial possessions. They also adhered to a rudimentary code of international law. A noteworthy "modern" goal of these city-states was to achieve a *balance of power,* a situation in which no city-state would be so weak or so isolated that it might be confronted by an overwhelming force of enemies. An outstanding illustration of this principle occurred during the Peloponnesian War, involving Athens and its allies against Sparta and its allies; to overcome Athenian superiority—in modern terms, to "redress the balance of power"—the Spartans asked and received aid from Persia, which helped them defeat the Athenians. The

Greeks even formed intertribal associations, which were rude predecessors of the United Nations, composed of representatives from a dozen or more city-states. The most famous, the Delphian Amphictyony, lasted from before 600 B.C. until after 100 A.D.; its main function was the protection of two religious shrines.

The Roman Empire. The Roman Empire was probably the greatest political and legal achievement of ancient times. Rome originated as a small city-state in Italy. The Roman people expanded their state first by conquering the other city-states and peoples of Italy, and then by overrunning and absorbing western Europe, northern Africa, and much of western Asia. In its most flourishing years, the first two centuries of the Christian Era, the imperial government brought a prosperity and a stability to the lives of the one hundred million inhabitants of the Empire that has ever since been termed the *Pax Romana*. This vast structure was united by the combined forces of Roman law, the bureaucracy, the army, an excellent system of roads, and a prosperous and interdependent economic network. From about the year 200 A.D., however, the Roman Empire slowly disintegrated as a result of such factors as the high taxes needed to support the Roman "welfare state" and the military predominance in the government, until 476, when Germanic tribes that had invaded the Empire seized control of the government. The Roman Empire was best known in later years as a regime that, in the era of the *Pax Romana*, had assured order under law. It is significant that, since the Romans controlled almost all of what they knew of the world, they never developed a concept of international relations.

The Early Middle Ages. During the Early Middle Ages, a period that is commonly dated from 476 A.D. until about 1000 A.D., political organization in western Europe gradually deteriorated into the pattern known as *feudalism*. Under feudalism there was a complicated patchwork of tiny political units governed by a multitude of petty rulers. Warfare among these rulers was so commonplace that this was one of the most disorderly periods in history. There were two agencies that strove to repress this disorder. One was the Roman Catholic Church, whose leaders, the popes, by the year 1000 were making claims to extensive political power as well as religious authority. The second was the revived Roman Empire, which, it was hoped, would restore the *Pax Romana*. By the year 1000 the Empire—later called the Holy Roman Empire—consisted of little more than the area of modern Germany, Austria, and northern Italy; yet it was supposed to be universal, the temporal counterpart of the universal Church. Significantly, at this time the emperor received his crown from the pope, a ceremony meant to symbolize the

subordination of the Empire to the Church. The rest of Europe was occupied by a host of small countries, all of whose rulers presumably were
subject to both the pope and the head of the Empire.

The High and Later Middle Ages. The High and Later Middle
Ages, which extended roughly from 1000 to 1500, were an era of great
political and economic developments. The period opened with a titanic
struggle between the Empire and the Church for political power, a struggle that ended only when each had effectively destroyed the political
power of the other outside its respective boundaries. By the year 1500
the direct political power of the Church was confined to a small area in
Italy called the Papal States. Yet the Church still exercised great political influence throughout western Europe; and the popes began depu-
tizing representatives, similar to ambassadors, to uphold the interests of
the Church outside the Papal States. Meanwhile the direct political
power of the Empire had been limited to the territory of the Empire
itself. Within the Empire, the emperors no longer received their crown
from the pope, and they had little real authority except over the "crown
lands"—the areas belonging to the imperial family. In most of the German part of the Empire and in most of eastern Europe the feudal lords
were still supreme. There was, however, a loose federation of merchant
groups in cities from London across the Empire to Novgorod, banded
together as the Hanseatic League. This league signalized the rebirth of
trade in northern Europe. Finally, in Italy there developed several vigorous city-states much like those of ancient Greece. They waged wars,
formed alliances, strove for a balance of power, exchanged diplomats,
and altogether provided a model for western European politics in the
coming centuries.

EMERGENCE OF THE NATION-STATE

The nation-state, which ever since about 1500 has been the increasingly predominant form of sovereign political unit, emerged as a combination of a strong, centralized monarchic form of government with the
sentiment of nationalism.

The Rise of the Centralized Monarchies. The first strong, centralized monarchies of modern times were those that arose in the western
European countries of England, France, Spain, and Portugal, during the
Later Middle Ages. In these countries the monarchs acquired the
strength to subdue the feudal lords in the course of fulfilling military
needs. The kings of England and France, for example, created effective
military forces to wage the Hundred Years' War (1337–1453); the
rulers in Spain and Portugal created such forces to expel the Moham-

medans from their realms. Efforts elsewhere in Europe to establish strong governments had varying success. For instance, the rulers of the Holy Roman Empire waged the Thirty Years' War in part to create such a regime. However, after this war the Empire—that is to say, Germany—was still a decentralized state and remained so for over two centuries more. In Poland, the feudal lords were so strong, and so jealous of their prerogatives, that no king ever subjugated them. In Russia, Tsars Ivan IV (the Terrible) (1547–84) and Peter I (the Great) (1689–1725) laid the basis for a government similar to those of the western monarchies. In these centralized monarchies the kings generally enjoyed the support of the local clergy and the growing merchant class in their struggle with the feudal lords. These governments were held together by strong royal armies, relatively efficient fiscal systems, and a flourishing economic life.

Character of the Nation-State. The nation-state is a governmental entity that, ideally at least, includes the people of only one nation, and *all* the people of that nation. The term *nation*, although often used interchangeably with the term *country*, means specifically a group of people possessing a sense of unity derived from one or more of such common traits as language, social or cultural patterns, religion, traditions, and government. The people of a nation generally possess symbols of their unity; in the period from about 1500 until about 1800 the symbols of most nations were their ruling houses, or dynasties, such as the Bourbons of France and the Tudors of England. Hence the sentiment at the base of their unity is called *dynastic nationalism*. It must be emphasized that the sentiment of nationalism, whether dynastic or otherwise, has not come to all peoples at the same time. As early as the fifteenth century the French people experienced a sense of nationalism with the exploits of the "warrior-saint," Joan of Arc. On the other hand, it would be difficult to find an instance of Russian nationalism before the Napoleonic invasion of 1812. The sense of nationalism that is widely attributed to the African peoples today actually involves only a very small number of political leaders.

Governments of the Early Nation-States. The governments of almost all the nation-states prior to the French Revolution of 1789 were absolute monarchies. The king generally claimed that he ruled by "divine right"—that is, that he had secured his powers directly from God, and was responsible to God alone. Such kings were subject to little, if any, formal control. The chief exception was England, where during the seventeenth century certain leaders in Parliament succeeded in transforming the government into a limited monarchy, in which the king was subordinate to Parliament. Under this regime the English people were assured certain political and judicial rights that protected them from arbitrary acts by government officials; by the year 1700 English politicians had founded the basis for a two-party system. Still, only a relatively small percentage of the population was qualified to vote or sit in Parliament.

Economic Principles of the Early Nation-States. The economic principles of the early nation-states comprised a system called *mercantilism*. Under mercantilism, the governments of the nation-states attempted to control economic life for the benefit of the country and the government. According to mercantilist theory, the economic strength of a nation could be measured by the quantity of gold and silver it possessed. This gold and silver was to be obtained by the sale of goods—preferably manufactured—to the people of other countries. Hence to achieve wealth and power, a nation must possess considerable industry, enjoy a favorable balance of trade, and secure numerous colonies as sources of raw materials.

Interrelations among the Nation-States in Europe, 1500–1789. The interrelations among the nation-states in Europe from about the year 1500 until 1789 were typified chiefly by power politics conducted for the benefit of, or at least in the name of, the principal dynasties. Only in England after 1603 and in Holland and Poland were dynastic interests rather unimportant. In France, Spain, and Sweden, among other countries, the rulers engaged in numerous aggressive wars to increase their power and that of their country at the expense of neighboring countries and dynasties. The reasons for which they sought to increase their power included the love of power for its own sake, the quest for military glory, the wish to enforce acceptance of their religious faith, and the hope for economic gain. Among the instruments they used in seeking these goals were war, threats of war, alliances, economic competition (often piratical), and marriage. The struggles among these nation-states fell generally into two rather distinct areas, western Europe and eastern Europe; however, sometimes a struggle involved countries from both areas.

WESTERN EUROPE. In western Europe, the sixteenth, seventeenth, and eighteenth centuries included a series of struggles for power among France, Spain, and England. The Spanish reached the peak of their power early in the sixteenth century and thereafter underwent a series of failures culminating in the defeat of Spain and its allies in the Thirty Years' War. The Spanish waged this war in alliance with the chief Catholics of the Empire against the Protestants of the Empire, the

Danes, the Swedes, and the French. The Treaty of Westphalia, which ended the war, gave the Dutch national independence and made the hundreds of German princes autonomous within the Empire. Furthermore, this treaty drew the boundaries of European countries that have been fundamental to this day. Finally, it provided a code of rules for the practices of diplomats that is one of the bases of modern international law.

France now became the most powerful country in western Europe. Against it were arrayed, at different times, the Spanish and Austrian Hapsburgs, the English, the Dutch, and, for a time, the Hohenzollerns of Prussia. After a lengthy series of wars France was in 1789 still the most powerful country in Europe, but its treasury was bankrupt. The wars of this period often had as their aim the maintenance, or the restoration, of the balance of power—a situation in which no one country or group of countries would be able to dominate all Europe. The treaties that ended these wars reflected this aim; they were negotiated by representatives of both the victors and the vanquished, and they awarded to the victors only a portion of their demands.

EASTERN EUROPE. Two of the main developments in eastern Europe between 1500 and 1789 were the decline of the Ottoman Empire and the rise of Russia. At one time powerful enough to besiege Vienna, the Turks after 1683 rapidly lost power and yielded many of their European territories to the Austrians and the Russians. Meanwhile Russia, under Tsar Peter I and Tsarina Catherine II (the Great) (1762–96), underwent reorganization and modernization and emerged as a great power in eastern Europe. Of the other countries of eastern Europe, Poland lacked the central power necessary to assert itself, and Sweden enjoyed several major successes but overreached itself and went into a decline after 1660.

THE EXPANSION OF EUROPE

Beginning in the later fifteenth century the powers of Europe expanded their possessions and influence throughout a large part of the world by creating vast colonial empires. The efforts to create these empires brought on struggles that paralleled and complemented those in Europe.

The Nature of Imperialism. Imperialism is a process by which a country extends its power. In the past, this was accomplished often by the acquisition of land, but today gaining controlling influence over the internal and external affairs of another state is more common. Sometimes imperialism may be exercised against neighboring areas, as by

Rome during ancient times and by Russia in modern times. Such areas are often incorporated into the territory of the imperialistic power. On other occasions, imperialism involves territorial acquisitions and the extension of power to areas remote from the imperialistic country, or "overseas," such as the western European powers conducted in the New World between 1492 and 1763. These areas are rarely incorporated into the territory of the imperialistic power, but instead remain colonies. This "colonial imperialism" was very important from the fifteenth century on and brought about what is termed the "expansion of Europe." Europeans expected colonies to perform one or more of several functions: sources for raw materials and precious metals; markets for industrial products; naval bases; areas for the settlement of surplus populations; targets for civilization and Christianization; and grounds for dynastic or national pride. Colonial imperialism, which involved chiefly Spain, Portugal, France, Holland, and England, also had an important part in the struggles in Europe itself.

Competition for Colonial Empires. Beginning with Portuguese voyages down the west coast of Africa, European governments sent out their ships to explore new lands. The Spanish were the first to explore the New World and circumnavigate the globe; but the French, British, and Dutch soon joined the search for new lands and new trade routes. All these voyages added greatly to European knowledge about the surface of the earth and introduced the people of Europe to the vast natural resources of the Americas. Perhaps even more important, they laid the basis for the colonial empires that the European powers afterward established and that afforded the grounds for numerous wars.

The Spanish occupied most of South and Central America, and the Portuguese founded trading posts in Asia and secured title to Brazil. Soon the French, Dutch, and English began establishing colonies and soon, too, they fought over them. By defeating first the Dutch and then the French, by 1763 England had established its imperial supremacy both in North America and in India.

The Birth of the United States. One of the results of English colonization was the birth of the United States. The inhabitants of the English North American colonies objected to certain taxes levied by the English government and demanded the restoration of their traditional political and judicial rights. The ensuing dispute between the English and the colonists led to the outbreak of the American Revolution in 1775. Faced by a combination of enemies in Europe, the English in 1783 conceded independence to the United States. At the outset the United States was not a great power, but its success in winning independence set an important precedent for colonies in the Americas and elsewhere.

Review Questions

1. In terms of origins, government, and external policy, how did the early empires compare with the United States? the USSR? the Roman Empire?

2. How did the relations among the Greek city-states differ from those among the early empires? Why?

3. During the Middle Ages, what two institutions in western Europe made the greatest claims to political power? What had happened to each of them by the year 1500?

4. Describe the main political and economic characteristics of the nation-states of western Europe up to 1789.

5. Narrate how, between 1500 and 1789, some European nation-states gained in power while others were losing power.

6. What were the principal imperialistic states in Europe between 1500 and 1789? What were the main reasons for which they sought empires?

3 WORLD POLITICS FROM 1789 TO 1900

The era from 1789 until 1900 was one of great importance politically and economically. For one thing, the principle of dynastic nationalism gave way, in one country after another, to the principle of democratic nationalism. Moreover, in the first part of this era some governments discarded, to some degree, the principles of mercantilism, in favor of arrangements permitting greater economic freedom. Later, however, some thinkers developed the philosophy of socialism, which called for a revival and extension of government controls over the national economy. Political and economic events during these years were substantially modified by the industrial revolution. Furthermore, a number of new countries came into being, and leaders in many countries sought to increase the amount of political power entrusted to the people. Near the end of the era, several of the great European powers, joined by Japan, resumed the quest for colonial empires and parceled out among themselves most of the remaining parts of the world.

THE BACKGROUND OF POLITICAL CHANGE

The political changes of the nineteenth century had as a background the evolution of dynastic nationalism into democratic nationalism, the emergence of two new systems of economic thought, and several other developments in economic and social life.

The Rise of Democratic Nationalism. Democratic nationalism, which in one country after another evolved from dynastic nationalism, is a type of nationalism in which the people itself is the symbol of the nation. Such a belief also involves a much greater public participation in the government, through a wider franchise, low qualifications for office-holding, and mass political parties. Moreover, it has the corollary of *national self-determination,* according to which every group of people that senses itself to be a nation has the right to exist as a separate country under a government of its own choosing. Thus the principle of democratic nationalism is used to justify both rebellion against an autocratic government at home and war against other countries to seize territory populated by fellow nationals. Democratic nationalism came into being in western Europe, was spread by the French Revolution to other parts of Europe, and afterward influenced peoples of America, Asia, and Africa.

New Systems of Economic Thought. During the nineteenth century two new systems of economic thought emerged. One was the principles of free enterprise, a rejection of mercantilism and the basis of nineteenth-century "liberalism." The other comprised the principles of socialism, which was in so many ways a revival of mercantilism that it is sometimes termed "neomercantilism" and which, in a limited form, is the basis for present-day "liberalism."

Free Enterprise. The most significant principle of the free-enterprise system was that the government should interfere as little as possible in the national economic life. As distinct from the mercantilist system, the national economy under free enterprise would be regulated by certain economic laws such as that of supply and demand, which the government must permit to operate freely. The functions of government would therefore consist of little more than protecting the rights and liberties of the people. In no country was total free enterprise put into effect, but the British went very far toward accepting it, especially by repealing tariffs on grain imports just before the year 1850.

Socialism. The principles of socialism, which became prominent somewhat after the dissemination of the concepts of free enterprise, called to some degree for a revival of mercantilism, although with a different rationale. The principles of socialism received their greatest impetus from the writings of Karl Marx and Friedrich Engels, especially *The Communist Manifesto* (1848) and *Capital* (1867). According to the socialists, the means of production in every country should be owned, not by a small group of people, but by the entire populace. In effect, therefore the government should own the means of production. The government should also strictly regulate all economic activity by the people, with the asserted goal of assuring a maximum of the production and distribution of goods and services. By 1900 no government had adopted the principles of socialism, but these principles had had some effect on political leaders and in many countries were the guiding body of thought for political parties, notably the German Social Democratic Party.

Other Related Changes. A number of other changes took place in these years that were related to political and economic developments. For one thing, the countries of Europe—beginning with England about 1750—underwent the industrial revolution, resulting in immensely greater production of goods and giving new importance to such matters as sources of raw materials, trade routes, and markets. Also, governments vastly increased their armed forces. One government after another adopted universal military training, which contributed to the growth of democratic nationalism. Also, in one country after another, tax-supported schooling became universal and compulsory, another stimulus for democratic nationalism. All these changes contributed to the process whereby political, economic, and social privileges for the few were eroded away in Europe, and a general trend set in toward domination of all aspects of life by a large middle class.

DOMESTIC POLITICAL DEVELOPMENTS

Domestic political developments between 1789 and 1900 revolved largely about the efforts of political leaders who had adopted the principles of democratic nationalism to put these principles into effect. In a series of revolutions extending through those of 1848, these leaders' efforts were not very successful. After 1848, however, leaders in a number of countries, especially Germany, Italy, and Japan, succeeded in realizing at least some principles of democratic nationalism.

The Wars of the French Revolution and Napoleon (1789–1815). From 1789 to 1815 France underwent a series of rapid and drastic changes, beginning with an attempt to reform the monarchy and continuing with the establishment of a republic, a military dictatorship, and finally an empire under Napoleon Bonaparte. At the same time France fought a series of wars against the nations whose aim it was to return France to its status before the revolution. Under Napoleon's leadership French armies defeated most of the countries of Europe. In 1812, however, Napoleon suffered catastrophe when he tried to conquer Russia. All the enemies of France, headed by Russia and Great Britain, now formed a grand alliance that by 1815 had overrun France and sent Napoleon into exile. These campaigns were outstanding illustrations of deliberate efforts to restore the balance of power.

The Congress of Vienna. The Congress of Vienna, an assembly of European rulers that met in 1814 and 1815, was intended to bring peace to Europe after 25 years of almost continuous warfare. The Congress included representatives from all the countries that had participated in the recent wars. It is significant that France was admitted to the Congress as an equal member once the Bourbons had been restored to the throne. The statesmen at the Congress were in general agreed that the main threat to peace was not any one country but democratic nationalism. Hence they strove to repress this concept and to restore Europe as nearly as possible to its state before 1789. To maintain the peace settlements, the governments of Great Britain, Prussia, Austria, and Russia formed the Quadruple Alliance, which in 1818 was enlarged to the Quintuple Alliance by the admission of France. These great powers, functioning as the Concert of Europe, were to guarantee peace.

The Failure of Democratic Nationalism. Between 1815 and 1848, a number of movements for democratic nationalism took place in Europe, most of them failures. Consistently they met opposition from one or more members of the Quintuple Alliance, more than once in the form of an army sent by a member of the Alliance. In 1848 the French did succeed in overthrowing their monarchy and established a republic. Within four years, however, this republic had been transformed into an empire, with another member of the Bonaparte family, Napoleon III, on the throne. Thus in the main the members of the Quintuple Alliance, despite the withdrawal of both Great Britain and France long before 1848, succeeded in quelling revolutions. Furthermore, working as the Concert of Europe, they prevented the outbreak of war among the great powers for more than thirty years.

The Triumph of Democratic Nationalism, 1848–78. Between 1848 and 1878 the principle of democratic nationalism triumphed in many countries around the world. In Great Britain and France it took form mainly in a far broader franchise. Elsewhere, a number of new countries came into existence or else for the first time achieved prominence in world politics. Most notable of all, as a result of the Civil War, was the United States—the topic of the next chapter. Others were Germany, Italy, and Japan; finally, some new small states arose in the Balkan portions of the disintegrating Turkish Empire. It must be stressed that after 1848 democratic nationalism was considerably different from what it had been before 1848. In the earlier period, it had generally been associated with policies aimed at assuring more powers and liberties to the individual members of society. After 1848, however, democratic nationalism came to be associated with policies tending to limit the powers and liberties of individuals. Hence democratic nationalism, which had been spread among the *peoples* of Europe by the armies of the French Revolution and Napoleon, now was adopted by the *rulers* of Europe as an instrument for increasing their powers and acquiring more territories. At the same time popular movements tended to advocate collectivistic, rather than individualistic, legislation.

GERMANY. Up until 1871 Germany was essentially a geographical expression, a loosely bound confederation of states. The principal German countries were Prussia and Austria, which vied for control of all Germany. Up until about 1860 Austria generally prevailed in these contests. However, Prussia was rapidly gaining in comparative strength, partly through a tariff union, the *Zollverein,* which included almost all the German states except Austria and which Prussia tended to dominate. In the 1860's Prussia under King William I and Chancellor Otto von Bismarck brought most of Germany under its control by defeating first Denmark and then Austria in war. Next, in 1870, Prussia defeated France, took the provinces of Alsace and Lorraine from France, and united all Germany save Austria into the German Empire. Finally, owing to internal reorganization in 1867, the Austrian Empire became Austria-Hungary or the Austro-Hungarian Empire.

ITALY. Like Germany, Italy until it completed unification in 1871 was mainly a geographical expression. Italy had been subdivided into several independent political units. Furthermore, Austria owned Lombardy and the city and territory of Venice. Leadership in the movement toward Italian unification came chiefly from the country of Piedmont, under its king, Victor Emmanuel II, and his chief minister, Count Camillo Cavour. In 1859 and 1860 the Piedmontese with the help of the French brought much of Italy under their control. Then, in 1866, they were the allies of Prussia in a war against Austria and seized Venice. Finally, in 1871, after the Prussians had defeated the French and the French troops had been withdrawn from the Papal States, an Italian army marched into Rome. Italian unification was now almost completed. Still, Austria kept some territory populated mainly by Italians, such as the province of Trento and the city of Trieste, so that the Italian government had a firm basis for hostility to Austria.

JAPAN. Japan had been politically united for centuries and was at least potentially able to play an important part in world politics. However, since the 1500's the Japanese had maintained a policy of isolating Japan from the world. As a consequence, Japan had no part in international relations and contributed almost nothing to international trade. Then, in the 1850's, the United States forced the Japanese to open their harbors to the ships of other countries. Americans also introduced the Japanese to western technology, which the Japanese greatly admired and began to imitate. Beginning in the 1860's Japanese leaders completely discarded their principles of isolationism, reformed their government so that it resembled those of western Europe, and commenced building an industrial complex. When Japanese armies handily defeated the Chinese in the 1890's, it was clear that there was a new great power in Asia and that Orientals were just as capable as Occidentals of mastering industrial techniques.

NEW BALKAN COUNTRIES. The emergence of new countries in the Balkan peninsula out of the ruins of the Turkish Empire was largely a result of the struggles among the great European powers for influence and territory in this region. A series of controversies involving Russia, Turkey, Great Britain, and Austria-Hungary led in 1878 to the Congress of Berlin, where Bismarck was to function as an "honest broker" to distribute the spoils of a Russian victory over Turkey. The Turks were allowed to keep some territory in the Balkans, but there were created the independent countries of Romania, Bulgaria, Serbia, Montenegro, Albania, and Greece. In the following years these small countries, which owed their birth to the principle of national self-determination, were pawns in the conflicting Balkan policies of the great powers, especially Austria-Hungary and Russia. Also, owing to the irregular and uncertain demographic boundaries, relations among the Balkan countries themselves were often tense, as the various governments tried to seize lands populated by what they claimed were their co-nationals.

THE RESURGENCE OF COLONIAL IMPERIALISM

During the 1870's the great powers of Europe resumed the quest for colonies, on a far vaster scale than before.

Reasons for the New Colonial Imperialism. There were various reasons for the resurgence of colonial imperialism in the 1870's. There were still the traditional economic motives of securing markets and sources of raw materials, which had become far more important because of the industrial revolution. A new economic reason was the desire to have areas in which capital could be profitably invested. Also, governments wanted to have outposts situated so as to protect their main trade routes and to serve as naval bases. Then, some countries alleged a need and desire for colonies to reduce overpopulation at home; however, relatively few people moved from overpopulated countries to colonial areas. An important reason was the aim of enhancing national pride, a factor of exceptional importance for the rulers and peoples of such new countries as Germany and Italy. One other very important motive was the desire to end slavery among the African natives. *I bet.*

Patterns of the New Colonial Imperialism. The colonial imperialism of the nineteenth century was aimed at Africa, Asia, and the islands of the Pacific. In Africa the principal European powers, especially Great Britain and France, seized vast areas that they incorporated into their empires. The Germans and Italians entered the scramble for empire comparatively late, so that they had only a small stake in Africa. In Asia the British stood in India, Burma, and Malaya; the French were in Indochina; the Dutch, in Indonesia. In China, the imperialist countries did not incorporate vast areas, but instead secured only ports and then claimed trading privileges in the hinterland. Thus China was subdivided not into colonies but "spheres of interest," among the British, French, Germans, Russians, and Japanese.

Consequences of the New Colonial Imperialism. The quest for colonial possessions led to many disputes among the great powers. Moreover, the colonies themselves in some cases, by providing manpower, natural resources, industrial facilities, or military bases, strengthened the powers for conducting these disputes. Meanwhile the resources of these colonies enriched the imperialist powers, and in turn the imperialist governments brought some benefits to the peoples of their colonies —mainly greater peace and order, some new economic techniques, and various social changes whose merits were highly controversial.

Review Questions

1. How did democratic nationalism differ from dynastic nationalism?

2. What two systems of economic thought emerged in the nineteenth century? To what degree were they put into effect?

3. What was the principal goal of the rulers who met at the Congress of Vienna, and how did they strive to achieve this goal?

4. Compare the emergence of Japan into world prominence with the similar emergence of Germany and Italy.

5. What important change took place in democratic nationalism about the year 1848? Who were some of the chief figures sharing in, and profiting from, this change?

6. Compare nineteenth-century colonial imperialism with that of the sixteenth, seventeenth, and eighteenth centuries, in terms of participants, areas involved, motives, and consequences.

7. What effects did democratic nationalism have on the course of war and peace in the nineteenth century?

4 THE GROWTH OF THE UNITED STATES, 1789 TO 1917

Between 1789 and 1917 the United States developed from a weak, ill-united group of commonwealths along the Atlantic coast of North America into a continental state with a vast population, the greatest industrial plant in the world, and a considerable overseas empire. Only at the very end of this period did the United States take a significant part in world politics; however, almost from its beginning there had been a United States foreign policy that government leaders had clung to rather consistently.

EARLY STATEMENTS OF UNITED STATES FOREIGN POLICY

The early statements of United States foreign policy, which still profoundly influence its relations with all other countries, include George Washington's Farewell Address, the Monroe Doctrine, and Pan-Americanism.

Washington's Farewell Address. The first formal statement of United States foreign policy occurred in 1797, when George Washington delivered his farewell address as he stepped down from the presidency. The section of this address devoted to foreign policy upheld a principle that is best termed *continentalism*. According to this principle, the chief interests of the United States lie in the New World. Washington urged adoption of a policy that would involve the United States in no *permanent* alliances with any European countries. Clearly he felt that the United States was much too weak to participate in the European diplomatic cockpit. This recommendation was especially appropriate at the time, for the wars of the French Revolution were raging in Europe and each side had its partisans in the United States. Hence, as

Washington saw matters, the American people should devote themselves to the settling and civilizing of their own great western hinterland.

The Monroe Doctrine. The Monroe Doctrine, enunciated in 1823 by President James Monroe, was in effect an extension of the principle of continentalism to the entire New World.

BACKGROUND. The Monroe Doctrine was set forth in response to suggestions that France and Spain together might seek to restore Spanish rule to South America, where the former colonial peoples had just won national independence; and in response to the slow encroachment southward of the Russians along the western coast of North America, where they had already reached California. Alone among the powers of Europe, the British government wanted the new South American countries to retain their independence, in order to prevent the restoration of the Spanish empire in America and to maintain the profitable trade that the British had established with South America. Hence it urged joint action with the United States to keep the Spanish and the French out. President Monroe at first was hospitable to this proposal. Later, swayed by the arguments of Secretary of State John Quincy Adams, who feared lest execution of the British proposal put the United States in a subordinate position, Monroe shifted his position to one of independent action by the United States government.

CONTENTS AND EARLY EFFECTS. The Monroe Doctrine as finally set forth asserts that the United States government will not interfere with any existing European colonies in the New World but that European powers are not to establish any new colonies. Meanwhile, it pledges a policy of nonintervention by the United States government in the domestic affairs of European countries. The Monroe Doctrine for many years depended upon the British navy for its effect. The only important threat to the Doctrine came in the 1860's, during the Civil War, when the French tried to establish an empire in Mexico. When the war ended, the United States government made it clear to the French that they must leave or face the possibility of war with the United States. Shortly afterward the whole French project collapsed.

Pan-Americanism. Pan-Americanism, which to a considerable degree is the child of James Blaine, twice Secretary of State in the 1880's, is in effect a supplement to the Monroe Doctrine. Probably its chief distinguishing feature is its implication, at least, that the countries of the New World are equals. Up to 1900 the main emphasis of Pan-Americanism was economic and took the form of efforts to improve trade relations among New World countries and to lessen commercial barriers.

ESTABLISHMENT OF THE UNITED STATES OVERSEAS EMPIRE

The United States overseas empire was entirely created after the Civil War. The seeming delay in the establishment of an overseas empire resulted from several factors. Among other things, the American people had once themselves been part of an empire and disliked, or at least mistrusted, the concept of empire. Besides, Americans had been devoting whatever expansive and acquisitive feelings they had to reaching the Pacific Coast and settling the land between the two oceans. It is noteworthy that the American empire overseas, unlike the British and the French, was not scattered over the surface of the globe in a rather piecemeal fashion. To the contrary, it was situated entirely in the Caribbean and the Pacific, and every unit in this empire was clearly associated with a long-standing interest of the United States in those regions.

First Interests and Acquisitions. Although some United States officials, especially certain spokesmen for the slave-owning interests, had shown concern even before the Civil War in getting some lands in Latin America, the first United States overseas acquisition was Alaska. The Russian government had decided that its efforts to establish a colony in the New World had not been worth the cost; meanwhile certain Americans, especially Secretary of State William H. Seward, viewed Alaska as a desirable base for the conduct of United States policies respecting the Pacific. Consequently, in 1867 the United States bought Alaska from Russia for $7,200,000. Before 1900 the United States had secured two Pacific island bases as well. It annexed the Hawaiian Islands, at the urging of groups in both the United States and Hawaii. Also, it obtained harbor privileges in Samoa, although here it had to share its concerns with Great Britain and Germany.

United States Policy toward Latin America, 1865–98. Between 1865 and 1898, the United States had acquired no land in Latin America, but United States policy toward this area was made very clear in 1895. At that time, the British government seemed on the verge of using force in order to settle a boundary dispute with the government of Venezuela. In response, Secretary of State Richard Olney informed the British government that the will of the United States government was practically absolute in the Americas. Soon, partly because the British wanted assurance of American help in case of an Anglo-German naval war, the British government agreed to submit the dispute to arbitration.

The Spanish-American War. The Spanish-American War, which occurred within the single year 1898, led to a great expansion of the American overseas empire. The immediate cause of the war was a rebellion in Cuba against Spanish rule; the Spanish proceeded to deal with the rebels in a particularly brutal fashion. Then, in February, 1898, the United States battleship "Maine," which had been sent to Cuba to protect and perhaps evacuate Americans there, blew up in the harbor of Havana. Although the cause of the explosion was never clearly established, many Americans held the Spanish guilty. Despite considerable domestic opposition, Congress declared war on Spain in April. In a short time an American fleet sailed into the harbor of Manila in the Philippines and destroyed the Spanish fleet there. American ships in the Caribbean defeated a Spanish fleet sent to defend Cuba, and American land forces occupied Cuba and Puerto Rico. The warring countries signed an armistice in August. By the Treaty of Paris, signed in December, the Spanish gave up Cuba, Puerto Rico, the Philippines, and Guam, in exchange for $20,000,000 from the United States. A few years later the United States granted formal independence to Cuba but kept the remaining areas. Acquisition of the Philippines was especially important, since it was almost certain to involve the United States in any Far Eastern quarrels among Great Britain, Japan, and Russia over spoils in China.

THE OPEN DOOR POLICY

The Open Door Policy, first set forth by Secretary of State John Hay in 1899, was the chief declaration of United States policy regarding the Far East. It reflected the type of imperialism that other countries had been practicing in China and the facts that the United States had just acquired the Philippines and that it had no "sphere" in China. Hay merely suggested to all powers concerned in China that each respect both the trading privileges of all other countries and the territorial and political integrity of China. Only the British accepted this proposal without reservation; the other governments, however, indicated a sufficient degree of approval to embolden Hay in 1900 to issue a declaration asserting that the Open Door Policy was in effect. In the same year a group of Chinese revolutionaries, the "Boxers," tried to expel the foreigners, but were repressed by the combined forces of the imperial nations. Together the great powers then made several demands upon the Chinese government, including an indemnity for damage to their property and for the death and injury of their nationals. Later the United States government considerably reduced its share of the indemnity, and the Chinese government used some of these funds to send Chinese students to schools in the United States. Meanwhile most of the great powers, with the particular exception of Russia, gave the appearance of agreeing to the principles of the Open Door Policy. However, the United States government never supported this Far Eastern commitment to the degree to which it backed the Monroe Doctrine.

THE ACQUISITION OF NEW COLONIES

Between 1900 and 1917 the United States acquired the Canal Zone and the Virgin Islands as new colonies.

The Canal Zone and the Panama Canal. In 1903 the United States obtained the Canal Zone as a colony, from the Central American republic of Panama; in 1914 the first ocean-going vessel sailed through the Panama Canal, built by the United States in the Zone. To permit the United States exclusive control over the canal, the British government in 1900–1901 agreed to the Hay-Pauncefote Treaty with the United States. This treaty was valuable for the British since it implied United States protection for British colonies in the West Indies. Next the United States government tried to obtain permission from the government of Colombia, which then held Panama, to build the canal; but Colombia refused. Thereupon the people of Panama, evidently with United States support, rebelled against Colombia, established an independent republic, and agreed to allow the United States to build the canal. The canal has accentuated United States interests in the Caribbean and the Pacific.

The Virgin Islands. In 1917 the United States bought the Virgin Islands, or Danish West Indies, from Denmark. The United States had been trying unsuccessfully to buy them for many years. The construction of the Panama Canal made their possession even more desirable. Then, from 1914 on, some Americans began to fear lest the Germans seize them and threaten the Panama Canal. Finally, under some pressure from the United States government, the Danes gave up the islands in exchange for $25,000,000.

RELATIONS WITH LATIN AMERICA

The relations of the United States with Latin American countries, especially those in the Caribbean area, displayed a vigorous policy of the United States government toward both these Latin American countries and the European countries that interceded in Latin American affairs.

Cuba. In 1902 the United States government gave Cuba formal independence. At the same time, Congress required the Cuban people to insert in their constitution a series of clauses known all together as the Platt Amendment, which in effect gave the United States government the power to interfere in Cuban domestic upheavals and to assure that Cuban foreign policy was friendly toward the United States. In later years the United States sent military forces to quell revolutions in Cuba. One aim of the Platt Amendment was clearly to guarantee United States supremacy in the Caribbean. It was also intended to help the United States government protect the substantial American business interests in Cuba, connected particularly with the growing and milling of sugar cane.

Venezuela. In 1902, during a quarrel between Venezuela and certain European powers, the United States government apparently interfered behind the scenes to uphold the Monroe Doctrine. When the government of Venezuela failed to pay debts it owed to the governments of Great Britain and Germany and even refused to negotiate concerning the matter, the British and the German governments first consulted with the United States government; then their fleets blockaded Venezuela and shelled a Venezuelan port. The Venezuelan government now agreed to arbitrate the dispute. Discussing the affair years later, Theodore Roosevelt, who had been President in 1902, seems to have given an exaggerated account of his influence. It does, however, appear that the British and German governments felt it wise to assure the United States government that they intended no annexations before they took the steps they did.

The "Roosevelt Corollary." The "Roosevelt Corollary," first stated in 1904 in conjunction with the difficulties of the Dominican Republic, was an important amendment to the Monroe Doctrine. The Dominican government was heavily in debt to Europeans and was often overthrown by revolutions. When it seemed that European governments might interfere in the Dominican government to obtain satisfaction for these debts, President Roosevelt asserted that in cases in which some government in the New World could not manage its debts or was generally quite unstable, the government of the United States might intervene to restore solvency and civil order. During 1904–5, with the consent of Dominican authorities, the United States government took over the administration of Dominican finances in order to repay European creditors, and in 1907 the United States and the Dominican governments negotiated a treaty providing for a considerable loan to the Dominican government from a New York bank. Thus the United States government rescued the Dominican government from both bankruptcy and possible intervention by European powers.

"Dollar Diplomacy." "Dollar diplomacy" is the term applied, usually by its enemies, to the Caribbean policy of Roosevelt's successors, notably Taft and Wilson. These two Presidents on occasion interfered in the domestic concerns of several Caribbean states, such as the Dominican Republic, Haiti, and Nicaragua. Generally, on these occasions United States officials supervised national finances, and United States marines sought to end civil disorder. Critics of these activities termed them "dollar diplomacy" because, they charged, the activities were designed chiefly if not solely to protect the investments of Americans who had bought the bonds of these governments or undertaken such private enterprises as fruit- or sugar-growing. No doubt, protection of this sort was one motive for these activities. However, there were also such motives as the defense of the Panama Canal and of American naval bases in the Caribbean, the establishment of orderly governments, and the conquest of disease. American investors may have benefited from these interventions, but the majority of the native populations did also.

Mexico. In 1910 a revolution broke out in Mexico against the dictator, Porfirio Diaz. It lasted for several years; deeply involved the United States; and led to an unusual declaration of foreign policy by the United States government, which set a rather commonplace diplomatic practice—the granting of diplomatic recognition—on a moral basis. In 1911 Diaz fled the country and was succeeded in control by Francisco Madero; Madero's political principles were generally acceptable in the United States. Early in 1913, however, Madero was overthrown and murdered by Victoriano Huerta and his followers. Shortly afterward, Woodrow Wilson, who had just become President, announced that he would not recognize the Huerta government as legitimate because of the way by which it had come to power. Consequently he refused to exchange ambassadors or ministers. Ordinarily the United States, like other countries, granted recognition to any government that appeared capable of holding power, regardless of how it secured power. On this occasion, however, Wilson introduced a moral element and provided an example that other American Presidents have occasionally followed. In part because of Wilson's policy, but also because of American military intervention in Mexico, Huerta resigned in favor of Venustiano Carranza, whose government Wilson later recognized. One other important feature of this dispute was that peace between the United States and Mexico was restored with the help of the governments of Argentina, Brazil, and Chile—an illustration of the growing tendency in the United States to view at least some Latin American countries as equals.

RELATIONS WITH THE FAR EAST

Relations with the Far East in these years revolved mainly around the problems associated with the expansion and the ambitions of the Japanese.

The Russo-Japanese War. The Russo-Japanese War (1904–5) provided the world with another proof that Japan was in fact a great power and it also furnished the United States with an opportunity to be a peacemaker. This war broke out mainly because of the competition between the two countries over influence in Manchuria and Korea. The Japanese Navy destroyed the Russian Far Eastern fleet; and the Japanese Army in Manchuria inflicted severe losses on the Russian Army. American public opinion generally favored the Japanese; President Roosevelt warned the French and the Germans not to assist Russia, on pain of seeing the United States go to the aid of Japan. Finally, at Roosevelt's invitation, representatives of both Japan and Russia met at Portsmouth, New Hampshire, where late in 1905 they signed the Treaty of Portsmouth. By the terms of this treaty, negotiated with the help of Roosevelt's mediation, Russia turned over certain commercial privileges and some land to Japan. Korea became officially a Japanese possession in 1910. A significant side to this affair was that, whether or not deliberately, Roosevelt's action contributed to maintaining a balance of power in the Far East. The war itself had the special importance of being the first in which an Asiatic country defeated a European great power.

The Open Door Policy and Japan. As suggested before, after the proclamation of the Open Door Policy the United States government did little to back it. In 1903, for instance, the United States government made little formal protest when the Russians made it clear that they regarded Manchuria their sphere of interest. After the Russo-Japanese War, however, Japan became the principal threat to the Open Door Policy. The Japanese felt that Roosevelt had kept them from getting all they deserved in the Treaty of Portsmouth. Furthermore, the Japanese resented the treatment afforded Japanese immigrants into the United States. Being members of a nonwhite race, the Japanese, particularly in California, were subjected to various discriminatory measures. The Japanese quickly made it evident that they wanted to control Manchuria, so that they could exploit its natural resources for the needs of their growing heavy industry. Meanwhile relations between the United

States and Japan became so tense that some observers feared lest war break out. In 1907 President Roosevelt sent the American battle fleet around the world, at least partly in order to impress the Japanese. Finally, in 1908, the two governments reached the Root-Takahira Agreement, according to which each would respect the interests of the other in the Far East and at the same time preserve the integrity of China. Still, such an agreement was little of a real guarantee for the Open Door Policy.

Review Questions

1. Summarize each of the three early statements of United States foreign policy. How can each of these statements be related to the power status and the domestic and foreign interests of the United States at the time?

2. In what specific way did the location of the United States overseas empire differ from the location of the British and French overseas empires? Give illustrations.

3. How did the activities of the United States in Latin America between 1890 and 1917 conform to the three early statements of United States foreign policy? Show how these activities were connected with the power status and the domestic and foreign interests of the United States betwen 1890 and 1917.

4. Suggest some reasons why the United States government never supported the Open Door Policy to the degree to which it backed the Monroe Doctrine.

5. Compare the foreign policy recommended in Washington's Farewell Address with the policy conducted by Theodore Roosevelt. What may have been some of the reasons for the differences?

6. Suppose that the United States government had vigorously intervened in Latin American affairs in the early nineteenth century and helped the peoples there win self-government—as it might have done if Aaron Burr had been elected President in 1800 and re-elected in 1804. What might have been some of the effects?

5 THE BACKGROUND AND CAMPAIGNS OF WORLD WAR I

The background of World War I goes back at least as far as the year 1871—the close of the Franco-Prussian War. Its causes include four main groups of phenomena: nationalism; imperialism; militarism; and an alliance system. It involved most of the civilized nations of the world and led to the defeat of Germany and its allies.

CONTRIBUTORY FACTORS TO WORLD WAR I

The main contributory factors to World War I were, as noted above, nationalism, imperialism, militarism, and an alliance system.

Nationalism. The essentials of nationalism, and the ways in which it might contribute to international tensions, are described in a preceding section. There were certain phases of nationalism that especially contributed to the outbreak of World War I. One was the sentiment of a desire for revenge that developed in France as a consequence of the Franco-Prussian War and the loss of Alsace and Lorraine. Another was the sense of nationalism that developed among the subject peoples of the Austro-Hungarian and Turkish Empires and of the small countries of the Balkans, leading these peoples to feel that war was the best instrument for breaking up these empires and enabling these peoples to enjoy their right to national self-determination. A third important phase of nationalism was that stimulated by the commercial and naval rivalry between Great Britain and Germany.

Imperialism. The essentials of imperialism, and the ways in which it might contribute to international tensions, are also described previously. Certain phases of imperialism also contributed to the outbreak of World War I. In general it can be said that rivalry for distant overseas colonies was not an important cause; instead, the areas for which the continental powers were competing were in or near Europe. One of these was the Balkans, where Russia and Austria-Hungary were the main contenders for influence, with other European powers having secondary roles. Another was the Turkish Empire in Asia as well as in Europe. The Russians wanted Constantinople, then capital of the Empire; the Germans wanted to build a "Berlin-to-Baghdad" railroad to assure economic ties with the Empire; and the British wanted to protect their economic interests in the Empire against German competition, yet keep the Empire from dissolving so as to bar Russia from Constantinople. This sort of imperialism was largely commercial and typified the trade rivalry between Great Britain and Germany then going on all over the world.

Militarism. From the 1870's on, all the great powers on the European continent as well as Japan vastly increased their land forces. Also, small countries with aggressive policies or fears of attack, such as Serbia, Romania, and Bulgaria, maintained what were for them very large armies. Meanwhile Great Britain and Germany engaged in a spirited naval race. Finally, both the United States and Japan were building large war fleets; by 1900 that of the United States was second only to that of the British. This military competition among the powers led all governments to feel somewhat insecure if they were isolated and to seek alliances.

The Alliance System. Most nations in 1914 were either members of, or associated with, two major alliances: the Triple Alliance and the Triple Entente. The dominating power of the first was Germany; the dominating powers of the second were Great Britain and France. Among the great powers, only the United States had no formal bond with either group.

THE TRIPLE ALLIANCE. The Triple Alliance stemmed from the efforts of the German government to forestall a revival of France by isolating it from the rest of Europe. Throughout the period from 1871 until 1914 the closest ties of Germany were with Austria-Hungary. However, during part of the 1870's and the 1880's it was a member of the Three Emperors' League, with Austria-Hungary and Russia. Then, in 1882, the Italians joined the Germans and the Austro-Hungarians in the Triple Alliance. Next, relations between Germany and Russia gradually cooled, for the German government had placed a high tariff on imports of grain, had curtailed German loans to Russia, and seemed prepared to back Austria-Hungary in the Balkans. In 1890 the alliance between Germany and Russia came to an end. Afterward, mainly in order to prevent a two-front war against both France and Russia, the Germans signed various friendship agreements with the Russians. However, they found it difficult if not impossible to back simultaneously the Balkan projects of both Austria-Hungary and Russia. Among other countries, at the beginning of World War I Turkey and Bulgaria were associated with the Triple Alliance.

THE TRIPLE ENTENTE. The Triple Entente resulted from parallel and more or less independent diplomatic maneuverings by the French and the British.

The French Phase. The French phase of the Triple Entente arose from the success of France in emerging from the isolation imposed on it for two decades after the Franco-Prussian War. During the 1870's and 1880's, despite their efforts to secure allies for a war against Germany, the French were an outcast nation. They had expected the support of the Italians, whom they had helped to achieve national unity in 1859–60; but they alienated the Italians by seizing Tunisia in 1882. Later, when the German-Russian alliance disintegrated, the French stepped forward, first of all by lending money to the Russian government. Subsequently, in 1893, Russia and France formed a military alliance, which was known as the Dual Entente. To a very considerable degree this pact brought about the restoration of the balance of power in continental Europe. The British, during much of the latter half of the nineteenth century, maintained a policy of isolation.

The British Phase. The British phase of the Triple Entente rose from the decision by the British government that it should discard the policy of "splendid isolation" to which it had adhered for several decades. It was already confident of at least the friendship of the United States, thanks to the peaceful settlement of various disputes in the 1800's and the Hay-Pauncefote Treaty of 1900–1901. Then, in 1902, it reached a naval alliance with Japan, directed chiefly against Russian expansion in China. Regarding Europe, the British hoped to negotiate a treaty with Germany, since they were involved in disputes with both Russia and France. The British, however, refused to join the Triple Alliance, a condition set by Germany, if only because their colonial interests clashed with those of the Germans. Hence the British turned to France, which was increasingly desirous of support against Germany, and in 1904 the two countries signed a treaty settling their disputes in northern Africa. The new relation between the French and the British was called the *Entente Cordiale.* Finally, in 1907 the British and the Russians signed a treaty to settle disputes over Persia (now Iran), Afghanistan, and China. This last treaty brought the Triple Entente into being. As for other countries, by 1914 Serbia and Portugal tended to favor the Entente powers.

THE HAGUE CONFERENCES

The Hague Conferences of 1899 and 1907 were international gatherings with the general aim of preventing war. The first, called by the Russian tsar, had the initial goal of reaching disarmament pacts. Such pacts would have been extremely useful to Russia, in view of its military and industrial inferiority to Germany. The members of the conference could reach no agreement on this matter, but they did unite in suggesting various means for the peaceful settlement of international disputes. They also provided for the establishment of an international tribunal which came to be known as the Hague Court and was officially called the Permanent Court of Arbitration. It was not a court in the usual sense, but a group of jurists from which arbiters might be chosen to handle disputes between governments. The Venezuelan dispute of 1902 was resolved by this court. The second conference, also called by the tsar, likewise could reach no conclusion on disarmament; it was clear on this occasion that the main conflict was between Great Britain as a naval power and Germany as a land power. The members of this conference tried, with little success, to draft a code of the laws of war. The chief contribution of the United States was a proposal that the Permanent Court of Arbitration be made a real court, dealing with matters under international law, but other governments offered little support for this proposal. In any case, the United States government after 1899 reached agreements with a number of other governments that disputes between them would be submitted to the Hague Court.

DIPLOMATIC CRISES, 1905–14

From 1905 until 1914, before World War I began, the powers of Europe went through a series of diplomatic crises, all save the last resolved without war among the great powers. This last one led to World War I.

The Moroccan Crises. The two crises over Morocco, in 1905 and 1911, both involved attempts by France to assert its influence over this region, and in each case the chief rival of France was Germany. In 1905, after the French had secured the consent of both the British and the Italians to establish a protectorate over Morocco, the Germans demanded that all countries enjoy equal privileges in Morocco. With Europe on the verge of war, the French agreed to turn the matter over to an international conference at Algeciras, Spain, in 1906, called partly at the urging of the United States. The British supported the French, and the conferees, although they proclaimed their intention of assuring the territorial integrity of Morocco and the right of all nations to trade there on an equal basis, also provided that order in Morocco be maintained by a local police force supervised by France and Spain—a considerable setback for Germany. The crisis simmered until 1911, when France sent an army deep into Morocco for the asserted purpose of ending a civil war among rival Moroccan factions. The Germans responded by sending a warship to the Moroccan port of Agadir, presumably to defend German interests. Again the British supported the French, and Germany and France reached a settlement by which France assumed a protectorate over Morocco but guaranteed Germany the freedom to trade there and ceded to Germany some territory in Central Africa. Neither power was satisfied.

The Balkan Crises. In 1908 Austria-Hungary incorporated Bosnia and Herzegovina, two former Turkish provinces near the Adriatic. This action was particularly offensive to Russia and Serbia, for both feared the expansion of Austro-Hungarian power. Serbia, in addition, had been hoping to annex the provinces itself, for without them Serbia was landlocked. Trouble recurred in the Balkans in the wars of 1912 and 1913. In the first of these Bulgaria, Greece, Montenegro, and Serbia defeated Turkey and forced it to give up all of its European possessions except Constantinople and a small adjacent tract. In a short time, however, the victors were quarreling over the spoils; in June, 1913, Bulgaria went to war against Greece and Serbia, which were soon aided by Romania and Turkey. Bulgaria went down to a quick defeat. The consequences of the Balkan crises were an increased hostility between Serbia and Austria-Hungary and a closer bond between Bulgaria and the Triple Alliance. In addition, Serbia had drawn closer to Russia.

The Turco-Italian War. The Turco-Italian War of 1911, another factor in the downfall of Turkey, resulted from the efforts of the Italians to acquire the Turkish African province of Tripoli. After a brief struggle the Italians proclaimed their annexation of Tripoli, and a treaty in 1912 confirmed this proclamation. One important aspect of this war was that it involved one member of the Triple Alliance—Italy—battling the Turkish Empire, a friend of the other two members of the Triple Alliance—Germany and Austria-Hungary. It showed, in short, a weakness in the Triple Alliance.

The Austro-Serbian Crisis of 1914. The Austro-Serbian crisis of 1914 was the immediate cause of World War I.

BACKGROUND OF THE CRISIS. By the end of the second Balkan War, in 1913, the hostility between Austria-Hungary and Serbia had become extreme. One of the chief points of contention between them was the status of the Slavic peoples in the Austro-Hungarian Empire. The Serbians wanted to annex them, and the Austro-Hungarians resented the propaganda the Serbians were conducting among the Slavs in Austria-Hungary. A number of Austro-Hungarian leaders, including the heir to the Austro-Hungarian throne, Archduke Francis Ferdinand, were especially eager to reconcile the Slavs in the Empire and therefore became particularly hateful to the Serbians. Consequently, when it was known that in June, 1914, the archduke was to visit Bosnia, the Serbian government co-operated with a Serbian secret society to plan his assassination. Accordingly, on June 28, 1914, agents of the secret society assassinated the archduke and his wife in the Bosnian city of Sarajevo.

THE AUSTRO-HUNGARIAN DECLARATION OF WAR ON SERBIA. Austro-Hungarian leaders, convinced that the Serbian government had had a part in the assassination, determined to punish Serbia. However, they wanted to go no farther than a local war involving only Austria-Hungary and Serbia. First, they obtained assurance of backing from Germany; then, they sent a group of demands to the Serbian government so extreme that the Serbian government was expected to refuse them, in which case Austria-Hungary would declare war. Meantime the Russian government had warned the Austro-Hungarians not to go too far, and the French government had offered the Russians its support. Shortly after Serbian officials received the Austro-Hungarian demands, they received also certain guarantees from the Russian government. Consequently they rejected a portion of the demands; yet in many respects their reply appeared satisfactory. Nevertheless the Austro-Hungarians, whom the Germans were now trying to restrain, declared war on Serbia on July 28.

ENTRY OF GERMANY, RUSSIA, FRANCE, AND GREAT BRITAIN INTO THE WAR. Then the Germans, in an effort to confine the struggle to a war between Austria-Hungary and Serbia, demanded that the Russians cease mobilizing. However, after some fumbling by government officials, Russian mobilization continued; hence, on August 1, Germany declared war on Russia. To protect themselves from having to fight a war on two fronts, the Germans insisted that the French announce their neutrality; when the French refused, Germany declared war on France, on August 3. Finally, when the Germans in implementing their plans for a campaign against France invaded Belgium, thus breaking a treaty guaranteeing Belgian neutrality and threatening to gain a foothold in the Lowlands, the British declared war on the Germans.

ENTRY OF THE OTHER COUNTRIES INTO THE WAR. Among the other countries, Japan declared war on Germany on August 23, both in simple fulfillment of its treaty obligations to the British and with the aim of expanding its Far Eastern holdings at the expense of Germany. Meanwhile the countries of the Triple Entente, or Allied Powers, had been seeking to keep the Turks neutral. However, the Turks were already so closely bound to Germany and Austria-Hungary, or the Central Powers, that with German aid they established a fleet on the Black Sea that bombarded Russian ports. Thereupon, early in November, the Allies declared war on the Turkish Empire. Italy, meanwhile, had remained neutral. As shown previously, the Italians had border disputes with Austria-Hungary and therefore were not anxious to join the Central Powers. At length, having been promised a number of territorial acquisitions by the Allies, the Italian government on May 23, 1915, declared war on Austria-Hungary. Among the lesser countries, Montenegro and Romania joined the Allies; Bulgaria joined the Central Powers; and Greece, despite efforts to stay neutral, was occupied by the Allied Powers.

WORLD WAR I, 1914–17

The military campaigns of World War I from 1914 until 1917 involved primarily two massive offensives: one by the Germans against the French and the British; and one by the Germans and Austro-Hungarians against the Russians. One particular phase of the offensive against the British, German submarine warfare, was probably the most important single event bringing the United States into the war.

Campaigns, 1914–17. The Germans marched through Belgium into France; after initial successes against the British and the French, they were stopped in the First Battle of the Marne in September, 1914. The Germans then extended their right wing to the English Channel, and both sides dug in for the trench warfare that was to last until the early part of 1918. The entry of Italy into the war had little effect on the Western front. On the Eastern front, the Russians advanced at first, but with the arrival of additional German troops from the Western front they were defeated in the battles of Tannenberg and the Masurian Lakes. Then the entry of the Turkish Empire into the war later in 1914 cut the Russians off from shipments of war goods through the Black Sea. By 1917 the armies of the Central Powers had advanced well into Russia and had greatly diminished the ability of the Russians to resist.

Entry of the United States into World War I. Entry of the United States into World War I occurred officially in 1917, but the United States government and many of the American people had in one way or another been partisans of the Allies since almost the very beginning of the war.

UNITED STATES FOREIGN POLICY, 1914–17. With the beginning of hostilities in Europe, President Wilson declared the neutrality of the United States, calling on the American people to be neutral in thought as well as in deed. Nevertheless, the United States soon moved to a position of support for the Allied Powers. There were, first of all, close ties between the United States and Britain, and both Britain and France seemed to many Americans to be defending the system of political freedoms against the asserted tyranny of the Kaiser. Then, the United States little by little acquired an economic stake in Allied victory, through selling war materials to the Allies that could be paid for only if the Allies won the war. Although the British did often interfere with American shipping, such proceedings did not threaten the lives of Americans, and the British seemed ready to compensate American shippers after the war for their losses.

The Germans, in addition to being viewed as tyrants, had reaped much ill will by their invasion of Belgium. Following this act it was not difficult for Americans to believe the many tales of German atrocities, both true and false, supplied to them in their daily newspapers. What most harmed the Germans' reputation in the United States, however, was their submarine warfare. Because of their nature, submarines could not satisfy certain requirements of international law, such as that the crew and passengers of a ship must be warned before the ship is sunk and must be cared for after a ship is sunk. Up to January, 1917, the Germans attacked only one American ship; however, their sinking of the vessels of other countries, notably the British "Lusitania," that carried Americans as passengers, more than once brought Germany and the United States close to war. By 1916, however, the Germans had promised to restrict their submarine warfare and were in the main keeping their promise.

UNITED STATES DECLARATION OF WAR. The United States declaration of war, on April 6, 1917, came chiefly because in January, 1917, the Germans announced that they were about to resume unrestricted submarine warfare. Two events speeded up American action. One was the publication of the so-called "Zimmermann Note," an invitation to the Mexican government to declare war on the United States as an ally of Germany; in exchange, Mexico would receive Texas, New Mexico, and Arizona after the defeat of the United States. The other event was the March Revolution in Russia, aimed at overthrowing the autocratic government there. This event made it easier for Americans to believe that they would join a band of nations dedicated to human freedom in a struggle against tyranny. Hence, at Wilson's request, Congress on April 6 declared war on Germany. Several months later, Congress voted a declaration of war on Austria-Hungary. The United States never went to war against the other Central Powers.

WORLD WAR I, 1917–18

The campaigns of 1917–18 began very favorably for the Central Powers, since a group of revolutionaries seized power in Russia and negotiated a separate peace treaty with Germany. The Germans were therefore able to increase the strength of their armies in the West and begin a series of offensives in 1918 that nearly broke through the Allied lines in France. However, the declining strength of Germany, the collapse of the other Central Powers, and the additional strength that the United States brought the Allies, led the Germans to sue for an armistice.

The Russian Revolutions. The Russian Revolutions, in March and November, 1917, were in many ways the most important events of World War I. They were partly a consequence of the war itself, and they very much influenced the conduct as well as the outcome of the war.

GROUNDS FOR THE RUSSIAN REVOLUTIONS. Some grounds for these revolutions, such as the low standard of living in Russia compared with that in most European countries, the corruption and inefficiency of the Russian government, and the existence of active subversive groups, went well back in Russian history. More immediate were the defeats of the Russian army, the low morale of Russian troops, and the insistence of the other Allies that Russia stay in the war. The tsar and the members of the nobility that supported his regime were, in the main, personally weak. Although the Russian government had enacted a broad labor code to regulate working conditions, it was not very well enforced, and this situation coupled with the generally low wages laid the basis for strong feelings of resentment, if not hatred, among workers toward employers.

THE MARCH REVOLUTION. The March Revolution, which started as a bread riot in Petrograd, led to the overthrow of the tsar and the establishment of a provisional government headed by Octobrists and Kadets (Constitutional Democrats), the most moderate of the four revolutionary parties. The original leaders were then gradually replaced by figures from the Socialist Revolutionary Party and the Menshevik faction of the Social Democratic Party. These four groups, however, seemed desirous of remaining in the war; the government launched one more military offensive against the Germans, which led to a catastrophic defeat for the Russians. The Bolshevik faction of the Social Democratic Party was the one group that called for peace, which seemed the desire of most peasants and workers. It was also the desire of the Germans; consequently they arranged for the transportation into Russia of the most important Bolshevik, Nikolai Lenin, who had been living in exile in Switzerland. The Bolsheviks commenced propagandizing vigorously and effectively among the soldiers for an end to the war.

THE NOVEMBER REVOLUTION. The November Revolution ("October Revolution" according to the calendar then used in Russia), organized and led by the Bolsheviks, was an uprising that overthrew the provisional government and placed the Bolsheviks in control. In January, 1918, representatives of the various parties met in a convention intended to draft a new constitution. The members of this convention had been chosen in a free popular election—the last to be held in Russia—and the Bolsheviks were in a minority. Since their party alone contained an organized armed force, the Bolsheviks dissolved the convention and established a "dictatorship of the proletariat" under Lenin and his chief lieutenant, Leon Trotsky.

THE TREATY OF BREST-LITOVSK. The Treaty of Brest-Litovsk, signed by the Germans and the Russians in March, 1918, constituted a Russian surrender. By the terms of this treaty the Russians gave up large areas along the Baltic and Black Seas. These areas, the most important of which was Ukraina, became formally independent countries, but in each one the government was dominated by Germany. These areas included the best farming land and most of the industry in Russia; consequently the Treaty of Brest-Litovsk is often held up as a demonstration of German war aims. Yet, since these areas were inhabited mainly by non-Russian peoples, the Germans could and did claim that they were only adhering to the principle of national self-determination. Lenin and Trotsky defended the treaty on the ground that the peace it brought would enable the Bolsheviks to establish in Russia a government and society founded on Marxist doctrines.

United States War Aims. United States war aims, especially as set forth by President Wilson, had a considerable part in ending the war. The chief statement of these aims was the "Fourteen Points," announced by Wilson in January, 1918. They fell into two general groups: (1) proposals for redrawing the map of Europe along the lines of national self-determination; and (2) recommendations for steps to be taken for preventing the outbreak of another war. The Fourteen Points were disseminated throughout the world. Furthermore, the President earlier had asserted that "the world must be made safe for democracy." Hence the United States government assumed leadership of a "crusade" aimed at assuring all people national independence and individual liberties.

End of Military Resistance by the Central Powers. The end of military resistance by the Central Powers late in 1918 resulted from the exhaustion of their human and material resources, the disintegration of their will to resist, and the dissolution of their political structures. Actually, in 1917 and in early 1918 the Central Powers enjoyed a number of major successes. Yet the allies of Germany were on the brink of collapse. Hence early in 1918, strengthened by troops drawn from the Eastern front, German armies launched one last series of attacks on the Allies in the West, with the especial goal of ending the war before the Americans could arrive. The first German assaults succeeded, but soon the Americans had arrived in sufficient numbers to halt the Germans at the Second Battle of the Marne. From that time on the German armies were pressed slowly but steadily back. Then, in September, Bulgaria surrendered; now divided from its allies, the Turkish Empire yielded in October; and the Austro-Hungarians gave up on November 3. German leaders, who had been trying for some time to end the war but would not accept the terms of the Allied Powers, refused to continue alone and signed an armistice on November 11, 1918.

The Armistice with Germany. The armistice with Germany was signed only after the Germans had agreed to comply with the Fourteen Points and had in certain other ways satisfied requirements that Wilson had fixed for them. As early as September the German government had begun asking for an armistice, but this government was the autocratic regime to which the United States had declared its hostility. Then, in October, this government was succeeded by one that, although still monarchical, gave promise of extending to the German people more political powers and individual liberties. Wilson at last agreed to an armistice with this regime. However, revolutionaries overturned the German monarchy, the Kaiser fled into exile in neutral Holland, and the leaders of the principal antimonarchist parties established a republic—the Weimar Republic. Representatives of this republican government, which evidently satisfied Wilson, signed the armistice. According to the terms of this armistice, the Germans had to renounce their peace treaties with Russia and Romania; withdraw their troops from Allied territory; surrender most of their armaments; pay civilians for damages German armed forces had inflicted on them; and consent to occupation of strategic points on their soil by Allied forces. Final peace terms would be drafted at an international conference later. This was an armistice so severe that only a country about to be overwhelmed on the field would have accepted it.

Review Questions

1. Outline the four factors that contributed to bringing on World War I. Can it be said that any of the four is more nearly "cause," and any of the four more nearly "effect"? Explain your answer.

2. What was the main reason for the summoning of the Hague Conferences, and what did the members of the conferences achieve?

3. In what area or areas did the chief diplomatic crises between 1905 and 1913 occur? Who were the main participants in these crises? To what degree did the crises involve the different alliances?

4. What were the chief points of contention between Austria-Hungary and Serbia in 1914?

5. After the Austro-Hungarians had invaded Serbia, what were the reasons, respectively, for which the Russians, the Germans, the French, the British, and the Italians entered the war?

6. Describe how the United States government gradually shifted from a policy of neutrality to a declaration of war against Germany.

7. Describe the events in Russia during 1917 and 1918 that led up to the Treaty of Brest-Litovsk. How would you react to the charge that Lenin was an agent of the German government?

8. How did the terms of the armistice with Germany deal with the capability of Germany to wage war?

6 THE PEACE SETTLEMENT AFTER WORLD WAR I

The peace settlement after World War I involved drafting peace treaties with the defeated powers as well as the Covenant, or charter, of the League of Nations. The way in which the drafting was conducted, and its consequences, showed how the distribution of power in the world had changed since 1914. When World War I started, there were six great powers in Europe: Great Britain, France, Germany, Italy, Austria-Hungary, and Russia; there was also one important medium-sized power lying partly in Asia: the Turkish Empire. At the close of the war, Austria-Hungary and the Turkish Empire had disintegrated; Germany had been defeated; Russia was in the throes of revolution and incapable of exercising a significant foreign policy; and Italy, although on the side of the victors, was greatly weakened. Hence the only true great powers in Europe in 1918 were Great Britain and France. Meanwhile the United States and Japan, already important non-European powers before the war, had gained both relatively and absolutely in power during the war. The peace treaties and the Covenant of the League of Nations were designed in part to maintain this new distribution of power.

THE PEACE TREATIES

The peace treaties—one for each of the defeated Central Powers—were drawn up in various suburbs of Paris. Each takes its name from the particular suburb in which it was signed, and the treaties all together are known as the Peace of Paris of 1919. Likewise, the whole international gathering is called the Conference of Paris.

The Conference of Paris. The work of the Conference of Paris was deeply influenced by the personalities of the chief figures and by the organization within which they did their tasks. At the same time this work was handicapped by the widespread hatred for Germany, the contents of the secret wartime treaties, and the world-revolutionary aims of Soviet Russia.

COMPOSITION OF THE CONFERENCE. The Conference was composed of representatives from all the countries that had shared in defeating the Central Powers. The representatives included such government leaders as President Wilson, Prime Minister David Lloyd George of Great Britain, Premier Georges Clemenceau of France, and Premier Vittorio Orlando of Italy. All together the Conference included hundreds of people, for the representatives from every important country brought with them "experts" on political, economic, social, and other problems. An outstanding fact was the exclusion of representatives from the defeated powers. Hence arose the claim that this was not a "negotiated" peace but a *Diktat* or "dictated" peace.

ORGANIZATION OF THE CONFERENCE. Although each country supposedly was equal to each other at the Conference, the spokesmen for the chief powers soon assumed control. At first the dominant body was the "Council of Ten," comprised of two representatives each from the United States, Great Britain, France, Italy, and Japan. Then, for various reasons, notably the disinterest of Japan in European questions, the "Council of Four"—Wilson, Lloyd George, Clemenceau, and Orlando—took up the reins. Indeed, for a time there was only a group of three, since Orlando left in reaction to alleged slights to Italian ambitions. In effect this small group made the principal decisions of the Conference. In the "Council of Four" appeared the great division between the Allies. On the one hand was Wilson, who had general and what might be termed "idealistic" aims. Opposing him were the other three, especially Clemenceau, with specific, "realistic" aims. In other terms, Wilson sought to establish a world political order in which wars, or at least major wars, would no longer occur; Lloyd George, Clemenceau, and Orlando intended to obtain the spoils of victory and were interested in preventing future wars largely as a means for assuring their possession of their spoils. Wilson, a highly moral individual who was a poor bargainer and a reluctant compromiser, was at a great disadvantage and often failed to secure his ends.

HANDICAPS OF THE CONFERENCE. Apart from the major division over principles between Wilson and the spokesmen for the other three Allied Powers, there were three specific handicaps under which the Conference operated.

Extensive Hatred for Germany. After World War I there was an extensive hatred for Germany, not only in the areas that German armies had invaded but also elsewhere. This hatred was evident in the 1918 parliamentary elections in Great Britain, which Lloyd George and his party had won on a campaign promising severe treatment of Germany. Holding the peace conference in Paris exposed its members to waves of this sentiment. It would be difficult for any conference gathered in such an atmosphere to produce a moderate peace treaty.

The Secret Treaties. During the war the Allied Powers had made various secret treaties among themselves dividing up territories of the Central Powers. For instance, to get Italy and Romania into the war on their side, Great Britain and France had made treaties with them promising large accessions of land. Also, the British, French, and Russians had subdivided the Turkish Empire among themselves. At the Conference the victors expected the terms of these treaties to be carried out in the peace settlement, or at least to serve as a basis for the peace settlement. Wilson, however, refused to accept these secret pacts; indeed, he asserted to a committee of the United States Senate that before going to Europe he had not even known they existed, in spite of the fact that the Russian Bolshevik government had disclosed their contents shortly after assuming power in November, 1917. In any case, Wilson's rejection of the terms of these secret treaties made it difficult for him to agree with the spokesmen of the other Allied Powers on what the peace settlement should include.

The Bolshevik Government in Russia. As discussed previously, the Bolshevik faction in November, 1917, won control in Russia, now known as *Soviet Russia.* This Soviet government performed a number of acts that angered the Allied Powers. It made a separate peace with Germany (Brest-Litovsk); it repudiated the debts of the old Russian government; it strove to foment revolution in as many countries as possible, to establish Soviet governments there; and, in effect, it declared war on every other country in the world, without resorting to conventional military operations. During 1918, armies of the various Allied Powers had invaded Russia, in part to keep military supplies there from the hands of the Germans. Japanese troops landed in Eastern Siberia to annex it to the Japanese Empire. With the end of the war the Allied armies might have left, except that by this time they had begun cooperating with the several anti-Bolshevik armies on Russian soil. Hence Soviet Russia took no part in the peace deliberations and was not included in the peace settlement.

Terms of the Treaty of Versailles. The terms of the Treaty of Versailles, which the Germans were compelled to sign on June 28, 1919, were quite severe; they reflected both the French desire to limit German military and economic strength, and the British desire to curtail the German navy and German colonial and imperial activities. First, Germany surrendered territories to France, Belgium, and Poland. The territory given to Poland included the so-called "Polish Corridor," a strip of eastern Germany that was designed to give Poland a seaport and that cut Germany into two parts. In this area the predominantly German city of Danzig was made a separate political unit, a "free city," supervised by the League of Nations. Other lands given to Poland contained much heavy industry. After a plebiscite, Denmark too received some German territory. Germany also gave up the Saar Basin, which was put under League supervision, and the French received the Saar coal mines outright. The Germans were permitted only small armed forces, and they were forced to *demilitarize,* or keep unfortified, an area along the Rhine called the Rhineland. The Germans further had to give up all their colonies to the League of Nations; the League in turn was to assign them to certain of the Allied Powers under the *mandate system,* under which League officials would supervise the administration of these areas. Finally, the Germans were forced to agree to the "war guilt" clause, whereby they admitted responsibility for starting the war. To compensate for the losses they were supposedly accountable for inflicting upon the Allied Powers, they consented to pay an undetermined sum of money termed *reparations;* until the sum was fixed they were to surrender a certain amount of gold, merchant ships, and commodities.

Terms of the Treaties with the Other Central Powers. The treaties with the other Central Powers all resembled the Treaty of Versailles. However, far more than the Treaty of Versailles, they were involved with the problem of national self-determination; there had been relatively few members of national minorities in Germany, but many millions of them in Austria-Hungary and the Turkish Empire. The Treaty of St. Germain-en-Laye with the new republic of Austria acknowledged and formalized the end of the Austro-Hungarian Empire, which had dissolved under nationalist pressures at the end of the war. This treaty conferred sections of the Empire upon Italy, Czechoslovakia, Poland, Romania, and Yugoslavia. Furthermore, it barred a future union between Austria and Germany. It limited Austrian armed forces and made the Austrian government liable to pay reparations. The Treaty of Trianon, with Hungary, awarded sections of the Empire to Czechoslovakia, Romania, Yugoslavia, and Austria. It limited Hungarian armed forces and made the Hungarian government liable to pay reparations. The Treaty of Neuilly with Bulgaria awarded some territories of prewar Bulgaria to Greece and Yugoslavia, limited Bulgarian armed forces, and imposed reparations payments upon the Bulgarian government. The Treaty of Sèvres, with Turkey, took away almost all territory inhabited by non-Turkish populations. Most of this territory was placed under the mandate system. The treaty also internationalized the Dardanelles. The Turkish government of the day signed the treaty but was soon overthrown by a nationalistic uprising, which installed a new regime that rejected the treaty. In 1923 this new regime agreed to the Treaty of Lausanne, which was considerably less severe.

THE LEAGUE OF NATIONS

The League of Nations was the first association of countries that was intended to be permanent and that was designed to cope with a variety of problems. Its Covenant, at the insistence of Wilson, was made a part of the peace treaties. The League was not a "supergovernment"; it comprised representatives of the governments of all member countries and was to serve as a mechanism through which these governments might achieve certain political, diplomatic, and economic goals. Hence it is never correct to assert that the League "failed" or "succeeded" in any undertaking; instead, it was governments, seeking to use League machinery for some end, that "failed" or "succeeded."

Structure of the League of Nations. As provided by the Covenant, the structure of the League included three bodies. One was the Assembly, in which each member country might have as many as three representatives but only one vote. The Assembly was to meet at least once annually. The second body was the Council, which originally was to have representatives from the great powers—the United States, Great Britain, France, Italy, and Japan—and from each of four other countries to be named by the Assembly. The great powers were to hold their seats permanently; the other countries were to have theirs for three-year terms. Since the United States did not join the League, it never sat on the Council; however, when Germany and the Soviet Union joined the League, they were granted permanent Council seats. The third body, the Secretariat, was to be a sort of League civil service headed by a Secretary-General chosen by the Council. Two important bodies associated with the League were the Permanent Court of International Justice, or World Court, and the International Labor Office; their titles indicate their functions.

Functions of the League of Nations. The two chief functions of the League of Nations were to maintain peace and to promote international co-operation. In pursuance of these goals, the Assembly was to serve as a forum where representatives of member countries might air the grievances of their governments; the Council, whose members could reach a decision only by a unanimous vote, might recommend positive action against a country whose actions might threaten war. The member countries were to work through the League machinery for the keeping of the peace on the principle that a threat of war to one country was equivalent to a threat of war to every country. Supposedly all international disputes that might lead to war were to be discussed before the League Assembly. If any country were to go to war, the League members were to halt financial and trade relations with the aggressor country. If this failed to restrain the aggressor, members of the Council might propose armed action. One other function of the League, in a distinct field, was the administration of the former colonies of Germany and the Turkish Empire under the mandate system.

Disputes Referred to League Mechanisms. From 1919 on, a number of international disputes were referred for settlement to the mechanisms of the League. For instance, the member countries helped resolve a dispute in 1920–21 between Sweden and Finland over the Åland Islands. They also ended the contest between Great Britain and Turkey over a part of Iraq. In 1925, war between Greece and Bulgaria halted when League members brought the League Council to intercede. On the other hand, when Poland took Vilna from Lithuania in 1920, when Japan invaded Manchuria in 1931, and when Italy attacked Ethiopia in 1935, the other countries could not, through the League, end these aggressions. Thus the machinery of the League might be serviceable in dealing with conflicts between small powers but was of no avail when a large power assumed the offensive. It must again be stressed that this situation reflected not a failure of the League but the unwillingness of League members to use the League machinery to deal with these aggressions or to abide by the terms of treaties they had signed.

Criticisms and Weaknesses of the League. Doubtless the commonest and strongest criticism of the League was that it did not carry out the function it was expected to carry out—the prevention of war. This criticism showed in many people a failure to understand that the League by itself had no power to compel any country or individual. To give the League such power would have required national governments to yield up their sovereignty, something they would have been very unwilling to do and something that without question would have injured the citizens of some countries. A criticism that had considerable basis in fact was that the British and the French viewed the League as no more than an instrument by which they might guarantee the arrangements reached in the Peace of Paris of 1919. Another weakness of the

League was that its machinery was organized to deal almost exclusively with political and military issues. Those who drafted the Covenant took little heed of the effect that economic, social, or psychological questions may have upon world politics and created few organisms to deal with them. Of course, the greatest source of the weakness of the League was the refusal of the United States to join it.

THE UNITED STATES AND THE PEACE TREATIES

The United States government never ratified any of the peace treaties negotiated at Paris in 1919. Although President Wilson signed them, the Senate refused to give its approval. United States ratification was therefore impossible. The refusal of the Senate to give its approval had several bases. One was partisan: some members of the Republican Party, which had won control of Congress in 1918 and which was led by Henry Cabot Lodge, a foe of Wilson, opposed the treaty simply because they felt it had too much of a Democratic Party stamp. This feeling was reinforced by the fact that Wilson had taken no important Republican with him to Paris. As for the treaty itself, probably more senators were alienated by the inclusion of the League Covenant than by any other feature. Yet when the treaty first came before the Senate, a majority of the senators would have accepted it at least in part; that is, some senators would have voted for the treaty with certain "reservations," or changes. However, Wilson wanted the text of the treaty just as he had signed it, and instructed the Democratic senators to accept no changes. Hence in the three times the senators voted on the treaty they never gave it the required two-thirds majority vote of approval. Finally, in 1922 the United States made separate treaties with Germany, Austria, and Hungary, that did not include the League.

Review Questions

1. Describe the organization of the Conference of Paris of 1919. How was this organization different from that of the Congress of Vienna in 1814–15? What may have caused this difference?

2. Describe the origins of the secret treaties, their contents, and their effects upon the Peace of Paris.

3. What major country besides Germany was not represented at the Conference of Paris? Why? What effect may its absence have had upon the Peace of Paris and world politics afterward?

4. What was the most important difference between the Treaty of Versailles and the treaties with the other defeated countries? Compare the Treaty of Trianon

with the Treaty of Brest-Litovsk, not in terms of areas concerned but in terms of general spirit and apparent intent.

5. Describe the chief bodies in the structure of the League of Nations. Could a difference in League structure have made it easier for countries to use the League mechanism to prevent war?

6. Discuss the various disputes that were handled through the League mechanism in the 1920's and early 1930's. Can any general rule be drawn from the conclusions reached in the handling of these disputes?

7. What reason or reasons lay behind the failure of the United States government to ratify the Treaty of Versailles?

7 THE PERIOD OF FALSE STABILITY, 1919 TO 1929

The years from 1919 until 1929 may well be termed the "period of false stability." These were years of peace; however, this peace resulted not from the settlement of all major international disputes but from the inability of the nations dissatisfied with the status quo to change matters. In Great Britain and France, the dominant military powers of Europe, the leaders were relatively content with the Peace of Paris and wanted to keep the essentials of the status quo. The Soviet Union, potentially the greatest source of problems concerning world peace, suffered political and economic chaos that kept it from being very influential in world politics. The Italians, victorious but resentful, were still only preparing to change some provisions in the peace settlement. The Japanese were biding their time. The Germans, militarily impotent, at least seemed willing to accept the decisions of 1919. The people of the United States appeared to have resolved that it was of little use for them to interfere in the politics of Europe. Meanwhile the various governments signed a number of pacts obliging them to carry out a degree of disarmament and to pledge the avoidance of war.

TOTALITARIANISM IN THE SOVIET UNION AND ITALY

Totalitarianism is a political system in which the government seeks to control all political, economic, social, and cultural activities of the people. The leaders obtain and exercise their control by persuasion if possible and by force if necessary. A totalitarian government is always a dictatorship. However, not all dictatorships are totalitarian; the dictatorships that arose after World War I in such countries as Poland were not totalitarian. These dictatorships emerged chiefly because the leaders and the peoples of these countries were unable to rule themselves under the limited governments they adopted, or that were imposed upon them, after World War I. They were designed primarily to regulate political behavior. Totalitarianism, by contrast, involves efforts to regulate all phases of behavior.

The Soviet Union. During this period the leaders of the Soviet Union were concerned chiefly with assuring their hold on the government and with repairing the enormous damages the November Revolution and the civil war had inflicted on the country. Not until 1928 did the Soviet government introduce a planned, socialistic national economy.

EMERGENCE OF THE SOVIET UNION. As discussed above, the withdrawal of Soviet Russia from World War I early in 1918 was followed by some years of civil war and foreign intervention in Soviet Russian affairs. Little by little, however, the Bolsheviks overcame their domestic opponents, and foreign governments concluded that the expense of intervention was greater than the advantages they might reap from it. The last strong effort to overthrow the Bolshevik regime was carried out by Poland, which with French support invaded Russia in 1920. In 1921 Soviet forces expelled the Polish troops, so that the Bolsheviks now controlled a large part of the territory taken from Russia by the Treaty of Brest-Litovsk. The Soviet Russian government made three "separate" Soviet states out of this area: the Ukraine, White Russia, and Transcaucasia. In 1923 these were combined with Soviet Russia into a new state, the Union of Soviet Socialist Republics (USSR), or Soviet Union. In later years, as the Soviet Union obtained more territories, they also were transformed into "Soviet Republics" and added to this nominally federal structure.

INTERNAL DEVELOPMENTS. Between 1919 and 1929 the USSR acquired a paper constitution for its government and underwent a great deal of economic experimentation. In 1923 Soviet leaders adopted a republican and federal constitution, which was in fact only a façade for a dictatorship of the Bolshevik, or Communist, Party. In 1924 Lenin died; and after a short struggle with Trotsky, Joseph Stalin, Secretary of the Party Central Committee, became the dictator of the Soviet Union. There was much economic experimentation. After the economy based on "pure communism" instituted in 1918 had failed, Lenin in 1921 proclaimed the "New Economic Policy," under which the government permitted some privately owned business undertakings and reduced its controls over the peasants. Then, in 1928, Stalin introduced the first Five-Year Plan, which was designed, through government planning of the national economy, to make Soviet industry and agriculture as extensive and as productive as possible. This Plan has been followed by several others and was the basis for the present form of the Soviet national economy.

FOREIGN POLICY. Long-range Soviet foreign policy since the Revolution has not varied; its goal has been consistently the conquest of the world. However, the particular attitudes and means of the time have changed periodically with changes in internal affairs or the foreign situation. During the first years of the Bolshevik regime, in the era of "pure communism," Soviet foreign policy was one of undisguised hostility toward non-Soviet countries as Communist Parties outside Russia sought to win control of the governments in their countries. Their efforts were seconded by the Communist International (Comintern), a world-wide association of Communist Parties established in Moscow in 1919. However, the result of these efforts was only two short-lived Bolshevik regimes, in Bavaria and Hungary. Then, under the "New Economic Policy," the USSR was much more conciliatory toward other countries. In appearance it discarded its policy of backing revolutions elsewhere; reached nonaggression treaties with other powers, which were one by one extending diplomatic recognition to the Soviet Union; and sought investments from abroad. Then, in 1928, with the first Five-Year Plan and the revival of outspoken hostility to capitalism, Soviet foreign policy again became openly inimical toward other countries, as Soviet leaders claimed that their regime would never be safe so long as there was a single non-Communist power in the world.

Italy. Although Italy had been among the victorious powers in World War I, during the postwar years it was the scene of much political unrest and economic distress. Finally, in order to save the country from what seemed to be impending internal collapse, King Victor Emmanuel III was impelled to name as prime minister Benito Mussolini, who had long been asserting that he and his Fascist Party alone could restore order and dignity to Italy.

THE POSTWAR SITUATION IN ITALY. The postwar situation in Italy was marked by political and economic chaos. The economy suffered from inflation and unemployment; in addition, the Italian people were dissatisfied with what Italy had gained from the war. Communists threatened a revolution. Into this crisis came Benito Mussolini, a former socialist newspaper editor, and his Fascist Party, which combined the principles of socialism, nationalism, and militarism. By 1921, 35 Fascists had been elected to parliament. To hasten matters, Fascist Party members, organized as Mussolini's private army, marched into Rome on October 28, 1922; on October 30 Victor Emmanuel asked Mussolini to become premier.

AFFAIRS IN FASCIST ITALY UNTIL 1929. Gradually Mussolini assumed absolute power for himself and the Fascist Party. By 1924 he had overcome all major opposition in Italy. Mussolini now instituted a government-planned economy, emphasizing self-sufficiency in heavy industry and agriculture and including numerous public works and various social-welfare measures. He also increased the size of the army to give Italy greater force in diplomatic negotiations. In foreign affairs the Italians obtained only the city of Fiume, but Mussolini soon commenced readying the Italian people for aggressive war by claiming such places as Nice, Savoy, Corsica, and Tunisia—all of them belonging to France.

THE OTHER GREAT POWERS

During the 1920's the other great powers included the United States, Great Britain, France, Germany, Japan, and China. In each one there was a considerable tendency toward economic nationalism, only somewhat less emphatic and deliberate than that of the totalitarian states. In the United States during this period there was considerable prosperity, but in the other countries there were varying degrees of economic want and political disorder.

The United States. The United States more than any other great power enjoyed prosperity between 1919 and 1929, save for the brief yet severe depression of 1921. Many Americans had prospered because of the stimulus the war had given industry and agriculture; the national economy had suffered little because of the war; and the national government had not incurred a large debt. One phase of the quest for prosperity was the many loans and investments that American citizens made abroad, notably by the purchase of German government bonds. These overseas financial activities had considerable effect upon world politics, as is shown below. During this same period the American public paid relatively little attention to the political and economic difficulties of other countries, and the national government mirrored this unconcern. Indeed, the United States government probably contributed to worsening these difficulties in some countries by demanding that the European governments to which it had lent money during and after the war repay their debts and by placing a high tariff on imported goods, so that Europeans could not sell their products in the United States and thus obtain money with which to pay their debts. On the other hand, it should be noted that the United States government, although not a member of the League, participated in some League activities by sending representatives to certain League gatherings; and it co-operated in various ways with other countries to reduce armaments and to try to prevent the outbreak of war.

Great Britain. The chief events concerning Great Britain during this period were, in domestic affairs, a realignment of political parties and, in foreign affairs, a reorganization of the British Empire.

DOMESTIC AFFAIRS. Great Britain experienced a brief spurt of prosperity just after the war. Yet, because of the debt incurred during the war, the sale of numerous overseas investments, and the loss of many foreign markets to such competitors as the United States, for the rest of the time up to 1929 at least some part of the British national economy was depressed. In politics, elections after the war made it clear that the Liberal Party had given way to the Labor Party, which henceforth would share the stage with the Conservative Party.

FOREIGN AFFAIRS. The chief event in foreign and colonial affairs was the granting of what amounted to national independence to the dominions in the Empire—Canada, Newfoundland (until 1934), the Union of South Africa, Australia, New Zealand, and the Irish Free State (1921–49). This major change in British imperial policy actually had been developing since before the war, because for a number of years the dominion governments had been performing such acts as signing treaties and appointing diplomatic representatives that are regarded as the functions of independent states. According to the Balfour Report of 1926, the dominions were to be only "united by a common allegiance to the Crown, and freely associated as members of the British Commonwealth of Nations." This principle became law by the Statute of Westminster in 1931. In their foreign policy the British seemed concerned mainly with reviving the balance of power in Europe and, as one step in this process, restoring the economy of Germany.

France. France enjoyed only a relatively small measure of the prosperity that Americans experienced after the war. France had suffered more from the war than any other western European country; French territory had been occupied, French property had been destroyed, and over a million French soldiers had been killed. The French government spent large sums to help the rebuilding of devastated areas, expecting to be recompensed by German reparations payments; but, as indicated below, these payments for a long time were not forthcoming. France also underwent a long period of inflation, which threatened the very existence of the large investor group in the country but which gave certain other groups the sensation of prosperity. Politically the French were still divided into numerous parties, none of which commanded a majority of the voters or in the parliament; hence it was difficult for a French government to take a stand on any issue. In foreign affairs, the French were concerned chiefly with keeping Germany weak and assuring their own military supremacy in Europe. In 1929 they started building the Maginot Line, a string of fortifications along the German frontier.

Germany. During this decade the Germans were concerned primarily with internal affairs, especially the payment of reparations.

REPARATIONS. As noted previously, the total sum of reparations was to be fixed some time after the Treaty of Versailles was signed; meanwhile the Germans were to make a substantial "down payment." In 1921 an international Reparation Commission dominated by France announced that Germany should pay about $32 billion plus interest, in semi-annual installments. The Germans paid the first installment, then asked for a moratorium. In fact, the Germans were opposed to reparations payments. Besides, in order to make these payments they had to have a favorable balance of trade so as to obtain the money; but after the war they had an unfavorable balance. In order to avoid deficits, the government resorted to monetary inflation. In 1923, the French declared the Germans in default on their reparations payments and, as permitted by the Versailles Treaty, occupied the industrial Ruhr Valley. Germany united in resistance, and chaos reigned. Finally, an international commission headed by an American financier, General Charles G. Dawes, drafted a new plan for reparations that came into effect in 1924. This plan made it somewhat easier for the Germans to make payments; under it, German inflation halted and the Germans began making payments. Yet there still was dissatisfaction, in part because the plan involved foreign supervision of German finances. In 1929 another committee, under the American industrialist, Owen D. Young, drafted a new plan that reduced the total to be paid and removed most foreign controls. This plan was in effect only a short time because of the depression that started in 1929. Perhaps the greatest problem raised by reparations was the insistence of European governments that they could not pay their debts to the United States without reparations and the refusal of the United States government to reduce or "forgive" these debts.

OTHER DOMESTIC CONCERNS. As a defeated power, Germany suffered considerably for years after the war, both because of the war itself and because of the reparations Germany was forced to pay. At the same time these losses indirectly promoted business undertakings. For instance, in turning over steamships to the Allies the Germans encouraged their own shipbuilding industry (and depressed that of Great Britain); by furnishing the Allies with industrial machinery from their factories, the Germans made it possible to introduce the latest type of manufacturing equipment into their own plants. As a result, after German finances had been stabilized under the Dawes Plan, Germany quickly regained many of its prewar markets and experienced some years of considerable prosperity. One important factor was the billions of dollars invested in Germany by American citizens. One of the greatest difficulties for Germany was the Weimar Republic itself. It assured so many political freedoms to the people that it could hardly protect itself from its domestic enemies; it had little backing from other countries; and it was despised by many Germans, especially the nationalists and the militarists, for signing the Treaty of Versailles.

FOREIGN AFFAIRS. In foreign affairs Germany had relatively little influence, for it was an "outcast" power and had been disarmed. German military leaders, however, saw to it that the small army Germany had been allowed would be so organized as to provide a framework for a much larger army, should it some day be permitted to have one. The Germans also arranged with the Soviet Union, likewise an "outcast," for German officers to get experience by commanding Soviet troops in practice maneuvers. Partly in exchange, German engineers supervised the erection of armaments plants in the USSR. After 1924, however, other countries began making treaties with Germany, and Germany was admitted to the League of Nations.

Japan. The period after World War I saw the expansion of Japanese power in the Far East. In 1915 the Japanese forced upon the Chinese government the so-called "Twenty-one Demands," which were intended to make China virtually a Japanese protectorate. The Chinese government, however, never ratified them. Then, at the end of the war, Japan received mandates over certain former German Pacific islands and outright possession of German properties in China. The Japanese had trifling military expenditures during the war and greatly expanded their exports, especially in Asia, at the expense of the belligerents. After the war the Japanese for some time continued to enjoy prosperity, to a large degree because of their exports of silk to the United States. With the increased use of rayon in the United States, however, Japanese exports and national income began to decline. The Japanese government tried unsuccessfully to cope with the worsening depression by inflating the money supply. Government officials also sought to encourage further growth in Japanese industry, but the economy was handicapped by the shortage of raw materials in Japan and the high Japanese birth rate. Finally, the government, the major industries, and the banks united to keep prices artificially high, with a resulting surplus of imports over exports, a dangerous situation for a country that had to sell fabricated goods abroad so as to be able to secure the raw materials essential for its industry.

China. During most of the 1920's China underwent widespread political disorder, since no Chinese leader was able to establish a stable regime after the overthrow of the imperial government in 1912. Although it did declare war on Germany, China played a very small part in World War I. After the war, when the Japanese obtained the former German areas and rights in China, the Chinese government rejected the Treaty of Versailles and entered the League of Nations only by signing the Treaty of St. Germain. Nevertheless, Sino-Japanese relations gradually became less hostile, and in 1923 the two countries reached an agreement according to which the Japanese were to turn over to the Chinese the Shantung peninsula, formerly a German sphere of interest. The most important leader in China was Sun Yat-sen, founder and head of the Nationalist Party, or *Kuomintang*. In the early 1920's this party received considerable assistance from the Soviet Union, working through the Comintern. Soviet leaders instructed the Chinese Communist Party to join the Kuomintang and to follow its dictates. It was Stalin's belief that the principles set forth by the Kuomintang would lay the foundations for the first stage of the revolution, the bourgeois revolution stage, after which the Communists would carry out the second stage, a revolution of the proletariat, and thus put China under the rule of the USSR. During his lifetime, Sun was able to control the two dissident groups in his party—the Communists and those members of the Kuomintang who suspected them of subversion. But in 1925 he died. His successor, Chiang Kai-shek, took a more direct approach. He expelled the advisers of the USSR and afterward began a civil war against the Chinese Communists. Meanwhile the Kuomintang had established a weak one-party government for China.

THE SEARCH FOR SECURITY AND PEACE

The search for security and peace between 1919 and 1929, a movement led chiefly by France, resulted in the formation of military alliances, the drafting of treaties to guarantee frontiers and possessions, and the negotiation of a pact that "outlawed" war.

The System of Military Alliances. The system of military alliances that developed in Europe after 1919 was built and dominated by France. To defend themselves against Germany, the French arranged military alliances with both Belgium and Poland that provided for mutual assistance in case of military attack, presumably by the Germans. Meanwhile the governments of Romania, Yugoslavia, and Czechoslovakia—the "Little Entente"—formed a group of military alliances among themselves; later they established ties with Poland as well. These countries, each of which had secured land from either Austria or Hungary, or both, wanted to protect themselves against Austrian or Hungarian aggression. Finally, in the mid-1920's, all the Little Entente countries became allies of France, so that they were now also concerned with restraining German aggression. This whole system of alliances was intended by the French to assure their hegemony in Europe. The Soviet Union and Italy also negotiated treaties with several other countries during the 1920's. These latter treaties, however, were not firm military alliances but simply friendship and nonaggression pacts.

Treaties to Guarantee International Frontiers. During the 1920's all of the great powers except the USSR, as well as some of the lesser powers, signed one or more treaties designed to guarantee frontiers and possessions.

THE LOCARNO TREATIES. The seven Locarno Treaties, first proposed by the German government and signed in 1925, included agreements among Germany, France, Great Britain, Belgium, Italy, Czechoslovakia, and Poland. The governments concerned promised to maintain the western frontier of Germany with Belgium and France, as fixed by the Treaty of Versailles, and the demilitarization of the German Rhineland; to settle all disputes by peaceful means, resorting to war only for purposes of defense or to uphold treaty obligations; and to assist one another against any country violating the treaty. These treaties were drafted in an atmosphere of great friendliness that came to be termed the "spirit of Locarno." They had, however, the major fault of not guaranteeing the eastern frontiers of Germany.

THE FOUR-POWER AND NINE-POWER TREATIES. The Four-Power and Nine-Power Treaties, signed at Washington, D.C., in 1922, were designed primarily to maintain the status quo in the western Pacific Ocean and the Far East. The Four-Power Treaty, signed by the United States, Great Britain, France, and Japan, constituted an agreement among the four signatories that they would respect the Far Eastern interests of each other. The Nine-Power Treaty, signed by these four countries and Belgium, the Netherlands, Portugal, Italy, and China, pledged the independence of China and the maintenance of the Open Door Policy.

A Pact to "Outlaw" War. The pact to "outlaw" war was the Pact of Paris, or Kellogg-Briand Pact, negotiated in 1928. It resulted from a suggestion by French Foreign Minister Aristide Briand to United States Secretary of State Frank Kellogg that France and the United States cooperate in inducing a number of countries to sign an antiwar treaty. Immediately after the pact was drafted, representatives from fifteen countries signed it; eventually there were 64 signatories. Despite the publicity surrounding this pact, the signatories had not agreed to "outlaw" war; they had only agreed to "condemn recourse to war" and to "renounce it as an instrument of national policy." Even viewed in this light, the pact contained an outstanding weakness: it provided no machinery for its enforcement. Nevertheless, at the time it was signed, many people believed it could effectively prevent the outbreak of war. After World War II it was used as the basis for the trials of certain German and Japanese leaders, who were accused of having committed a crime by violating it.

EFFORTS TO ACHIEVE DISARMAMENT

Efforts to achieve disarmament between 1919 and 1929 were of two sorts: those aimed at general disarmament, and those aimed at naval disarmament.

General Disarmament Undertakings. Undertakings to reach agreements on general disarmament ran almost continuously between 1919 and 1929. The chief immediate cause for their failure lay in the inability of the powers concerned to reach a satisfactory compromise between French demands for security and German insistence on military equality. Still more important was the mistaken view of government leaders that disarmament in itself could prevent war without a reduction of the causes that motivated countries to arm themselves in preparation for war.

THE VERSAILLES TREATY. The Versailles Treaty laid the basis for a general disarmament by limiting the military forces of the defeated nations. Although this seemed to be a unilateral action, Clemenceau assured the world that this would be a "first step" toward a "general reduction and limitation of armaments." In fact, according to one provision of the League Covenant, the members of the League held that the "maintenance of peace" demands the "reduction of national armaments." The United States and Great Britain did reduce their armies. However, other European countries did not, on the ground that without large military forces they would be insecure.

LATER ATTEMPTS TO AGREE ON DISARMAMENT. Later attempts to agree on disarmament were conducted chiefly through the League of Nations. The most important of these attempts began in 1925, when the League Council named a Preparatory Commission for a disarmament conference. After submitting a questionnaire to the governments involved and after analyzing the answers received, the Commission submitted the draft of a treaty that embodied the points agreed upon, to be read before the entire League in 1929. Subsequently the League Council called for a world disarmament conference, to meet at Geneva in 1932. It had by now become evident, however, that governments were acting more according to self-interest than according to a genuine desire for disarmament.

Naval Disarmament Treaties. Although the various nations had failed to reach an agreement on general disarmament by working through the League, the great naval powers negotiated two important naval disarmament pacts outside League mechanisms.

THE NAVAL ARMAMENTS TREATY (1922). In 1921–22, representatives of the United States, Great Britain, Japan, France, and Italy gathered at Washington, D.C., to consider, among other things, a limitation on naval forces. The resulting Naval Armaments Treaty forbade construction of any new battleships except to replace those more than twenty years old. It also provided that the nations concerned, in the order listed above, might have battleship tonnages in the ratio of 5:5:3:1.67:1.67 and aircraft-carrier tonnages in the ratio of 5:5:3:2.22:2.22. Finally, the treaty required most of its signatories, particularly the United States, to scrap some new ships and some under construction.

THE LONDON NAVAL TREATY (1930). Since the Naval Armaments Treaty fixed no limits for smaller ships, representatives of these five powers assembled in London in 1930 to draft a second treaty. Here the French and the Italians could reach no agreement, owing to their rivalry in the Mediterranean. The Americans, British, and Japanese, however, concurred on limits for cruisers, destroyers, and submarines. One other noteworthy clause in the London Naval Treaty permitted any of the signatory powers to build ships beyond the quota assigned to it if it believed itself imperiled by new construction on the part of a nonsignatory country. It needed only inform the other signatories, so that they could increase their navies proportionately. This treaty was to last until 1936.

Review Questions

1. Why can the years from 1919 until 1929 be termed a "period of false stability"?

2. What were the three types of economic systems that prevailed in the Soviet Union between 1919 and 1929? Was there any correlation between these systems and the attitudes that Soviet leaders adopted toward other countries?

3. Compare Fascist Italy with the Soviet Union during the 1920's in terms of (a) the acquisition of power by a party of totalitarian principles; (b) political and economic structure; and (c) foreign policy.

4. What major change occurred in the structure of the British Empire between 1918 and 1931?

5. What were the various arrangements under which the Germans were to pay reparations? What was the impact of reparations upon other international financial transactions?

6. In what country during the 1920's were agents of the USSR most active? What did they do, and how successful were they? Why was this country a particular target of Soviet imperialism at this time?

7. During the 1920's, which European state was most interested in preserving the status quo, and what steps did it take to achieve this goal?

8. Describe the negotiations and contents of the Kellogg-Briand Pact.

9. Discuss the various disarmament undertakings after World War I, not as a narrative but in terms of the strategic interests of the great powers concerned.

8 THE BACKGROUND OF WORLD WAR II, 1929 TO 1939

Beginning with the year 1929 the economic and political structure erected during and after the war rapidly disintegrated. Economic prosperity ended as a depression struck first the United States then western Europe. The League of Nations showed itself a weak if not useless mechanism for preventing war when Japan and Italy committed aggression and went unpunished. Western Europe neared the verge of war as Adolf Hitler became dictator of Germany and launched an aggressive policy toward the neighbors of Germany. While Germany and Japan continued their militaristic policies, Great Britain and France at first did almost nothing. Gradually, however, the British and the French became aware of the menacing policies of these aggressive powers and felt concern about their own safety. The United States first indicated that it was not going to try to settle differences in Europe but slowly began to sympathize with Britain and France. During this period, the Soviet Union maintained its policy of hostility toward all non-Soviet states. War broke out in 1939 after the Soviet and German governments signed a treaty dividing Eastern Europe between them. By so doing, Soviet leaders, tacitly at least, encouraged the Germans to attack Great Britain and France.

THE ECONOMIC DEPRESSION OF 1929

Starting with the New York Stock Exchange crash of 1929, a major depression spread through the United States, with economic and political repercussions all over the world. Its causes are still not completely clear, but among them were speculation and various unsound financial practices by both government officials and businessmen. Its first effects in the United States were the spreading of unemployment and the slowing down of industry and commerce. As far as world politics was concerned, one of its most important early effects was the Hawley-Smoot Tariff of 1930, which imposed the highest tariff rates in American history. Among the later effects of the depression was the introduction of the New Deal by Franklin D. Roosevelt in 1933, involving, among other programs, a program of monetary inflation designed to promote economic recovery. Most important for world politics, Roosevelt secured from Congress a bill taking the United States off the gold standard. Also, in June, 1933, he withdrew the United States from the London Economic Conference, which had gathered especially to consider ways to stabilize the moneys of the world. Thus the United States government adopted a policy of economic nationalism. The depression spread quickly to Europe. European countries lost not only their markets in the United States but, even worse, the American investments in business equities and government bonds. The whole system of international payments stemming from the Treaty of Versailles broke down. The refusal or inability of Americans to buy German government bonds impeded German reparations payments; it thus became difficult or impossible for the British, French, and others to pay their war debts to the United States. In 1931 President Hoover urged a moratorium on all debt payments for one year, and when the moratorium ended in 1932 only Finland resumed full payments to the United States. Great Britain and other important countries went off the gold standard. Thus the depression speeded the world-wide tendency toward *autarchy*—the quest for economic self-sufficiency.

JAPANESE AGGRESSION IN THE FAR EAST

Japanese aggression in the Far East involved a successful military campaign in 1931–32 whereby the Japanese seized Manchuria from China. It was the first of a series of moves by Japanese military leaders, who in the 1930's dominated the government. It provided the first illustration of how the members of the League would not use League machinery to restrain a major power, and it was one occasion when the United States government took a firm stand against aggression.

The Japanese Occupation of Manchuria. In 1931 the Japanese opened a wide-scale invasion of Manchuria, an area then and today of great strategic and economic significance. The Japanese had been investing in Manchurian business undertakings for some years. They owned the South Manchuria Railway, and Japanese troops patrolled its right-of-way. In 1931 Japan was nearing an economic crisis, particularly because it was losing its foreign trade. For several years the Japanese government had been adopting the principles of autarchy, and in

1931 it went off the gold standard. With China in political turmoil, the Japanese seized upon an explosion that damaged the South Manchuria Railway as an excuse to send troops to Manchuria; since China was almost powerless to resist, Japan quickly overran Manchuria, detached it from China, and transformed it into an "independent," puppet state, Manchukuo. When the Chinese tried to halt Japanese aggression with an economic boycott, the Japanese seized Shanghai and forced an end to the boycott before withdrawing. By the end of 1933 the Japanese appeared to be firmly in control of all Manchukuo.

International Reactions to the "Manchurian Incident." Almost at once after the beginning of the "Manchurian Incident," as the Japanese termed their aggression in China, there were international reactions. The principal arena for these reactions was the League of Nations, to which China appealed soon after the Japanese invasion. The members of the League did not invoke any of the sanctions available to them through League machinery; instead, they appointed an investigatory commission to survey matters and propose a solution. The report of the commission, ten months later, was very guarded, and made no propositions for the use of military or even economic restraints against Japan. Nevertheless, this report, and the apparent attitude of League members, so irritated the Japanese that in March, 1933, they announced their intention to withdraw from the League. Meanwhile the United States government independently had taken a much firmer stand regarding the Japanese aggression. Before the League commission issued its report, Secretary of State Henry L. Stimson announced that the United States government viewed the Japanese action as a violation of the Kellogg-Briand Pact and that the United States would not recognize any conquest or new states arising from such a violation. This "Stimson Doctrine" was an effort to uphold the Open Door Policy, but it won little support in Europe. When the Japanese attacked Shanghai, Stimson proposed even stronger action, but the British refused to cooperate. Thus the Japanese succeeded in flouting the principles of the League.

THE RISE OF NAZISM IN GERMANY

From 1929 until 1933 the situation in Germany was one of a growing political and economic crisis that finally subverted the Weimar Republic and established the National Socialist, or Nazi, Party in power.

The Rise of the National Socialist Party. The depression of the late 1920's and the early 1930's brought with it the rise of the National Socialist (Nazi) Party, led by Adolf Hitler, a socialist and anti-Semite.

The Nazi Party was dedicated to the belief in the superiority of the Nordic peoples and to the cult of the state. It united nationalists, small businessmen, veterans, former government officials, anti-Semites, and a few wealthy capitalists. Largely because of the economic conditions in Germany and widespread opposition to the domestic and foreign policies of the Weimar Republic, the Nazi Party grew until in the election of 1932 it became the largest party in the German parliament (*Reichstag*). In January, 1933, Hitler became Chancellor, or prime minister.

First Acts of the Nazis in Power. One of the first acts of the Nazis after Hitler became Chancellor was to assure their control of the government. In a terror-filled election in 1933, they and the allied German National People's Party won a majority of the legislative seats. The legislature then surrendered most of its power to the cabinet, meaning in effect to the Nazi Party. The Nazis also transformed the more or less sovereign states of Germany into mere administrative units, so that Germany now had a unitary rather than a federal government. They inaugurated a public works program to lessen unemployment; and they instituted a planned economy designed to achieve autarchy, in part to strengthen the country for military purposes. In this early period of Nazi control the Germans were still too weak to commit any foreign aggression. However, they did withdraw from the Geneva Disarmament Conference, which had gathered in 1932 to discuss the draft treaty mentioned above. At the same time they announced their intention to withdraw from the League. Thus by 1933 two great powers, Japan and Germany, had officially rejected the Treaty of Versailles and the League of Nations. Moreover, the principles of human liberty and capitalism that during the 1920's had seemed predominant in all great powers save Italy and the USSR had been formally cast aside in two other great powers and threatened elsewhere.

THE FIRST STEPS OF NAZI GERMANY, 1934–35

The first steps of Nazi Germany, in 1934 and 1935, showed the Nazis' expansionist ambitions. One of Hitler's first goals was to annex Austria, and to this end he nurtured a Nazi Party in that country. However, a revolt by the Austrian Nazis in 1934 was quelled by the Austrian government, which at the time enjoyed Mussolini's sympathy. Also in 1934, Germany signed a nonaggression pact with Poland, which had become convinced that France was too weak to protect it against Germany. This treaty heralded the breakdown of the French security system in central and eastern Europe. Then, early in 1935, the residents of the Saar voted by an overwhelming majority to rejoin Germany in a plebiscite administered by the League of Nations. German repossession of this area substantially increased German coal resources and strengthened German industry. Also, Hitler announced the revival of military conscription in Germany. These German undertakings evoked some important reactions from other countries. Great Britain, France, and Italy combined into a more or less anti-German group, the "Stresa Front," mainly concerned with keeping Germany from annexing Austria. The Soviet Union began to regard Germany as its greatest foe, secured diplomatic recognition from the United States, unleashed a world-wide campaign against Fascism and Nazism, and became the leading supporter of collective security. Soviet propagandists adopted the fiction that Fascism and Nazism were dictatorships of big businessmen; Soviet leaders instructed Communists around the world to join with other "anti-Fascist," anti-big-business parties to establish pro-Soviet "Popular Front" governments. The USSR also made an alliance with France.

THE ITALIAN CONQUEST OF ETHIOPIA

In 1935 and 1936 the Italians executed a military conquest of Ethiopia, a backward yet independent country that was a member of the League. Again, the other great powers failed to use the League machinery for preventing or halting an aggression.

The Military Campaigns. In October, 1935, after a number of border clashes, Italian armies based in the Italian East African colonies invaded Ethiopia. The well-equipped Italian army and the Italian air force had comparatively little difficulty in overcoming the primitive Ethiopian forces opposing them and found their chief hardship to be the mountainous terrain. In May, 1936, Mussolini proclaimed that Ethiopia had been conquered and comprised a new element in the Italian overseas empire.

International Reactions. There was a group of major international reactions to the Italian aggression against Ethiopia.

EFFORTS TO END THE WAR. Governments of several countries made efforts to end the war, both through the League and independently. Even before large-scale fighting broke out, a League commission had investigated the armed clashes on the borders of Ethiopia. Late in 1935 the League membership except for Italy undertook to end the war. However, the British and the French were divided as to their degree of interference. The British asserted that the war must be halted and that they would support vigorous action through the League. The French, by contrast, tried to restrain the British from very strong measures. Perhaps the chief reason for their differing views lay in the fact that the British were concerned almost entirely with limiting Italian aggression whereas the French were concerned with keeping Italian friendship in the event of German aggression. In any case, the members of the League voted to impose economic sanctions on Italy, meaning that they would sell the Italian government no munitions. However, the German government, hoping to secure the alliance of Italy, willingly provided the Italians with all the goods they needed. The government of the United States also embargoed shipments of war materials to both Italy and Ethiopia but did not curtail shipments of oil. In fact, Mussolini threatened to expand the war to Europe if he were denied oil. With the end of hostilities in Ethiopia, Italy left the League, having succeeded in violating the League Covenant without being punished.

The Deterioration of the French Military Situation. The Italo-Ethiopian War also led to a deterioration of the French military situation, as governments in other countries saw that the French were unwilling to go to war. In March, 1936, while the attention of the world was focused on Ethiopia, Hitler announced that Germany was going to remilitarize the Rhineland, in defiance of the Versailles Treaty. Actually, he sent very small forces into the Rhineland at first, and German military leaders trembled at the thought of how easy it would be for the French to expel them and overrun Germany. Hitler's boldness and his success in this venture greatly strengthened his hand in dealing with German army leaders in the future and magnified his own confidence in his military competence. The Germans soon commenced building a line of fortifications in the Rhineland, the West Wall. This step made the French still less anxious to impose sanctions upon Italy. It also so weakened Belgian confidence in France that late in 1936 the Belgian government broke its alliance with France and announced its neutrality. This act by the Belgians imposed on France the need for extending the Maginot Line to the English Channel, but the French never carried out this task. The entire sequence of events greatly weakened the reliance that the Little Entente countries had placed in French military power and dealt the whole French security system a blow from which it never recovered.

THE SPANISH CIVIL WAR

Between 1936 and 1939 a civil war raged in Spain, with major repercussions on all the great powers of Europe.

Events in Spain. In 1936 a civil war broke out in Spain between "Loyalists," who supported the Spanish republican government, and "Rebels," or "Nationalists," led by General Francisco Franco, who opposed it. The outbreak of this war climaxed years of political instability in Spain, where in 1931 the monarchy had been overthrown and a republic installed in its place. In the republican government some socialists and Communists held important posts, and in 1936 the government was dominated by a Popular Front cabinet. The republican government tended to be hostile toward the army, the Catholic Church, and the landlords. As a consequence, representatives of these three groups banded together under General Franco in an effort to overthrow the republic.

International Reactions. The Spanish civil war had far-flung international reactions. The Nationalists received troops, munitions, and money from Fascist Italy. Nazi Germany also contributed to the Nationalist cause. The Loyalists received help from the USSR at the beginning of hostilities, but later the Soviet government ceased its support. The British and the French, although friendly toward the Loyalists, officially were neutral and supposedly did not contribute to either side. The United States government took the exceptional step of placing an embargo on munitions to Spain. This measure helped the Nationalists, since they had relatively few sympathizers in the United States and were receiving arms from Italy and Germany. The British and the French initiated the formation of an international nonintervention committee that was supposed to patrol the Spanish frontiers, but war materials were nonetheless brought in to both sides. The Nationalists obtained far more of this sort of help than the Loyalists and in 1939 were able to bring hostilities to a victorious close, with General Franco becoming dictator of Spain.

Formation of the Axis. The formation of the Berlin-Rome-Tokyo Axis was one of the chief results of the Spanish civil war. In 1936 the German and Italian governments, which had already been associated in aggressions in Ethiopia and Spain, were termed by Mussolini "an axis around which all European states animated by the desire for peace might collaborate." Later that year, Germany and Japan signed the Anti-Comintern Pact, openly directed against the USSR. In 1937 the Italian government also signed this treaty, completing the formation of the Axis. At the beginning the Axis seemed most concerned with an ideological war against the USSR, but Axis leaders soon made it clear they were preparing for hostile action against other non-Axis states such as Great Britain and France.

Other Consequences of the Spanish Civil War. The Spanish civil war had other consequences for world politics. It furnished another demonstration that neither the British nor the French were willing to go to war to halt aggressions, so that their prestige throughout Europe dropped sharply. Their stand during the war made Soviet leaders especially suspicious; utterances by both some British and some French leaders disclosed that they were more friendly toward Fascist Italy and Nazi Germany than they were toward the USSR. Consequently, Soviet leaders concluded that their military alliance with France might be of little avail in a war, and that they should pursue a more nearly independent course. Meanwhile the French now had a hostile country on their southern border, and the British had before them the possibility that in time of war the Spanish might capture Gibraltar. Finally, all countries that had provided war materials had had an opportunity to test new weapons and the techniques of using them.

THE FOREIGN POLICY OF THE UNITED STATES, 1933–39

The foreign policy of the United States between 1933 and 1939 involved generally distant relations with European and Asiatic countries but much closer ties with Latin American states.

Relations with European and Asiatic Countries. Between 1933 and 1939 the United States showed only slight interest in events outside the Western Hemisphere. One important change came in 1933, when President Roosevelt extended diplomatic recognition to the USSR. Soviet leaders promised to maintain no revolutionary political groups in the United States, but never kept this pledge. The belief that the United States should concern itself with its own economic problems, shown in 1933 by its withdrawal from the London Economic Conference, was reflected the following year in the Johnson Act, which forbade loans by the United States to the government of any country that had defaulted on its debt to the United States. In 1935, 1936, and 1937, Congress passed Neutrality Acts designed to keep the United States out of war by forbidding, among other things, the sale of arms to belligerents. Late in 1937, however, President Roosevelt urged that those responsible for "lawlessness" in the world be "quarantined." Nevertheless, the United States government took no immediate steps to implement this proposal.

Relations with Latin American Countries. In the years between 1933 and 1939 the relations of the United States with Latin American countries became much closer and more cordial. This change had been foreshadowed in the 1920's and early 1930's, especially in Hoover's presidency. However, it was Roosevelt who publicized it as the "Good Neighbor Policy." The United States government discarded "dollar diplomacy" and made it a point to deal with Latin American governments as equals. A major change in 1934 was the abrogation of the Platt Amendment, so that for the first time Cuba was genuinely independent. Also, at the urging of Secretary of State Cordell Hull, who wanted to stimulate foreign trade, Congress in 1934 passed the Reciprocal Trade Agreements Act. This law, which was intended to lower the rates of the Hawley-Smoot Tariff, empowered the President to negotiate agreements with other countries to lower tariff rates. In the next few years Roosevelt made such agreements with the governments of about twenty countries, most of them in Latin America.

GERMAN ABSORPTION OF AUSTRIA AND CZECHOSLOVAKIA

In 1938 and 1939 Germany absorbed both Austria and Czechoslovakia, without effective opposition from Great Britain or France and with Italy in a position of benevolent neutrality if not open support.

Austria. Although, as noted above, Germany was unable to secure Austria in 1934, the German government never ceased working toward this goal. It continued to support a powerful Nazi Party in Austria. Agitation in Austria for union, or *Anschluss,* with Germany increased, and the Italian government made it clear that it might not protect Austria again in case Hitler sought annexation. Finally, in March, 1938, Austrian Chancellor Kurt von Schuschnigg announced that voters in Austria would be asked in a plebiscite whether or not they wanted Austria to remain independent. Afraid that a fair election might produce an anti-Nazi majority, Hitler threatened to invade Austria if the vote were held. Schuschnigg resigned; an Austrian Nazi became Chancellor and invited the German army to "restore order" in Austria; and Hitler soon proclaimed the *Anschluss.* The British and the French protested, but took no steps to prevent Hitler from completing his aims. The Italian government made no open complaint.

Czechoslovakia. For economic, military, geographic, and demographic reasons, Czechoslovakia appeared desirable for German absorption. Consequently Hitler inaugurated a campaign of propaganda, threats, and abuse, that resulted in German occupation of Czechoslovakia, in two stages, the first of which had the support of the British and the French governments.

GERMAN AMBITIONS FOR CZECHOSLOVAKIA. Of all the countries that first appeared after the collapse of the Austro-Hungarian Empire, Czechoslovakia was by far the most prosperous and the most stable politically. It had a well balanced economy, a well trained army, and strong fortifications along its border with Germany. It was both a valuable prize for Hitler and a roadblock to German expansion eastward. The excuse that Hitler used for interfering in Czech affairs was the German minority residing mostly in the area of Czechoslovakia known as the Sudetenland, along the German frontier. Claiming that Germans in Czechoslovakia were being mistreated by the Czech government, Hitler began threatening in 1938 to march into Czechoslovakia to "protect" the Germans there. Czechoslovakia had a military pact with the USSR and, as a member of the Little Entente, was allied with France. France and the Soviet Union, as well as Great Britain, therefore rallied to the support of the Czechs against Hitler. Their support, however, was more apparent than real, for the Soviets promised to help the Czechs only if the French helped them, and the French government had a marked anti-Soviet bent. The same was true of the British government. In September, 1938, British Prime Minister Neville Chamberlain began a series of negotiations with Hitler, culminating in a meeting at Munich among Hitler, Mussolini, Chamberlain, and French Premier Edouard Daladier. Although the Czechs at the time were willing to go to war in their own defense, the British and French governments were not willing to go to war in defense of the Czechs. Therefore they agreed to a plan that would satisfy Hitler, that ultimately dismembered Czechoslovakia, and that Chamberlain proclaimed would bring "peace in our time."

RESULTS OF THE MUNICH AGREEMENT. According to the Munich agreement, Germany was to receive the Sudetenland. This area happened to include much of the industry of the country, including the Skoda munitions works and the fortifications facing Germany. As a result, Czechoslovakia became a weak and almost defenseless agrarian state. The Polish and Hungarian governments also helped themselves to regions of Czechoslovakia inhabited mainly by their co-nationals. The repercussions of the Munich agreement were world-wide. By their actions the British and the French had revealed that they were willing to sacrifice a small nation in order to prevent war. The French security system in eastern Europe vanished. Leaders in the USSR were especially put on guard, for the Munich agreement had been reached without their participation, and its terms removed Czechoslovakia as a barrier to German expansion eastward. It was not difficult for Soviet leaders to conclude that in British and French ruling circles there was considerable willingness to appease Germany in an effort to keep Soviet influence from extending farther west. Soviet leaders probably found it easier than before to decide that the best defense of the USSR lay in putting the Axis and non-Axis powers at each others' throats.

DISAPPEARANCE OF THE CZECH REPUBLIC. In March, 1939, Hitler brought about the disappearance of the Czech republic. Germany annexed the remainder of Bohemia-Moravia; Slovakia became an "autonomous" state that was actually a Nazi puppet; and Hungary annexed Ruthenia. Hitler carried out this aggression in spite of his pledges at Munich to seize no more Czech territory and in spite of the guarantees the British and the French had given the Czechs at Munich. This latest annexation offended many British and French leaders who countenanced earlier German aggressions since they had involved territories populated mainly by Germans. The British and the French still took no steps against Germany, but they speeded their armament programs. Also, since annexation of Bohemia-Moravia had enabled Germany to outflank Poland militarily, the British and the French started assuring the Poles of support in case of German attack. The Germans meanwhile seized the old German city of Memel from Lithuania, and the Italians profited by the confusion to occupy Albania. Southeastern Europe was becoming more and more dependent on Germany, not only because Germany had been rearming but also because German goods had replaced those of Great Britain and France in southeastern European markets.

THE GERMAN ATTACK ON POLAND

The German attack on Poland in 1939 opened much like that on Czechoslovakia, with a diplomatic and propaganda offensive. On this occasion, however, the result was war, because the British and the French decided to resist further German expansion whereas the Soviet government gave the Germans a free hand in Poland.

Opening of the German Offensive against Poland. Shortly after Hitler completed the annexation of Bohemia-Moravia he opened a diplomatic offensive against Poland. His chief demands were the return of Danzig, a former German city now under League supervision but important to the Polish economy since it controlled trade on the Vistula, the chief river of Poland; and the right to have a highway and a railroad across the Polish Corridor linking East Prussia with the rest of Germany. In exchange, he pledged to guarantee the borders of the Polish state. The British and the French proclaimed that they would defend Poland against a German attack, and they also promised help to Greece and Romania in case of German attack. Furthermore, they commenced efforts to reach an agreement with the USSR. The efforts went on for weeks, as Hitler uttered his typical charges that German minorities in Poland were being persecuted and denounced the German-Polish nonaggression pact of 1934. In May, the German and Italian governments signed a ten-year alliance.

The Soviet-German Pacts. In August, 1939, the governments of the USSR and Germany signed three treaties. One provided for an exchange of goods, particularly those Germany needed for war. A second was a pledge that neither country would wage war on the other for a ten-year period. The third, which was secret, arranged for the division of eastern Europe into spheres of interest, including a mutual partition of Poland. Considering how the governments of the two countries had been waging propaganda war on each other for several years, these agreements astonished many people. However, the Soviet Union had decided well beforehand that a treaty with Great Britain and France would do it little good; Soviet leaders distrusted British and French views on Germany, and still bore ill will toward them for omission of the USSR from the Munich discussions in 1938. (Maxim Litvinov, a leading supporter of the League of Nations, had therefore been replaced as foreign commissar by V. M. Molotov, who held to a more nearly "nationalistic" foreign policy.) The treaties showed the Soviet conviction that all non-Communist countries might band together for an attack on the USSR and that its best protection lay in permitting or even encouraging these countries to fight one another. By signing these treaties Soviet leaders freed Germany from the dangers of a war on two fronts and thus bear a major part of the responsibility for the outbreak of World War II.

The Beginning of Military Operations. With the negotiation of the Soviet-German pacts, events moved swiftly toward the beginning of military operations. A Nazi became head of the Danzig government, and Hitler made it clear he would not hesitate to go to war to secure his other demands—outright annexation of Danzig, certain privileges in the Polish Corridor, and a cessation of "atrocities" against Germans in Poland. Evidently Hitler believed that despite their pledges the British and French would not go to war in defense of Poland. While such other leaders as Pope Pius XI, King Leopold of Belgium, and President Roosevelt tried to forestall war, Hitler demanded that the Polish government send a plenipotentiary to Berlin to reach a settlement. On August 31 the German government broadcast to the world a group of sixteen demands that it supposedly was making on the Polish government to resolve differences between the two countries; however, the Germans severed communication links between Germany and Poland so that these demands could not be submitted officially to the Polish government. The German government also asserted that since the Poles had not sent the plenipotentiary, as they had been asked to do, they had rejected German peace suggestions. Hence on the morning of September 1, German troops invaded Poland, and German planes bombed Polish cities. The British and French governments now demanded that German forces withdraw from Poland; when the Germans continued their offensive, the British and French on September 3 declared war on Germany. Italy as in 1914 announced its neutrality.

Review Questions

1. Describe the various international reactions to the Japanese conquest of Manchuria. Why would the United States take a stand on this issue much different from the stand it adopted regarding the Italian invasion of Ethiopia?

2. Define *autarchy* and show its impact on the policies of the various great powers. What effect was autarchy apt to have on international relations?

3. Compare Nazi Germany with Fascist Italy and the USSR, in terms of (a) the acquisition of power by a party of totalitarian principles; (b) political and economic structure; and (c) foreign policy.

4. How did the Soviet government react to the Japanese conquest of Manchuria, the rise of Fascism in Italy, and the rise of Nazism in Germany? Try to account for the differences.

5. What effects did the Italian invasion and conquest of Ethiopia have on world politics? Suggest reasons for the differing reactions of the other great powers.

6. What was the Maginot Line? How was it related to the Little Entente? to Belgium?

7. What changes in the world situation made Germany, Italy, and Japan allies in 1937 when they were not allies in 1914 or on the same side in World War I?

8. Compare the German absorption of Czechoslovakia with that of Austria, in terms of (a) German interest in the two countries; (b) the reactions of other governments at the time; and (c) the ultimate consequences of these two acts.

9. Outline the general trends of United States foreign policy between 1929 and 1939 and suggest some of the domestic conditions that influenced this policy.

10. Why would the British and the French be willing to fight over Poland when they refused to go to war over Austria or Czechoslovakia?

11. All things considered, would you say the German government was more aggressive in 1914 or 1939?

9 THE CAMPAIGNS OF WORLD WAR II

The campaigns of World War II from 1939 until almost the end of 1941 took place, with minor exceptions, in Europe. These campaigns involved first an era of Soviet-German co-operation in partitioning eastern Europe, followed by a series of lightning military offensives by which German armies overran western Europe. Meanwhile both governmental and nongovernmental leaders in the United States were gradually adopting a policy of assisting the anti-Nazi forces. Then, in 1941, the Germans consolidated their hold over southeastern Europe and finally invaded the Soviet Union. At last, in December, 1941, United States resistance to Japanese aggressions in the Far East brought a Japanese attack on the United States. The war had now become worldwide. Axis advances continued through most of 1942, but by the end of the year the tide had turned. Soviet armies soon expelled German troops from the USSR, and Anglo-American forces expelled German and Italian troops from Africa and then invaded Italy. Meanwhile the Allies conducted air raids on Germany. The defeat of Germany came after Anglo-American troops had landed in France and marched into Germany. Finally, United States troops in the Pacific drove the Japanese out of one island outpost after another, sank the Japanese navy and merchant fleet, and bombarded the Japanese home islands, until Japan surrendered.

SOVIET–GERMAN CO–OPERATION IN EASTERN EUROPE, 1939–40

The conquest of Poland by joint Soviet-German action was only a matter of weeks. The Germans, numerically and technically far superior to the Poles, quickly overran western Poland. Then, on September 17, Soviet troops entered Poland from the east. On September 27, Warsaw surrendered, and on the following day the Soviets and the Nazis divided Poland between them. Almost immediately afterward, Soviet leaders compelled the governments of Estonia, Latvia, and Lithuania to sign mutual-assistance treaties that granted the USSR military bases in each of these countries. These treaties might be regarded as defensive actions by the USSR, to establish buffers between itself and Germany. They should also be considered as offensive steps, that is, as parts of the over-all Soviet project of extending Soviet power and influence into western Europe. Soviet leaders clearly aimed at using German preoccupation with Great Britain and France to conduct this expansion without interference. In October the Soviet government made similar demands upon the Finnish government, this time requiring also the cession of some territory near Leningrad. The Finns, however, rejected these demands. Hence, on November 30, Soviet military forces attacked Finland. On this occasion the members of the League of Nations acted quickly, declaring the USSR an aggressor and expelling it from League membership. Numerous members of the League then provided the Finns with various, though insufficient, kinds of military assistance. However, the Finns were severely handicapped by the refusal of the Norwegian and Swedish governments to allow British and French troops to cross their territory; they wanted to maintain their neutrality. The Finns fought off the Russians for three months, but finally, in March, 1940, the Finns surrendered. They then had to cede considerably more territory than the USSR had at first demanded.

THE GERMAN CONQUEST OF WESTERN EUROPE

The Germans did not inaugurate their campaigns in western Europe until several months after they had overrun Poland. Actually, the British and the French had no great desire to fight. Also, Hitler continued to believe, or at least to hope, that Britain and France would give up the struggle. Moreover, Germany was not yet prepared for war with Britain and France, at least in the judgment of German army leaders; some appear to have been so fearful of defeat that they even considered trying to overthrow Hitler. Indeed, German industrial production did not reach its peak until the years from 1942 until 1944. Nevertheless, since Hitler felt confident of victory, the Germans launched campaigns that before the end of 1940 had conquered all western Europe except Great Britain.

Denmark and Norway. The first important German move in western Europe came in April, 1940, when the Germans attacked Denmark and Norway. For one thing, the Germans had learned that the British planned to occupy at least Norway for use as a base, and the Germans meant to forestall such an occupation. Also, they could make good use of Norwegian harbors as submarine bases facing the Atlantic. Occupation of Denmark would help them control the entrance into the Baltic and prevent the British from mining these waters. On being invaded, the Danes offered very little resistance, and the Danish government surrendered almost at once. In Norway, by contrast, the Germans met considerable resistance. There, also, they first combined a new type of warfare with their use of conventional weapons—a "fifth column" of sympathizers led by a Norwegian Nazi, Vidkun Quisling, who thereby conferred his name upon all non-German Nazi leaders. The British and the French sent sizable military forces to several points along the Norwegian coast, but they failed to dislodge the Germans. Armed hostilities ended in June when the Norwegian government surrendered.

Belgium and the Netherlands. In May, while their forces were still fighting in Norway, the Germans launched an invasion of Belgium, the Netherlands, and France. The attack on the Netherlands included a heavy air bombing of Rotterdam, the landing of parachute troops behind enemy lines, and considerable fifth column activities. In five days the Netherlands government surrendered. Meanwhile other German forces continued their invasion of Belgium; and still other German armies pierced into France, moved against little opposition down the valley of the Somme River, and reached the English Channel. Late in May the Belgians also surrendered. A major result of this German offensive, together with that against Denmark and Norway, was that Winston Churchill replaced Neville Chamberlain as British prime minister.

The British Evacuation of the Continent. The surrender of Belgium left more than 200,000 British troops almost surrounded by German forces in Belgium and northern France; these troops now evacuated the continent and returned to Great Britain through the port of Dunkirk. At this point the Germans could have practically destroyed the remains of the British army in Europe; however, the German army was forbidden to press on its attack by direct orders from Hitler. Nevertheless, the British left almost all their weapons in France and Belgium, so that Great Britain for a time was nearly defenseless.

The Defeat of France. As the British were evacuating the continent, the Germans directed their attention to the French armies. With little more difficulty than they had had in Poland, German forces cut up the French into disorganized groups, and circled to the rear of the Maginot Line. On June 10, Italian armies began an invasion of southern

France. In a few days most French military commanders had decided that all was lost, and, on June 16, Marshall Philippe Pétain became head of the government with the principal task of making an armistice. Fighting ceased on June 25. The Germans occupied more than half of France, demilitarized what remained, and planned to integrate the French national economy into the German war machine. The unoccupied district, known from its capital city as Vichy France, acquired a new government somewhat like that of Nazi Germany, under Pétain and former premier Pierre Laval. Still, there were many "Free French," led chiefly by General Charles de Gaulle, who were determined to carry on the war against Germany from Great Britain and the French colonies.

The "Battle of Britain." The "Battle of Britain" was the struggle, waged almost entirely in the air, between the British and the Germans in the months after the surrender of France. It involved a German attempt either to defeat the British solely by aerial bombardment or to prepare the way for a German invasion of England. From the first, however, German aviators found themselves opposed in the air as never before. By the early part of 1941 the Royal Air Force had shot down so many German planes, and so much of the German air force was being sent east in preparation for an attack on the USSR, that invasion plans were canceled and the "Battle of Britain" ended.

THE FOREIGN POLICY OF THE UNITED STATES, 1939–41

Between 1939 and 1941 the foreign policy of the United States moved step by step from one of neutrality to one of open and unneutral support of the countries opposing the Axis.

Neutrality Legislation. One of the first indications of the foreign policy of the United States after World War II broke out was a change in neutrality legislation that was urged by President Roosevelt and enacted by Congress. The Neutrality Act of 1939, which amended the Act of 1937, authorized foreign governments to purchase weapons from the United States on a "cash-and-carry" basis. It was evidently designed to benefit Great Britain and France, whose navies could keep Axis vessels from United States ports. This Act also authorized the President to forbid United States ships entry into the ports of belligerents.

Relations with Latin American Countries. As suggested previously, the United States government even before 1939 had been improving its relations with Latin American countries, partly with the aim of improving co-operative defenses for the New World. In 1938, for instance, representatives of the New World governments at a Pan-American Conference asserted that they were united by "continental solidarity" and that they would defend themselves against "all foreign interventions." Late in 1939, spokesmen at another conference declared the right of their governments to resist any acts of aggression. Here they also established a "neutral zone" 300 miles wide and reaching from Maine to Cape Horn, in which ships of warring powers were not to engage in military actions. In July, 1940, the New World countries arranged for the administration of all French and Dutch colonies in the New World to keep them from capture by the Germans.

Supplying Weapons to the British. After the Germans had overrun western Europe, President Roosevelt began supplying weapons to the British in ways that were technically neutral but that demonstrated the intention of the United States government to help the British. Most disputed was an exchange that Roosevelt brought about by which the British obtained fifty old United States destroyers and the Americans secured bases in each of eight British New World colonies. After the presidential election of 1940, in which foreign policy had not been an issue, Roosevelt steered through Congress the Lend-Lease Act. The Act provided that the United States government might sell, lend, or lease armaments to any country whose defense the President asserted was necessary for the defense of the United States. The United States at once began shipping goods to the British and the Chinese; when the USSR entered the war, it too obtained arms and industrial equipment. To assure the safety of ships carrying these goods, the United States later in 1941 occupied both Iceland and Greenland, and sent warships to escort the merchant vessels. German submarines began firing on these American ships, so that Roosevelt issued a "shoot-on-sight" order to American naval commanders. Hence by the fall of 1941 the United States and Germany were in an undeclared naval war.

Declarations of War Aims. In 1941 President Roosevelt began making declarations of United States war aims. Inasmuch as the United States was not at war, this was an exceptional and unneutral procedure. It was also a type of propaganda weapon. He made the first of these declarations in January, 1941, when asking Congress to pass a lend-lease bill. He then declared that the defeat of the Axis powers could lead to a world based on the "four freedoms"—freedom of speech and expression, freedom of worship, freedom from want, and freedom from fear. Another major declaration was the Atlantic Charter, written by Roosevelt and Churchill at a secret conference in August, 1941. The Atlantic Charter was much more general than Wilson's Fourteen Points. Among other goals, it declared that all nations should have governments of their own choosing; that natural resources should be freely available to all countries; that all governments should co-operate to raise standards of living; and that all governments should strive for world disarmament.

THE AXIS, EASTERN EUROPE, AND THE USSR— 1940–41

After the fall of France, the Soviet Union expanded its control in eastern Europe by absorbing the three Baltic states and a part of Romania. Later in 1940 and during the first months of 1941, Germany expanded its control in eastern Europe by establishing pro-Nazi governments in Romania and Bulgaria and by conquering Greece and Yugoslavia. Finally, in June, 1941, the Germans commenced an invasion of the USSR.

Further Soviet Expansion in Eastern Europe, 1940. In June, 1940, as the Germans were overwhelming the French, the Soviet government charged the governments of Estonia, Latvia, and Lithuania with "unfriendly" acts. On the demand of the USSR, government chiefs resigned in all three countries; Soviet troops occupied these areas, which were then incorporated as "republics" into the USSR. A few days later, Soviet officials demanded that Romania surrender its provinces of Bessarabia, once a part of Russia, and Northern Bukovina, whose people were related to the Ukrainians; defenseless, the Romanian government complied. Bessarabia became another "republic" of the USSR, and Northern Bukovina was added to the Ukraine.

Expansion of Axis Power in Eastern Europe, 1940–41. During 1940 the Axis too expanded its power in eastern Europe. For one thing, the German government recompensed two countries that had lost in the 1919 Peace of Paris, at the expense of one country that had gained, by forcing Romania to yield Southern Dobruja to Bulgaria and Transylvania to Hungary. When opponents of these cessions commenced a revolt against the Romanian government, German troops in September, 1940, occupied the country. Finally, in November, the governments of Hungary, Romania, and Slovakia joined the Axis military alliance. These expansions of German power were intended in considerable part to assure German control of Hungarian grain and Romanian oil. In October, 1940, Italian forces attacked Greece, with disastrous results for Italy. To the astonishment of most of the world, the Greeks not only halted the Italians but by 1941 had driven them back into Albania. The reasons for Italian defeat included excellent Greek tactics; the difficulties of Italian mechanized equipment in the Greek mountains; the assistance the Greeks obtained from Great Britain; and the unwillingness of many Italian soldiers to fight. The defeat of the Italians by the

Greeks, and their own plans for an attack on the USSR, led the Germans to expand still further their control over eastern Europe in early 1941. In March Bulgaria joined the Axis, partly to regain from Greece the territory it had lost in 1919. Then early in April German armies invaded Yugoslavia, and Greece as well. After a campaign of about two weeks, the Yugoslav and Greek forces were overpowered and the governments went into exile. The following month German paratroops captured Crete, whose defense the British tried to help. Now every state on the continent of Europe save Portugal, Sweden, Switzerland, and Turkey was dominated by either the Germans or the Soviets; and the blocs of German- and Soviet-ruled territory extended from the Baltic Sea to the Black Sea.

The German Attack on the USSR. The German attack on the USSR not only did not result in a quick triumph for the German armies but brought well-organized, often Communist-led campaigns of guerrilla warfare and industrial sabotage all over Europe.

THE CAMPAIGNS OF 1941. On June 22, 1941, German forces invaded the USSR. This campaign, which Hitler had promoted but which many Germans who had fought in Russia during World War I had opposed, at first enjoyed immense success. Although outnumbered by the Soviets, the Germans were better led, better equipped, and more experienced; also, for a while no Soviet air force appeared, and the Germans controlled the skies. Indeed, the Soviet government appeared to have taken few preparations for such an attack, and Soviet troops at and near the frontier offered little resistance. Hence the Germans in these first weeks cut up Soviet armies and surrounded hundreds of thousands of Soviet troops. Hitler announced that the USSR would soon surrender. In Germany, the production of armaments was reduced. At length the German troops outran their supplies and slowed their advance. Then, in the autumn, as the Russian winter approached, German leaders delayed several weeks choosing the principal goal for the campaign. When they finally selected Moscow and set out toward it, they found new, better prepared, and more resolute Soviet armies facing them. As winter set in, it became clear that neither German troops nor German equipment was prepared for the cold. Finally, in December, the Soviet troops halted the Germans short of Moscow and then began pressing them slowly back. However, because Hitler commanded his forces not to retreat, the Germans did not suffer a catastrophic withdrawal such as that of Napoleon in 1812.

FIRST EFFECTS OF THE CAMPAIGN IN THE USSR. One of the first effects of the campaign in the USSR was the Communist effort to get the

United States into the war. Communist leaders who had opposed United States aid to Great Britain were now the strongest backers of United States help and even entry into hostilities. Another effect was the resistance to the Nazis that now sprang up all over Europe. Among the "professions" for which Communists are especially trained are guerrilla fighting and industrial sabotage. Not all anti-Nazi guerrillas were Communists, but those trained in Moscow were often leaders of such bands. These groups were generally termed "Partisans." One of the most important bands of Partisans was that in Yugoslavia, headed by a devoted Communist, Josip Brozovich or "Tito." A chief practice of these Partisans was to attack not only Nazi troops and supplies, and Nazi sympathizers, but also anti-Communists. Still another result of the German campaign in the USSR was the fact that the failure of the Germans to capture Moscow somewhat reduced both the renown of the might of the German armies and the reputation of Hitler as a brilliant military planner.

THE HIGH SEAS, THE MIDDLE EAST, AND THE FAR EAST

On the high seas, where the Germans were even more inferior to the British than they had been in World War I, the Germans as in World War I relied chiefly upon the submarine. They entered the war with what German naval commanders thought a dangerously small submarine fleet, but they quickly expanded it. German submarines attacked British merchant shipping in groups known as "wolf packs." Soon they were sinking British vessels more rapidly than new ones were being launched, but the British made up some of their losses by taking over the merchant fleets of such countries as Norway that the Germans had overrun. As for surface vessels, the Germans soon lost two of their best battleships, the "Graf Spee" and the "Bismarck." Also, in November, 1940, the British almost totally destroyed the Italian surface fleet in the Mediterranean.

In the Middle East and Africa, Italian forces attempted to win British colonies and the Suez Canal, but after several reverses the British repulsed the Italians and occupied the Italian colonial empire. They also made Ethiopia once again an independent country. Meanwhile the British occupied Syria, Iraq, and Iran—countries that seemed about to fall to Axis agents. In the Far East the Japanese, taking advantage of the surrender of France to German troops, occupied northern Indochina, and a Japanese attack on the Dutch East Indies seemed likewise imminent.

THE ENTRY OF THE UNITED STATES INTO THE WAR

It was an attack by Japan on the United States base at Pearl Harbor in the Hawaiian Islands, and not, as many Americans had anticipated, an attack by Germany, that brought the United States into World War II.

Preliminary Japanese Moves. During 1940 and 1941, relations between the governments of Japan and the United States grew rapidly worse. The worsening in their relations actually started in 1937, when the Japanese opened an offensive against China proper. In that year they also attacked an American ship, the "Panay," which was legally in Chinese waters; the Japanese did apologize and pay an indemnity, but some Americans remembered this act. About this time Japanese leaders also began speaking of the "new order" in the Far East that they would create; it supposedly would follow the motto "Asia for the Asiatics," but clearly would result in "Asia for the Japanese." In 1940 the Japanese not only moved into Indochina but also demanded that the British close the Burma Road, the route by which the Chinese received supplies. Facing Germany alone, the British had to obey. Then, in April, 1941, the Japanese signed a nonaggression treaty with the Soviet Union, freeing the Japanese for a war with the United States. This treaty was another illustration of the Soviet policy of allowing non-Communist countries to fight each other. In July, the Japanese completed their occupation of Indochina.

United States Resistance and the Raid on Pearl Harbor. By this time the United States government was taking a firm stand. For one thing, it "froze" all Japanese assets in the United States and started banning the export of certain goods to the Japanese that would enable them to carry on their aggressions. Representatives of the two govern-ments continued to exchange demands; the Japanese held that they must have a free hand in Asia, and the Americans maintained that the Japanese must cease their aggression. While such conversations were go-ing on in Washington, the Japanese without a declaration of war carried out an air raid on Pearl Harbor, sinking most of the American fleet there; attacked such other American possessions as the Philippines and Guam; and struck at British and Dutch Far Eastern colonies.

The Controversy over the Attack on Pearl Harbor. Almost immediately after this attack on Pearl Harbor, a controversy developed in the United States that has not yet ended. The controversy has had a pro-Roosevelt, pro-British group on one side, and an anti-Roosevelt, proneutrality group on the other. According to the first group, the United States was acting wisely in helping the British, and correctly in negotiating with the Japanese. Meanwhile the Japanese were preparing for war against the United States. At the same time, United States officials were sending details of preparations by, and threats of, the Japanese, to the army and navy commanders at Pearl Harbor. Consequently, this group argues, the attack on Pearl Harbor showed infamy on the part of the Japanese and negligence or incompetence on the part of the military chiefs at Pearl Harbor. According to the second group, the United States government was acting in an improper fashion in the degree to which it helped the British. Moreover, President Roosevelt and his followers wanted badly to get the United States into the war. Hence they deliberately goaded the Japanese into an attack and withheld knowledge of Japanese plans and activities from the commanders at Hawaii. Several government committees, generally bipartisan, have investigated the matter since 1941, and there has been no final decision. This controversy demonstrates, if nothing else, the problems of determining foreign policy and of assigning responsibility for it.

ALLIED VICTORY IN AFRICA AND ITALY

Early in 1942 the Germans and Italians made their deepest penetration into Egypt. Within the next two years the forces of the Allies (the United States, Great Britain, and associated countries) defeated the Axis armies in Africa and then conquered Sicily and invaded the mainland of Italy. The Italian government thereupon surrendered, but German armies continued to occupy most of the country.

The Defeat of the Axis in Northern Africa. In 1941 German and Italian troops under the command of German General Erwin Rommel pushed the British out of Libya and invaded Egypt. The Axis advance did not come to a halt until it had reached El Alamein, only seventy miles from Alexandria, but here it was finally stopped. First, in October, 1942, British forces led by General Sir Bernard L. Montgomery opened a major attack on the German positions at El Alamein and forced Rommel to retreat. Meanwhile, in November, an Anglo-American army under General Dwight D. Eisenhower landed at various points in the French colonies of northwest Africa. Pursued by Allied forces both in the east and the west, the Axis armies retreated to Tunisia, which they turned into a powerful stronghold. Nevertheless, they were at last outnumbered and outgunned; they surrendered in May, 1943. Thus the first great Allied amphibious invasion had succeeded.

The Allied Invasion of Sicily. After their victory in Africa the Allies turned their attention to the proposed invasion of Sicily and Italy. There was considerable argument over the desirability of such action. Its opponents held that the main task was the defeat of Germany and that this area, though it might be called the "soft underbelly of Europe," was actually separated by mountains from the rest of the continent; hence its conquest would not provide a base for a large-scale invasion of Germany. Proponents of the attack on Sicily and Italy, however, argued that the Italians would not be able to remain in the war much longer and that their defeat would diminish the Nazis' allies by one. Furthermore, they asserted, Italy would furnish excellent bases for Allied planes to raid previously "safe" parts of Germany. In any case, in July, 1943, the Allies landed in Sicily. The Germans there resisted vigorously, but hosts of Italian troops surrendered. Leading Italians compelled Mussolini to resign, and Marshal Pietro Badoglio became head of a new Italian government. The Allies completed the conquest of Sicily in 39 days.

The Allied Invasion of Italy. On September 3, 1943, the Allies invaded Italy from Sicily. This invasion came only after confused negotiations between representatives of the new Italian government and the Allies, as a result of which on the day of the invasion the Italians signed an armistice providing for unconditional surrender as of September 8. Allied leaders had agreed in January, 1943, that all Axis powers must surrender unconditionally. This surrender, however, was of little avail to the Italians, since German troops had by now occupied most of Italy. Fighting often on difficult terrain and under bad climatic conditions, the Allies pushed the Germans slowly back and in June, 1944, took Rome. Thereafter the Western Allies concentrated on their invasion of France and their subsequent march into Germany.

ALLIED VICTORY OVER GERMANY

Allied victory over Germany was the product of a continuing advance by Soviet armies, heavy bombing by Anglo-American aircraft, and an Allied invasion of Germany by way of France.

The Advance of Soviet Forces. In the Soviet Union in 1942 the Germans had launched an offensive directed chiefly at the oil fields of the Caucasus, with a secondary offensive against the Volga River city of Stalingrad. By August the Germans had reached the westernmost oil fields; however, owing to shortage of fuel for their tanks and other motorized equipment, they were never able to advance to the main fields. Besides, Soviet armies were making a stand before Stalingrad, and, although this was supposed to be only a secondary goal, more and more German troops were deployed to reinforce those before this city. Here, in the fall of 1942, the Germans were halted, and here Soviet forces began the offensive that ultimately took them into Berlin. Soviet factories, many of them east of the Urals, had by this time started producing large quantities of war goods, and the USSR had received vast amounts of lend-lease goods from the United States. The Soviets pushed the Germans out of the Caucasus, captured the German armies at Stalingrad, and in 1943 proceeded to push the Germans out of the Ukraine. A last German offensive in the spring of 1943 failed, and Soviet armies were soon marching through Poland.

Anglo-American Air Raids on Germany. By 1943 the United States and British air forces were conducting daily bomber raids on Germany and German-held territory. The results of such bombings have been controversial; however, studies after the war have shown that they did not greatly injure the morale of German civilians and that until the second half of 1944 they did not lessen very much the output of German factories. Perhaps the most effective of these raids were those late in the war that were directed at such specialized targets as aircraft plants, ball-bearing factories, electric power generating stations, and railroads.

The Anglo-American Invasion of France. On June 6, 1944, American and British soldiers began landing on the beaches of Normandy. After days of bitter fighting they assured their foothold and secured Brittany to their rear. Next the Allied armored and motorized columns began dashing across France, and the Germans, hoping at least to keep the Allies from Germany, withdrew to the remains of their West Wall. They had meanwhile opened an attack on Great Britain, with "robot bombs" and "rocket bombs," which caused considerable damage but was too late to be effective. With the help of another Allied invasion into southern France, the Allies had expelled German troops from almost all of France by the autumn of 1944.

The Last Days of Nazi Germany. In spite of stiff resistance at the West Wall and a German counteroffensive known as the "Battle of the Bulge," the Anglo-American forces continued their advance and in March, 1945, crossed the Rhine. Meanwhile, Soviet forces were marching through Germany to meet Anglo-American troops at the Elbe. The last days of Nazi Germany were typified not only by utter German military collapse but also by great confusion as to the area of Germany that Anglo-American forces should conquer and occupy. It is important that for months some German military leaders would have given up but were deterred by such factors as the Allied demand for unconditional surrender and Hitler's continued popularity among the German people. On May 2, the German armies in Italy, where no Soviet forces had participated, surrendered to the Allied armies. In Germany, after the Anglo-American armies had crossed the Rhine, they were evidently in a position to cross Germany and at least share in the capture of Berlin, if not take it themselves. Also, it seems that they could have entered Czechoslovakia and seized Prague. In keeping with agreements made beforehand, however, Anglo-American troops were held back and the Soviets captured Berlin and eastern Germany. On or about April 30 Hitler committed suicide, and Admiral Karl Doenitz assumed control of Germany. In the following week German armies surrendered piecemeal, and on May 7 a representative of the German government surrendered unconditionally to the Allies.

ALLIED VICTORY OVER JAPAN

Allied victory over Japan resulted from a series of campaigns conducted primarily by American forces that ousted the Japanese from their island fortresses, swept the Japanese Navy and merchant marine from the seas, and rained bombs on Japanese cities. The Japanese government surrendered soon after American planes dropped atomic bombs on two Japanese cities and Soviet armies invaded Manchuria.

Island-Hopping Campaigns. At the farthest extent of Japanese conquest Japan possessed numerous Pacific islands, including the Philippines, Guam, Wake, and some of the Aleutians, the East Indies, and almost all of southeast Asia; and Japanese forces were threatening India. The Japanese were finally halted by units of the American Navy in May and June, 1942, at the battles of the Coral Sea and of Midway. After these battles the Allied offensive against Japan took chiefly the form of "island-hopping" campaigns, whereby Allied forces—mainly Americans under the command of General Douglas MacArthur—seized one Japanese outpost after another. One series of campaigns led to the capture of Guadalcanal, New Guinea, and then the Philippines; and another, directed at Japan itself, brought the conquest of the Gilbert and Ellice Islands, Kwajalein, Saipan, and Iwo. Meanwhile, on the mainland British troops struggled with the Japanese in Burma, and the Chinese, helped by lend-lease materials flown to them over the Himalayas, sought to resist Japanese occupation of China.

Air and Sea War against Japan. While Allied troops were warring with the Japanese on the Pacific Islands and the Asiatic mainland, Allied planes and ships were attacking Japanese outposts, the Japanese merchant fleet, and finally Japan itself. Japanese naval vessels on several occasions came to grips with the Allied navies, and, in a number of great sea battles, especially those of the Philippine Sea, the Allies sank most of the Japanese navy. Finally, the Allies carried out air raids on Japan itself, seeking to destroy Japanese factories and depress Japanese morale.

The Surrender of Japan. By mid-1945 Japan had been cut off from its colonies and driven from one fortified island after another. Allied forces were now in control of Okinawa and were clearly preparing for an invasion of Japan. Under these circumstances the Japanese tried to get the USSR, with which they were not then at war, to negotiate a surrender with the Allies. Soviet leaders refused to do so, evidently because they wanted to enter the war against Japan and seize Manchuria. American leaders were aware of this Japanese attempt to surrender but did nothing about it. At length, after the Japanese had rejected an ultimatum to surrender unconditionally, a single American plane dropped an atomic bomb on the city of Hiroshima, on August 6, 1945. Two days later the Soviet Union declared war on Japan and began an invasion of Manchuria. On the following day the Americans dropped an atomic bomb on Nagasaki. The Japanese did not know that these were all the atomic bombs the United States then had; fearing total destruction of all their cities, they now agreed to surrender unconditionally with the one exception that their emperor be permitted to retain his throne. On September 2, 1945, Japanese envoys surrendered to General MacArthur as the representative of the Allies.

Review Questions

1. Show how Soviet policies and actions regarding eastern Europe during 1939–40 (a) complemented German policies and actions; (b) conflicted with German policies and actions; and (c) reflected Soviet policy toward Great Britain and France.

2. Why did the Germans feel it necessary to conquer Norway and Denmark? What may have been the reason or reasons for their refusal to attack neighboring Sweden as well?

3. What were the similarities and the differences between United States foreign policy from 1914 until 1917 and from 1939 until 1941? Suggest explanations for the differences.

4. Describe the course of the German campaign against the USSR in 1941 and some of the consequences of this campaign.

5. Assume that in 1941 the Japanese had attacked only the British, French, and Dutch possessions in the Pacific. What might have been the subsequent policies of the United States?

6. Offer arguments for and against the Anglo-American policy of attacking the Axis forces in Africa and invading Italy before making an assault on Germany.

7. Outline the various Anglo-American and Soviet campaigns against Germany from 1942 through 1945.

8. Describe the several ways in which the campaigns and factors that brought about the defeat of Japan were different from those that brought about the defeat of Germany.

9. How much military value does there seem to have been in dropping atomic bombs on Japan? What were the moral aspects of these acts?

10. What may have been the effects of implementing the doctrine of unconditional surrender? Do you see any connection between this doctrine and the American military tradition based upon fighting Indian wars?

10 THE PEACE SETTLEMENT AFTER WORLD WAR II

The peace settlement after World War II differed markedly from that after World War I. In the first place, representatives of the Allies had conferred several times to agree not only on the conduct of the war but also on certain principles and arrangements for the peace settlement. In the second place, after World War II there was no single peace settlement analogous to the Peace of Paris in 1919. Instead, the Allies together first reached treaties with the lesser Axis countries. Then, most of the non-Communist countries that had been at war with Japan reached a treaty with the Japanese. By contrast, as of the end of 1961 there was not yet a general peace settlement with Germany. The one major combined achievement of the Allies was the establishment of the United Nations organization, which occurred before the war was over and while the Allies were still held together fairly closely by military needs. The failure of the Allies to co-operate after World War II must be attributed almost entirely to the existence of a condition that may be termed *bipolarity*, in which control of most of the world fell into the hands of two "superpowers," the United States and the USSR. When relations between the two countries became openly hostile and the "Cold War" resulted, general agreements between the leaders of the superpowers became almost impossible. The consequence was their failure to achieve a general peace settlement.

WARTIME CONFERENCES AMONG THE ALLIED POWERS

The wartime conferences among the Allied Powers, as indicated above, dealt not only with means for defeating the Axis powers but also with arrangements for the postwar world. This section deals primarily with these arrangements.

The Moscow Conference. The Moscow Conference, in October, 1943, included United States Secretary of State Cordell Hull, British Foreign Secretary Anthony Eden, and Soviet Foreign Commissar Vyacheslav M. Molotov. The Chinese ambassador to the USSR was also present. The conference yielded a general agreement that after the war there should be an international organization to guarantee the maintenance of peace. It also produced an assurance that the Italians would be prevailed upon to establish a non-Fascist government; an assertion that the postwar treatment of the Austrians would depend on their throwing off German domination; and a promise of punishment for Nazis who had committed crimes against Allied personnel or citizens of occupied countries.

The Cairo Conference. The Cairo Conference, in November, 1943, included President Roosevelt, Prime Minister Churchill, and Generalissimo Chiang Kai-shek of China. They agreed that Japan must yield all the territory it had acquired during the two world wars and all the territory otherwise taken from China. They also pledged national independence for Korea.

The Tehran Conference. The Tehran Conference, in November, 1943, came just after the Cairo Conference; it included Roosevelt, Churchill, and Soviet Premier Stalin. At this conference these three leaders drafted a general plan for the postwar world. For example, Roosevelt agreed in substance with Stalin's view that Poland should be established as an independent country but that it should surrender certain of its eastern territories to the USSR and should be compensated by a portion of eastern Germany. Moreover, whereas Churchill apparently wanted Anglo-American forces to invade the Balkans, Roosevelt and Stalin agreed that they should establish a second front in France in 1944. Adoption of this policy left the Balkans open to Soviet occupation. So far as the conduct of the war was concerned, Stalin at Tehran asserted that after the defeat of Germany it would be possible for Soviet armies to begin an offensive against Japan.

The Yalta Conference. The Yalta Conference, in February, 1945, with Roosevelt, Churchill, and Stalin, in the main filled in the outlines drawn at Tehran. Among other things, it produced several agreements regarding the postwar administration of Germany. Germany was to be divided into three occupation zones, one for each country represented at the conference; a fourth might be established for the French, if they wanted one, which they did. A central control commission in Berlin was to co-ordinate the administration of these zones. The Allies would wipe out Nazism, disband the German general staff, and punish Nazis guilty of war crimes. Germany would pay reparations to nations that had suffered damage from the Nazis. Other agreements at the Yalta Conference provided for an international gathering to devise a permanent international organization; fixed the voting procedure in this organization; dealt with the Polish government and Polish boundaries; and recommended establishment of a multiparty government for Yugoslavia. Secret agreements recognized Soviet domination of Outer Mongolia and gave Japanese territories and privileges in Manchuria to the USSR. Finally, and perhaps most crucial, the conference confirmed Soviet entry into the war against Japan.

The Potsdam Conference. The Potsdam Conference, in July, 1945, included at first President Harry Truman from the United States, Churchill, and Stalin. Then, when Churchill's party lost its majority in an election during the conference, Churchill was replaced by the new British prime minister, Clement Attlee. This conference yielded more details on the treatment of Germany. It set forth, among other provisions, the boundaries of the four occupation zones and provided that although Germany was to be viewed as an economic unit there would for a time be no central government. The members of the conference further arranged that peace treaties with the lesser Axis powers should be negotiated before those with Germany and Japan. To prepare drafts of these treaties they founded the Council of Foreign Ministers of the four countries occupying Germany.

CREATION OF THE UNITED NATIONS ORGANIZATION

The creation of the United Nations organization (UN), which was completed at the San Francisco Conference in June, 1945, differed in important ways from the creation of the League of Nations. In the first place, creation of the organization was preceded by a number of international conferences in which various aspects and problems of such an organization were discussed. Second, the countries that made the core of the UN organization had already gained experience in collaborating in another international body, the United Nations Relief and Rehabilitation Administration (UNRRA). Finally, the San Francisco Conference dealt solely with creating the UN permanent organization; it was not concerned with the drafting of a peace treaty also, as was the case in 1919 when the League Covenant was inserted in all the major peace treaties.

Preliminary Actions and Conferences. The actions and conferences preliminary to the establishment of the United Nations organization comprised mainly the signing of the United Nations Declaration, by countries opposed to the Axis; the Bretton Woods Conference, where international economic problems were discussed; and the Dumbarton Oaks Conference, where a draft Charter for the United Nations organization was prepared.

THE UNITED NATIONS DECLARATION. The United Nations Declaration, signed on January 1, 1942, by representatives of the United States, Great Britain, the USSR, and China, pledged each of the signatory powers to use all its resources for the defeat of the Axis powers and promised that none of the signatories would make a separate peace with the Axis governments. Subsequently the governments of 43 other countries adhered to this Declaration, a dozen of them after the decision at Yalta that only the signatories of the Declaration could share in drafting the United Nations Charter. This Declaration illustrates the belief, widespread at the time, that only the Axis countries were warlike and that their defeat was all that was necessary to bring about a peaceful world. Supposedly, as a corollary, war would be prevented by a continuing alliance among the United States, Great Britain, the USSR, and China.

THE BRETTON WOODS CONFERENCE. The Bretton Woods Conference (1944), with representatives from 44 countries, was concerned with economic matters. It showed how political leaders by the 1940's were convinced that peace could reign only in a world that was economically prosperous and orderly. The Conference dealt with plans to unite the world economically through free trade and international facilities for the exchange of moneys. The conferees provided for the establishment of two agencies: (1) the International Monetary Fund, to lower barriers in international exchange, thus clearing international balances; and (2) the International Bank for Reconstruction and Development, to lend money for projects connected with the reconstruction or development of a given country. Each agency was to be financed largely by the United States government.

THE DUMBARTON OAKS CONFERENCE. The Dumbarton Oaks Conference, including representatives of the "Big Four"—the United States, Great Britain, the USSR, and China—meeting in August–October, 1944, laid the foundation for the structure of the UN organization. A draft for a United Nations charter prepared at this Conference was the basis for negotiations at San Francisco in the following year. Certain questions that were not settled at this Conference, especially that of voting procedure, were resolved at the Yalta Conference in the following February.

The United Nations Relief and Rehabilitation Administration. The United Nations Relief and Rehabilitation Administration (UNRRA), established formally in February, 1943, was the first formal agency through which the Big Four and their allies co-operated toward a particular end. The establishment of UNRRA was in a way prefaced by the United Nations Conference on Food and Agriculture, which included representatives of 44 countries meeting in May, 1943, to study world food needs and to make recommendations for coping with them. These, however, were to be long-range projects; the requirement at the time was an organization to deal with the emergency food situation that prevailed in the devastated countries. Partly because of urging by the United States, representatives of several countries late in 1943 founded UNRRA; subsequently it had more than 40 member nations. Financed largely by the United States and headed by former Governor Herbert Lehman of New York, it inaugurated a program of relief for millions of needy people in a number of countries. UNRRA certainly saved the lives of hosts of individuals and afforded an opportunity for international co-operation among the countries at war with the Axis. However, leaders in some countries such as Yugoslavia commenced using UNRRA goods to strengthen their control. Furthermore, some influential congressmen in the United States opposed the whole principle of UNRRA. As a result, UNRRA was dissolved in 1947, its functions being given to appropriate agencies in the United Nations.

The San Francisco Conference. At the San Francisco Conference, in 1945, delegates from 50 countries wrote the charter for the UN organization.

MEMBERSHIP AND ORGANIZATION. The San Francisco Conference, which met from April to July, 1945, included delegates from 50 countries. Although the small countries were theoretically equal to the large ones, the Conference was dominated by the "Big Five"—the Big Four plus France. President Roosevelt, who probably more than any other one person was responsible for this gathering, died before it met. However, before his death he had chosen as United States representatives at the Conference Secretary of State Edward R. Stettinius, leading congressmen from both political parties, and two important private citizens. Thus Roosevelt sought to avoid at least one of Wilson's difficulties in 1919—the resentment of his partisan foes that had contributed to senatorial rejection of the Treaty of Versailles and the League of Nations.

ACTIVITIES. The activities of the Conference revolved about the drafting of a charter for the United Nations organization, on the basis of prior agreements reached at Dumbarton Oaks and Yalta. The conclusions reached at the Conference became parts of this charter and are therefore discussed in the chapter concerned with the United Nations. The significant point here is that the disputes arising at this conference, like the conclusions stemming from them, were an early indication of the hardening split of the world into pro-Soviet and anti-Soviet blocs. It should be noted that in previous discussions the Soviet representatives had been more flexible, mainly because the war with Germany was still going on and the Soviet government was willing to make some concessions in order to assure itself of continued Anglo-American help. By the time of the Conference, however, the war against Germany was almost over; it ended during the Conference. As a result Soviet delegates at San Francisco were much less yielding over disputed points; on one occasion they even threatened to leave the Conference unless their demands were satisfied. Soviet spokesmen were clearly intent on gaining as much as possible from these deliberations and were less desirous than the spokesmen for other countries of establishing an international body with powers to assure peace.

PEACE TREATIES WITH THE DEFEATED POWERS

Representatives of the Allied Powers negotiated peace treaties with the lesser Axis countries, Austria, and Japan. However, because of the "Cold War," they have failed to agree on a treaty with Germany.

Lesser Axis Countries. Peace treaties with the lesser Axis countries—Italy, Hungary, Romania, Bulgaria, and Finland—were signed in 1947. Drafting of these treaties began in the Council of Foreign Ministers founded at the Potsdam Conference. Almost from the beginning, however, it was clear that Soviet representatives in the Council expected the discussions and the peace treaties to confirm the domination of Eastern Europe that Soviet armies had secured during the war. Nevertheless, by mid-1946 the Council had proceeded far enough with the drafting of these treaties to summon the Paris Conference, which included spokesmen from all UN members that had fought the Axis in Europe. After weeks of discussion, prolonged and complicated by the Soviets, the Conference turned its work over to the Council for final rewriting. Italy gave up certain areas to France, Yugoslavia, Albania, and Greece, as well as its entire prewar colonial empire. It had to pay reparations to Yugoslavia, Greece, the USSR, Ethiopia, and Albania; and it was to have only small armed forces. Hungary lost territory to Czechoslovakia and Romania, and was to pay reparations to the USSR, Czechoslovakia, and Yugoslavia. Romania confirmed its previous grants of land to the USSR and Bulgaria, in 1940, but regained its former losses to Hungary; it agreed to pay reparations to the USSR. Bulgaria yielded no land and kept Southern Dobruja; it was obliged to pay reparations to Greece and Yugoslavia. Finland confirmed its earlier cessions to the USSR and contracted to pay reparations to the USSR.

Austria. Although Austria had been only an administrative unit of Nazi Germany when the war started, it was viewed at the end of the war as one of the defeated countries. Like Germany it was divided into four occupation zones. In 1946 the United States and Great Britain proposed treaties, but the USSR rejected these proposals. Later Soviet actions made it evident that the USSR wanted to get reparations from Austria and wanted an excuse to maintain troops in such countries as Hungary and Romania on the ground that they were essential to protect Soviet communications with Austria. At last, in 1955, when pro-Soviet governments had been founded in Hungary and Romania, so that Soviet troops were no longer necessary, and when the USSR had secured large quantities of reparations from Austria, representatives of the four countries drafted and signed a treaty with Austria restoring it its national independence. The treaty also forbade a German-Austrian union and guaranteed the military neutrality of Austria.

Japan. A peace treaty between Japan and most of the countries with which it had been at war—with the notable exceptions of the Soviet Union and China—was signed in 1951. That a treaty could be negotiated with Japan whereas none has yet been reached with Germany reflects mainly the different ways in which the two countries were occupied. Japan, unlike Germany, was not partitioned into zones; in fact, under occupation it was administered at the direction of one person—General MacArthur. Moreover, the Japanese government, unlike that of Germany, was not overthrown, so that MacArthur had a legitimate native authority through which to transmit his orders. At MacArthur's direction, the postwar Japanese leaders drafted a constitution for a government that conferred more political power upon the voters. They and MacArthur also attempted to decentralize the control of Japanese industry. The treaty the Japanese signed in 1951 with their former enemies limited Japanese political rule to their four chief islands. Unlike the other peace treaties, it did not impose a large quantity of reparations. Subsequently the Japanese signed a treaty with Nationalist China and a "declaration" with the Soviet Union ending the state of war between them.

Germany. As of 1961 there still was no conclusive peace treaty with Germany. Indeed, there was no single German government with which such a treaty could be negotiated. The postwar treatment of Germany disclosed as well as any other international situation of the time the difference between the goals of the USSR and those of the United States, Great Britain, and France. As agreed at the Potsdam Conference, Germany was divided into four occupation zones. Berlin likewise was divided into four zones; however, by some inadvertence the Americans, British, and French did not insist on a guaranteed land corridor for themselves from western Germany into Berlin, so that the city became an island in the Soviet zone. It soon became apparent that Soviet policy aimed at turning all Germany into a Soviet workshop; by contrast, American, British, and French policy aimed at restoring political independence and unity to the Germans, but under a government that could not and would not wage aggressive war. Repeated discussions among the four occupying powers achieved no decisions concerning a peace treaty. Finally, the Americans, British, and French united their three zones into a single economic and political body, and in May, 1955, granted it full national independence. In the meantime, the USSR in March, 1954, declared its zone a sovereign state. Thus in 1962 there are two "Germanies," a pro-Western Federal Republic of Germany and a Soviet-controlled German Democratic Republic.

The Trials of German and Japanese Leaders. As promised during the war, the Allies in 1945 started a series of trials of certain German and Japanese leaders. The German leaders were first to go on trial—at Nuremberg. Some were charged with violations of the rules of war, as offenses against military prisoners and against noncombatant civilian groups such as the Jews. Such acts had been defined as crimes by the international law to which most countries adhered. A related charge was of crimes against humanity, which stemmed from the idea that it was illegal for government leaders—the Nazis—to persecute innocent persons or groups. Those charged with these two classes of offenses were generally found guilty in the "Nuremberg Trials" and sentenced either to death or to long prison terms. Another group of leaders (including some of the first) were charged with having violated the Kellogg-Briand Pact by waging aggressive warfare. They received either death sentences or long prison terms. Numerous Japanese leaders were afterward dealt with likewise. There has always been some question as to the legality of these convictions because, it has been held, the Kellogg-Briand Pact includes no stipulations for punishing those who violate it. Also, it has been suggested that in the future the leaders of any country that has engaged in war *and lost* may afterward be charged with, and sentenced to a capital punishment for, waging aggressive warfare. Still, the Nuremberg Trials and the Japanese trials set a forceful example on behalf of the principle that individuals may be held responsible by an international court for the types of aggressive and ruthless practices engaged in by many Nazis and their cohorts.

Review Questions

1. Show how the steps taken to achieve a peace settlement after World War II differed in several ways from the analogous steps for a peace settlement after World War I.

2. From what is now known of the agenda of the various wartime conferences, which seems to have been the most important? Or were they all equally important, with emphases on different problems?

3. How did the creation of the United Nations differ from the creation of the League of Nations?

4. Can you see any reason or reasons why the treaties with the minor powers were negotiated first after World War II, whereas all the treaties were negotiated together at the Paris Conference of 1919? Would either arrangement tend to work to the advantage or disadvantage of any country?

5. How did the postwar administration of Japan differ from that of Germany? What was probably the chief reason for this difference? What might have happened if Japan had been administered in the way Germany was? if Germany had been administered in the way Japan was?

6. What were the unusual features of the postwar trials of German and Japanese leaders? What objections have been raised to these trials?

11 *THE POSTWAR CONFLICT, 1945 TO 1962*

World politics since 1945 has revolved chiefly about the conflict between the United States and its allies on one hand and the Soviet Union and its satellites on the other. This conflict has been simply a continuation of the war that the Bolsheviks declared on the non-Bolshevik world when they came to power in Russia in 1917. Since 1945 it has become more intense than ever before, largely because the USSR is relatively more powerful than at any time in the past. In the process of this conflict the Soviet Union has transformed eastern Europe into a group of small countries that are its dependents and satellites. It has also aided Communists in China to win power there, and has laid the basis for Communist infiltration from China into the states of Southeast Asia. In response, the United States, which typically disarmed soon after World War II ended, has rearmed itself; formed military alliances with countries all over the world; and granted billions of dollars for military and economic aid to countries that leaders in the American government believed must be defended from communism.

TRAITS OF THE POSTWAR CONFLICT

The postwar conflict, or "Cold War," is a political war of the most intense sort. It involves a struggle between governments for certain objectives in which the opposing sides employ many instruments but do not resort to large-scale military operations. In some instances the opponents engage in guerrilla warfare, and even make limited use of regular troops. A conflict of this general sort is not unique; often in the past countries have vied bitterly with one another in pursuit of certain goals without using numerous conventional armed forces. What distinguishes the current political war is the scope of the arena, the stakes, the combination of instruments, and the way the instruments are used.

Bipolarity. Bipolarity is a term used to describe the present strategic configuration of political, economic, and military forces in the world, in which there are just two centers of power—the United States and the USSR. This is a unique situation; never before has the world contained only two major and competing political centers. Even at the time of the Roman Empire, which is sometimes thought of as a world-empire, there were comparable mighty states in Persia, India, and China. Bipolarity has not extinguished the balance of power, for the two superpowers more or less balance one another. However, it has led to a different sort of balance of power, one that lacks a major traditional element—the "equalizer." An "equalizer" may be defined as a country that is closely attached to neither of two competing power centers; in the event one of these centers becomes substantially inferior to the other, leaders in the "equalizer" can redress the balance by allying their government with the weaker center. Great Britain has often played the role of an "equalizer." During the Russo-Japanese War, when it seemed that France and Germany might help Russia, Theodore Roosevelt threatened to intervene in behalf of Japan; here the United States was the "equalizer." Today there is no country with strength close enough to that of either the United States or the USSR to exercise a decisive effect upon their comparative power standing. A united western Europe might conceivably play such a role in the future.

Universalism. Universalism describes the present effort by both the United States and the USSR to spread their power to every government and area in the world. Universalism was beyond question introduced by the USSR, with its ideology that Marxist principles and practices must rule the earth. The United States has developed its own universalism in response to that of the USSR, often unskillfully and with many compromises and hesitations. The consequence of universalism appears in the views of United States and Soviet officials that there must be no neutrals in the present conflict. In previous struggles between countries there have been of course strenuous contests to win over neutrals. It is improbable, however, that neutrals have at any past time been wooed so vigorously. If, however, leaders in the superpowers succeed in compelling all countries to adopt a positive stand for one side or the other, the frontiers of influence and power of the United States and the USSR will abut directly upon one another everywhere. There will be no "buffer states," such as Siam in the nineteenth century between British Burma and French Indochina. Figuratively, at least, there will be no room for maneuver and compromise. Finally, this means that for the first time there will be a genuine and deliberate "world war." The several "world wars" of the past commenced as wars of limited objective and only after their outbreak developed into world-wide struggles. Austria wanted to regain Silesia in 1756; Austria-Hungary wanted to humiliate Serbia in 1914; Germany wanted to reincorporate Danzig and the Polish Corridor in 1939. Present-day universalism prohibits such limited goals.

Political Ideologies. Political ideologies are systems of beliefs, or programs, held by political groups, which aim at particular political goals and which interpret events and institutions in terms of those goals. Governments and nations in the past have adopted ideologies to justify their behavior, and have patterned their behavior after the precepts of a given ideology. The leaders of the French Revolution expressed their ideology in the slogan "liberty, equality, fraternity." Today, ideologies can be and are much more rigidly controlled by the government; and they can be disseminated farther through the press, tax-supported schools, and conscript armies. Of the two superpowers, the USSR has by far the more highly developed ideology. Certain of its main doctrines, such as the inevitable collapse of capitalism, are unchanging bases of Soviet foreign policy. On the other hand, secondary principles, such as the need of a violent revolution, can be manipulated and altered to serve particular circumstances. Acceptance of this ideology is compulsory for Soviet citizens. Yet the very compulsion that supports this ideology may weaken its hold upon the Soviet citizenry. By contrast, in the non-Soviet world there are many ideologies, most but not all of which clash with beliefs held by the USSR. This variety stems not only from the diversities among the peoples that are associated with the United States but also from the unwillingness of leaders in the United States to compel adherence to one system of thought. Ideologies such as that of the USSR have a pseudoreligious nature that makes their adherents fanatic believers. In this respect, at least, the USSR has a certain advantage over the United States.

Interventionism. Interventionism in international politics consists of the efforts made by the government of one country to alter the attitudes or behavior of the government in another country. It is quite an old practice; for example, the members of the Quintuple Alliance in the early nineteenth century intervened regularly in the affairs of countries where any of the principles of the French Revolution seemed to be alive.

SOVIET INTERVENTIONISM. In the present conflict, the Soviet Union in particular intervenes in countries all over the world, seeking to win local adoption of pro-Soviet views. For such undertakings it has the most extensive assortment of tools available to any state in history. It can use not only such traditional implements as bribery and assassination but also the unique world-wide Communist Party with its various fronts and affiliates. If possible, the USSR foments a revolution that installs a pro-Soviet government. Where such a procedure would be difficult or impossible, Soviet agents endeavor to lessen the hostility of officials toward the USSR or in some other way divert the policy of the country from an anti-Soviet bias.

UNITED STATES INTERVENTIONISM. The government of the United States suffers considerable handicaps in such activities. For one thing, the United States has a tradition dating back to Washington's Farewell Address of avoiding intervention in the domestic affairs of European countries. Moreover, many American leaders view intervention as a denial of the right of national self-determination. Yet the necessities of the "Cold War" work for some degree of interventionism. The United States formerly intervened rather often in domestic Latin American politics; it does so less today. The Marshall Plan and succeeding foreign aid programs are a type of intervention, yet United States officials in granting aid under this and later programs rarely asked for drastic changes in policy by the recipient government. The refusal of the United States government to intervene effectively against the Castro regime in Cuba during 1960 and 1961 maintained this pattern of hesitant and restrained interventionism.

The Transformation of Diplomacy. In the present conflict, diplomacy has acquired a major complication both in method and in aim. Diplomacy is always conducted in at least relative secrecy—despite the first of Wilson's Fourteen Points—and a principal aim is often the resolution of international disputes through compromise. Today, in part because of the United Nations, much diplomacy is conducted in public. A considerable body of opinion holds that this is the proper method for carrying on discussions between governments, and the various media of public information have a vested interest in such a practice. Furthermore, some government leaders find it to their advantage to have open discussions. As a result, negotiating is used frequently not to achieve a settlement but to publicize the stand of a government all over the world and to gain support from its own people and from other governments. Thus sometimes, when leaders wish to compromise, their publics, which have been introduced to the issues in public debate, wish to remain inflexible, and vice versa. It cannot be maintained that the results are always disadvantageous, but certainly political leaders encounter more difficulties in conducting foreign policy, a fact manifest in negotiations like those over disarmament, German unification, and the status of Berlin.

Economic Competition. Economic competition is one of the oldest forms of nonmilitary warfare; however, today it takes a form quite different from that in the past. Usually, economic competition has involved struggles for sources of raw materials, precious metals, and markets. Such activities had political overtones, but in general they were monetarily rewarding. The economic competition being waged by the superpowers today, on the contrary, is motivated chiefly by political considerations and in some cases results in a net monetary loss. For one thing, through grants and loans of government money, and through furnishing technical aid, the United States and the USSR are trying to win allies by raising living standards in other countries. This, it may be noted, is a drastic about-face for the USSR: Marxist theory holds that communist revolutions break out because of the workers' poverty, so that until recently Soviet agents promoted economic disorganization. Another phase of the economic competition has seen efforts by each superpower to raise the well-being of its own people in attempts to prove to other nations the superiority of its economic system. One other phase of this competition has been the limitations placed upon foreign trade, especially by the United States, to keep the enemy from receiving certain goods believed essential for its economy.

CREATION OF THE SOVIET BLOC, 1939–49

The creation of the Soviet Bloc was accomplished mainly between 1945 and 1949, but it actually began in 1939.

The Soviet Attitude toward World War II. Even during the war, when the Soviet Union appeared on the verge of destruction by Axis forces, Soviet leaders took steps to assure their postwar dominance of eastern Europe. These steps were noteworthy for providing illustrations of how the Soviet view of the war differed from the Anglo-American view. Anglo-American leaders regarded the war chiefly as a struggle to defeat the Axis powers. Soviet leaders viewed it as an opportunity for having one set of their enemies—the United States, Great Britain, France, and China—mortally injure another set of their enemies— Germany, Italy, and Japan—and at the same time gravely weaken themselves. In addition, the Soviets paved the way to control eastern Europe by fostering bands of Partisans, who fought not only the Nazis but all other anti-Soviet groups. Thus the USSR supported Tito's pro-Soviet guerrillas in Yugoslavia but sought to destroy the anti-Soviet guerrillas in both Yugoslavia and Poland. Yet during the war Soviet leaders took various steps to convince Anglo-American chiefs that they had discarded the policy of world revolution; for instance, in 1943 they dissolved the Comintern, and claimed that American Communists would no longer receive their instructions from Moscow.

Postwar Measures in Europe. Postwar Soviet measures in Europe involved annexation of certain lands from neighboring small countries, or official confirmation of annexations already made; and the establishment of pro-Soviet governments in lands abutting on the USSR. The lands annexed to the USSR included districts taken from Finland, Poland, Czechoslovakia, and Romania. Estonia, Latvia, and Lithuania were annexed outright. Soviet authorities established pro-Soviet governments in Poland, Hungary, Romania, Albania, Bulgaria, and Czechoslovakia. The general practice was that when Soviet armies occupied these countries they installed a coalition, Popular Front government and placed local Communists in such strategic ministries as those of Education, Justice, and Interior (which controlled the police). Later, under the protection of the Soviet armies, the local Communist Party took over all cabinet posts. The situation in Yugoslavia was different, for there the local Communists, under Tito, already comprised an army that could secure dominance. In 1947, partly to insure its supremacy over Eastern Europe, the government of the USSR created the Communist Information Bureau (Cominform). It included representatives from all Soviet-Bloc nations except Albania, along with delegates from France and Italy. It was not a revived Comintern, but mainly a propaganda agency. In 1948 Soviet leaders expelled Yugoslavia from the Cominform, because Tito would not allow as much Soviet intervention in Yugoslavia as Soviet rulers wished.

Postwar Measures in Asia. Postwar Soviet measures in Asia through 1949 included chiefly the conquest of China by the Chinese Communists. During World War II the Chinese Communists, whose headquarters were in northern China, had co-operated with the Chinese government—the Nationalists or Kuomintang—in fighting the Japanese. However, they greatly profited from the Soviet invasion of Manchuria; for Soviet leaders turned over to the Chinese Communists the weapons they took from Japanese soldiers and the industry in Manchuria that they did not dismantle and transport west for their own use. Civil war now broke out in earnest in China. The Nationalists, headed by Chiang Kai-shek, were handicapped by various factors. One was their lack of support from many of the Chinese people. Another was the corruption and inefficiency of certain elements in Chiang's own government. The United States recommended various reforms to the Nationalist government. It also suggested that the Nationalists and Communists co-operate in forming a new government and integrating their forces. But both sides violated all agreements that stipulated co-operation. In addition, the lack of reliable information on the actual situation in China led to a generally indecisive policy on the part of the United States government. The Soviets, in the meantime, provided the Communists with captured Japanese equipment and facilitated their take-over of Manchuria. By 1949 the Chinese Communists had secured control of China, with their leader, Mao Tse-tung, at the head of the government. The Nationalist leaders and many of their troops withdrew to the island of Formosa, where they were still recognized by the United States as the government of China.

RESISTANCE TO SOVIET EXPANSION, 1946–49

Organized resistance to Soviet expansion did not begin until 1947, when the United States government appropriated money for the governments of Greece and Turkey, which were under constant and severe attack by the Communists. Soon afterward the United States government adopted the policy of expending huge sums abroad for the asserted purpose of limiting Soviet expansion.

Winston Churchill and the "Iron Curtain." Although certain influential people in the Anglo-American world had for years been warning about the threat posed by the USSR, the first major public utterance to this effect came in mid-1946, when Winston Churchill spoke of the "iron curtain" that had descended across Europe from the Baltic to the Adriatic. He was referring to the fact of Soviet domination over Eastern Europe, and the growing division between "East"—represented by the USSR—and "West"—represented by the United States and Great Britain. Churchill urged greater co-operation between the American and British governments, and perhaps even an alliance between them.

The "Truman Doctrine"—Greece and Turkey. Early in 1947, when President Truman was at last convinced that the Soviet Union was a threat to the United States, he enunciated the "Truman Doctrine." According to the Doctrine, the United States government was to "support free peoples who are resisting attempted subjugation by armed minorities or by outside pressures." This principle applied at this time to two countries, Greece and Turkey. Greece at this time was in the throes of a civil war, in which Greek Communists receiving supplies through Yugoslavia and Bulgaria were trying to overthrow the anti-Communist Greek government. Turkey was undergoing pressure from the USSR both for the cession of certain northeastern provinces on the

Soviet frontier and for the easing of restraints on shipping through the Dardanelles. Ordinarily the British would have supported the Greeks, if not the Turks, to keep Soviet naval vessels out of the Mediterranean; however, the British were in such financial difficulty at the time that they announced their inability to protect the Greeks. Hence President Truman and his advisers decided that the United States government must assume this burden. At their urging, Congress appropriated $400,000,000 for aid to these two countries.

The Marshall Plan. In June, 1947, Secretary of State George C. Marshall called on all European governments to draft plans for the reduction of hunger and misery and offered United States assistance. This program was to amount essentially to a reorganization and extension of the various aid programs the United States government was already financing, notably UNRRA. However, the government of the Soviet Union denounced the proposal as one aimed at spreading American imperialism. It refused to participate, and forbade the governments of its satellites to take part. The sixteen governments that did draft plans for the European Recovery Program (ERP) in 1947 were therefore all from Western European countries. It is noteworthy that in the same period the Communist leaders met at Warsaw to found the Cominform. In any case, the plan submitted by the Western European governments met strong resistance in Congress until early in 1948, when Communists seized power in Czechoslovakia. Thereupon Congress appropriated $5.3 billion for the first year and established the Economic Co-operation Administration (ECA) to supervise the funds.

The Berlin Blockade and "Airlift." In 1948, largely in response to the consolidation of the three western zones of Germany, the Soviet Union commenced a blockade of all rail, highway, and canal traffic into Berlin. Evidently the Soviet government wanted the other occupying powers either to give up their plans for creating a "West Germany" or else to surrender Berlin itself. The Americans, British, and French thereupon instituted an "airlift," whereby essential goods were brought into Berlin by airplanes. Though the flying was often hazardous, they succeeded in importing enough goods to keep the two million residents of their sectors of Berlin from starving and freezing. At length, almost a year later, the USSR ended the blockade.

The North Atlantic Treaty Organization (NATO). The North Atlantic Treaty Organization (NATO), formed in 1949, was a military alliance of 12 anti-Communist powers on both sides of the Atlantic. It was foreshadowed in 1948 by a military alliance formed among Great Britain, France, and the Benelux countries (Belgium, the Netherlands, and Luxemburg). Leaders not merely in these countries but also in the United States soon realized that effective resistance to the USSR could be mustered only with the collaboration of the United States. Hence in April, 1949, these countries and the United States, together with six other countries, formed the North Atlantic Treaty Organization. The terms of the treaty provided that an attack on any one signatory would be regarded as an attack on all other signatories. In other words, this treaty might require the United States to go to war because of a military attack on another country. After considerable debate the Senate voted to approve of the treaty. This was the first military alliance for the United States since that negotiated with France in 1778.

The "Point Four" Program. The "Point Four" Program, enunciated by President Truman in 1949, called for United States action to help "undeveloped" areas achieve a higher level of agricultural and industrial productiveness. The presumption here was much like that underlying the ERP—that a prosperous nation was less likely to turn to communism than an impoverished one. Under the Point Four Program the United States has reached agreements with numerous countries in Latin America, Africa, and Asia to supply technicians and goods for modernizing the economic systems of these countries. Still, Congressional appropriations for the program have not been large. It should also be noted that private business organizations since the war have invested billions of dollars in such countries for various industrial and commercial tasks.

Inter-American Relations, 1945–49. Inter-American relations after World War II continued in much the same path as before, that of the Good Neighbor Policy and of "hemispheric solidarity." For instance, in 1945, the United States and all the Latin American countries save Argentina signed the Act of Chapultepec, according to which a military attack on one American country was to be regarded as an attack on all. The Act was really directed against Argentina, whose government under its dictator, Juan Perón, had tended to favor the Axis during World War II and seemed after the war on the verge of aggressions against its neighbors. By 1947, however, when the threat of the USSR had appeared much more dangerous than that of Argentina, delegates from the United States, Argentina, and most other Latin American countries agreed to the Treaty of Rio de Janeiro; in effect it repeated the terms of the Act of Chapultepec. It also transformed the Monroe Doctrine officially into a hemispheric responsibility. Subsequently, in 1948, at Bogotá, Colombia, delegates from the American governments created the Organization of American States (OAS). Essentially the functions of the OAS are to keep the peace in the Americas, increase co-operation among American countries, and provide for their defense from outside attack. The OAS, a "regional organization" within the United Nations, replaced the Pan American Union.

THE WAR IN KOREA, 1950–53

The war in Korea, from 1950 until 1953, was the first armed clash between Soviet-Bloc troops and anti-Soviet troops. Although military campaigning officially ceased early in 1953, there was by 1962 still no formal peace.

Korean Developments, 1945–50. The Korean people, for many years colonial dependents of the Japanese, were promised national independence at the Cairo Conference. Then the leaders at the Potsdam Conference agreed that until the Koreans were ready for self-government their country would be divided at the 38th parallel, the United States to administer the southern half and the USSR the northern half. In 1947 a United Nations commission visited Korea to help establish a government for the whole country. Soviet officials, however, would not allow the commission to enter the Soviet-administered area. Hence the government for Korea that was approved by the United Nations commission and recognized by the United States was that of the United States-administered area. Soviet authorities created a pro-Soviet regime in their area (North Korea), supplied it copiously with arms, and withdrew Soviet troops in 1948. The United States government terminated the occupation of its area (South Korea) in 1949. United States authorities, however, had not provided very well for the arming of South Korea.

The Attack on South Korea and United Nations Reaction. On June 25, 1950, troops from North Korea crossed the 38th parallel and invaded South Korea. The United Nations Security Council on the same day termed the attack a "breach of the peace" and demanded that North Korean forces withdraw. This action was possible only because the USSR was then "boycotting" the Council since it would not admit Communist China to its membership. Next, on June 27, President Truman directed United States air and naval forces to help South Korea. He also ordered the commanders of American naval ships near Formosa to keep the Nationalist Chinese from intervening in Korea. Later that day the UN Security Council urged all UN members to assist the South Koreans, another action made possible by the absence of any Soviet delegate. On June 30, United States army units from Japan landed in South Korea. Early in July the Security Council authorized the creation of a combined United Nations military force and, duly empowered by the UN to do so, President Truman named General MacArthur head of this force. Most other UN members contributed only token elements to this force, so that the undertaking was conducted almost entirely by the troops of the United States and South Korea. Some 37 countries in all gave supplies of some kind to the UN forces.

The Military Campaigns in Korea. The battle lines in Korea moved up and down the peninsula. After the North Koreans had overrun almost all Korea, the UN forces compelled North Korean troops to withdraw and eventually expelled them from all of South Korea. MacArthur then halted the UN advance to receive further instructions. Early in October, the UN General Assembly voted that "all appropriate steps be taken to ensure conditions of stability throughout Korea." MacArthur interpreted this resolution as leave to invade North Korea and promptly did so, pushing the North Koreans back toward the Chinese Manchurian border. Within a few days the UN forces began encountering Chinese Communist "volunteers" who in November mounted a powerful offensive that drove UN troops back into South Korea. Then, in January, 1951, the UN armies once more advanced, driving the North Koreans and Chinese Communists out of South Korea. A battle line was stabilized just north of the 38th parallel. In April, 1951, when General MacArthur apparently wanted to bomb military bases in Manchuria, against the wishes of other American and UN authorities, President Truman dismissed him from command of the UN forces. This action led to a great debate on foreign policy in the United States, but Truman's action remained the authoritative expression of policy.

The Truce in Korea. In June, 1951, the Soviet government proposed that the two sides in Korea make a truce. Reaching the truce, however, required many months, largely because of the numerous barriers the North Korean negotiators erected. Perhaps the most important barrier involved the disposition of prisoners held by the UN forces who did not wish to return home, either to North Korea or to Communist China. At length the Communist negotiators agreed that such prisoners need not be forced to go home if they were unwilling, provided that first the Communists be allowed to try to persuade them to return voluntarily. Subsequently a few of these prisoners were persuaded to return home, but the bulk of those who at first refused to go home held to their decision. The truce came into effect in July, 1953, but there is still no conclusive peace treaty.

NATIONALISM AND NEUTRALISM IN ASIA
AND AFRICA

Although many countries in the world, especially in Europe and the Americas, took a firm stand on either the pro-Soviet or the anti-Soviet side, various other countries, chiefly in Asia and Africa, did not. Instead, they adopted, or tried to adopt, a position of neutralism. A significant feature was that in general these were new countries, resulting from the disintegration of the British and French colonial empires after 1945, and their neutralism was in large part the consequence of the strong feelings of nationalism that their leaders and elites were undergoing.

Nationalism. The sense of nationalism in these new countries had some unusual causes and led to profound complexities in politics.

CAUSES AND ACHIEVEMENTS. The nationalism that became prominent and influential after World War II stemmed from various causes. For one thing, the leaders and elites of Asia and Africa were becoming more educated, and became aware of the bonds among individuals and groups that underlie nationalism. Also, many of them accepted the teachings of the USSR, which disseminated nationalist propaganda among them in efforts to break down the colonial empires. Another cause was the strong antiwhite feelings of these people, which had been furthered by the military triumphs of the Japanese—a nonwhite nation—during the war. This nationalism has resulted in the creation of over 40 new countries in Asia and Africa since the end of the war. Yet political independence for these nations has not always been accompanied by political freedom for individual citizens. For example, in Ghana today it is legal for the government to "detain" a person for as long as five years without a trial.

COMPLEXITIES. The new nationalism and the responses to it involved profound complexities. The new countries in the main followed the borders established when they were colonies, for the simple reason that the European governments were extending national independence to specific colonies. However, the borders of the colonies had seldom been drawn according to the territories of native tribes or cultural groups. As a consequence, a single new country might in fact include several national groups or tribes. The division of British India into India and Pakistan was a recognition of this fact. Moreover, particularly in Africa, some tribes in a given colony were apt to be more advanced culturally than other tribes in the same colony, and hence their leaders were more aware of "nationhood." Therefore national independence for a one-time colony might mean the right to national self-determination for only one country in the Middle East that desires military help from the United States may have it.

The Economic Struggle. The economic struggle between the pro-Communist and anti-Communist groups has involved a contest as to the relative productivity of the United States and the USSR, and competition by economic means to win the support of neutralist states.

THE CONTEST OVER PRODUCTIVITY. In the contest over domestic productivity, Soviet leaders have made sweeping claims for a high rate of increase in their economic output, and many Americans have not only accepted the Soviet figures but expressed considerable alarm at them. Different sets of statistics have given different and often opposite results. However, according to an American study published in 1961, since 1913 the rate of increase in Soviet output per man-hour in all economic fields has been much lower than that in the United States, and the high Soviet rate of increase from 1948 until 1953 was to be expected of any country whose productive facilities had been seriously damaged in war. Whatever the facts, this competition was an important propaganda undertaking for Soviet leaders, since it was designed to prove that communism is more efficient than capitalism in industrializing a country.

THE COMPETITION FOR THE TRADE OF NEUTRALIST COUNTRIES. In the competition for the trade of neutralist countries, the USSR and Communist China have resorted to practices that were monetarily unrewarding but—at least in appearance—politically profitable. For instance, they sold goods below the cost of producing them. Also, they bought such items as sugar from Cuba for which the USSR had no need. The United States government could subsidize American products and sell them abroad at a low price, but in doing so it might undersell the goods of a friendly country and thereby arouse rancor in that country.

THE COMPETITION TO PROMOTE INDUSTRY. Finally, the USSR and Communist China have entered into competition with the United State in efforts to promote industry in the "underdeveloped" countries. Th USSR, however, does not give away money in the fashion of the Unit States but relies instead upon loans at low interest rates. This proced by 1960 had not extended more than a small fraction of the quantity aid the United States had granted. From 1954 through 1960 the So Bloc countries together provided $4.6 billion in aid, only $193,00 of which was in grants. At the same time, the fact that Soviet ai not take the form of outright gifts may be psychologically advant for the USSR. Certainly the United States has harvested a large of resentment from people overseas as a result of the Marshall P its successors.

tribe out of several in the country. Besides, as in the case of Sudan, this tribe could be a minority, though dominant. As a result, when the presently retarded tribal groups acquire a higher cultural level and a stronger national sense, their leaders may demand autonomy within these new countries, or they may even attempt to secede and form distinct new nation-states. Conceivably, a state such as Nigeria may some day undergo the same internal problems as those experienced by the Austro-Hungarian Empire before 1914. One final point is that the bulk of the population in many of these new African countries is tribalistic rather than nationalistic and may suffer acute psychological and social distress from its inability to understand the nationalism of its leaders.

Neutralism. The neutralism that was common in these new countries after 1945 was a corollary of their nationalism. Such older countries as China, Japan, and Turkey, which had long enjoyed self-government, were not neutral. Rather, it was generally new states such as India, Indonesia, and Guinea that became neutral. (Exceptions were Israel, Pakistan, and the Republic of the Philippines.) In their neutralism these governments tend to deal with the USSR and Communist China on the same basis as with the United States. They have become the targets of the political, economic, and propaganda war that the United States and the USSR are waging all over the world.

THE CONFLICT IN THE 1950's

During the 1950's the conflict between the pro-Soviet and the anti-Soviet countries acquired some new aspects and emphases. One important cause for these changes was the death of Joseph Stalin in 1953. His eventual successor, Premier Nikita Khrushchev, tended to assume the appearances of friendliness toward non-Communist governments. At the same time the government of the USSR was still willing on occasion to use force to repress opposition and extend its influence. Meanwhile the Communist Chinese government was less and less willing to obey Soviet commands. A final, and general, change was that the Soviet Bloc discarded the industrialized states as its immediate targets in favor of the economically more or less backward countries of Asia, Africa, and Latin America.

Soviet Pretenses of Friendliness. The Soviet government under Khrushchev, especially from 1956 on, made various pretenses of friendliness toward non-Communist countries. For example, in 1956 Khrushchev denounced Stalin as a tyrant and dictator who had made many errors and committed many brutalities. Also in 1956, the Soviet Union dissolved the Cominform and established closer relations with Yugoslavia. Khrushchev, with his then chief associate, Marshal Nikolai Bulganin, toured from one European capital to another. Khrushchev met leaders of important non-Soviet countries at Geneva, and there urged a policy of "peaceful coexistence" under which capitalism and communism would vie in economic competition. In 1959 Khrushchev visited the United States at President Eisenhower's invitation, reaping a huge propaganda victory. On the other hand, at a "summit conference" of American, British, French, and Soviet leaders in 1960, Khrushchev was extremely insulting toward the President, using as one pretext the fact that a United States reconnaissance aircraft had been brought down in the USSR just before the conference met. He remained hostile until the end of Eisenhower's presidency in 1961. No sooner had John F. Kennedy become President than the Soviet government released two American flyers who had been imprisoned in the USSR. Khrushchev discarded the pretense of friendliness later in 1961 when he ordered a resumption of atmospheric nuclear tests.

Soviet Uses of Force. On various occasions the Soviet Union used force both to repress opposition within its domains and to expand its influence outside the Soviet Bloc. For instance, when the people in the Soviet sector of Berlin started rioting against Soviet rule in 1953, the Soviet government rushed troops and equipment to the city, and put down the rioters with tanks. In 1956 certain Hungarian leaders tried to uproot Soviet controls, but they were overcome by Soviet armed forces. The Soviet government through local Communist Parties sought by forceful means as well as by others to win control, or at least predominance, in such countries as Iraq and Egypt. In the Americas, the USSR contributed to the establishment of the pro-Soviet Castro regime in Cuba. Cuba is now the principal staging area for Soviet guerrilla operations and subversive activities throughout Latin America. In Asia, the USSR supported the uprising of pro-Soviet groups in Laos. These uses of force, however, have sometimes alienated other governments. For instance, it appears certain that the government of Iceland, once friendly toward the USSR, became very cool after the Soviet repression of the Hungarians.

Communist Chinese Aggressions. The Communist Chinese were a great deal more aggressive than the leaders of the USSR and made little pretense toward friendly relations with their neighbors. In Southeast Asia the Chinese Communists were especially active in their support of local Communist groups. They enjoyed a notable victory in 1954, when the Communists of Vietnam defeated the anti-Communist forces there and compelled the establishment of a pro-Communist North Vietnam

government. Subsequently they helped the Communist North namese make forays into South Vietnam. In 1959 they overran T forcing the ruler of Tibet, the Dalai Lama, to flee, and began exte nating the Tibetan people. They attacked traditional border outpos India, leading even the neutralist Indian prime minister, Jawaha Nehru, to protest. Some of these actions displeased Soviet leaders, there is little doubt that on occasion they urged Communist Chin leaders to adopt a more moderate policy. Furthermore, after Stali death the Communist Chinese leaders made strong claims to dominat world communism and asserted that they had been responsible for i portant changes in Communist doctrine and practice for gaining cont of a nonindustrialized country. In 1961 the Communist Chinese acquir a European base in Albania when Albanian leaders broke with th USSR and established close ties with Communist China. Still, despit their claims of ideological independence, the Communist Chines will be materially dependent on the USSR for many years. Sovie withdrawal of its technical aid from Communist China in 1961 and 1962 worsened the already bad economic conditions prevailing in China.

Military Alliances. During the 1950's both the Soviet-Bloc countries and the anti-Soviet countries formed a number of military alliances. The chief alliance of Soviet-Bloc countries was established by the Warsaw Pact, negotiated in 1955 between the USSR and the seven Eastern European satellites. The Communist Chinese did not formally join the countries signing this pact, but a leading Chinese Communist was present at the negotiations. As for the anti-Communist countries, the United States became the center of a group of military alliances encircling the Soviet Union. In addition to being a member of NATO, it was a member of the Southeast Asia Treaty Organization (SEATO), created in 1954 by the United States, Great Britain, France, Australia, New Zealand, the Republic of the Philippines, Thailand, and Pakistan. Another group, which does not include the United States as a member but which has its backing, was first termed the Middle East Treaty Organization (METO); at one time it comprised Great Britain, Turkey, Iraq, Iran, and Pakistan. Later, however, the anti-Communist government of Iraq was replaced by one more friendly to the USSR, and Iraq in effect withdrew from this body. Its name was also changed, to the Central Treaty Organization (CENTO). Furthermore, the United States has separate military alliances with such countries as South Korea, Nationalist China, and Japan. Finally, in 1957, the United States government proclaimed the "Eisenhower Doctrine," under which any

Review Questions

1. Discuss the traits of the postwar conflict. Correlate these traits with such matters as the industrial revolution, present-day communications media, and compulsory tax-supported schooling. Does any of these traits seem more nearly "cause," and any other more nearly "effect"?

2. Describe the Soviet attitude toward World War II. Was there any analogous view held in certain circles before and during the war in the United States, Great Britain, and France?

3. How was the establishment of a Communist regime in Yugoslavia different from that in the other Eastern European countries? What factors in the history and geography of Yugoslavia may have contributed to this difference?

4. How did the Marshall Plan differ from the "Truman Doctrine"? Were there any later plans, applicable to other countries, that resembled the "Truman Doctrine"?

5. How have the foreign-aid programs that began with the Marshall Plan evolved up to the present, in terms of recipients, aims, and administrative structure in the United States? What factors, both in the United States and abroad, may have contributed to this evolution?

6. Describe the relations between the United States and the countries of Latin America since 1945. To what degree has the United States government regarded these countries as elements in the security of the United States?

7. Compare the roles of the United States and the United Nations in the Korean War.

8. Discuss postwar nationalism and neutralism in Africa and Asia. Try to find examples from countries not mentioned in the text.

9. What might be the reasons why Soviet leaders pretend friendliness on some occasions and use force on others?

10. How does the imperialism of Communist China today resemble the imperialistic activities of China in centuries past, and how does it differ from them?

11. What are the relative advantages of the United States and the Soviet Union in their economic competition?

PART 2 STRUCTURE OF WORLD POWER

12 FUNDAMENTAL PRINCIPLES OF NATIONAL POWER

National power comprises the strength that the government of a country can bring to bear in its effort to carry out its foreign policy. It is the strength a government may use to secure what it wants from other governments. Exactly which elements constitute national power is a matter of some controversy among students of the subject. There is fairly general agreement, however, that they include population, territorial extent, natural resources, technology, national unity or national morale, military preparedness, and diplomacy. The relative importance of these forces is changing all the time; moreover, the degree to which each country and its government possess them is also constantly changing, both absolutely and relatively to other countries. As a consequence, there is a continuous process of fluctuation in national power. This chapter discusses first the elements underlying national power. Then, in terms of these elements, it deals with fluctuations in national power that have occurred in the past and those that may occur in the future. The remaining chapters of Part Two describe the main countries and areas of the world in terms of these elements.

ELEMENTS UNDERLYING NATIONAL POWER

The elements that underlie national power can be listed under the categories of population, territorial extent, natural resources, technology, national unity (or national morale), military preparedness, and diplomacy.

Population. Population as an element of national power is important both quantitatively and qualitatively. For one thing, it is assumed that any country must have a large population to be strong, for today a large population is essential for manning the armed forces and the national economy. That Germany became more populous than France in

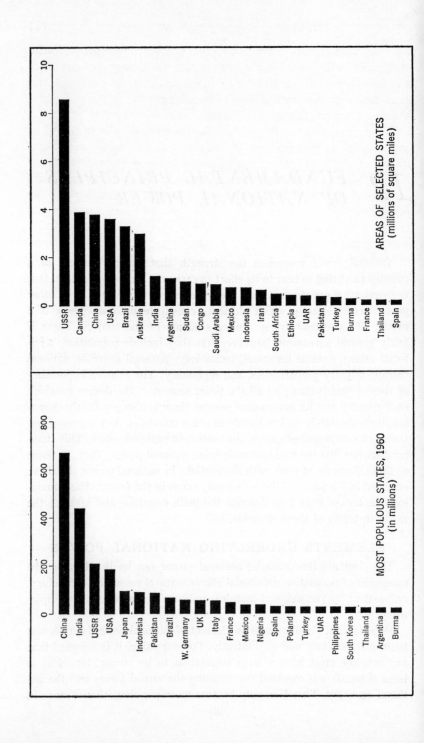

AREAS OF SELECTED STATES
(millions of square miles)

USSR · Canada · China · USA · Brazil · Australia · India · Argentina · Sudan · Congo · Saudi Arabia · Mexico · Indonesia · Iran · South Africa · Ethiopia · UAR · Pakistan · Turkey · Burma · France · Thailand · Spain

MOST POPULOUS STATES, 1960
(in millions)

China · India · USSR · USA · Japan · Indonesia · Pakistan · Brazil · W. Germany · UK · Italy · France · Mexico · Nigeria · Spain · Poland · Turkey · UAR · Philippines · South Korea · Thailand · Argentina · Burma the nineteenth century was an important cause for the relative decline of France. On the other hand, a large population in itself does not make a country powerful; for many years China has been the most populous of all countries, but until recently it has occupied the status of a quasi-colony. Where the population is greater than the ability of a national economy to support it and therefore hinders the formation of capital, a country may be weakened. Also, the population must be healthy and have a good morale. Sickly people do not make good soldiers, diplomats, or business directors. When the people of a country such as India are almost universally ill nourished, the country is weak. Finally, the population should be more or less evenly divided between the sexes and contain a substantial percentage of men of working and fighting age. The reluctance of the French government to send its troops into battle in 1939 was doubtless based in part upon the tremendous losses in manpower the French suffered during World War I.

Territorial Extent. The territorial extent of a country must be rather large for that country to be strong. Today the two superpowers, the United States and the USSR, are both continental in extent. Yet Canada, Brazil, Australia, and China are likewise continental; but, because they lack such other forces as population or technology, none of them ranks with the superpowers. On the other hand, a comparatively small country such as Germany or Japan may be very strong if it possesses an exceptionally high level of technology, military preparedness, and national unity.

FUNCTIONS OF TERRITORIAL EXTENT. One leading function of territorial extent that Soviet leaders exploited during World War II is the space it provides for military withdrawal. When time permits—it may not in another war—territorial extent also allows the relocation of industry behind the lines, as Soviet engineers demonstrated during World War II. In any war waged with missiles it enables a government to disperse both its launching bases and its industry, so that the enemy has more difficulty in locating and hitting the vital targets. It is significant that the principal military commands of the United States today are situated not in New York, Washington, Chicago, or San Francisco, but near Omaha and Colorado Springs. One other advantage of a great territorial extent is that it makes political and military control by an invading army very difficult; it encourages guerrilla action, as the British discovered in the American Revolution and as Union generals found out in the American Civil War.

EFFECTS OF LOSSES OR GAINS OF TERRITORY. Loss of a comparatively small area need not greatly weaken a country; it may even firm the morale of the people. French loss of Alsace-Lorraine in 1871 led to a desire for revenge that helped bring on World War I. Yet a rather small area may for particular reasons be so important to a country that its loss will result in a drastic fall in power; the Sudetenland, which the Germans took from Czechoslovakia in 1938, contained so much industry and so large a proportion of Czech fortifications that its loss made Czechoslovakia defenseless against German troops. On the other hand, an increase of territory may in some ways weaken a country. German acquisition of Austria in 1938 was an economic loss; however, it was a military and a moral gain. Likewise, the loss of an extensive area need not weaken a country; Great Britain is stronger today without India than it would be with India and the obligation to defend it. Nevertheless, the loss of considerable territories may at times greatly weaken a country or indicate the fact that the country has become too weak to defend these territories. For instance, in the seventeenth century Sweden was a powerful country occupying much of northeastern Europe; during the eighteenth century the neighbors of Sweden, especially Russia, took away much of this territory, and Sweden gradually lapsed into the position of a minor power. Finally, all the territory of a country may be taken away, so that the country disappears; Poland thus vanished in 1795. Yet the feeling of nationalism among the people concerned may urge them to regain the status of national independence; thus Poland reappeared after World War I.

Natural Resources. Not only the possession of natural resources, but also their ownership and control, are important elements underlying national power.

THE SECURING OF NATURAL RESOURCES. Natural resources are essential for national power. Some countries, such as the United States, may possess most important natural resources within their own boundaries. Other countries, such as Germany, may possess some important resources but have to acquire a considerable number of others elsewhere. Yet other countries, such as Japan, may have very few resources but a talented and aggressive population determined to fill its needs. Nations may engage in bitter conflict for possession of important resources; the British and the Turks nearly went to war in the 1920's over the Mosul oil fields. Countries may seek colonies to provide their wants; North Carolina was valuable to the English in the eighteenth century for the naval stores, especially pitch, that it furnished. Loss of the supply of a particular resource may weaken a country. According to one school of thought, the Italian city-states, especially Venice, that flourished on trade during the Renaissance declined from about 1500 on because the

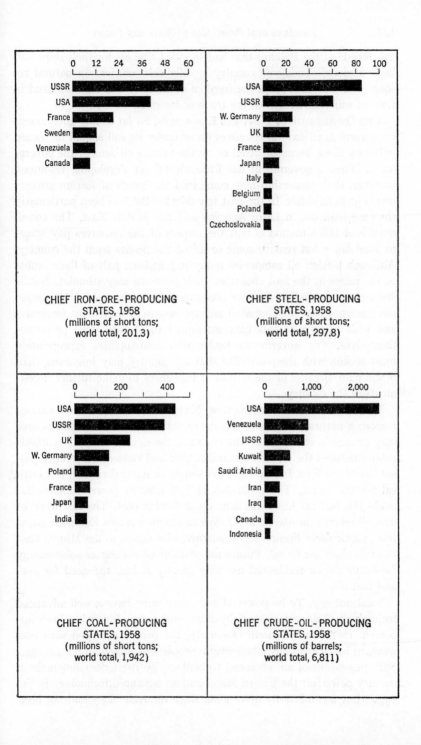

CHIEF IRON-ORE-PRODUCING
STATES, 1958
(millions of short tons;
world total, 201.3)

CHIEF STEEL-PRODUCING
STATES, 1958
(millions of short tons;
world total, 297.8)

CHIEF COAL-PRODUCING
STATES, 1958
(millions of short tons;
world total, 1,942)

CHIEF CRUDE-OIL-PRODUCING
STATES, 1958
(millions of barrels;
world total, 6,811)

oak forests of the Balkans that had supplied timbers for their ships had been depleted. Today no country is fully self-sufficient in natural resources; hence each seeks the freedom of trade on the high seas and in time of war interferes with the trade of its enemies.

THE OWNERSHIP OF NATURAL RESOURCES. So far as any government is concerned, all natural resources on or under its soil should be owned either by the government itself or by the private citizens of the government. When a government has little capital for developing resources, however, their ownership may come into the hands of foreign governments or individuals. In the past few decades this has been particularly the case with oil, in Latin America and the Middle East. The consequence of this situation is that the owners of the resources pay wages to local labor but remove some or all of the profits from the country. Although foreign oil companies today pay at least half of their profits to the rulers of the host countries, their presence may stimulate hostile feelings of nationalism that are encouraged by Soviet agents. Numerous governments have expropriated natural resources owned by foreigners and with varying success have attempted to operate these properties themselves. Any government leader who contemplates expropriation must reckon with the possibility that his country may lose more than it will gain, because of the refusal of foreigners to make further investments in the country.

THE CHANGING IMPORTANCE OF NATURAL RESOURCES. For various reasons a natural resource or a country that supplies a natural resource may change in importance. For instance, the development of synthetic rubber reduced the value of natural rubber and consequently made possession of the East Indies, the chief source of natural rubber, less critical for the Dutch. The expansion of hydroelectric power supplies has made the Italians less dependent upon British coal. The discovery of vast oil reserves in Algeria and Libya has made western European countries, particularly France, less concerned with access to the Middle East through the Suez Canal. Future adaptations of nuclear or solar energy for industrial or residential use may greatly reduce the need for coal and fuel oil.

Technology. To be powerful a country must have a well advanced technology. This seems especially important today, but it has been important in the past as well. Obviously, the people equipped with iron weapons had a great advantage over a people equipped with bronze ones. Still, possession of an advanced technology by itself does not make a country powerful; the United States had an advanced technology in the 1930's but was militarily quite weak since the technology had not been

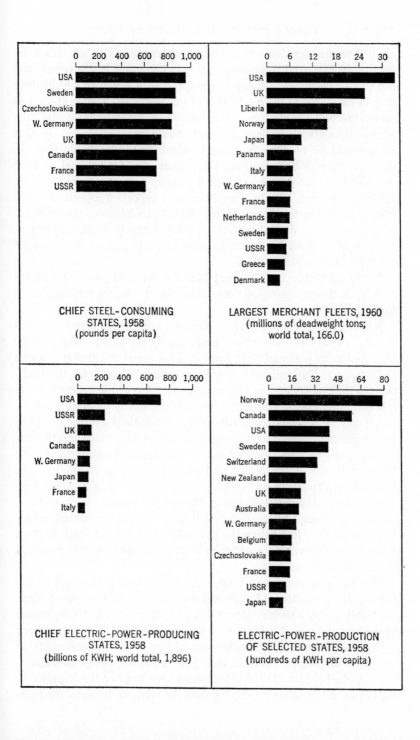

CHIEF STEEL-CONSUMING
STATES, 1958
(pounds per capita)

LARGEST MERCHANT FLEETS, 1960
(millions of deadweight tons;
world total, 166.0)

CHIEF ELECTRIC-POWER-PRODUCING
STATES, 1958
(billions of KWH; world total, 1,896)

ELECTRIC-POWER-PRODUCTION
OF SELECTED STATES, 1958
(hundreds of KWH per capita)

applied to the large-scale manufacture of armaments. A significant aspect of an industrial technology that was important in the recent past but can be meaningless today is the speed with which this technology may be converted to the production of war materials. Today, at least as some observers see matters, a war carried on by intercontinental missiles equipped with nuclear warheads would be over so quickly that there would be no time to convert industries to war production. As these people view the situation, the critical issue for national survival and victory is the degree to which a country possesses weapons ready for immediate use. Finally, one of the most important aspects of world history in the nineteenth and twentieth centuries has been the extension of advanced technological methods to many formerly "backward" countries, enabling them to play major roles in world politics once reserved for Western European powers.

National Unity, or National Morale. National unity, or national morale, is the psychological foundation for the successful conduct of foreign policy.

NATURE OF NATIONAL UNITY. National unity is, in terms of world politics, a consensus or near consensus among the citizens of a country that the foreign policy of their government is sound and that it deserves their support. National unity requires a general respect for the traditions of the country and an adherence to the aims of the government. It is a condition that is stimulated by such devices as national symbols, which may be propagated by educational institutions and the media of mass communications. Some government leaders have made effective use of scapegoats as well—the "aristos" of the French revolutionaries, the "inferior races" of the Nazis, and the "decadent capitalists" of the Communists. Today in particular, leaders also rely upon a comprehensive ideology disseminated among the public. Finally, a government leader may attempt to create national unity by a deliberate adventure in world politics; just before the Civil War, Secretary of State William Seward urged provoking a war with France and Spain to end Southern threats of secession.

THE ROLE OF NATIONAL UNITY. A country with a low level of national unity, regardless of its possession of other elements of power, finds it difficult to play a successful part in world politics. For instance, France in the first years of World War II was weakened by dissension stirred up by the Communists, who because of the Soviet-German pacts of 1939 were helping the Nazis in their war on France. Religious disunity has disturbed Ceylon. Tribal antagonisms have wracked the Republic of the Congo. National unity also involves the relations between the leaders and the mass of the population. Russia in World War I was weak partly because the Russian people did not back the tsar; on the other hand, Germany in World War II was immensely strong in part because the people supported Hitler. Great Britain became much stronger in 1940 when Winston Churchill, an advocate of resistance to Germany, replaced Neville Chamberlain, whom the majority of the British people identified with a policy of yielding to the Germans. Finally, national unity stemming from a particular event may strengthen a country; the national unity that emerged in the United States after the Japanese attack on Pearl Harbor almost overnight readied the United States psychologically for a positive and aggressive role in world politics.

Military Preparedness. Military preparedness is a major element underlying national power, but its importance may be overemphasized. Certainly the United States was much more powerful in 1944 than in 1941, for by 1944 it had created vast armed forces. On the other hand, when the Germans triumphed over the British and the French in the Czechoslovakian crisis by threatening war, they conducted a superb game of bluff, for they were not really prepared for war. Military preparedness also involves having the most effective weapons. One reason for German victory over France in 1940 was the great superiority of German tanks. Later in the war, the Germans were forced to retreat in the USSR partly because Soviet tanks were even better. In the current era of potential nuclear and missile warfare, military preparedness is perhaps more important than ever before. Military preparedness today is aimed not only at assuring the ability to fight a war but also, perhaps even more, at deterring a possible aggressor from starting a war.

Diplomacy. Diplomacy is the procedures and personnel by which the government of one country applies the principles of its foreign policy in dealing with the governments of other countries. It has often been charged that the diplomatic mishaps of the United States after 1945, such as the hostility shown Vice President Nixon on his Latin American tour during 1958, resulted partly from the inability of United States ambassadors and ministers to deal with people of other countries in their native tongues and from their ignorance of foreign customs and practices. The diplomatic representative of any country may be able to exploit his knowledge of foreign tongues and civilizations, or any other personal trait, in such a way that his influence is much greater than the power status of his country seems to warrant. Finally, in the past two decades there has been an increasing tendency for foreign ministers and even heads of state to conduct diplomatic negotiations for their governments. However, after Soviet Premier Khrushchev abruptly terminated the "summit meeting" at Paris in 1960, many officials of the United States government began questioning the merits of this practice. Nevertheless, shortly after his inauguration President Kennedy went to Vienna to meet Khrushchev.

SHIFTS IN NATIONAL POWER

The period since 1500 may be divided into three distinct eras in terms of concentrations of national power. The period as a whole manifests two primary trends: (1) the transference of power from European countries to non-European countries and (2) the diminution in the number of relatively equal, first-rate powers from a half dozen or more to only two.

The Era of European Supremacy, 1500–1800. The era generally viewed as "modern," beginning in about 1500, opened with a major shift in national power, from the Italian city-states and the Mediterranean to the more populous, territorially larger western European monarchies and the Atlantic. At first, Spain and Portugal were the chief Atlantic powers; however, they soon dissipated their energies and their wealth. During the early seventeenth century the Dutch, who had developed a considerable sense of national unity from their wars with the Spanish, became a major nation. Holland, however, was simply not populous enough to be able to resist the English, who had also acquired a sense of national unity in fighting the Spanish and who now undertook empire-building seriously. On the continent, France, with a large population and area, an excellent army, and outstanding diplomatic negotiators, became the most important country in the west in the seventeenth century. In central Europe, the Holy Roman Empire was almost destroyed as an effective political unit by the Thirty Years' War, and the chief states to emerge were Prussia and Austria. In eastern Europe, Poland, lacking national unity, vanished; and Sweden, strong for a time because of its diplomats and its armies, slowly weakened and lost its territories. Russia, on the other hand, which had been small in 1500, slowly gained a sense of national unity, an improved technology, and effective armies; and by 1800 it was geographically immense. Meanwhile the Ottoman Empire, with deteriorating armies and national unity, was gradually yielding before the advance of the Russians.

The Challenge to European Supremacy, 1800–1900. During the years from 1800 to 1900 the chief power in the world was Great Britain; its navy dominated world politics and its factories dominated the world economy. On the continent, France was the strongest country in 1800; by 1900, however, it had two new rivals, Germany and Italy. By 1900

Germany had defeated France in war, and was more populous and more productive economically. Germany was a threat to Great Britain as well, for German goods began invading British markets and the German Navy challenged British maritime supremacy. Russia and Austria-Hungary dominated eastern Europe, but Austro-Hungarian unity was being rapidly undermined by the growing nationalistic sentiments of the subject minorities. Meanwhile the influence of Russia in the Far East was threatened by Japan; the Japanese, who had undertaken no role in world politics until after 1850, by 1900 had adopted a modern technology, started building a large army and navy, and developed a sense of national unity that aimed, among other things, at controlling eastern Asia. One other major power in 1900 was the United States, which by this time could outproduce Great Britain and Germany combined. It, too, had a large navy and in 1898 had secured an overseas empire by defeating the Spanish in the Caribbean and the western Pacific. Thus by 1900 political power had clearly moved away from the European Atlantic-coast countries to other parts of Europe, to Asia, and to North America.

The Emergence of the Superpowers, 1900–1962. Between 1900 and 1962 the center of political power shifted still more away from Europe. The two world wars did not increase the power of European states such as Great Britain, France, Germany, and Italy; correspondingly, they strengthened the United States and the USSR. By 1962 these two countries so far outranked all others in their possession of the various elements underlying national power that they alone could be called "superpowers." Furthermore, the disintegration of the British, French, and Dutch colonial empires led to the establishment of many new countries; some of these, such as India, Pakistan, and Indonesia, were—at least in terms of population, area, and natural resources—the repositories of considerable political power. Also, China at last emerged from its quasi-colonial status and, having acquired a sense of national unity under the Communists, adopted a vigorous foreign policy. One other feature of this time was the growing population along both coasts of the Pacific, as the Soviet government colonized Siberia; as millions of Americans moved to California, Oregon, and Washington; and as the populations of China, Japan, India, and the neighboring countries tended to grow at a faster rate than those of European countries. Hence, by 1962, in spite of a great revival in Europe after World War II, political power was concentrated in large measure along the Pacific coasts and in Southeast Asia.

Possible Future Shifts and Developments. With respect to possible future shifts and developments in political power, the areas of the greatest importance are the superpowers, Western Europe, the Far East, and Latin America.

THE SUPERPOWERS. The power status of the superpowers relative to one another is likely to remain more or less constant for years to come. Their comparative equality might be overthrown by such possible events as a revolution in the USSR, a technological development by one superpower that would nullify the weapons of the other, or a great increase in the number of allies of the Soviet Union. It is true that the rate of increase in the manufacturing output of the USSR appears to be somewhat larger than that of the United States; however, the rate of increase of tsarist Russia was also larger than the rate of the contemporary United States. Russia and the Soviet Union simply started from a smaller manufacturing base. The rate of increase will decline in the Soviet Union as the Soviet industrial base widens. Meanwhile the manufacturing output of the United States is still increasing by more in an absolute sense. Furthermore, the Soviet rate of output in such other economic activities as agriculture and housing construction is increasing very slowly or even declining.

WESTERN EUROPE. Western Europe might be the scene of important future developments in national power. The chief countries of the Western European mainland—France, Italy, West Germany, and the Benelux countries—together have a population approximately as great as that of the USSR and an industrial output even greater. They are, however, not well equipped militarily, and their relatively small area makes them vulnerable to attack by land or air. They have established an economic union, but they are not united politically. They do share a common anti-Soviet policy, but that bond might break if the USSR should cast aside its present expansionist policy or perhaps disintegrate. All these countries, and even Great Britain as well, might some day form a single political unit. In 1961 the members of the economic union were taking steps toward this goal. In the same year the British government announced its desire to join this union.

THE FAR EAST. In the Far East, the new countries seem likely to increase in power relative to Europe and to even the superpowers. Yet, despite their efforts to industrialize their economies, these countries suffer such technological backwardness and lack of fundamental resources that it will take them a long time to challenge Japan or the states of Western Europe. Communist China has both the population and the area to rank with the superpowers. It also has a long tradition of political domination over its neighbors and today has considerable national unity. At present, however, it is the target of extreme hostility on the part of the United States and numerous other countries; furthermore, as it becomes increasingly a rival of the Soviet Union for influence in the Far East and over the economically backward countries of Africa and Latin America, its relations with the USSR will cool. Hence Communist China will have diminishing opportunities for securing the capital and technical assistance it needs for expanding its industrial system, whose present smallness is the main reason that the country is not ranked as a superpower.

LATIN AMERICA. In Latin America, too, especially in Mexico, Brazil, and Argentina, there are apt to be greater concentrations of power. The population of Latin America is increasing more rapidly than that of any other continent—and more rapidly than the local food supply. Although these countries do have important stocks of essential resources, they are technologically retarded and need the help of the United States to accelerate their industrial development. In 1961 the leaders of most Latin American states united to propose a ten-year industrialization project that would be financed by $20 billion from outside sources. One important natural handicap is the almost unbearable climate of a large part of Latin America. Another handicap is that the most nearly central of the important Latin American states, and by far the largest, is Brazil, which might seem a "natural" core for a Latin American union; yet the people of Brazil speak Portuguese, a linguistic difference that sets off Brazilians from all other Latin Americans. The two other strong Latin American countries are Mexico and Argentina, but both are peripheral. Prussia, however, was peripheral in Germany, and Piedmont was peripheral in Italy; yet each was the core of a new state.

Review Questions

1. On the basis of your present knowledge, make a table that ranks each of the following countries in terms of the elements underlying national power: the United States; the Soviet Union; the United Kingdom; France; West Germany; Italy; Communist China; Japan; Indonesia; India; Pakistan; Brazil; and Canada. How much confidence do you have in your rankings?

2. How has the relative importance of the elements underlying national power changed since 1500? Is it possible that in the future one or more of these elements may become insignificant in the determination of national power?

3. What specific elements of national power have had the principal roles in determining the relative status of the following countries since 1500: the United States; the Soviet Union (Russia before 1918); the United Kingdom; France; Spain; Germany; India; Communist China (China before 1949); and Japan?

13 THE UNITED STATES

The United States is one of the two superpowers in the world today. In population as in area it is one of the largest countries in the world, but its great strength results mainly from its industrial capacity. It possesses a limited government that has been held up as a model for the other nations of the non-Communist world. Its government has a foreign policy aimed at achieving peace through the United Nations, through negotiations, through a series of alliances, and through economic programs designed to raise living standards in most countries of the world.

POPULATION AND GEOGRAPHY

The United States has a population of more than 185,000,000, including people of diverse national and racial origins, increasingly concentrated in urban areas. Geographically, the United States is a huge country that can be divided into four distinct regions.

Number and Distribution of the People. In 1962 the total population of the United States numbered about 186,000,000. This figure makes the United States the fourth most populous country in the world, being surpassed in this respect only by China, India, and the USSR. This figure also reveals that the American population increased more in the 1950's than in any other decade. The average density is somewhat greater than 50 per square mile, which is low in comparison with such countries as Great Britain, Belgium, and Japan. It is concentrated in the northeastern States, around the Great Lakes, and on the Pacific Coast. It is also highly urban; more than one half of the people live in the 212 districts that the Census Bureau terms "metropolitan." Rural areas generally, and especially in the South and Midwest, are losing population as their residents move to the cities. Finally, although the number of elderly people has greatly increased, the present high birth rate has made the average age of Americans lower today than it was in 1950.

National and Racial Backgrounds of the People. The American people have a great variety of national and racial backgrounds. According to the 1950 census there were about 10,000,000 foreign-born persons in the United States; millions of other Americans have at least one parent or grandparent of foreign birth. Because of limits on immigration, the percentage of foreign-born in the entire population is steadily falling. At first the area that became the United States was colonized chiefly by people from the British Isles, so that it started out as a predominantly English-speaking country. Later, immigrants began arriving from such varied places as Germany, Scandinavia, southeastern Europe, the Far East, and Latin America. Racially, most Americans are Caucasian; about ten per cent of the population is Negro.

Other Characteristics of the People. The proportionate distribution of trades and professions among American workers has undergone steady change, in keeping with such factors as the urbanization of the population and the adoption of labor-saving equipment by manufacturers. Thus the absolute number of farmers has been dropping, and that of factory operatives has risen only slightly since 1950. Domestic servants have almost vanished, but the number of people employed in other "service" trades and professions has been increasing rapidly. With respect to religion, by 1962 over 110,000,000 Americans were members of some church body. The majority of them belonged to some Protestant sect, but the number of Catholics—23 per cent of all Americans in 1960—was increasing at a greater proportional rate. In every State the government provided tax-supported schools open to all children and required attendance at some sort of school; only a very small percentage of the population was illiterate. Such features as the nationwide distribution of goods and universal tax-supported school systems, together with the vast amount of internal migration in the country, made the American people quite uniform in many respects despite their varied national and racial backgrounds.

The Land of the United States and Its Subdivisions. The land of the United States is subdivided politically into fifty States, occupying an area of more than 3,600,000 square miles, an area surpassed only by those of the USSR, Canada, and Communist China with its dependencies. The United States may be divided into four regions. The Northeast is the most densely populated and highly urbanized region of the United States and contains much light industry, coal mining, and shipping. The Midwest includes, near the Great Lakes, probably the

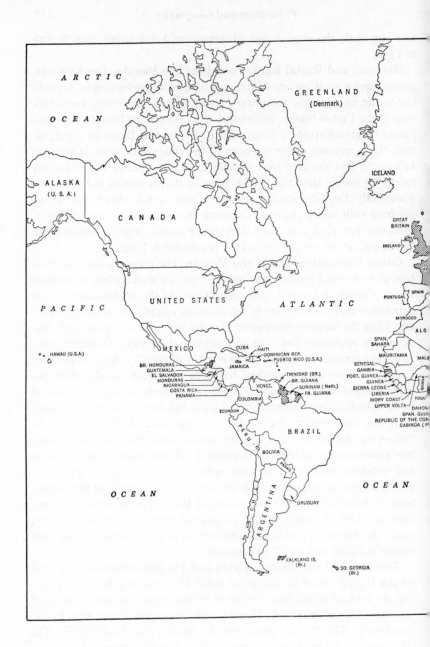

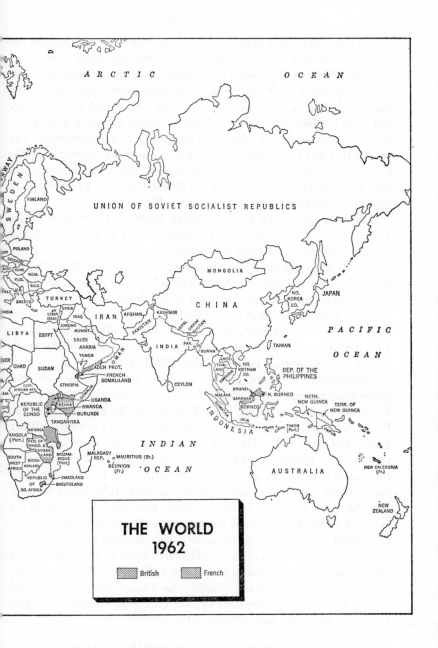

THE WORLD
1962

British   French

largest concentration of heavy industry in the world; it also provides the United States with significant mineral resources and large amounts of grain and livestock. The South is the most rural part of the country, but it has acquired a great deal of manufacturing since 1900. Finally, the West, including Alaska and Hawaii, is the largest and most sparsely settled of the four regions. Its economy is varied, including mining, agriculture, and, especially along the Pacific coast, manufacturing. The factors that distinguish the sections from one another, especially political party orientation, economic interests, and geographic location, also encourage the political leaders of the different sections to endorse and promote distinctive foreign policies for the United States.

Other Areas under United States Control. Other areas under United States control include the Commonwealth of Puerto Rico and various territorial possessions and military bases.

PUERTO RICO. Puerto Rico occupies a unique situation in which it is politically almost independent and yet enjoys the protection of the United States government. Members of the legislative and executive branches of the government are elected by the voters of Puerto Rico; by contrast, the courts of Puerto Rico are part of the judicial branch of the United States government, and the judges are appointed by the President. Puerto Ricans are citizens of the United States.

POSSESSIONS AND BASES. The United States also has a few territorial possessions, and numerous military bases around the world. In the New World the possessions are the Canal Zone and the Virgin Islands; in the Pacific they include Guam, American Samoa, the Midway Islands, Wake Island, and some other islands. Apart from the Canal Zone, whose first function is to transfer ships between two great oceans, the chief use of these areas is to furnish the United States with bases to protect its various political, commercial, and strategic interests. Inhabitants of these areas have few powers of self-government; their officials in general are members of the United States Department of the Interior. In addition, the United States has leased areas in many countries to serve as military bases for the needs of the "Cold War." Bases of this type exist in such places as Japan, South Korea, the Philippines, Okinawa, Spain, West Germany, and Iceland. Finally, the United States has a naval base in Cuba, at Guantánamo Bay; the Castro government that rules Cuba is hostile to the maintenance of this base.

RESOURCES AND ECONOMIC LIFE

With great stocks of natural resources, a fruitful agricultural system, diversified industry, and a comprehensive transportation network, the

United States possesses the most productive and complicated national economy in the world.

Resources and Industry. With the exception of a few minerals, the United States is self-sufficient in natural resources. Chief among the minerals that the United States must import are copper, lead, zinc, manganese, mercury, bauxite, chromite, nickel, tin, antimony, and graphite. Other minerals, such as oil, iron, coal, salt, magnesium, potash, molybdenum, uranium, and sulfur, have so far been found in sufficient quantities in the United States. The United States is likewise self-sufficient in agriculture and has enough lumber to satisfy its needs. In manufacturing and transportation the United States leads the world. It has half the productive factory capacity of the world and the world's most highly developed transportation system.

Foreign Trade. Foreign trade is only a minor fraction of all United States commerce, amounting to about five per cent of the total. Since World War II, however, foreign trade has become increasingly important as an instrument of foreign policy. The chief customer of the United States is Canada. Other major customers are Great Britain and Japan. Patterns of United States foreign trade have changed somewhat in recent years because, among other things, United States prices have risen considerably more than those elsewhere in the world. Typically the United States has exported such finished or semifinished goods as steel, machinery, automobiles, and refined petroleum products, as well as cotton, wheat, and meat. Meanwhile it has imported significant raw materials such as tin and chromite, as well as such foods as coffee and sugar. In the past few years, however, with the recovery of European and Japanese industry, the United States has been importing large amounts of steel and automobiles. For many years the United States has had a *favorable balance of trade*—that is, it has exported more than it has imported. By 1959, however, when foreign aid payments were united with payments for goods imported from overseas, the United States was sending out more money than it was receiving. An important consequence of this situation was a reduction of the United States gold supply, leading to a weakening of the dollar by comparison with other moneys.

GOVERNMENT

The structure of the United States government has certain distinctive characteristics related to the formation and execution of foreign policy.

Exclusive Formal Control of the National Government. The national government has exclusive formal control over the formation and execution of United States foreign policy. That is, the Constitution forbids the States to negotiate agreements with foreign countries or to maintain armed forces in time of war. Furthermore, the powers of the national government in the realm of foreign relations are inherent, and therefore unlimited, as distinct from the enumerated, limited powers it enjoys in domestic affairs. Any treaty negotiated by the executive branch of the government and concurred with by two-thirds of the Senate becomes part of the "law of the land" and is tantamount to a constitutional provision. As a consequence, by making a treaty with the government of some other country, officials of the United States government can actually amend the Constitution.

Partisan and Regional Influences. Notwithstanding the formal exclusive control over foreign policy vested in the national government, partisan and regional influences have considerable impact upon the foreign relations of the United States. So far as partisan influences are concerned, government leaders have held up bipartisanship as an ideal. They have not, however, consistently practiced it. For example, as far back as the French Revolution there was a patent split, with Federalists opposing the Jacobins and Republicans supporting them. Likewise, the people of the different regions vary on foreign policy. An outstanding illustration concerns the South. Three decades ago the South was largely an exporter of cotton and importer of manufactured goods; it backed free trade. Today the South has major industries; it is opposed to free trade. Such differing partisan and regional influences dilute the formal control that the national government has over foreign policy.

The Creation of Foreign Policy. The creation of foreign policy is a highly complicated procedure. Actually the President bears the chief responsibility in this area and is vested with full powers for the task. His chief advisor is expected to be the Secretary of State. Some Presidents, such as Franklin D. Roosevelt and Truman, have tended to be their own Secretaries of State. Eisenhower, by contrast, placed great reliance in Secretary of State John Foster Dulles. During the first year under Kennedy it was almost impossible to determine responsibility in foreign-policy decision-making. The Secretary himself must depend upon his subordinates in the State Department for counsel. There is a host of other agencies in the national government that contribute to foreign policy making. One of the most important is the National Security Council, which includes the President. Certain congressmen, especially members of the Senate Committee on Foreign Relations, counsel the President. Recently, Presidents have also been turning to high military officers for advice. Finally, private individuals and groups may bring pressure upon the President, or upon some influential government official. What policy is chosen is contingent upon many factors, such as the various phases of the situation being dealt with and the personalities of the President and the other individuals concerned.

The Execution of Foreign Policy. The execution of foreign policy is somewhat less involved than its creation. Here again the President has full power and bears entire formal responsibility. Again, the Secretary of State is his principal advisor. The immediate executors of foreign policy include primarily the members of the Foreign Service of the State Department. Foreign Service members range from the ambassadors and ministers heading embassies and legations abroad down to the various levels of clerks. Most of these personnel are recruited through a system of difficult tests. Even ambassadors, although they do not hold their posts on the basis of a classified system, are more and more being appointed from the ranks of career Foreign Service Officers. Outside the State Department are various other national agencies that execute foreign policy. For example, the Department of Commerce determines what goods manufactured in the United States may be shipped abroad.

MILITARY FORCES AND STRATEGIC SITUATION

The military forces of the United States, which are ultimately under civilian control, include the army, the navy, and the air force. To a certain degree they are "unified," yet each branch retains special and discrete interests. The military policy of the United States government calls for organizing and distributing these forces in terms of the national strategic situation.

Structure of the Armed Forces. The supreme chiefs of the United States armed forces are civilians. The commander in chief of the army, the navy, and the air force is the President. The principal civilian agency for the armed forces is the Department of Defense, whose head, the Secretary of Defense, is a presidential appointee and a member of the Cabinet. Subordinate to the Defense Department are the Departments of the Army, the Navy, and the Air Force. Each is headed by a Secretary, who is chosen by the President but who is not a member of the Cabinet. Each of these Departments has over 300,000 civilian employees, all charged with duties connected with maintaining the armed forces. The highest-ranking military officers are subordinate to these Secretaries. The armed forces of the United States today are regarded as "unified," that is, as a single military arm for the United States government. This structure was initiated in 1947, in an effort both to end the rivalry between the army and the navy and to give the air force equal status. By 1961, however, despite major advances toward true "unification," there was still a great deal of competition among the three branches, especially over shares of congressional appropriations. The military group heading the armed forces is the Joint Chiefs of Staff, comprising a chairman and the chief of staff of each of the three military services.

General Traits of the Armed Forces. The armed forces have undergone vast changes since 1945, not only because of their unification but also because of such technical factors as the atomic bomb, the nuclear-powered submarine, and the ballistic missile. The armed forces are organized today, at least in appearance, according to the fundamental principle that the United States will engage in either large-scale wars with unrestricted use of nuclear weapons, or in small-scale, "brushfire" wars. In 1961, however, President Kennedy instituted changes in the direction of enabling the land forces to undertake conventional warfare on a large scale. Under unification the air force has secured the lion's share of the funds. It possesses great numbers of long-range bombers stationed all over the world. Also, it is gradually developing intermediate range ballistic missiles (IRBM's) and intercontinental ballistic missiles (ICBM's). The army is now comparatively small, but heavily armed; it is equipped with, among other things, some missiles and some tactical atomic cannon. The navy has decommissioned all its battleships and is concentrating on nuclear-powered, missile-firing submarines and on aircraft carriers. In any future conflict the role of the navy would be not so much to engage in surface clashes as to provide floating bases for air attacks on the Soviet Union.

Strategic Situation. The strategic situation of the United States is based on a favorable geographic location, relative parity of armaments with the other competing superpower, and military alliances with many countries.

GEOGRAPHIC LOCATION. The strategic situation of the United States in terms of its geographic location is very favorable. It is separated from Europe by the Atlantic and from Asia by the Pacific; it is bounded on the north by friendly Canada and on the south by small, nonaggressive Mexico. But this geographic isolation by itself is not enough. It is sometimes said that although this isolation protected the United States from invasion in 1914 and 1939 it would not today, since transportation facilities are much better. The fact is that the United States was invaded from overseas in 1814, in the era of sailing ships. What is important is that the United States Navy did not control the neighboring seas in 1814, but it did in 1914 and 1939. Today the navy and the air force appear still capable of repelling any surface-borne attack on the

United States. At the same time, the consensus is that a bombing attack carried out by manned aircraft, by ICBM's, or by IRBM's fired from submarines, could inflict grave damage on the United States. Another new development is that the United States for the first time is confronted with the possibility of war on three fronts—the Atlantic, Pacific, and Arctic Oceans, for attacks by missiles or long-range aircraft can come over any of these.

COMPARATIVE ARMAMENT. In comparative armaments the United States and the Soviet Union are closely matched. The armies of the Soviet Union may be numerous and well enough equipped to be able to reach the Pyrenees in a few months against the opposition of armies of the United States and its European allies. On the other hand, the United States is much better provided with long-range bombing aircraft. The United States has a much larger surface naval fleet than the Soviet Union but far fewer submarines. However, the capabilities of American submarines appear superior. The United States had a monopoly on the atomic bomb only until 1949; in that year the USSR, thanks to its own scientists, German scientists and artisans captured during the war, and the work of its spies in the United States, was able to explode its own nuclear weapon. The United States probably does not surpass the Soviet Union in the capability for delivering an atomic or a hydrogen bomb by a missile; indeed, Soviet technicians have built missiles with far greater carrying capacity than those of the United States. The supply of nuclear weapons in the hands of both powers is large enough to threaten mutual damage of vast extent.

ALLIES. In its struggle with the Soviet Union since 1945, the United States has formed a number of military alliances with various countries around the world. It is, however, always difficult to foretell the usefulness of alliances. Their purposes are many, and not only military but cultural and economic. Like different resources and weapons, allies may never be called on to play a critical role in events, or some of them may be placed directly in the role of defending American (and their own) interests. The United States government has been investing a larger percentage of national income in armaments than have the governments of the other NATO countries, the chief United States military alliance. Moreover, certain of these allies are not completely reliable. In some countries there are influential voices in behalf of neutralism or communism. Finally, it is difficult to estimate the number of individual supporters the United States has behind the "Iron Curtain" who will function as saboteurs and insurrectionists against the Soviet Union in case of war.

FOREIGN POLICY

The foreign policy of the United States today has extended far beyond its traditional concerns in the New World and the Far East, and is now involved with problems in so many other countries and regions that it is "universalist."

Traditional Foreign Policy. The traditional foreign policy of the United States, as created and executed up to 1914, included three major points, all discussed in previous chapters. To repeat, they were:

1. Noninvolvement in European affairs.
2. Protection of Latin American national independence.
3. Freedom of trade in the Far East.

Disputes over Foreign Policy. Ever since 1914 there have been more or less continuous disputes as to just what the general pattern of United States foreign policy ought to be. Two groups, perhaps best termed "internationalists" and "independents," have had the main roles in these disputes. (It should be clear that, in the heat of debate, various self-flattering and uncomplimentary names have been commonly given to both groups.)

THE INTERNATIONALIST POSITION. According to the internationalists, traditional United States foreign policy is today unsuited to be the basis for the relations between the United States and other countries. They contend that World Wars I and II proved that an aggressive country in Europe is a menace to the United States, and they add that improved means of transportation would enable a foreign power to invade the United States if it managed to overrun Europe. They further hold that the well-being of peoples everywhere is the concern of the United States and that a world in which everyone has material plenty would be peaceful. As a consequence, they argue that the United States should make alliances with friendly countries to discourage any other country from resorting to aggression and that the United States government should invest large sums in programs to raise world living standards.

THE INDEPENDENT POSITION. The independents, on the other hand, maintain that the two world wars did not prove that the existence of an aggressive country in Europe necessarily menaces the United States. They also insist that the United States should negotiate temporary alliances where they would be of value, but not to the extent of weakening the United States itself. It is their position that the best defense of the United States lies in its own national strength, and here they emphasize air and sea power. Finally, they are skeptical of assertions that economic improvement abroad will necessarily increase the desire for peace.

A Summary of Present-Day Foreign Policy. A summary of present-day foreign policy shows that in the main the views of the internationalists have triumphed. Underlying current United States foreign policy are the following principles:

1. Hemispheric solidarity, including Canada, with joint strategic planning for the defense of the New World.

2. Control over the western Pacific, with a friendly Japan, an independent Formosa, an independent South Korea, and bases on various islands.

3. Amicable relations and a military alliance with states in Southeastern Asia.

4. Support for anti-Communist states of the Middle East.

5. Supremacy in the Mediterranean, with bases in the area and protection for Greece and Turkey.

6. A military alliance with the states of Western Europe.

7. Extension of economic aid to almost any country that, whether or not it is in the Soviet Bloc, in the eyes of American officials deserves it.

8. Disarmament of all countries, at least to the extent of international control over nuclear weapons.

9. The strengthening and greater use of the machinery of the United Nations.

10. Freer trade among the non-Communist countries.

Review Questions

1. What features of the population and geography of the United States add to the national power of the country, and what other features of these elements detract from it?

2. What areas besides the fifty States are under the jurisdiction of the United States government? What are the services that these areas perform for the United States? Are there still other areas of the world that might be termed "semi-colonies" or "wards" of the United States?

3. What is the nature of United States foreign trade? Is the role of this trade chiefly economic or chiefly political, or does the role vary according to the other party and the commodity involved?

4. What different factors enter into both the creation and the execution of United States foreign policy?

5. Analyze United States foreign policy today in terms of the three traditional points in United States foreign policy. According to this analysis, what may be the special problems of any individual or group seeking to influence the public about foreign policy, either in defense of or in opposition to the policy that is being conducted today?

14 THE SOVIET UNION

The Union of Soviet Socialist Republics (USSR) is the other super-power of the world. It too has a large population and occupies a huge area. It has a totalitarian government, which its leaders declare is essential for the achievement of certain economic and strategic goals. Its over-all industrial output is much less than that of the United States, even though its industry is growing rapidly; in its military potential it probably matches the United States. Its chief aim is world domination.

POPULATION AND GEOGRAPHY

The more than 210,000,000 people of the Soviet Union have greater national and racial heterogeneity than the people of the United States. The Soviet population, which is about one-half rural, is scattered over a generally monotonous landscape of more than 8,000,000 square miles.

Number and Distribution of the People. In 1960 the total population of the Soviet Union numbered about 210,000,000. The Soviet Union experienced enormous population losses in World War II, not only from military and civilian deaths but also from a huge deficit in births. As a result, whereas the Soviet population exceeded that of the United States by 46 per cent before the war, it now exceeds it by only 18 per cent. Moreover, the Soviet population of working and military age is increasing much less rapidly than that of the United States, and the Soviet Union has an immense relative shortage of men. Consequently, the Soviet Union and the United States today are countries with practically the same population. The average density of the Soviet population is about 25 per square mile, which is quite low. It is still concentrated in European Russia. There has been a considerable movement into the Asiatic provinces, but not so great as officials have tried to promote. Although the Soviet population is still proportionately more rural than that of the United States, it is becoming urbanized. The USSR contains over twenty cities with more than 500,000 people each, the largest being Moscow (metropolitan area, 7,000,000) and Leningrad (3,300,000). Urbanization of the Soviet Union is essential for the fulfillment of Soviet economic plans.

National and Racial Backgrounds of the People. The Soviet people have a great variety of national and racial backgrounds. In keeping with its asserted tolerance of national differences, the Soviet government has encouraged the cultural development of numerous minority groups so long as the development does not conflict with the political and economic purposes of the Soviet government. All together there are about 180 different nationalities, speaking almost fifty distinct languages. The largest national groups are the Great Russians, who include more than half the total; the Ukrainians or Little Russians; and the Kazakhs, in Asia. The predominant group is Slav, and Caucasian; but there are many Turks and other Asiatic peoples, a large part of whom are Mongolian.

Other Characteristics. As in the United States, the proportion of the Soviet labor force in agriculture has been falling, and that in industry rising. Wage and salary workers in the USSR totaled 13.5 per cent of the labor force in 1928, and 44.2 per cent in 1955. Yet the percentage of the labor force in the USSR employed in agriculture is still much greater than that in the United States. Furthermore, only a small percentage of Soviet workers are in mercantile or service pursuits. There are also much greater differences in wage levels in the Soviet Union than there are in the United States. Soviet officials have concentrated on expanding a tax-supported school system; in 1917 more than half the people of the USSR were illiterate, but today scarcely any of them are. Soviet schools emphasize instruction in the sciences, mathematics, foreign languages, and the concepts of Marxism-Leninism. Officially the Soviet Union is an atheistic country; its leaders profess atheism, and discourage religious practices. Nevertheless, the exercise of religion is to some extent tolerated, but Soviet leaders are forthrightly hostile to Judaism, branding it a nationalist movement inimical to communism, and they discriminate against Jews in such matters as admission to the universities and the professions. The most important religious body in the USSR is the Russian Orthodox Church. There are also many Moslems in the Soviet Union.

The Land of the Soviet Union and Its Subdivisions. The Soviet Union, occupying an area of about 8,600,000 square miles, is the largest country in the world. It is essentially a "natural" geographic unit con-

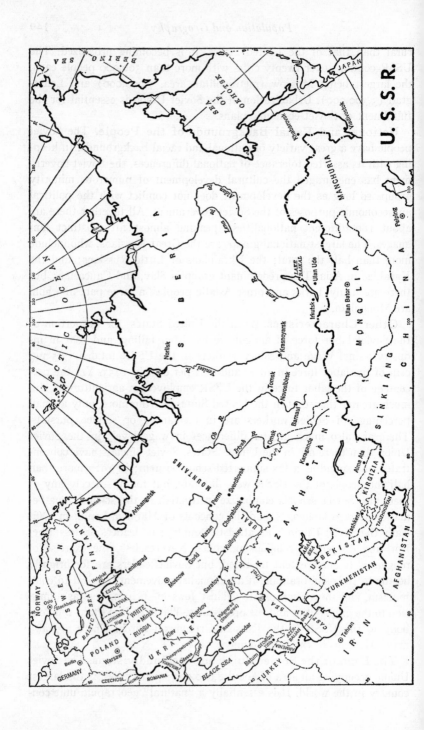

sisting of the plains north and northwest of a series of mountain ranges extending across Asia roughly from east to west. These plains are almost unbroken; the Ural Mountains form no real division between Europe and Asia. The Soviet Union may be divided into four zones, or belts, differing from each other in climate and vegetation. Northernmost lies the tundra, barren but useful for defense outposts. South of it is the forest zone, which contains Leningrad, Moscow, and the Asiatic cities of Tomsk, Irkutsk, and Vladivostok, the last being the eastern terminal of the Trans-Siberian Railroad. This zone includes a large part of the industry of the USSR, and it is also the seat of considerable agriculture. The best farm land in the Soviet Union, however, is located in the Ukraine, which is in the third zone, the steppes. In this zone too there are such industrial centers as Kharkov and Volgograd, along with such harbors as Rostov and Odessa. Southernmost is a belt consisting of deserts and mountains. The western end of this zone, the Caucasus, contains major oil deposits and such metropolises as Batum and Baku. This zone, furthermore, borders on some Middle Eastern countries, which the Soviet Union is trying to incorporate into its bloc.

RESOURCES AND ECONOMIC LIFE

The hallmark of the Soviet national economy is that it is almost entirely subject to government planning and control. The Soviet economy is quite productive, although not nearly so much as that of the United States; moreover, its absolute rate of increase is smaller, and it seems capable of little inventiveness save in the design and construction of military equipment.

The Government-Planned Economy. The government-planned economy of the USSR has had various goals, but all its goals have been politically motivated. One of the chief goals has been to arm the Soviet Union both to defend itself and to undertake aggression against other countries. Another goal has been the establishment of the USSR as an industrial power, in great part for purposes of propaganda. A last goal is to furnish Soviet citizens with enough necessities to keep them relatively contented and working efficiently. To achieve these goals, the Soviet Union has put into effect a series of plans. The authorities are able to draft and impose these plans because the government owns all of the principal aspects of production—raw materials, agriculture, industry, transportation, and power. Although, for the needs of propaganda, government plans have usually extended over periods of five or seven years, actual economic planning is done on an annual basis. The principal agency is the State Planning Committee, which, working through republic and regional bodies, indicates to each enterprise what it shall produce for the following year. Managers of the enterprises then draft outlines of what they will need to fulfill their quotas and transmit them upward to the State Planning Committee, which in turn allocates supplies, especially of raw and semifinished materials, as they are available. The results of this system are open to dispute. The Soviet economy does have sound achievements to its credit. It has laid the basis for major heavy industrial plants in the USSR and has accomplished a rate of manufacturing growth somewhat higher than that of the United States. It has done so, however, only at the cost of hardship and deprivation for most of its population.

Mineral and Other Resources. Since the USSR withholds exact statements about much of its mineral production, it is not possible to make accurate calculations about it. From all appearances, however, the USSR ranks with the United States as a country endowed with mineral deposits. Yet each country is deficient in some minerals that the other has a sufficiency or even a surplus of. The Soviet Union is especially rich in iron, coal, and oil. On the other hand, the USSR apparently lacks sufficient quantities of zinc, copper, lead, mercury, tungsten, antimony, tin, nickel, and iodine. However, all of these are available in Soviet-dominated countries and can come by land routes. The USSR has one major advantage over the United States in that it can provide its own manganese for its steel mills.

Agriculture. One of the chief problems of Soviet leaders has been agriculture. Among all phases of the Soviet economy it has had the lowest proportional increase in output since 1913—in spite of massive attempts by the Soviet government to stimulate it. Although there is still some very productive nongovernmental farming left, most agriculture is government-managed either in the form of a *kolkhoz,* a collective farm where the workers are paid by shares of the income of the farm, or a *sovkhoz,* a state farm where the workers are state employees. Collectivization of farms ran into much resistance from farmers, and the *sovkhoz,* in which much hope was once placed, has proved to be quite disappointing. Attempts to mechanize farms, to grow corn, and to increase the supply of meat have had no more than partial success. In short, the output of Soviet agriculture lags far behind that of the United States; at best, the Soviet citizen eats just adequately.

Manufacturing and Transportation. The Soviet Union has the second greatest manufacturing output of any country on earth, being surpassed only by the United States. This output has, however, been concentrated in heavy industry, and moreover, when measured against the huge Soviet population, is less per capita than that of several other countries. In light industry, especially that producing consumers' goods, the Soviet Union has lagged. Also, the quality of Soviet producers' goods is high, whereas that of consumers' goods is shoddy. Probably the most backward of all Soviet industries has been construction. Soviet leaders in 1961 were boasting that they would soon overtake the United States in the production not only of steel but also of consumers' goods; however, there seems little likelihood of such an accomplishment. For transportation the Soviet Union relies chiefly on railroads. Some of the waterways are important, but most of them run north-and-south. There are few automobiles and trucks, and the highway system is poor. To a growing degree passenger transportation in the USSR is being conducted by airplane.

Foreign Trade. The foreign trade of the USSR is fairly important to the Soviet Union. The majority of this trade is with the satellite countries; it is controlled by the government and is therefore conducted for both economic and political purposes. Soviet exports include such raw materials as iron ore, manganese, and petroleum; some finished goods, among them machinery; and foods. Imports comprise in large part the minerals needed for Soviet industry, such as bauxite from Hungary and zinc from Poland. This particular trade is apt to grow in volume as Soviet industry increases beyond the ability of Soviet mines to produce essential raw materials. The Soviet government also makes widespread use of foreign trade for political purposes, chiefly to expel the goods of the United States and its allies from the markets of countries whose governments have not definitely aligned themselves in the "Cold War" and to secure admittance of Soviet technicians, with subsequent Soviet influence, into these countries. The Soviet government has the great advantage of being able to disregard monetary profit and can therefore sell commodities cheaply. For example, it has offered oil to India at a very low price, and school-laboratory equipment similarly to various other countries. Buyers afterward may find that the goods they have purchased are poorly fabricated or that spare parts are unavailable. The Soviet government also buys goods that other countries have produced in surplus quantities, as, for instance, cotton from Egypt, tobacco from Greece, and various agricultural items from Latin America. However, the seller may have to accept payment in the form of Soviet goods. Furthermore, the Egyptians and the Greeks have found that the Soviet Union afterward was selling their cotton and tobacco at very low prices in the Egyptians' and the Greeks' traditional European markets.

GOVERNMENT

The government of the Soviet Union, which formally comprises a federal republic, is in fact a unitary totalitarian dictatorship under the Communist Party.

A Federal Structure. On paper, the government of the Soviet Union has a federal structure. That is, there is the national government centered at Moscow; then, there are the governments of the fifteen republics comprising the USSR. One of these republics, the Russian Soviet Federal Socialist Republic, contains more than half the area and half the population of the whole USSR. Again on paper, these republics have far more powers than do the States of the United States. For instance, they are authorized to secede. Even more notable, they may establish foreign offices and exchange representatives with the governments of other countries. This power underlies the three votes the USSR has in the United Nations—one each for the Soviet Union and the Ukrainian and White Russian (Byelorussian) Republics.

The National Government of the USSR. The national government of the USSR possesses legislative, executive, and judicial branches. The legislative branch consists of a bicameral assembly, the Supreme Soviet; its chambers have equal powers. One house, the Soviet of the Union, is elected according to population; the other, the Soviet of Nationalities, is elected according to territorial area. The Supreme Soviet actually has very little power; its main function is to approve formally the legislative proposals submitted by the executive chiefs. The executive branch is headed by the Council of Ministers, a cabinet elected by and supposedly responsible to the Supreme Soviet. The Chairman of the Council is the Premier of the USSR. Members of the Council are the heads of the great administrative departments. The judicial branch comprises a hierarchy of courts; judges of the lower courts are popularly elected, and those of the Supreme Court are chosen by the Supreme Soviet. The government of each republic is similar to that of the USSR.

The Communist Party. Despite this impressive official structure, the real government of the USSR is the Communist Party (once the Bolshevik Party). The Party now has about 8,000,000 members, organized into groups at every level of the government. Presumably the chief organ of the Party is the All-Union Congress, a body resembling a convention, with over 1,000 members. The real controlling agency of the Party is the Presidium of the Central Committee, a group that includes between 20 and 30 of the most important figures in the USSR. One other major executive body is the Secretariat, which has great control over Party personnel and organization. Its head, the Secretary of the Central Committee of the Party, is apt to be the most powerful or second most powerful member of the Party; both Stalin and Khrushchev held this post before rising to premier. In fact, Stalin, by virtue of this post, was dictator of the USSR even before becoming premier. The political omnipotence of the Party makes fictions of both the federal structure and the parliamentary apparatus.

The Creation of Foreign Policy. The creation of foreign policy in the USSR is a much simpler process than it is in the United States, but it is probably more complicated than it seems. The Presidium of the Communist Party creates and promulgates Soviet foreign policy. This body assumes an appearance of unanimity in this process, but it is likely that within the closed sessions of the Presidium there are some intense debates over the emphases of foreign policy. The main features of this process that make it simpler than policy making in the United States are the absence of private interest groups and minority political parties, and the unitary nature of the Soviet state that eliminates clashing regional concerns.

The Execution of Foreign Policy. The foreign policy of the USSR is executed by a variety of agents and agencies, some of which have no counterpart in any non-Communist country. All Soviet officials in these agencies must turn to Soviet authorities in Moscow for decisions about even trifling matters. First of all, the Soviet government includes a typical foreign office, the Ministry of Foreign Affairs. It also has the usual body of ambassadors, consuls, and their subordinates, to function as its official representatives abroad. The Soviet government also sends out and maintains a variety of formal missions, dealing with such matters as foreign trade, all of which execute Soviet foreign policy. Furthermore, Communists in the governments of the satellites carry out Soviet foreign aims. Indeed, the Soviet government may even use a Communist not in the satellite area for a major task; an outstanding example was Jacques Duclos, a leading French Communist, whose article, published in a French Communist magazine in 1945, gave the signal for unseating Earl Browder as head of the Communist Party in the United States. Indeed, all Communist Party members are explicitly directed to further the overseas aspirations of the USSR. Then, certain agencies in the Soviet government, such as the Soviet Army, maintain their own corps of overseas agents. Finally, the USSR may count on great numbers of persons outside its jurisdiction who, although not party members, sympathize with the USSR and will to some degree perform errands for it.

MILITARY FORCES AND STRATEGIC SITUATION

The Soviet Union has powerful military forces and occupies a generally advantageous strategic situation.

Supreme Control of the Armed Forces. The supreme control of Soviet armed forces apparently lies in the hands of Party chiefs. Army leaders today can be viewed as trustworthy Party members or at least as reliable supporters of the Party line. Stalin sometimes appointed "military commissars"—Party representatives—to high military rank, to assure loyalty to the Party among military personnel. Doubtless today there still are such agents in the armed forces, or would be in any unit whose loyalty was doubtful.

Structure and General Traits of the Armed Forces. The Soviet Army, Navy, and Air Force are governed by a single Ministry of Defense. The Soviet Army is the largest in the world, with perhaps 3,000,000 men organized into 175 or 200 divisions. Soviet government leaders explain both to their own people and to the rest of the world that such vast forces are essential for protecting the "Soviet homeland" from the "capitalist-imperialist" attack that they say may occur at any time. These forces are stationed along the Soviet frontiers, within the USSR as police forces, and as occupation troops in some of the satellites. They are well drilled, ably led, heavily armed, and extensively mechanized. The Soviet Air Force is probably the second-largest in the world. It has a considerable fleet of long-range bombers; it also has many smaller craft designed for tactical purposes in conjunction with the land forces. Like the United States, the USSR has been experimenting successfully with ICBM's and IRBM's. Nevertheless, a Soviet military display in July, 1961, emphasized fighter and bomber aircraft. The Soviet Navy has a comparatively small surface fleet; however, it contains about 500 submarines, some of which—Soviet authorities have announced—are nuclear-powered. Finally, the Soviet Union now has not only the atomic bomb but also the hydrogen bomb.

Strategic Situation. The Soviet Union occupies a strategic situation typified by an excellent geographical location, a favorable comparative status in armaments, and a weak alliance system.

GEOGRAPHIC LOCATION. The strategic situation of the USSR in terms of its geographic location is excellent, both for defense and for offense.

Halford Mackinder, in a book called *Democratic Ideals and Reality* (1919), wrote: "Who rules East Europe commands the Heartland: Who rules the Heartland commands the World-Island: Who rules the World-Island commands the world." Nevertheless, like the United States the Soviet Union today must face the possibility of a three-front war. For defensive purposes, the USSR confronts the invader with an immense spread of territory whose occupation alone would require millions of troops. Moreover, Soviet authorities have reduced the industrial concentration near the Soviet western frontier by constructing many new industrial plants in Asia. Hence invading forces must go deep within the USSR in order to strike a mortal blow at its munitions output. Furthermore, most of the Soviet Union experiences winters severe enough to disable any army not especially equipped for them. However, these traditional protections, just like the oceans around the United States, have to some extent been nullified by the long-range bombing plane and the missile. For offensive purposes, the USSR includes the "heartland," the geographic core of the Old World, whose control theoretically enables its master to gain world domination. The "heartland" is encircled on every side but the north by the "rimland," in which are located most of the countries of Europe and Asia. Soviet foreign policy calls for, among other things, absorption of all the "rimland." Situated as it is, the USSR can easily attack almost any part of the "rimland" and profit from the time it will require to oppose this attack because of the long lines of communication among "rimland" countries.

COMPARATIVE ARMAMENT. To summarize and put into context what was said in the preceding chapter, in terms of comparative armament the USSR enjoys an advantage in some fields and a disadvantage in others. The Soviet land forces available for immediate service in Eastern Europe are at least double the size of those the United States and its allies can put into action. Besides, the Soviet Union has several times as many troops in reserve. Its surface fleet is much smaller than that of the United States, but its submarine fleet is far greater. It has very large numbers of tactical aircraft to escort its land forces but comparatively smaller numbers of long-range bombing planes. Furthermore, these bombers would encounter a United States plane-to-plane missile, the "Sidewinder," that in tests and in use by the Nationalist Chinese Air Force has been extremely effective. The Soviet Union has developed missiles of various sizes, and its use of them for space probes shows that it has rocket engines more powerful than any of the United States. Finally, although the extent of the Soviet nuclear-weapon stockpile is unknown, it is assumed to be large enough so that the USSR and the

United States could mutually annihilate one another. Perhaps the greatest present weakness of the USSR in terms of comparative armaments lies in the fact that it is ringed about by United States air bases and has no similar ring of its own about the United States. An effective Soviet ICBM, however, would offset this disadvantage.

ALLIES. At least on paper, and probably in fact, the Soviet position relative to allies is less advantageous than that of the United States. The principal military alliance system of the USSR was formalized by the Warsaw Pact of 1955, between the USSR and its European satellites. In Asia its chief ally is Communist China. However, all these countries except Czechoslovakia are so backward industrially that the USSR must provide them with the bulk of their munitions. Furthermore, events in Poland, East Germany, and Hungary have indicated that the Eastern European countries are not reliable allies. In fact, in 1961 the Albanian government withdrew itself entirely from the Soviet camp. Moreover, the Communist Chinese with their aspirations of becoming a world power have adopted a foreign policy in some ways independent of that of the USSR and by some aggressive move opposed by the Soviet leaders might draw the USSR into a war not wanted by the Soviet Presidium. Perhaps the chief asset of the Soviet Union in the rest of the world is its ability to deny allies to the United States. For instance, working through local Communist Parties, Communist fronts, and Communist sympathizers, the USSR strives to keep such countries as India and Indonesia neutral. It has tried to discredit the United States in Africa, in Latin America, and even in such countries as France and Great Britain. In case of war, many Communist groups can be expected to carry out sabotage operations in the United States and elsewhere.

FOREIGN POLICY

The foreign policy of the Soviet Union is forthrightly "universalist." It stems to a considerable degree from that of tsarist Russia, and expands it greatly.

Traditional Russian Foreign Policy. Traditional Russian foreign policy contained at least five outstanding trends.

THE DRIVE TO THE EAST. Since the fourteenth century the Russian people have pushed constantly toward the east, going through or around the Urals and across Siberia to the Pacific. In the nineteenth century this drive was altered into an offensive against the weak Chinese Empire, as the Russians encroached on the Chinese borders and staked out a sphere of interest.

THE QUEST FOR WARM-WATER PORTS. Originally a landlocked people in eastern Europe, the Russians have waged an unending quest for warm-water ports to the west, south, and east. Their chief goal, the Dardanelles, has so far been denied them. The Russians did secure the coast of the Baltic, where they built St. Petersburg—today Leningrad. To the south and farther east, they have aimed for the Persian Gulf. In the Far East the port they built at Vladivostok is not ice-free all year; hence they have sought Port Arthur and Dairen to the south, in Manchuria, where in about 1900 they secured trading privileges. They regained these privileges in 1945, by the Yalta Agreement.

THE SEARCH FOR AN ALLY IN WESTERN EUROPE. The Russians have generally sought to have at least one ally in western Europe, usually either France or Germany. This search arose in part from the Russian desire to maintain a balance of power in their own defense. It probably also had roots in the backwardness of Russian technology and in the Russians' fear that they might be without a sure source of armaments. Furthermore, a western European ally could furnish sorely needed capital for investment in Russian business enterprise—capital that the Russians themselves did not have.

THE PROTECTION OF SMALLER SLAV NATIONS. As Russia became a large country and replaced Poland as the most powerful Slav state, the Russians undertook the burden of protecting all the smaller Slav nations. Some Russians even proposed a great union of all Slav peoples, under the name of *Pan-Slavism*. Slav nations that especially benefited from Russian protection were the Bulgarians and the Serbs. This undertaking had the goal of barring further Austro-Hungarian expansion into the Balkans.

THE "MESSIANIC URGE." The Russian people, or at least their leaders, have long had a sort of "Messianic urge," whereby they proclaimed themselves, or the Slav peoples in general, superior to other nations and proposed to correct the shortcomings of other peoples. This was the direction of the "Slavophile" movement in the late nineteenth century.

Soviet Foreign Policy Today. Soviet foreign policy has had the one consistent aim of securing world domination for the USSR. In pursuance of this aim, Soviet authorities have adopted a policy toward every country and every international political issue.

SINGLE CONSISTENT AIM. Since 1917, Soviet foreign policy has aimed at the establishment of Soviet supremacy throughout the world. It is true that Soviet policy since 1917 has had several apparent shifts. Nevertheless, these shifts have been only tactical devices intended as the best means for achieving this single aim. These shifts have reflected what Soviet leaders thought were important changes either in the USSR or in the world outside the USSR.

PRESENT-DAY TACTICAL INSTRUMENTS OF SOVIET POLICY. The present-day tactical instruments of Soviet policy include the following:

1. Dominating the Eastern European satellites and controlling their foreign policy and foreign trade.

2. Maintaining an alliance with Communist China. This includes both restraining the more ambitious and aggressive moves of the Chinese and profiting wherever possible from Chinese conquests.

3. Weakening the alliance between Western European countries and the United States, especially so as to create a unified, Soviet-oriented Germany or at least to prevent the establishment of a unified anti-Soviet Germany.

4. Extending Soviet influence in the Middle East, particularly by such means as furnishing weapons for these countries and denouncing imperialism and colonialism.

5. Wooing former colonial peoples all over the world, and especially in Africa, by denouncing imperialism, with the particular goal of weakening the Western European countries that formerly possessed these colonies.

6. Promoting hostility to the United States in Latin America and weakening Latin American anti-Soviet groups.

7. Bringing pressure on Japan, especially by economic methods, to win the Japanese away from their alliance with the United States.

8. Sending "cultural missions" to the United States and maintaining espionage rings within the United States.

9. Denouncing the capitalist system, and all other non-Communist systems, in hopes that neutralist and economically backward countries will seek Soviet guidance.

10. Fomenting political, economic, and social disorder throughout the world in the hope that peoples will turn to communism.

11. Depicting the Soviet Union as peaceful and the United States as warlike in an attempt to anger people against the United States.

12. Using the machinery of the United Nations, notably the veto power in the Security Council, to bar efforts by other countries to bring about peace and world disarmament.

Review Questions

1. What features of the population and geography of the Soviet Union add to the national power of the country, and what other features of these elements detract from it?

2. What connections do the Soviet government and national economy have with Soviet foreign policy? Are there any similar connections in the United States?

3. What is the nature of Soviet foreign trade? Is the role of this trade chiefly economic or chiefly political, or does the role vary according to the other party and the commodity involved?

4. Compare the federalism of the USSR with that of the United States.

5. How do the creation and execution of foreign policy in the USSR differ from these proceedings in the United States?

6. Compare the strategic situation of the Soviet Union with that of the United States.

7. What specific points in present-day Soviet foreign policy go beyond traditional Russian foreign policy? To what extent have Soviet leaders accomplished the goals of traditional Russian foreign policy?

Review Questions

15 THE BRITISH COMMON-WEALTH OF NATIONS

The British Commonwealth of Nations—sometimes called simply the Commonwealth of Nations—is the group of countries making up what was once known as the British Empire. Its nucleus is the United Kingdom (UK) of England, Wales, Scotland, and Northern Ireland. It also includes a group of independent states that were formerly British colonies; their independence is perhaps best shown by their powers to determine their own foreign policy and to exchange representatives with other countries. Today they are rather infrequently called "dominions." Finally, the Commonwealth includes a number of colonies, protectorates, and trust territories. Although these countries are scattered about the globe, the Commonwealth may still be viewed in certain respects as a major power bloc. Its elements are united by such factors as a common attachment to the British royal family, widespread use of the English language, general belief in certain principles of government, and economic ties and interests. (See map, pp. 138–139.)

THE UNITED KINGDOM

The United Kingdom is the financial, industrial, commercial, and diplomatic heart of the Commonwealth, but it continues to lose importance by comparison with other Commonwealth members.

Population and Geography. According to a 1961 census, the population of the United Kingdom then was about 53,000,000, almost four-fifths of which was in England. This figure ranks the United Kingdom as less than one-third as populous as the United States, slightly less populous than West Germany, and somewhat more populous than France or Italy. Very densely populated, the United Kingdom has over 500 people per square mile. The population is concentrated around London, in central England, and in the Scottish Lowlands. It is highly urban, and will be increasingly so. The capital city, London, with more than eight million people, is larger than any other city in the world except Tokyo (and perhaps Shanghai and Calcutta); Birmingham and Glasgow each somewhat exceed one million, and numerous other cities contain more than 100,000 people. The British people are racially, nationally, and linguistically rather homogeneous. Probably one person in four belongs to a religious body, a much lower ratio than in the United States; most numerous are the Catholics, followed by the Church of England (Anglican) and the Church of Scotland (Presbyterian). All religions are officially tolerated. School attendance is compulsory in either a tax-supported school or some private establishment. The United Kingdom, consisting of England, Scotland, Wales, and Northern Ireland, has an area of about 94,000 square miles. The climate is mild, but much of the land is not fertile enough to be cultivated.

Economic Life. The British national economy, which after World War II underwent a large degree of nationalization, is devoted mainly to manufacturing and commerce.

RESOURCES AND INDUSTRY. Unlike the Soviet Union and the United States, the United Kingdom has few natural resources. It has large supplies of coal and iron ore, but even these materials must be imported to meet the needs of British steel mills. There is some very intensive farming in the United Kingdom, but most of the food consumed there must be imported. Manufacturing is the backbone of the British economy; among the goods fabricated in the United Kingdom are automobiles, machinery, cutlery, and other steel products, as well as textiles. The steel output is more than 20,000,000 tons annually, a total exceeded only by the mills of the United States, the USSR, and West Germany. The United Kingdom is also capable of manufacturing large quantities of munitions. It has a comprehensive transportation system, consisting of highways as well as railroads. The British economy has run into grave difficulties almost since World War I. The problems became so acute after World War II that the government introduced a number of "austerity" programs. The subsequent relaxation of some government controls enabled the people to enjoy a higher standard of living, but the whole economy is still very heavily taxed. The United Kingdom is far from overcoming its economic difficulties, and the government retains a controlling hand over most of the British economy.

FOREIGN TRADE. Foreign trade is necessary for the survival of the United Kingdom and has a major role in its economy. It is important enough that the British will disregard political considerations in their efforts to buy or sell a given commodity; British leaders have urged expanding trade with the USSR and Eastern Europe. Fundamentally, the United Kingdom imports raw materials and semifinished goods, and exports finished products. Almost half of British foreign trade today is with other members of the Commonwealth. An important feature of this foreign trade is that most of it is carried in British ships. The United Kingdom has an unfavorable balance of trade. It makes up the difference for its balance of payments from such sources as shipping fees, returns from its overseas investments, and the money spent in the United Kingdom by tourists.

Government and Foreign Policy. The government of the United Kingdom is a limited monarchy operating under a two-party system. Foreign policy is the responsibility mainly of the leaders of the majority party in Parliament.

STRUCTURE OF THE GOVERNMENT. The core of the government of the United Kingdom is a bicameral legislature, Parliament. The upper house, the House of Lords, whose members obtain their seats by inheritance or royal appointment, has practically no power. The lower house, the House of Commons, which is elected by the voters, exercises almost all the legislative powers in the government. Furthermore, the leaders of the majority party in Commons form the Cabinet, which is the chief executive agency. The Lord Chancellor, whose position is roughly analogous to that of the Chief Justice of the United States, is a member of the Cabinet. Thus the United Kingdom does not have the separation of powers characteristic of the United States government. The chief functions of the monarch are traditional and ceremonial. The United Kingdom is a unitary state. As for political parties, since 1945 party leaders have engaged in what were and are probably their most important debates in discussing foreign policy in the United Kingdom, particularly relations with the United States and the USSR. Chiefs of the Conservative Party have been consistently for a strong anti-Soviet policy. Labor Party leaders, on the other hand, have been divided; some of them have urged such policies as unilateral disarmament.

CREATION AND EXECUTION OF FOREIGN POLICY. Since the United Kingdom is a relatively small country with a unitary government, it does not experience the various sectional interests and pressures on the creation of foreign policy that the United States does. Consequently it is fair to say that the chief contests over foreign policy creation are between the two political parties. The chief government agency concerned with foreign policy is the Foreign Office, whose head is a leading member of the Cabinet. Sometimes the prime minister himself is the effective creator of foreign policy. In theory at least, the majority party is in full agreement as to what foreign policy should be and takes responsibility for it. Execution of British foreign policy is carried out by a typical diplomatic staff.

Strategic Situation. The relative weakness of the British military forces, the changing world situation, and advances in technology have reduced Britain to a position below the superpowers. It is, therefore, more dependent on its allies than ever before.

Geographic Location. The insularity of the United Kingdom has in the past been an important protection for the country. It has, in conjunction with British supremacy over the seas, kept the United Kingdom from invasion for many centuries. Its location has also made the United Kingdom a major base for operations against the continent. Today, however, new instruments of war have made the United Kingdom much more vulnerable than at any time in the past. Even during World War II, the country was severely damaged by raids of bombing planes and by rocket-propelled bombs. In the event of a war now, the country could be destroyed by missiles from the continent.

Allies. The British are favorably situated in terms of allies. Their principal ally is, of course, the United States. Furthermore, the British can expect support from most of the Commonwealth governments; however, they can not be sure of aid from India. Furthermore, the United Kingdom belongs to various alliance systems such as NATO, CENTO, and SEATO.

Foreign Policy. The principal features of British foreign policy today are:

1. Maintaining and protecting a network of oceanic trade routes that link the various elements of the Commonwealth with one another and also tie the United Kingdom to non-Commonwealth countries such as the United States.

2. Defending Western Europe from further expansion by the USSR.

3. Keeping friendly relations with the Moslem countries in the Middle East, both to bar the USSR from the Suez Canal and the Indian Ocean, and to assure the United Kingdom a supply of crude oil.

4. Preserving good relations with the United States, so as to enjoy its military, political, and economic co-operation.

5. Improving economic conditions in underdeveloped Commonwealth members through such projects as the Colombo Plan, which involves the United Kingdom, some Commonwealth and non-Commonwealth countries of Southeast Asia, the United States, Canada, and Japan.

6. Extending national independence to certain among the colonies,

especially in Asia, with an apparent narrowing of traditional imperial interests to little more than the continent of Africa.

7. Preparing a number of the African colonies for national independence.

8. Strengthening the United Nations.

SELF–GOVERNING COMMONWEALTH NATIONS

This section discusses the self-governing Commonwealth nations of Canada, Australia, and New Zealand, the three Commonwealth members most likely to assist the United Kingdom in time of crisis.

Canada. Among the self-governing Commonwealth nations with a fundamentally British culture, Canada is by far the most powerful and the most capable of an independent foreign policy.

POPULATION AND GEOGRAPHY. The population of Canada in 1961 was about 18,000,000. It is increasing fairly rapidly, as a result both of natural increase and of immigration from other countries, especially the United Kingdom. At the same time, Canada is losing emigrants to the United States. Since the northern part of Canada is mostly uninhabitable, the population is concentrated along the southern frontier of the country, close to the United States. It is becoming more urban, especially near the St. Lawrence River and on the shore of Lake Ontario. Canada is officially a bilingual country, with English and French equally recognized. The English-speaking population—chiefly of Scots-Irish extraction—has long been predominant, for Canada has been part of the British Empire since 1763. However, the French-speaking group, resident mainly in the province of Quebec, is increasing more rapidly than the English-speaking, and at the present rate will some day be the more numerous. Canada is a very large country; its area of about 3,850,000 square miles ranks it second only to the USSR. The topography has great variety; it includes the high Rocky Mountains of the Far West, broad plains in the Middle West, the rolling Laurentian Uplands in the Great Lakes area, the rugged East Coast, and the Northern sub-Arctic and Arctic areas.

RESOURCES AND ECONOMIC LIFE. Canada is very rich in resources, in some respects more so than the United States; and constant exploration is bringing more resources to light all the time. The most important recent discovery is that of petroleum, which now is monetarily the most valuable of all Canadian mineral resources. Canadian iron ore has an important place in United States steel production. Other minerals in significant amounts include gold, nickel, uranium, platinum, silver, and zinc. Nonmineral resources consist of fish, fur-bearing animals, and forests. Canada is a great agricultural country, with such major crops as wheat, oats, sugar beets, fruits, and tobacco. Despite its comparatively small population, it is a leading industrial country, producing a wide variety of goods. Much of the industry is owned by investors in the United States, a situation that arouses ill will in some circles. Canada has an extensive railroad system, more than half of which is government-owned. It depends also on the St. Lawrence River for transportation. It has a large foreign trade, about fifty per cent of which is with the United States; each country is the other's best customer.

GOVERNMENT. Like the United States, Canada has a federal type of government. The national government has a parliamentary structure resembling that of the United Kingdom, with a governor general appointed by the British crown as its representative. Foreign policy is the responsibility of the national government; it is conducted through the Department of External Affairs, whose head may also be the prime minister. The French-speaking population has a considerable, if mainly negative, impact upon the creating and executing of foreign policy. Fundamentally, this population holds that wars in Europe are not a proper concern for Canadians. Because of the opposition of the French-Canadians, there is no military conscription.

STRATEGIC SITUATION. Geographically, Canada occupies a very important strategic situation in that it lies between the United States and the USSR. An air-borne attack by one of the superpowers upon the other, unless launched from some other country or the ocean, would pass over Canada. Since Canadian relations with the United States are extremely friendly, the Canadians have co-operated with the United States in defense projects against the USSR. Perhaps most important, the two countries have established a network of radar stations for the detection of hostile aircraft; best known of these stations are those in a system far to the north called the Distant Early Warning (DEW) line. Thus, although Canada is a former British colony and part of the Commonwealth, its leaders look to the United States rather than to the United Kingdom for military support. In addition Canada has well armed military forces, many of which are assigned to NATO duty in Europe.

Australia. Australia geographically is almost as large as Canada, but its considerably smaller population and its nearness to potential enemies among the densely populated nations of Southeast Asia make Australia considerably weaker and less important in the world power structure.

POPULATION AND GEOGRAPHY. The population of Australia in 1961 totaled about 10,000,000. It is increasing rapidly; the birth rate is considerable, and the government encourages immigration from Europe. Apart from the aborigines, the population is almost entirely Caucasian and of British stock. The majority of the people live on or near the eastern coast, which receives from adequate to heavy rainfall. The interior is mostly desert and is therefore very thinly settled.

RESOURCES AND ECONOMIC LIFE. Australia is not so well endowed with resources as Canada, but it is nevertheless a rich country. Many of its potentialities are unknown or as yet little exploited. One of its chief resources is its land, much of which can be either cultivated or used for grazing. Among minerals, it possesses coal, iron, gold, silver, and copper. It is a major agricultural country, being the largest producer of wool in the world and having also considerable outputs of wheat and cattle. The hot and rainy northeastern corner yields sugar cane and tropical fruits. Australian industries include iron and steel, various types of machinery, paints, drugs, and chemicals. Yet the greatest industrial activity is the processing of farm goods. Much of this industry is owned by investors in the United States. Australia has a considerable railroad system, used mainly for bringing goods to coastal cities. Australia has a substantial foreign trade, especially with the United Kingdom, the United States, and Canada; it exports mainly food and raw wool, and imports mainly fabricated goods.

GOVERNMENT. The government of Australia, officially termed a Commonwealth, is federal, consisting of six states in Australia proper and of the island of Tasmania. The national government has a parliamentary structure, with a governor general representing the British crown. The national government administers foreign policy through a typical ministry of external affairs. Local interests do not appear to have much effect upon foreign-policy creation, especially since the population is unusually homogeneous.

OTHER AREAS CONTROLLED BY AUSTRALIA. The government of Australia controls a number of separate areas. Some of these—for instance, New Guinea and Nauru—are colonies that the German government surrendered to the League of Nations in 1919 and that are now governed under the trusteeship system administered by the United Nations. Over others the Australian government of itself assumed authority; these include the Cocos Islands and Christmas Island. Some of these islands have valuable mineral resources, and others produce tropical crops; still others are important chiefly for military bases. The population of most is quite small, consisting almost entirely of very primitive native tribes. These areas are generally viewed as unready for self-government.

STRATEGIC SITUATION. The strategic situation of Australia is such that the government is deeply concerned with affairs on the mainland of Asia and in Japan. The sparse population of Australia makes the country attractive to the peoples of China, Japan, and Southeast Asia, all of which are heavily populated. The Japanese came close to overrunning Australia in World War II, and it appears that the Communist Chinese today would do so if given the opportunity. The Australian government has supported the United Nations and may in general be expected to second the foreign policy of the United Kingdom. Australia also has large and well trained military forces. Like the Canadians, the Australians are apt to count more on the United States than on the United Kingdom for protection from attack.

New Zealand. The population of New Zealand is about 2,400,000 (1960). There are around 150,000 natives, the Maoris; the remainder of the population is almost entirely Caucasian. It is growing, although not very speedily, from both natural increase and immigration. The country comprises chiefly two islands east by southeast of Australia. It also includes a number of small islands, among them the trust territory of the former German colony of Samoa. The New Zealand economy is primarily agricultural; it produces wool, meat, and dairy products for export. The country also has small quantities of certain minerals, such as gold, coal, and petroleum. New Zealand has an elected unitary government and, with military conscription, has relatively strong armed forces. The strategic situation of New Zealand is much like that of Australia. The government generally supports the United Kingdom, favors the United Nations as machinery for reaching international agreements, and views the United States as a major element in its defense.

OTHER COMMONWEALTH AREAS

Other areas in the Commonwealth have a variety of relations with the United Kingdom. First, there are several fully self-governing states, such as India, Pakistan, Nigeria, and Ghana. They are not described here because they do not have a European culture and because they conduct relatively independent foreign policies. Then, there are the numerous areas that do not yet have full self-government; they are known by such titles as colonies, protectorates, and trusteeships. Some already have some powers of self-government; for instance, the voters of British Guiana elect officials who control their internal affairs, but

British officials still administer foreign policy and defense. The Federation of Rhodesia and Nyasaland has about the same status. British dependencies, located all over the world, perform various roles for the Commonwealth. Some are chiefly naval bases for the protection of sea lanes. Others are commercial outposts. Still others furnish the United Kingdom and other countries with food and industrial raw materials. For instance, much of the bauxite used in the United States comes from British Guiana. In some areas the United Kingdom has undergone great expenditures in manpower and money to maintain civil order; for example, in the early 1950's it put down a terroristic native group, the Mau Mau, in Kenya. Meanwhile British officials have striven to implant in the natives certain traditional British political concepts, notably that of the rule of law. Retention of many of these areas appears essential to assure the power of the United Kingdom.

Review Questions

1. Compare the role and importance of foreign trade for the United Kingdom with its role and importance for the United States and the Soviet Union.

2. Compare the creation and execution of foreign policy in the United Kingdom with the creation and execution of foreign policy in the United States and the Soviet Union.

3. Canada and Australia, although they are both large and sparsely populated countries, have somewhat different roles in world politics. Discuss the various reasons why.

4. Does the whole Commonwealth, as it is presently constituted, appear to add much to the national power of the United Kingdom? Has the evolution of the Commonwealth since 1945 added to this national power, detracted from it, or had no influence on it? Is the Commonwealth likely to evolve in the future in such a way as to make important changes in the national power of the United Kingdom?

16 *WESTERN EUROPE*

Western Europe, for the purposes of this text, includes all of Europe west of Finland, the Communist-Bloc countries, and Yugoslavia, except for the United Kingdom. Western Europe has great political, economic, social, and cultural diversity; yet there are common threads that link these nations. Compared with the United States, the government in every one of these countries has introduced a high degree of economic control, with variations from one country to another. Yet during the 1950's a number of political leaders have become disenchanted with certain controls and have discarded them. This is especially true of monetary inflation as a device for creating economic prosperity. This chapter describes the outstanding traits of the countries in this area.

FRANCE

France today is a country that retains only a small part of its once great power in Europe and its former vast empire overseas. However, its present leaders are attempting to revive French influence in the councils of Europe. Meanwhile the French government has loose ties with a minor fraction of its one-time colonial empire through an organization called the Remodeled French Community.

Population and Geography. The population of France in 1961 was about 46,000,000. It is very important that between 1870 and 1945 the population of France was almost stationary, whereas that of its principal rivals, Germany and Italy, was growing rapidly. The French population is nationally and racially rather heterogeneous, a reflection of the fact that France has been the crossroad of tremendous cultural migrations from almost every part of Europe and has become the home of immigrants from overseas territories. The French population is far less urbanized than that of England. Paris is the only French city with over

Murmansk

Arkhangelsk

U R A L

M O U N T A I N S

Sverdlovsk

FINLAND

Perm

Chelyabinsk

Helsinki

Izhevsk

Ufa

Leningrad

Magnitogorsk

Reval

Narwa

Volga R.

Kazan

Riga

Duna R.

Vitebsk

Kalinin

Ivanovo

Gorki

Moscow

Kuibyshev

Minsk

U. S.   S.   R.

Bryansk

Volga R.

Saratov

Warsaw

Ural R.

Kiev

Kharkov

Don R.

Volgograd
(Stalingrad)

Dnepr R.

Donez R.

Volga R.

Astrakhan

CASPIAN

Dnepropetrovsk

Rostov

Odessa

BLACK   SEA

Baku

ROMANIA

Bucharest

BULGARIA

Sofia

TURKEY

Istanbul

Ankara

Salonica

T U R K E Y

REECE

Athens

CRETE

CYPRUS

EUROPE

a million inhabitants, and only two other cities, Marseilles and Lyons, have over 300,000. Hence France is a country of medium-sized cities and small towns. Officially, most people belong to the Catholic Church; but there are many who are indifferent or positively hostile to organized religion. The area of France is about 213,000 square miles. Like the people, the geography of France presents much variety—mountain ranges, coastlines, rivers, and fertile plains. The climate, too, has considerable variety but is nowhere severe, and the rainfall except in the southeast is plentiful.

Resources and Industry. France contains large supplies of some mineral resources, such as iron ore, gas, petroleum, bauxite, antimony, fluorspar, potash, pyrite, and iodine. Its coal deposits, although considerable, are not sufficient for its steel industry. France produces some copper, lead, manganese, phosphates, and asbestos, but it must import all its tin, nickel, mercury, chromite, and tungsten. Another resource of France is its fertile soil. Agriculture comprises a major part of the French economy. A very important aspect of French agriculture is that farms generally are small or medium-sized and are owned by those who till them. France produces large amounts of wheat, sufficient for the needs of its people; such orchard products as apples; and a vast quantity of grapes, much of which is turned into wine. Then, there are root crops, especially sugar beets. Finally, there is much livestock, supplying both meat and dairy products. Industry in France is considerable, although not so extensive as in the United Kingdom and West Germany. To a much larger degree than in the United States, the United Kingdom, or Germany, it is organized in small units dependent on hand labor. There is much light industry, notably textiles, perfumes, and various types of small machinery. However, in the northeast there are numerous steel mills, with an annual output of about 15,000,000 tons. Other important heavy industries include automobiles and automobile accessories, shipbuilding, chemicals, and aluminum. France also has an important oil refining industry. Altogether, French industry is able to produce many war materials, but it depends upon German mines for much of its coal. France has an excellent transportation system—railroads, highways, waterways, and airlines.

Foreign Trade. Foreign trade is important to France, mainly to supply the country with certain raw materials. The French need to import only a few foods, such as coffee, tea, and citrus fruits. Among raw materials, however, they must import coal, crude oil, and other minerals noted above. French exports include iron ore, wines, perfumes, textiles, and automobiles. France has a good-sized merchant fleet, larger than the one it had before World War II yet surpassed by that of numerous other countries. One other major source of income for France that may be classed as foreign trade is the host of tourists from all over the world who visit the country every year; they help reduce the unfavorable balance of trade in commodities.

Government. The government of France today comprises the Fifth Republic, which was established in 1958.

ORIGINS OF THE FIFTH REPUBLIC. The Fifth Republic was the response to the demand that France have a stable and responsible government. It succeeded the Fourth Republic, established after World War II, which had a strong legislature and weak executive, and under which France suffered civil disorder and economic want at home and a loss of prestige abroad. General Charles de Gaulle, who had opposed the weak-executive system of the Fourth Republic and had retired after the creation of the Fourth Republic in 1946, was the chief moving force behind the creation of the Fifth Republic and became its first president.

STRUCTURE OF THE FIFTH REPUBLIC. France is a unitary state; its political subdivisions are all administered by governments directly responsible to national authorities. The government under the Fifth Republic is parliamentary, with a strong president. The president has wide powers, such as the dissolution of the legislature, the promulgation of laws, appointment of many administrative officers, the command of the armed forces, and the authority to assume almost all governmental powers in time of national emergency. In February, 1960, the French parliament conferred such powers upon President de Gaulle to help him cope with the political unrest that stemmed from an uprising of the French residents in Algeria. The president appoints the premier and his cabinet, which, in addition to its administrative functions, proposes bills for action by the legislature. If the legislature rejects a crucial bill submitted to it by the cabinet, the cabinet must resign. The great weakness of the Third and Fourth Republics was the stalemate over policy-making that might occur after the resignation of a cabinet. The constitution of the Fifth Republic not only makes it more difficult to remove a cabinet but also gives the president such strong powers that policy-making can continue without a cabinet. The creation and execution of foreign policy are entrusted to the president; he relies for counsel chiefly upon the Ministry of Foreign Affairs.

THE PARTY SYSTEM. The system of political parties in France has been and is very complex. France has been the outstanding example of a multiparty government in which no party has had a majority. This has been a major cause for the many cabinet upheavals in the Third and Fourth Republics. Since World War II the Communist Party has generally been the strongest, but Communists have not been appointed to cabinet posts. However, under the Fifth Republic, new voting laws and the wide popularity of General de Gaulle sharply reduced Communist parliamentary representation. Other leading parties are the Socialist, Popular Republican, and Radical Socialist (which is less "radical" than the Socialist). In the Fifth Republic, members of De Gaulle's "Union for the New Republic" coalition won many seats. Despite the instability that still resides in the government and the party system, there is one great political "flywheel"—the nonpartisan bureaucracy. The many civil service workers below the highest posts do not lose their offices when a cabinet resigns and keep most government functions in operation.

Power and Strategic Situation. France today, even in combination with the other states of the French Community, is a secondary power. Here lies one of the greatest difficulties of present-day France: President de Gaulle and some other French leaders refuse to accept this status and continue to think in terms of the past. The fact is that France today does have a moderately large and moderately well armed military establishment. Yet it does not compare with that of the United States or the USSR and is not even in a position to make France overshadow West Germany. In 1960 the French detonated their first nuclear apparatus in the Sahara, but still they have no large stockpile of nuclear weapons. Late in 1960 the French parliament by a rather narrow margin voted to accept President de Gaulle's program for a French nuclear striking force independent of NATO. Such a force will not be ready for action before 1965. Geographically the French are vulnerable to attack overland by Soviet armies through Germany and Belgium. They are members of NATO, but even with their allies they could not readily stop an invading army. They are in no position—militarily, politically, or economically—to increase their power by very much. By ending the war in Algeria, the French enabled themselves to make a great increase in their contribution to the NATO forces.

Foreign Policy. French foreign policy today is considerably more limited than in the past. However, under President de Gaulle the French have been striving to restore themselves to the ranks of the great powers. This is shown by their attempts to produce a nuclear weapon so as to be on a par with the United States, the USSR, and the United Kingdom. For some years after World War II the French continued to regard Germany as their chief enemy, even after the "Cold

War" had become apparent to leaders in most other countries. By the late 1950's, however, they had agreed to maintain comparatively friendly relations with West Germany and to co-operate in efforts to restrain Soviet expansionism. France is united with five other European countries to make an economic free-trade area—the European Common Market. To expedite achieving this aim the French government has abandoned the long-standing French policy of inflating French money, which had worked hardship on many people in France and made economic agreement with such "hard-money" countries as West Germany, Italy, and Holland almost impossible. However, the French have been reluctant to concede much political power to a "Government of Europe." France generally backs the United Nations, in which it has a permanent Security Council seat.

The Remodeled French Community. The French Community is a confederation of seven autonomous states—France and six African republics. In this organization France itself includes not only the traditional area in Europe but also certain non-European areas. Some of these areas, known as overseas departments, have the same status as the departments in European France: they are represented in the French Parliament, and their domestic affairs are administered by officials responsible to the government in Paris. Still other areas, known as overseas territories, are represented in the French Parliament, but their domestic affairs are administered by officials responsible to a local assembly.

GOVERNMENT OF THE REMODELED COMMUNITY. The Community has three principal branches of government. The executive branch is the Council of the Heads of State and of Government, including the President of France. The legislative branch of the Community is the Interparliamentary Consultative Senate. It discusses matters common to the whole Community. The judicial branch, the Court of Arbitration of the Community, is intended to resolve disputes among the member republics. Each republic is quite independent. Any member republic may secede from the Community. Every inhabitant of the Community possesses French citizenship.

NON-EUROPEAN AREAS OF THE COMMUNITY. The non-European areas of the Remodeled French Community are much smaller than the prewar French Empire. For one thing, the French have given up such regions as Algeria, Indochina, Tunisia, and Syria. Also, some of the new African states remained only briefly in the Community, and then severed their political ties; however, they still have economic and cultural bonds with the Community. The non-European areas in the Community contain about 1,200,000 square miles and somewhat more than 12,000,000 people, almost all of which are in Africa.

African Areas. The African areas of the Community, with one exception, are republics; the exception is Somaliland, which is an overseas territory. The population of most of these countries is predominantly Negro. Their governments all resemble one another and are similar to that of France. In most cases the legislative branch is a unicameral assembly; the executive, called either the president or the premier, is chosen by the legislature. Universal suffrage prevails, and the percentage of voters participating in elections is high. There are a number of quite active political parties. These republics conduct a foreign trade that is important both for them and for France. Their chief exports are agricultural, including livestock, tobacco, coffee, cocoa, peanuts, cotton, rice, sugar, sisal, and fish. They also yield such mineral goods as diamonds, lead, gold, graphite, mica, phosphates, and petroleum. Finally, they produce large quantities of lumber. Transportation facilities are still rather primitive, but there are some railroads. The economies of these republics have been stimulated by the investment of several billion dollars of French government funds. The French government has also helped in the organizing of such welfare activities as tax-supported schools and public health groups.

Non-African Areas. In the New World the only portions of the French Community are Guiana, Martinique, Guadeloupe, and St. Pierre and Miquelon. All but St. Pierre and Miquelon are overseas departments. Local Communist Parties have shown considerable strength in Martinique and Guadeloupe, which as West Indian islands are strategically placed in relation to the Panama Canal. Guiana is very heavily forested and produces gold. It raises various tropical crops, as do Martinique and Guadeloupe. St. Pierre and Miquelon yield little but fish. In the Indian and Pacific Oceans there are some other islands; Réunion alone is an overseas department. Réunion and the islands of French Polynesia and New Caledonia raise many tropical foods. There are also important mining enterprises in New Caledonia, yielding such minerals as nickel, manganese, cobalt, and chromite. Lastly, the French with the British have a condominium over the New Hebrides, a typical South Pacific island group.

WEST GERMANY

West Germany, officially the Federal Republic of Germany, is an independent country formed of the postwar American, British, and French zones of occupation.

Population and Geography. The population of West Germany in 1960 numbered about 56,000,000, somewhat less than one-third that of the United States. Since the war this population has risen at a slow pace. A major source of new residents has been the influx of refugees from East Germany, a high percentage of whom have been members of the professions and skilled workmen. The population is highly urban, and large cities are scattered about the country. Since West Berlin is a separate political entity, the largest city is Hamburg, with about 1,800,000; Munich has about 1,000,000; and there are nine other cities with populations in excess of 500,000. The people are almost all German-speaking, drawn from blond Nordic and brunet Alpine stocks. A high percentage is engaged in industrial or commercial pursuits, but the high level of prosperity has drawn many into the service trades and professions. The population is almost equally divided between Catholics and Protestants, and all religions are tolerated. The tax-supported school system in Germany has been used more than in any other country for the education of industrial technicians. West Germany has an area of about 96,000 square miles. The land presents no natural obstacles, being either flat or hilly, and it is well watered. The climate is rather mild, and the rainfall is sufficient for farming.

Resources and Economic Life. The West German economy today is renowned for its productiveness and its prosperity. With its comparative lack of government controls, it is often the subject of favorable comparison with the economies of the countries of Eastern Europe, especially East Germany.

RESOURCES AND AGRICULTURE. West Germany has considerable deposits of some resources but is entirely or almost entirely lacking in others. Perhaps its most important resource is coal. It also produces large quantities of fluorspar, graphite, and potash. It produces some iron, but not nearly enough for its steel mills. The soil is not very good, but German agriculture is very productive, because of the use of much labor and the application of fertilizer and good farming practices. Germany produces livestock and grains, as well as other crops, but it must still import a considerable amount of food.

INDUSTRY. West Germany is one of the most highly industralized countries on earth. This industrial complex depends not upon the availability of resources so much as upon the application of technological and administrative skills to resources imported from elsewhere. It should also be noted that there are fewer government controls on the German economy than on any other economy in Europe. West German steel production, which totals about 25,000,000 tons per year, is exceeded only by that of the United States and the USSR. West Germany produces more automobiles than any other country in the world except the United States. It also makes large quantities and numbers of chemicals, machinery of various sorts, electrical equipment, locomotives, steamships, textiles, aluminum, and synthetic oil. Germany has excellent railroad and highway networks, in addition to all other transportation facilities.

FOREIGN TRADE. The revival of West German industry has brought a resumption of large-scale foreign trade. Today the West Germans are challenging the British and the Americans in many regions, such as Asiatic and Latin American countries, that they seemed ten years ago to have lost forever as customers. In 1961, mainly to help stem the flow of gold out of the United States, the West German government even revalued its money upward. Yet the Germans have lost a great part of their once vast trade in Eastern Europe. The severance of these traditional commercial ties with Eastern Europe is perhaps as important as Soviet political and military domination over these countries in barring the way to a new German *Drang nach Osten* (push toward the east) and in turning West German interests toward Western Europe and the lands outside Europe. There is one exception to this rule: West German goods are so important to East Germany that a West German embargo on shipments would be catastrophic to the East German economy. East German goods are in no sense this important to the West German economy. The chief West German exports are coal, steel and steel products, automobiles, machinery, chemicals, and dyes. Leading imports are iron and other metallic ores, crude oil, and food. Although West Germany lost almost all its ships as a result of the war, since 1945 the West German shipbuilding industry has created a merchant fleet larger than that of France.

Government. The West German government is federal, consisting of a national level and a *Land,* or state, level. There are ten states, or *Laender,* with considerable powers. The government at the national level is parliamentary. There is a president, chosen indirectly by an electoral college; his functions are chiefly decorative and ceremonial. The true chief executive is the chancellor—similar to a prime minister, but somewhat more powerful—who is named by the parliament. The parliament is bicameral; the lower house represents the voters, and the upper house represents the state governments. West Germany, after twelve years under the Nazi one-party system, today has what amounts to a two-party system. The chief parties are the Christian Democratic Union and the Social Democratic Party. Other parties are the Christian Social Union and the German Party, which tend to side with the Christian Democratic Union; and the Free Democratic Party, which in 1961 held the balance of power in the German parliament and entered into a coalition with the Christian Democrats. Neo-Nazi and Communist Parties have been outlawed. Foreign policy is in the hands of a foreign minister; however, Chancellor Konrad Adenauer has to a considerable extent operated as his own foreign minister. On foreign policy the two major parties vary only in degree.

Power and Strategic Situation. West Germany has been allowed to rearm itself rather rapidly since World War II, mainly because of the "Cold War" and the development of considerable armed forces in East Germany by Soviet authorities. By 1960, however, despite encouragement and aid by the United States, the West German armed forces were not very strong. It is still important for West German defenses that there be strong United States bases in the country. Eventually the West German army is to be organized around tactical nuclear weapons. In a geographic sense, West Germany is ill-situated for its defense; its only "natural" boundary is to the south, and that divides it from neutral Switzerland and neutral Austria. However, this situation is traditional for Germany, and helps to account for the powerful military forces that the Germans have maintained in the past. Perhaps its chief problem now is that along its entire eastern frontier are ranged two hostile countries, East Germany and Czechoslovakia, each of which has the backing of the Soviet Army. West Germany does have allies, for it is a member of NATO; but it would be the first victim of any Soviet land advance westward.

Foreign Policy. The fundamental and almost exclusive positive goal of West German foreign policy has been to secure the reunification of all Germany, on non-Soviet terms. Its leaders, and leaders of countries friendly toward it, have suggested various sorts of unimpeded all-German elections as a plebiscite on the question of unification; but Soviet leaders have opposed them. One of the most ticklish issues here is that, when Soviet rulers after World War II incorporated into the USSR a large strip of eastern Poland, they allowed the Poles to recompense themselves by occupying a section of eastern Germany. Presumably one of the first acts of a reunited Germany would be to regain this lost territory—even though most of the Germans in it have been expelled or have fled. Consequently the Poles do not want a reunited Germany any more than the Soviets do. In other matters, the West Germans have been far more hesitant than the French to view themselves as a great power that can deal with the United States or the USSR as an equal. They have been at the forefront in the movement toward European co-operation.

ITALY

Although Italy was a member of the Axis in 1939, it was associated with the Allies at the close of World War II. Hence it was not saddled with a very burdensome peace treaty after the war, and today it has a repute and a legal status that differ little from those of the other wartime Allied Powers.

Population and Geography. The population of Italy in 1960 was about 51,000,000, approximately the same as those of the United Kingdom, France, and West Germany. It is increasing fairly rapidly, despite considerable emigration, for the birth rate is rather high and the death rate is falling. It has a density of over 400 per square mile. Much of it is rural. On the other hand, Rome contains over 2,000,000 people; Milan and Naples, more than 1,000,000 each; Turin, more than 900,000; and Genoa, more than 700,000. It is not very homogeneous; there are several important dialects. Southern Italians on the average have less schooling and lower incomes than northern Italians. Officially, almost all Italians are Catholics; nevertheless, anticlericalism is strong. Vatican City, home of the Pope, is in Rome, but it is an independent state. Italy has an area of about 116,400 square miles. A large part of Italy comprises a long peninsula extending southeast into the Mediterranean. Much of the country is mountainous, with the Alps in the north and the Apennines down the center of the peninsula. Northern Italy also contains a fertile plain, watered by the Po and other rivers coming down from the Alps. Northern Italy has adequate rainfall, but southern Italy does not. Italy includes two large islands as well, Sicily and Sardinia.

Resources and Economic Life. Although the Italian people today are generally among the more prosperous nations of the world, Italy is still a country with shortages of raw materials and an excessively specialized type of industry, and with serious problems of unemployment among unskilled workers and in the rural areas of the South.

RESOURCES AND INDUSTRY. Italy does not possess many important mineral resources. It does produce exportable surpluses of bauxite, zinc, mercury, sulfur, and pyrites. However, it must import all its needs of such ores as chromite, tin, and nickel; and it must also import large quantities of iron ore and coal. In recent years the Italians have been obtaining major quantities of natural gas from wells in the Po Valley, and petroleum from Sicily. Much of the soil of Italy, especially in the south, is not very fertile, and Italy is not well timbered. Agriculture in Italy received a great deal of attention from Mussolini and has continued to obtain government assistance since the end of World War II. Government activities have taken such forms as draining swamps, helping farmers to mechanize their operations, and giving instructions in the use of fertilizer and new techniques of cultivation. Italian agriculture is fairly productive, especially in the north, but still does not yield enough to support the Italian people. The Italian industrial plant has increased considerably since the end of the war, but Italy does not yet have nearly so much industry as other Western European countries with comparable populations. It does, however, make hundreds of thousands of automobiles annually and has many shipyards. It has gained world renown for its manufacture of such lighter goods as typewriters and sewing machines. Other notable industries are sugar-beet refining, chemicals, and cotton and silk spinning and weaving. Transportation depends largely on railroads, although they are not so concentrated as in some other countries; there is a good highway system as well. Inland waterways are unimportant; the Po is the only river carrying much commercial traffic.

FOREIGN TRADE. Foreign trade is very important for Italy. For example, Italy must import both coal and iron ore for its steel mills. It must also import food. At the same time, it can export, and has very successfully created foreign markets for, such goods as tropical fruits, automobiles, sewing machines, and office equipment. The Italian economy has become so prosperous that Italian businesses can even afford to invest capital abroad. Italy is also active in trade development in the Middle East, as well as in oil exploration there. By 1957, despite wartime losses, Italy had the seventh largest merchant fleet in the world. Part of its adverse balance of trade is recovered by the savings that Italians send home from abroad. Finally, as in France, tourism is an important aspect of foreign trade.

Government. By a plebiscite in 1946, Italian voters rejected the monarchy and established a republic. It has a typical parliamentary form. The titular executive is the president, elected by the national legislature, but he has little real power. The true executive is the prime minister, appointed by the president at the direction of the legislature; he must resign in case he loses a vote in the legislature. As in most countries, a foreign minister is in charge of foreign policy. The legislature is bicameral; each house is distributed roughly in proportion to population. The government of Italy is unitary; the chief executive officer in each of the regions is appointed by a minister in the national government. Italy has several large political parties, most important of which is the Christian Democratic Party. Other important parties are the Communist, Socialist (which once sided with the Communists), Democratic Socialist, and Neo-Fascist. There has been a broad division between the Christian Democrats on the one hand and the Communists and Socialists on the other as to the treatment that should be accorded the Soviet Union. It was significant that after the Soviet repression of the Hungarian uprising in 1956, some Socialists, including the party leader, Pietro Nenni, became less cordial toward the USSR than they had been in the past. The Christian Democratic Party, which runs the government, does not have a majority in the legislature and consequently must rule as the head of a coalition. In 1962 the Socialist Party broke with the Communists and agreed to back such a coalition; however, no Socialists were included in the cabinet formed in that year. Overturns of the prime minister have been rather frequent, but they do not seem to lead to the severe political crises that were common in the French Third and Fourth Republics.

Power and Strategic Situation. In terms of intrinsic power, Italy occupies a position somewhat inferior to that of France, for its industrial plant has less capacity to produce armaments. Since Italy has no colonies to tame or police, the rather considerable Italian Army, Navy, and Air Force can be entirely devoted to European problems. As a result, Italy has made a substantial contribution to the forces of NATO. Geographically, Italy seems relatively invulnerable by land, since it is cut off from Europe by the Alps. However, the Alpine passes make it more easy for an enemy to invade Italy than for the Italians to invade their neighbors. Italy today is on good terms with France; and, since the peaceful solution of the dispute over Trieste, it is on good terms with Yugoslavia as well. It need not fear an attack by sea so long as it keeps its present good relations with the United States and the United Kingdom, whose navies dominate the Mediterranean. Italy is a member of NATO and hence can expect the support of the United States in the event of war.

Foreign Policy. The foreign policy of Italy today is rather peaceable, if only because of the human, physical, and psychological losses it suffered in World War II. Apparently that war taught the majority of Italians that their country is not rich or productive enough to assume the role of a great power. Today, in spite of Communist opposition, the Italian government is anti-Soviet and co-operates with other governments in resisting further Soviet expansion. To assure its Mediterranean lifelines, it works to keep good relations with the United States and the United Kingdom. It usually supports undertakings carried on through the United Nations. Italy is engaged in a border dispute with Austria over the South Tyrol, an Italian province with a large German-speaking population. Although no settlement has yet been reached, the dispute does not seem to pose a serious threat to peace.

THE BENELUX COUNTRIES

The Benelux Countries (Belgium, the Netherlands, Luxemburg) work closely together politically and form practically an economic and cultural unit.

Population and Geography. The total population of the Benelux countries in 1959 was about 20,725,000 (Belgium, 9,100,000; the Netherlands, 11,300,000; and Luxemburg, 325,000)—less than half that of France. This population is not increasing very rapidly, for these countries have a rather low birth rate. All three countries are densely populated; the population is generally urban with only a small percentage engaged in farming. The only one of the three countries that has any problem concerning national groups is Belgium, which is officially bilingual; some of the people speak French, and others speak Flemish. Most of the people of the Benelux countries are concerned with industrial, commercial, and professional callings. In general they enjoy a high standard of living. The people of both Belgium and Luxemburg are mostly Catholics; the people of the Netherlands are almost equally divided between Catholics and Protestants. Geographically, this area consists of coastal plains and hills further inland. The climate is temperate and the rainfall conducive to prosperous farming.

Resources and Industry. The Benelux countries together have important natural resources. Perhaps the most important is coal, mined in both Belgium and the Netherlands. There are diminishing amounts of iron ore, found in Belgium and Luxemburg, and the Netherlands produces some crude oil. There are sand for glass, and clay for pottery. Much of the soil is fertile, and there are extensive forests. Although manufacturing is the most important economic field, there are significant agricultural undertakings in all three countries. For example, a considerable part of the arable land in the Netherlands has been reclaimed from the sea, and government officials are planning further reclamation projects. Farming is very intensive but does not produce enough to feed the people. All the Benelux countries are highly industrialized but depend on imports of most raw materials. Belgium has a good deal of heavy industry and is an important steel center. Other manufactures include chemicals, glass, pottery, and textiles. Belgians enjoyed considerable prosperity in the late 1940's and early 1950's, before West German industry recovered sufficiently to offer them serious competition. During the late 1950's, however, Belgian industry entered a period of relative decline. Luxemburg is also a steel-producing area. Industry in the Netherlands, apart from shipbuilding, is somewhat lighter, producing chemicals, textiles, and diamonds, among other products. For transportation the Benelux countries rely on waterways and railroads linking France and Germany.

Foreign Trade. Foreign trade is of great importance to all three countries; for they must import food and various raw materials, and export finished goods. Moreover, they handle much of the overseas trade of Germany. The Benelux countries are a customs union and impose the same general tariff levels. Both Belgium and the Netherlands have unfavorable trade balances, that of the Netherlands being larger. The Netherlands merchant fleet, however, is one of the largest in the world, and therefore the Dutch maintain a balance of payments through shipping fees. Each country also gets returns from overseas investments, for each is a major source of venture capital. (The rioting and property damage that occurred in the Congo after it received its independence was a severe, but not disastrous, economic blow to the Belgians.) Belgium and the Netherlands both also receive income from the "transit trade" they conduct of goods that simply pass through, using their ports. Hence a prosperous Germany, using the Lowlands, is a desirable condition for them. All Benelux countries have clung to an anti-inflationary monetary policy.

Government. Belgium and the Netherlands are both kingdoms; Luxemburg is a grand duchy. Each has a strong bicameral legislature. In all three, the true executive is a cabinet responsible to the legislature. The Netherlands to a degree has a federal government, for the members of one legislative house are elected by the provincial assemblies. Belgium has a fundamentally unitary government, although some members of the national upper house are elected indirectly. There is a vigorous party system in both Belgium and the Netherlands; that in the Netherlands is partly based on religion. The Communist Party is nowhere very strong.

Power and Strategic Situation. All three countries are connected with NATO; indeed, one reason for creating the Benelux union was military. This represents a considerable change of policy for Belgian leaders, since in both 1914 and the late 1930's they tried unsuccessfully to be neutral. The fact is that almost any conceivable overland attack on France must go through at least Luxemburg and Belgium, and in 1940 the Germans went through the Netherlands as well. All these countries maintain rather substantial military forces but in the long run depend upon stronger allies to protect them. Geographically they are quite vulnerable; in the Netherlands there are almost no natural defenses, and even flooding the country did not seem to hold back the Germans in 1940.

Foreign Policy. The foreign policy of all three countries today includes chiefly the support of the various anti-Soviet coalitions that involve Western Europe. Their geographic location and their extreme vulnerability to military attack have put their leaders among the chief proponents of European unification. The foreign policies of Belgium and the Netherlands also involve their colonies. Since World War II the Dutch have given up their largest colony, the East Indies, and rely upon the United States to restrain efforts to seize their New World properties. The Belgians have greatly cooled toward the United Nations and their own European allies as a result of the happenings since they gave the Congo its political independence. Leaders in the United Nations, the United States, and the various European countries have expressed a great deal of concern for the welfare of the Congolese people, but they have shown little inclination to protect either the Belgian settlers or the considerable Belgian properties in the Congo from being attacked or confiscated by the Congolese. In fact, United Nations representatives in the Congo have maintained that the Belgians must leave. Some Belgians complain that this UN policy is one more case in which leaders of the United Nations have not hesitated to deal much more harshly and rigorously with a small nation than they would have done had one of the larger powers been involved.

Overseas Territories. The Netherlands still possesses scattered remnants of a once vast colonial empire. In the Indonesian island chain the Netherlands holds part of the island of New Guinea, although the Indonesian Republic government claims it also. In the New World the Dutch have Guiana, or Surinam, and some West Indian islands collectively termed the Netherlands Antilles. These New World properties are self-governing in local affairs, and have a voice in the operation of the Netherlands government itself. These territories provide considerable wealth. For instance, most bauxite used in the United States comes from Surinam. New Guinea contains petroleum; and the Netherlands Antilles receive crude oil from Venezuela, only a short distance away, and refine it.

THE SCANDINAVIAN COUNTRIES

The Scandinavian countries include Denmark, Norway, Sweden, and Iceland. Except for Iceland, they form what amounts to a single geographic block. They have many political, economic, strategic, and cultural similarities and interrelations.

Population and Geography. The total population of all the Scandinavian countries in 1960 was about 15,700,000, running from 7,500,000 in Sweden to 170,000 in Iceland. Since these countries include about 350,000 square miles, the population is not very dense, being about 45 per square mile, and much of it is rural; among the relatively few good-sized cities are Stockholm (800,000), Copenhagen (785,000), and Oslo (460,000). In all these countries the people and their language are fundamentally Germanic. The commonest religious faith is the Lutheran. The people generally have a very high cultural level. Much of the land, as in Denmark and southeastern Sweden, is rather flat, and there are many fresh-water lakes; but there are important mountains in Sweden and Norway. The coast of Norway is deeply indented by many fjords. Some parts of Scandinavia have a fairly mild climate; in the north, however, the winters may be severe.

Resources and Economic Life. The Scandinavian people in general are exceptionally prosperous. Scandinavia possesses important resources. Sweden has one of the world's largest deposits of high-grade iron ore; it is significant that the German steel industry is better adapted than the British for using Swedish ore, which contains much phosphorus. Norway has significant amounts of silver, copper, nickel, lead molybdenum, and zinc. However, the Scandinavians must import coal and oil. Much of the land is not very fertile, but other parts are excellent for farming. In some sections there are huge and valuable forests, but much of the logging is done by Finns. Agriculture is a major phase of the economy; Scandinavia yields grains, potatoes, dairy products, and livestock. Denmark is predominantly agricultural and is economically dependent on British markets for its bacon, butter, and poultry. Commercial and subsistence fishing are widespread. Manufacturing is varied. Sweden, the principal manufacturing state, produces moderate amounts of very high quality steel and also fabricates the steel; other significant industries are wood pulp and lumber, chemicals, textiles, processed foods, and shipbuilding. Foreign trade is quite important for Scandinavia, since the people need many goods not produced there, and Norway and Denmark are well situated for oceanic commerce. Norway possesses one of the largest merchant fleets in the world.

Government. Governments in Scandinavia generally resemble one another; however, Iceland is a republic whereas the others are monarchies. All the governments are parliamentary; only in Sweden is the legislature bicameral. The titular executives generally have but slight powers; the real executives are the prime ministers and cabinets, which are responsible to the legislatures. Each country has several political parties, chief of which is usually the Social Democratic, or one with comparable policies. In Iceland the Communist Party is strong; elsewhere it is not. Scandinavian governments, especially in Sweden, have instituted major welfare programs. Foreign policy creation and execution are the responsibilities of the chief executive, the ministry of foreign affairs, and the diplomatic corps.

Power and Foreign Policy. The countries of Scandinavia all together have little power, for their populations and industrial plants are too small. Norway has a common frontier with the USSR, and all Scandinavia except Iceland is easily accessible to Soviet forces. Iceland, by contrast, is a major outpost in the United States defense system, but the Icelandic people have been quite hostile to American military personnel. Scandinavia lies on the air route between the eastern part of the United States and the western part of the USSR; moreover, the Norwegian fjords would make excellent bases for Soviet submarines. Hence these countries could scarcely escape direct involvement in a war between the superpowers. All these countries except Iceland have compulsory military service. Sweden is very heavily armed, but the other countries are not. All but Sweden belong to NATO. Sweden apparently wishes to retain the neutrality it practiced during World War II and is allied only with Iceland, Norway, and Denmark.

SWITZERLAND AND AUSTRIA

Switzerland and Austria are adjacent Alpine countries that are neutral. Otherwise the two countries differ substantially from one another.

Population and Geography. The population of Switzerland in 1959 was about 5,200,000; that of Austria, about 7,000,000. In neither country is the population increasing very rapidly. Austria is much more highly urbanized, for it contains Vienna, with about 1,700,000 inhabitants; the largest city in Switzerland is Zurich, with only 425,000. Switzerland is a multilingual state; over seventy per cent of the people speak German, over twenty per cent French, and about five per cent Italian. Austrians are mainly German-speaking; this fact has contributed to a traditional effort to unify Austria and Germany, but for many years there have been a considerable number of Austrians who feared or even hated Germany. In both countries a substantial part of the population is engaged in farming. In Switzerland, religious faiths are represented in a ratio of about four Protestants to three Catholics; in Austria, most people are Catholics. Switzerland is mountainous, as is much of Austria. A substantial part of Austria, on the other hand, is composed of the rather wide Danube Valley.

Resources and Economic Life. Switzerland does not contain many mineral resources; the most important is salt. Austria, by contrast, has a variety of mineral ores, including iron, copper, and bauxite, but they have not been very thoroughly exploited; Austria also produces coal and petroleum. Both countries have important lumber stands, but many of the forests in Switzerland have been cut down to create pastures. Austria produces considerable yields of staple crops, including grains, potatoes, and sugar beets; it also raises fruits and livestock. Farms in Switzerland grow staples, too, but they also produce many dairy goods such as cheese. Each country has important industries. Thanks to its resources, Austria has a considerable steel output; it also manufactures textiles and chemicals. Switzerland, by contrast, has a great deal of specialized industry, such as watchmaking, textile machinery, and drugs. Each country has a rather considerable foreign trade. Both must import food. Switzerland in particular fabricates goods with a world-wide market. Switzerland is an important international banking center, in part because of the peculiar Swiss law that forbids Swiss bankers to disclose the identity of their depositors; dictators and gangsters regularly use Swiss banks as hiding places for their liquid assets. In each country, tourists furnish a large share of the national income.

Government. In both Switzerland and Austria, the voters have major political powers; however, the governments differ considerably.

SWITZERLAND. Switzerland is a confederation that includes 22 cantons, each with its own government and with great power over matters of local concern. The national government has a bicameral legislature; in one house the cantons are equally represented, and in the other the members are apportioned according to population. Swiss voters exercise considerable direct legislative power through wide use of the initiative and the referendum. The executive branch is headed by a seven-member council; its president serves a one-year term and does not succeed himself. The national government has only the powers with which the cantons have vested it; these are somewhat greater than they were in the past but are still limited.

AUSTRIA. The government of Austria is federal and parliamentary. The legislature is bicameral, one house representing the nine provinces of the country and the other apportioned according to population. The titular executive is the president, but the actual executive is the chancellor and the cabinet. Austria operates under what is essentially a two-party system. Yet, because neither the People's (Conservative) Party nor the Socialists have been able to win a majority in the Assembly, the leaders of the two parties have formed an extragovernmental committee whose members determine which bills shall go to the legislature. This committee is the most important political agency in the country. The Communist Party has been losing both votes and representation.

Power and Foreign Policy. As noted above, both Switzerland and Austria are neutral; however, their power situations are profoundly different. For one thing, the Swiss have a long tradition of neutrality; the Austrians, by contrast, have been officially neutral only since 1955, when they signed a peace treaty with the Allies that affirmed their neutrality. Austria is much more vulnerable than Switzerland; the Danubian plain can be rather easily invaded and has been invaded many times in the past. Austria has almost no armed forces. In comparison, the Swiss have played a major part in the establishment of their own neutrality by expelling would-be invaders. Switzerland today is proportionately one of the most heavily armed countries in the world, and the Swiss have promised to oppose military force with military force. Furthermore, on the boundaries of Austria are some countries, especially Yugoslavia, with whom the Austrians have border disputes; contrariwise, none of the countries on the Swiss frontiers have aims on Swiss territory. The Swiss do not join international political or military agencies; Switzerland today does not belong to the United Nations or NATO and has no military allies. Austria, on the other hand, is a member of the United Nations and has a mutual security pact with the United States. In case of any war in Europe, it would be difficult for the Austrians to remain neutral.

SPAIN AND PORTUGAL

Spain and Portugal together occupy the Iberian peninsula. They have a number of important similarities.

Population and Geography. The population of Spain in 1960 was about 30,000,000; that of Portugal, about 9,000,000. Population density is about 150 per square mile in Spain, but over 250 per square mile in Portugal. In both countries a large percentage of the population is rural, but both countries also have large cities. Recently, many thousands of Spaniards have emigrated to become factory workers in more highly industrialized countries, especially West Germany. The population of

Spain is rather heterogeneous, consisting of such linguistically different groups as the Castilians, the Catalonians, the Galicians, and the
Basques. Most of the people in both countries are Catholics; Catholicism is the state religion of Spain. The schools in these countries prepare few students for technological careers, one index to Spanish and
Portuguese industrial backwardness. The land in Spain, except that in
Catalonia, is not very fertile; much of the country is a high, arid plateau. Portugal is mountainous, but it has some fertile areas with adequate rainfall. Parts of both countries have subtropical climates.

Resources and Economic Life. Spain is rather well endowed with
minerals, notably iron, copper, zinc, cobalt, and mercury. It also produces modest quantities of coal. Portugal, too, has a few coal mines;
and rather important deposits of lead, copper, tungsten, and tin as well.
These mines are generally owned by foreign interests. Portugal is well
forested, and cork is one of its most important products. Sheep grazing
is a major pursuit. Spanish farms yield a wide variety of crops, including grains, fruits, cotton, flax, and tobacco. The Portuguese grow
grains and fruits. In general, methods of tillage are primitive, and food
must be imported. Both countries have sufficient vineyards for noteworthy wine industries. Spanish manufacturing, which still suffers from
the civil war of the 1930's, is not very extensive; perhaps its most important side is the manufacture of textiles. Largely because of the shortage of coal, there is very little industry in Portugal. The Spanish, and
the Portuguese even more, process fish. Both countries suffer from poor
transportation facilities. Finally, Portugal is a tourist center, and Spain
seems well on its way to becoming one also.

Government. Although Portugal is a republic and Spain technically
is a monarchy, the governments of the two countries are rather similar.
They are both dictatorships; however, they are authoritarian rather
than totalitarian, for their leaders confine their interest mainly to the
political and economic activities of the people.

SPAIN. Spain is more nearly a totalitarian state. Its government is
actually a creature of Franco, the *Caudillo*. There is a single political
party, the Falange, which bears a superficial resemblance to the Fascist
and Nazi Parties. However, in free elections before Mussolini and Hitler
took power, the Fascist and Nazi Parties received millions of votes and
elected many government officeholders; the Falange never did likewise
in Spain before the civil war. Franco is of course executive chief of the
government. There is a legislature, the Cortes, whose members are partly
elected and partly appointed. A distinctive agency is the Regency Council, which in case Franco leaves office is to propose to the Cortes a can-

didate for the throne. The Spanish government has instituted a planned economy, with many welfare programs for laborers that are financed to a large degree by heavy taxes on the rich. The government has also introduced a farm-resettlement project. Still, the rise in material standards of living is very slow. Monopolies run most sectors of the economy. There is a strong but diminishing opposition to Franco that is suppressed by the army and the police. It lacks true inspiration and organization.

PORTUGAL. The dictatorship of Portugal is in the hands of one man, Antonio de Salazar, who has been premier since 1932. There is a bicameral legislature, one house being apportioned according to population and the other according to such functional groups as labor unions; thus Portugal has a partly corporative government. The government permits apparent opposition groups to run for office, but Salazar's candidates are almost always victorious. The Portuguese government takes a hand in regulating the national economy. Altogether, the Salazar dictatorship has been noteworthy for its comparative lack of brutality.

Power and Foreign Policy. The power status and the foreign policy of Spain are somewhat different from those of Portugal. At the end of the civil war, in spite of wartime losses the Nationalist army was still large, and Franco kept it large partly in order to prevent uprisings against him. Today this army is quite large, but it is not very well armed; it secures recruits by conscription. Spain also has a navy and an air force. In Portugal there is conscription as well, but the armed forces are not very large. Spain is protected from overland attack by the Pyrenees; this strategic insularity gives the country its chief military value. It is safe from attack by sea as long as it maintains friendly relations with the United States and the United Kingdom, which control the Atlantic and the Mediterranean. Spain for many years after its civil war was more or less an outcast nation; the Soviet Union and its sympathizers aroused as much public opinion as possible against the Franco government, and many people in the countries that had fought the Axis disliked Franco because he had won power with the assistance of Hitler and Mussolini. Today, however, Spain is a member of the United Nations and has a mutual security treaty with the United States. It contains a number of important United States bases. Portugal has a traditional alliance with Great Britain; it is a member of the United Nations and NATO. Owing to attacks on its administration of its African territories, the Portuguese government in 1961 threatened to withdraw from the UN. The Portuguese might be able to influence United States policy by hesitating to renew leases for United States military bases in the Azores.

Overseas Possessions. Both Spain and Portugal have overseas possessions, which amount to only a fraction of once vast colonial empires. The governments of both states contend that these possessions are integral parts of the mother countries; thus in their own eyes the Spanish and the Portuguese have no colonies. The Portuguese holdings are larger and more important. The chief Portuguese areas in Africa are Angola, Guinea, and Mozambique. They furnish a number of tropical products, such as ivory, coffee, cotton, and coconuts. They also yield minerals, including iron, copper, manganese, and gold; Angola has diamond mines. In the Atlantic Ocean, Portugal has the Azores, the Madeira Islands, and the Cape Verde Islands. In Asia the Portuguese territories are Macao, off the Chinese coast, and Timor, near Australia. Numerous observers now charge that the Portuguese government administers its African possessions in a repressive and unenlightened manner and that it is not preparing the native populations for the national independence they demand. In 1961, part of Angola was torn with rioting that brought death to both white and black inhabitants and severe damage to the many prosperous farms of the area. Spanish overseas possessions today are chiefly in northwestern Africa; the principal ones are Guinea and the Spanish Sahara. Guinea furnishes certain tropical products and gold.

THE REPUBLIC OF IRELAND

The Republic of Ireland is an independent state in Western Europe that from 1921 until 1949 had the status of a self-governing British dominion and that for centuries previously was ruled directly by the British government.

Population. The Republic of Ireland in 1960 had a population of about 2,800,000, with a density a little greater than 100 per square mile. The population is increasing little if at all. Emigration is still considerable, and marriage and birth rates are low. The population is about one-half rural, a very high percentage for a Western European country. The only large city is Dublin (540,000). The people of the Republic of Ireland are mainly Celts, related to the Welsh, Cornish, and Breton nations. The independent Irish government in the 1920's began reviving the study and use of the Irish language, but many Irish people still prefer English. Roman Catholicism is the official religion, but there is a small Protestant minority.

Geography and Economic Life. The Republic of Ireland occupies about five-sixths of the island of Ireland; the northeastern corner of Ireland, known generally but not quite accurately as Ulster, is part of the United Kingdom. The whole island is shaped somewhat like a saucer, comprising a central lowland rimmed with hills. It is poorly drained, so that much of the country is bog. The climate is warmer than that of England, but the rainfall in some places is too great for crops. The country has very few mineral resources; the peat, or "brown coal," has little industrial value. Farming is the mainstay of the national economy; farmers have been deserting crop growing for grazing. The chief industries are food processing, textiles, and brewing. The government is trying to increase industry and to harness the Shannon River for hydroelectric power. Foreign trade is mainly with the United Kingdom, despite Irish political independence.

Government and Foreign Policy. The government of the Republic of Ireland is based upon the doctrines of modern Roman Catholicism. It is a parliamentary republic. The titular executive is the popularly elected president; the actual executive is the prime minister with his cabinet. In the bicameral legislature, the lower house is directly chosen by the voters; the upper house contains some members who are appointed by the prime minister and other members who are elected according to economic groups, so that it furnishes functional representation. There are fairly vigorous political parties, which tend to differ with one another mainly over policy toward the United Kingdom. Party disputes may lead to violence on government officials, so that political freedoms are sometimes curtailed. There is no announced Communist Party in Ireland. In foreign policy Ireland has tended to be neutral; for example, during World War II it was still a member of the Commonwealth, but it did not declare war on Germany and refused Allied naval vessels the use of its harbors. The most important goal for the Irish is unification with Ulster, so that Ireland remains anti-British.

Review Questions

1. Compare the national power of France, West Germany, and Italy with that of the United Kingdom, in terms of population, geography, and economic capabilities. Which of the four would be most likely to dominate any political union of Western European states? Which might have the greatest ability for conciliating disputes among the others?

2. Compare the relations between France and the states of the French Community with the relations between the United Kingdom and the states of the Commonwealth. What factors help account for the differences? Which association is apt to have the longer life?

3. Compare the party systems of France, West Germany, and Italy with that in

the United Kingdom. In which country does the party system offer the greatest potential hindrance to the effective creation and execution of foreign policy?

4. Describe the chief contributions of the Benelux countries and the Scandinavian countries to the waging of the "Cold War."

5. If all of the great powers of Western Europe formed a political union and admitted Austria as an economic partner, how much of a chance would the Swiss have of maintaining their political independence?

6. Show how since 1945 the policies of the United States toward Spain and toward Portugal have moved in opposite directions. What factors account for such an evolution?

17 EASTERN EUROPE

Eastern Europe comprises all the countries between Western Europe and the Soviet Union. These countries have a number of unifying traits. For instance, in general they are small and militarily rather weak; they have tended to serve as pawns for the great powers in international politics. Likewise, they are not very strong economically; they have in the main functioned as sources of food and raw materials for larger and more industrialized states. Hence with a few exceptions they are chiefly agricultural. Furthermore, most of these countries have no more than a century of national independence; their peoples are politically inexperienced and sometimes disorderly. Today, in terms of world politics and international relations, the countries of Eastern Europe may be divided into three fairly distinct groups: (1) the satellite countries of the USSR; (2) the anti-Communist states; and (3) the neutralist states.

THE SATELLITE COUNTRIES OF THE USSR

The Eastern European satellite countries of the USSR include East Germany, Poland, Czechoslovakia, Hungary, Romania, Bulgaria, and Albania. All except Albania and, to some extent, Poland are completely dominated by the USSR. This domination was installed by Soviet troops. It is enforced today not so much by Soviet troops as by the national Communist Parties, which are dominated by the Communist Party of the Soviet Union and which have full control over the political, economic, and cultural lives of these peoples. Soviet troops, however, always lurk in the background, ready to crush any uprising against this rule; this became clear in 1956 in Hungary. Because of their domination by the USSR, these countries and governments have certain common characteristics. First, each has a government termed a "people's democracy," modeled after the government of the USSR. Second, each has a government-planned economy, which not only is patterned after that of the USSR but which also puts the resources and productive facilities of these countries at the disposal of the USSR. Third, the foreign policy of each country (except, in 1962, Albania) is subordinate to that of the USSR. Fourth, each country (with the probable exception, in 1962, of Albania) together with the USSR is a member of the Warsaw Pact, signed in 1955, which is primarily an anti-NATO military alliance. Yet, as was shown by such occurrences as the 1956 Hungarian uprising, the armed forces of these countries are not trustworthy allies for the Soviet Union. Finally, each country has such buildings as factories and such institutions as school systems that are slavish imitations of those in the USSR.

East Germany. East Germany was formed out of the Soviet occupation zone in Germany.

POPULATION AND GEOGRAPHY. The population of East Germany in 1959 was about 17,300,000. Until 1961, when the East German government halted emigration through East Berlin, this population was declining; great numbers of people from East Germany were taking refuge in Western Europe, at the rate of 200,000 per year in the 1950's. This was an especially serious matter, for at least three reasons. First, an unusually large percentage of these people were doctors, lawyers, and teachers, so that the number of professionally trained people in East Germany was being depleted. Second, this emigration was reducing the population of East Germany as compared to that of West Germany, so that in any free plebiscite of all German voters the anti-Soviet forces have had a growing advantage. Third, even with the ending of most of this emigration, Soviet authorities may move in large numbers of Poles, or members of some other non-Germanic people, to relieve the increasing labor shortage; such an act will dilute East German sentiment favoring unification with West Germany. The East German population is largely rural; since East Berlin is a separate political entity, the only city with more than 500,000 people is Leipzig (600,000). The area of East Germany is less than half of that of West Germany. Much of the country is lowland, extending from the glaciated and unproductive shores of the Baltic to the more fertile areas farther south.

ECONOMIC LIFE. The national economy, after stagnation during the late 1940's and early 1950's, by the late 1950's seemed to be perhaps the most prosperous in all Eastern Europe. By 1960, however, the constant westward emigration had resulted in a severe labor shortage that threatened a drastic cut in national output. East Germany has certain important minerals, notably bauxite, uranium, and salt. There is considerable industry, much of it new, as Soviet authorities have promoted the development of the country into a major "workshop" for the Soviet empire. Agriculture is also very important, but the collectivization of the land has prompted many farmers to emigrate.

INTERNATIONAL POLITICAL AND DIPLOMATIC STATUS. East Germany holds an unusual and important political and diplomatic status. For one thing, it is the only Soviet satellite that did not exist as a distinct country before 1939. It is also the only one to which the government of the United States has not extended diplomatic recognition. East Germany has become a vital part of Soviet foreign policy. In 1960 and 1961, Khrushchev provoked a crisis when he threatened to sign a separate peace treaty with the East German government and then turn East Berlin over to East German authorities—notwithstanding the provisions of the Potsdam agreement putting all Berlin under the joint jurisdiction of the four governments represented at Potsdam. Khrushchev has in the past indicated the long-range aim of using the East German government to secure control of all Germany. By 1961, however, it was clearer than ever, from conditions in East Germany, that the West German government would consent to unification only on its own terms. In fact, Khrushchev's behavior in 1961 suggested that he now wanted to maintain the "two-Germanies" situation permanently. The USSR has considerable opposition from East Germans, as shown by the popular uprising in 1953 against the Soviet armed forces. It seemed evident in 1961 that the East German government was surviving only on the basis of military force. East Germany has the very significant role of being the base from which any Soviet ground attack on Western Europe would be launched.

Poland. Poland is the largest of the Eastern European satellites. It is the one satellite, except for Hungary, that has a long tradition of real power in international relations. Today the Poles seem to enjoy a closer approximation to national sovereignty than the people of any other Eastern European satellite state.

POPULATION, GEOGRAPHY, AND ECONOMIC LIFE. Poland in 1960 had a population of about 29,700,000. The country suffered great population losses from World War II, because of military deaths, the Nazi slaughter of both Christians and Jews, and the westward movement of many Germans from Polish-occupied territory after the war. Today most of the people are Polish and are Roman Catholics. Though much of the population is rural, there are such urban centers as Warsaw (1,100,000), Lodz (700,000), and Krakow (500,000). By contrast with 1939, Poland today is smaller and farther west. After World War II it surrendered a large area in the east, populated chiefly by White Russians, to the USSR; it was compensated by being authorized to occupy part of East Germany, an area that the Polish government today gives no sign of planning to return to Germany. Like East Germany, Poland consists mainly of lowlands, most fertile in the central parts of the country. There are important mineral resources, such as coal, iron, zinc, salt, and petroleum. Polish farms have been subjected to less collectivization than those of any other Eastern European satellite. They are rather productive, being devoted mainly to grain, potatoes, and sugar beets. There is a good deal of industry, involving iron and steel, textiles, and chemicals.

INTERNATIONAL POLITICAL AND DIPLOMATIC STATUS. Of all the satellite countries, Poland comes nearest to enjoying independence from the USSR. It has occupied this status since 1956, when Polish Communist Party leaders restored Wladyslaw Gomulka to power as party chief; Gomulka had been deposed and imprisoned in 1951 at Stalin's orders. Khrushchev threatened to use Soviet troops to quell this near-revolt but did not carry out his threat. Subsequently Poland has become, according to American and West European observers, the one satellite in which open criticism of the Soviet Union is expressed. Furthermore, the Polish government is somewhat tolerant of the Catholic Church, which Soviet leaders view as one of their greatest enemies. At the same time, Polish government chiefs have been following the lead of the USSR in foreign affairs. Meanwhile the government of the United States has extended credit to the Polish government so that it can buy surplus United States grain. The Poles have a long tradition of hatred for the Russians; today, however, they seem even more hostile toward Germany. Polish leaders believe that a Germany united under an anti-Soviet regime would almost certainly try to regain the part of eastern Germany now occupied by Poland. In that case the Poles appear sure to turn to the USSR for assistance.

Czechoslovakia. Czechoslovakia has the most advanced technological and industrial system of any satellite nation.

POPULATION AND GEOGRAPHY. The population of Czechoslovakia in 1960 was about 13,600,000. An important fraction of it is rural, but Prague contains about 1,000,000 people, and there are several other medium-sized cities. The Czechoslovak population more than that of any other satellite country resembles the peoples of Western Europe in its possession of industrial skills. It comprises two distinct nationalities, the Czechs and the Slovaks, who have separate representation in the government. Relations between Czechs and Slovaks may be quite hostile, as was evident before and during World War II; many Czechs consider the Slovaks backward. Czechoslovakia has an excellent school system. The majority of the people are Roman Catholics. Much of Czechoslovakia is rimmed with mountains; it has excellent natural defenses to the west.

ECONOMIC LIFE AND INTERNATIONAL ROLE. Czechoslovakia has large quantities of such mineral resources as coal, oil, and iron ore; it is the leading European source of uranium. Its agriculture, which is very productive, yields large harvests of grains. It has a substantial industrial complex, manufacturing iron, steel, and machinery. The Lenin (formerly Skoda) armaments factory is one of the largest in Europe. Owing to its industrial facilities, Czechoslovakia sometimes performs an unusual role in the conduct of Soviet foreign policy. That is, non-Communist countries seeking fabricated goods from the Soviet Bloc may sometimes be directed to order them from Czechoslovakia rather than the USSR; for instance, Soviet weapons delivered to Egypt in the name of the Soviet Union were made in Czechoslovakia.

Hungary. Hungary offers the outstanding illustration of a satellite whose people almost succeeded in overthrowing Soviet rule. It has long been unique in other ways too.

POPULATION, GEOGRAPHY, AND ECONOMIC LIFE. The population of Hungary in 1960 was about 10,000,000. The Hungarian people are mainly of Alpine stock, but they speak an Asiatic tongue. Owing to a blurring of nationality lines, there are Hungarians also in Czechoslovakia and Yugoslavia; meanwhile Hungary itself has German and Slovak minorities, among others. Most of the population is rural; the only large city is Budapest (1,800,000). The majority of the people are Roman Catholics. Much of the country lies in the wide and fertile Danubian plain. Hungary contains some important mineral resources, such as bauxite, coal, and oil. Still, the chief economic activity of the Hungarians is farming; the principal crops are grains. There are modest industrial undertakings in iron and steel, machinery, chemicals, and textiles.

INTERNATIONAL STATUS. Hungary in an important way occupies a unique status among the satellite countries. It is the only one that has a considerable, and recent, tradition of dominion over neighboring peoples, stemming from its role in the Austro-Hungarian Empire. Partly as a consequence of this tradition, the Hungarians tend to stand apart from the Slavic nations. Hungarians also have a strong anti-Russian tradition, if only because during the nineteenth and early twentieth centuries they were rivals of the Russians for control in the Balkans. Furthermore, during the revolutions of 1848 Russian troops helped to quell an antimonarchist uprising in Hungary. Thus the intervention of Soviet troops in Hungary in 1956 had its precedent. The Communist regime in Hungary today survives only because of the continued threat of the Soviet Army.

Romania. Romania in 1960 had a population of about 18,400,000. Although the background of the Romanian people has been disputed, modern research has fairly well established that they are a Latin nation. Romania does include significant minority groups, notably Hungarians, Ukrainians, and Germans. The Romanian population is increasing at a rapid pace, because of a high birth rate. The population is chiefly rural; the only major city is Bucharest (1,200,000). Much of the country is a wide and fertile plain between the Danube and the Prut. The Carpathian Mountains and the Transylvania Highlands divide this plain from Transylvania, which is geographically part of Hungary but politically part of Romania. Romania is rich in certain minerals, such as oil, gas, iron, copper, and zinc. However, the Romanian people have shown little inclination to work them; under the Communist regime, this situation will probably change. The chief products of its normally fruitful agriculture are grains. There has been relatively little manufacturing in the past, but under the Communist, government-planned economy it is being increased. It is devoted to such enterprises as food processing, oil refining, agricultural equipment, and chemicals.

Bulgaria. The population of Bulgaria in 1959 was about 7,800,000. The Bulgarians were originally an Asiatic people that over the centuries has become Slavicized; they speak a Slavic tongue. Most of the population is rural; the one large city is Sofia (725,000). The country consists chiefly of two large plains separated by the Balkan Mountains, which extend from the west toward the Black Sea. There are not many mineral resources; the principal ones are coal and copper. Although much of the plains is fertile, backward farming techniques lead to comparatively low harvest yields. The main crops are grains and fruits, together with the roses that produce the famous attar. There is not much industry in Bulgaria. It seems that ambitious government plans for increases in manufacturing have been modified in favor of a project to convert much of the country into a tourist and resort center. In international relations, the Bulgarians have ancient disputes with the Greeks over Thrace and with the Yugoslavs over territory inhabited by the Macedonians.

Albania. Albania in 1959 had a population of about 1,600,000. Albanians are an Illyrian people speaking an old Indo-European tongue who centuries ago withdrew before stronger peoples, took refuge in the mountains, and preserved their culture there. The largest city is Tirana (60,000). The bulk of the people are Mohammedans. Most of the country is mountainous. There are relatively few developed mineral resources; the most important seems to be copper. The main crops in the small amount of arable land, which is very densely populated, are wheat, fruits, and tobacco. There is very little manufacturing. Albania in 1961 secured a unique international position: it became the only Soviet satellite that not only overthrew Soviet controls but also put itself under Communist Chinese influence. Apparently the Albanian government evicted Soviet troops and submarines from their base in Albania, and the Albanians accepted a loan and admitted technicians from Communist China. Why the Soviet government acceded to these moves is not clear, especially since Albania is very strategically situated on the Adriatic only about 50 miles from Italy. However, there probably is some connection with the fact that Albania does not touch any other Soviet satellite and could not therefore be invaded overland by Soviet forces, as was the case with Hungary in 1956.

THE ANTI-COMMUNIST STATES

The anti-Communist states of eastern Europe are Greece and Turkey. Although Turkey lies mainly in Asia and has important links with certain Asiatic countries, there are other circumstances such as its membership in NATO that make Turkey also a part of eastern Europe.

Greece. Greece is a weak and impoverished country whose importance stems mainly from its location on the Mediterranean.

Population, Geography, and Economic Life. The population of Greece in 1960 was about 8,300,000. The population is mainly rural; the chief cities are Athens (1,400,000) and Salonika (300,000). Many Greeks have emigrated to Western Europe, to work in factories there. There is a tax-supported school system, but widespread poverty makes enforcement of compulsory attendance laws difficult. Most Greeks belong to the Orthodox faith. The country is generally mountainous, and the irregular coastline includes many natural harbors. The port of Salonika serves much of the interior of the Balkans. The country is not well endowed with resources. It does produce some iron, copper, zinc, lead, bauxite, and marble. Most of the country is not very fertile; its forest areas, once stripped away, are being replaced. Agriculture is the chief economic undertaking; farmers raise grains, citrus fruits, olives, cotton, and tobacco. Nevertheless, the Greeks must import food. Industry is confined mainly to food processing, although United States aid programs have been aimed at raising factory output. Greek foreign trade generally has an unfavorable balance; the difference is partly made up through the ownership, by a few Greek citizens, of one of the largest merchant fleets in the world.

GOVERNMENT AND FOREIGN POLICY. The government of Greece is a limited monarchy. The king is primarily a figurehead, with little power. The actual executive is the prime minister with the cabinet; the legislature is unicameral. There is a strong pro-Soviet party, the Union of the Democratic Left, which in the elections of 1958 won about one-fourth of the seats in the legislature. The Greek Army, which is recruited by conscription, is not very strong. Greece has had long-standing disputes with Yugoslavia and Bulgaria over Macedonia, and with Bulgaria over Thrace. The most important international difficulty for Greece in recent years has been the threat of the Soviet Union to take over the country, by means of Greek Communists supplied from Yugoslavia. However, the Truman Doctrine provided weapons for the Greek government, and the expulsion of Yugoslavia from the Cominform in 1948 cut off supplies for the Greek Communists. Greece is a member of the United Nations and of NATO. It joined Turkey and Yugoslavia in a military alliance in 1954; but since Yugoslavia has revived friendly relations with the USSR that alliance seems meaningless.

Turkey. Turkey is a much larger and more populous country than Greece, possessing centuries-old traditions of dominion over other peoples and of warring with the Russians.

POPULATION, GEOGRAPHY, AND ECONOMIC LIFE. The population of Turkey in 1960 was approximately 27,800,000. The majority of the people dwell in rural areas; the chief cities are Istanbul (1,450,000) and Ankara (450,000). The shift of the Turkish capital to Ankara drastically reduced the importance of Istanbul. The people of Turkey comprise a mixture of various Asiatic nations that have settled in Asia Minor; their main bond is their common use of the Turkish language. In the process of modernizing their country in the 1920's, the Turks adopted the Roman alphabet. Almost all Turks are Moslems, but such Islamic symbols as veils for women and fezzes for men have been outlawed in the modernization process. Much of Turkey is a high plateau. Like Greece, it has a long coastline, though not so indented, and has several good harbors. Turkey has large mineral deposits, but they are just beginning to be exploited. It is the largest producer of chrome in the world and has large quantities of iron and copper. It has relatively smaller amounts of manganese, molybdenum, antimony, lead, silver, and zinc. It also has large fields of coal and petroleum. Agriculture still is the most important economic activity, the chief crops being tobacco, grains, and fruits. There are various industries, notably textiles, iron and steel, metal wares, and armaments. The government is encouraging foreigners to invest in plants in Turkey. Significant exports are foodstuffs, tobacco, and chrome.

GOVERNMENT AND FOREIGN POLICY. Turkey has a republican form of government, based on a constitution drafted in 1960 and 1961 largely under the supervision of army officers. The core of the government is a bicameral legislature. The upper house, or Senate, which is fairly powerful, contains some members who are popularly elected and others who are appointed by the president. The lower house, or Chamber of Representatives, is popularly elected with proportional representation. The titular executive chief is the president, who is elected by the two legislative houses; he does have the power to select the premier, who must also receive the approval of the legislature. The judiciary is selected independently. The Communist Party is banned. The Turkish army, which is recruited by conscription, is large but not well equipped. Since World War II the chief international dispute of Turkey has been with the USSR, whose government demanded that the Turks surrender territory to it from northeastern Turkey. This the Turks refused to do, and, like the Greeks, they received help from the United States under the Truman Doctrine. Today the main source of tension between the two governments is Turkish control of the Dardanelles, which blocks Soviet warships from the Mediterranean. Turkey is a member of the United Nations, NATO, and CENTO.

THE NEUTRALIST STATES

The neutralist states of Eastern Europe are Finland and Yugoslavia. These two countries are neutralist in different senses, and for different reasons. Finland is clearly more sympathetic toward the United States and the countries of Western Europe than toward the USSR and its satellites. Yugoslavia, by contrast, leans toward the Soviet Bloc. Finland is neutralist because it is forced to be, owing to the proximity of the USSR and the controls the Soviet government can exercise over it. Yugoslavia is neutralist because its leader, Marshal Tito, wants it to be.

Finland. During its short life of a little more than 40 years, Finland has received attention in America principally because of its efforts to pay its war debts in the 1930's and because of the strong resistance it offered to Soviet attack in 1939.

POPULATION, GEOGRAPHY, AND ECONOMIC LIFE. The population of Finland in 1960 was about 4,500,000. The population is chiefly rural; the one large city is Helsinki (450,000). The majority of the people are

of Nordic and East Baltic stock, but they speak a tongue distantly related to Hungarian. Most of the people are Lutheran. The country is
generally flat or somewhat rolling, with no important elevations. The
climate is rather cold. Finland does not have many important mineral
beds; its significant nickel deposits were taken away from it after the
Russo-Finnish War of 1939–40. Its greatest resources are its forests,
which cover most of the country. Despite the climate, Finnish agriculture produces grains and potatoes. Since the end of World War II the
Finns have erected many factories to make the goods needed to pay
reparations to the USSR. The reparations were all paid during the
1950's, but the Finns continued to fabricate goods in these plants since
they were up-to-date and their building had consumed much capital.
The chief market for these goods is the USSR; hence the USSR can
wield considerable influence over Finnish foreign policy by simply refusing to buy Finnish industrial products. However, the majority of
Finnish export trade is with Western Europe and the United States, and
the percentage of this trade is growing. Thus the USSR is losing its
ability to injure the Finnish economy.

GOVERNMENT AND FOREIGN POLICY. Finland is a parliamentary republic. The president, who has few powers, is chosen by an electoral
college. The real executive is the prime minister and the cabinet. The
legislature is unicameral and is elected according to proportional representation. The Communist Party is quite strong; in the elections of
1958 it won more seats than any other party, but it was still far from a
majority. In the elections of 1962, however, the Agrarian Party won the
largest number of seats, and the broad anti-Communist trend of the
voting was considered a rebuke to the USSR for Khrushchev's recent
interference in Finnish concerns. Generally the Communists are allotted
very little part in the execution of policy. In the main the Finns enjoy
political freedoms comparable to those in West European countries. The
Finnish armed forces, which are recruited by conscription, are not very
strong, for they are limited by the peace treaty of 1947. Sharing a long
common frontier with the Soviet Union and being remote from any possible strong defender, Finland is constantly exposed to the possibility of
Soviet armed invasion despite a treaty of friendship with the Soviet government. Thus, despite their evident repugnance for the USSR, going
back to a century of Russian domination, the Finns have been compelled
to maintain a neutralist foreign policy. This policy was threatened in
1961, when Khrushchev urged the Finns to sign a mutual-defense treaty
with the USSR as a "protection" against the alleged aggressiveness of
West Germany. Shortly afterward, however, Khrushchev withdrew the

proposal. Finland is a member of the United Nations but as of 1961 had no military allies.

Yugoslavia. Since 1948 the government of Yugoslavia has been conducting a neutralist foreign policy, which distinguishes it from all other Communist regimes.

POPULATION AND GEOGRAPHY. The population of Yugoslavia in 1961 was about 18,500,000. This population is chiefly rural; the principal city and capital is Belgrade (700,000), and the only other large city is Zagreb (450,000). The bulk of the people consist of three Slavic nations —the Serbs, Croats, and Slovenes. Other nationalities include Germans, Hungarians, and Romanians. Much of the country is very rugged, but an important fraction of the land, especially in the valley of the Danube, is fertile. The country has a lengthy coastline on the Adriatic; but most of the good harbors, such as Split and Kotor, have small trading areas, since the mountains lie very close to the sea. This situation explains Yugoslav interest in Fiume—now Yugoslav and called Rijeka—and Trieste—now Italian—both of which have considerable trading areas.

ECONOMIC LIFE. Immediately after World War II, when Yugoslavia was a Soviet satellite, Marshal Tito introduced a rigid, government-planned economy similar to that of the USSR. Later, after Yugoslavia had been expelled from the Cominform, and when peasant resistance and obvious inefficiencies had made some sectors of this program undesirable or unworkable, the government relaxed its controls and modified its plans. Yugoslavia is fairly rich in mineral resources, which at least until recent years have not been exploited very much. It is a major producer of copper and also yields coal, iron, bauxite, and chromite. It has quite valuable forests. Agriculture today, after some experiments with collectivization, is carried on chiefly by peasants owning small farms. The principal crops are grains, fruits, tobacco, and livestock. Government officials have striven to increase industrial output, but it is still not very large; leading industries include some metallurgical works, food processing, and oil refining. The main handicap for the Yugoslav economy appears to be the dearth of good internal transport, since railroad lines and connections are few and poor.

GOVERNMENT. The government of Yugoslavia is officially a federal republic. In the central government, as in the Soviet-Bloc countries, real authority is in the hands of the Communist Party chief, Marshal Tito. Tito is also president, through election by the legislature. The Yugoslav legislature is bicameral, one house representing national groups and the other representing economic groups. The federal structure embraces six "autonomous" republics: Serbia, Croatia, Slovenia, Montenegro,

Macedonia, and Bosnia-Herzegovina. The governments in these republics, too, are dominated by the Yugoslav Communist Party. Political freedoms are denied or at least drastically limited.

INTERNATIONAL STATUS AND FOREIGN POLICY. Yugoslavia occupies a unique international status: it is the only considerable country (see Albania) with a government and economy termed "Communist" that refuses to be subordinate to the USSR and has established its independence of Soviet controls. This situation resulted from a combination of factors. Perhaps most important, Yugoslavia is the only Eastern European country in which the Communist regime was established by natives instead of by the USSR; that is, Tito himself was the head of the army of Yugoslav Communists that erected the present Yugoslav government. Hence, unlike the government in any Soviet-Bloc country save perhaps Poland, the Yugoslav Communist regime has considerable popular backing. Also, Yugoslavia is cut off from the USSR by land, is easily aided from the West, and cannot be easily reached by sea. As a result, it would be difficult for the Soviet Union to restore its control there. Since 1956 relations between Yugoslavia and the USSR have been friendly, yet in 1960 the Soviet government forbade the erection of a Yugoslav cultural center in the USSR. Since 1948 the Yugoslav government has received large amounts of financial gifts from the United States government. Yugoslavia does have some not very severe disputes with Bulgaria, Greece, and Austria; its long dispute with Italy over Trieste has apparently been settled with mutual satisfaction. Yugoslavia is a member of the United Nations, but it belongs to neither NATO nor the Warsaw Pact. It has a military alliance only with Greece and Turkey.

Review Questions

1. Among the satellites of the USSR in Eastern Europe, which state is most capable of conducting *by itself* an anti-Soviet policy and most likely to do so? What are the possibilities that the satellites might combine as an anti-Soviet coalition? Which state might lead such a coalition?

2. Describe the various ways in which the satellites aid the USSR and the various ways in which they are a hindrance to the USSR.

3. Rank the satellite countries in the order in which you think they might become the focus of a major dispute between the NATO powers and the USSR. Explain your ranking.

4. Compare the value of Greece and Turkey as members of NATO.

5. Distinguish between the neutralism of Finland and the neutralism of Yugoslavia, and offer reasons why the leaders in each country have adopted their present policies.

18 *COMMUNIST CHINA*

Communist China—officially the People's Republic of China—includes all of what is traditionally termed "China" that is on the mainland of Asia. Nationalist, or non-Communist, China comprises Formosa and a number of smaller islands off the China coast; it is dealt with in the next chapter.

POPULATION AND GEOGRAPHY

Communist China possesses the largest population of any country on earth, occupying an area somewhat larger than that of the United States.

Number and Location of the People. Although no real census of China has ever been taken, it appears today that the population of Communist China is approaching 700,000,000—about one-quarter that of the entire globe. This population is increasing rapidly, so that by the end of the century it may reach or exceed one billion. It is notable that whereas government chiefs in many other countries show concern or even alarm at great population rises in their areas, Chinese leaders so far seem content to allow this increase to go on. The people are concentrated in the southeast—in China proper—and in the northeast—in Manchuria; some parts of western China are almost uninhabited. The population is still predominantly rural. There are some large cities; Shanghai may have as many as 9,000,000 people, Peiping has more than 4,000,000, and there are at least eight other cities with more than 1,000,000 people. Still, these are not large in proportion to the total population of the country.

Other Traits of the People. The people racially and nationally are rather homogeneous, being of Mongolian stock. The small groups of non-Mongolian peoples do not create minority problems. There are many dialects in China; one of them, Mandarin, predominates. The govern-

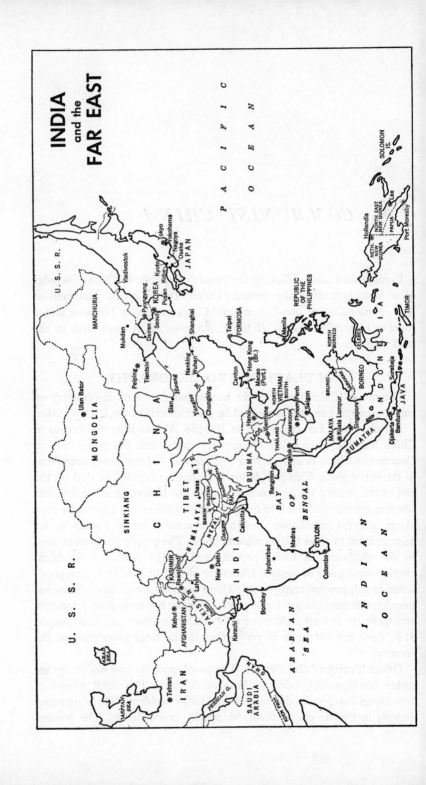

INDIA
and the
FAR EAST

ment is trying to impose Mandarin on the entire populace, and in 1956 introduced a thirty-letter, modified Roman alphabet in an attempt to reduce illiteracy from its present estimated level of 80 per cent. The peasants have traditionally made up the largest economic group in China; today an increasing number are being shifted to industry. The bureaucratic group, which has usually been large and occupied a high social position in China, under the Communists is more important than ever. Schooling has acquired new emphasis under the Communists, but Chinese rulers no longer permit the Christian mission schools that in the past filled many gaps in the tax-supported school system. Many Chinese belong to some religious group, such as the Buddhist, Confucianist, or Taoist. Confucianism has had profound effects upon traditional Chinese political and social institutions, yet Communist Party leaders have avoided attacking it directly; however, they have attacked it indirectly by their efforts to dissolve the institution of the family, which is central to Confucianist belief.

Geography. Communist China is a very large country; its area of about 3,750,000 square miles is exceeded only by those of the USSR and Canada. About three-fifths of this territory comprises China proper; the rest is included in the dependent regions of Kwangsi, Ningsia, Inner Mongolia, Sinkiang, and Tibet. Outer Mongolia is no longer a part of China. China proper is drained chiefly by three large rivers flowing to the east—the Hwang, Yangtze, and Si. Their valleys in their lower reaches are very fertile. In the southeastern part of China, near the coast, there are numerous mountains; a fairly high mountain range is the watershed between the Hwang and the Yangtze. In the north, Manchuria also contains very fertile plains. In the west the land rises into plateaus, and finally into mountains; the highest are in the southwest, in Tibet.

RESOURCES AND ECONOMIC LIFE

The national economy of Communist China is subject to more government control than that in any other country. All reliable evidence indicates that it has reduced the living standard of the individual Chinese and that it is accompanied by extremes of political and social regimentation.

The Government-Planned Economy. Like the Soviet Union, Communist China has a government-planned economy. Of course, it has been in effect a much shorter time—the first Chinese Five-Year Plan came into being in 1953. Moreover, this economy was launched in a country that was almost entirely agricultural—by contrast with the Soviet Union in 1917, which had a major industrial base. This factor underlies one

goal of the Communist Chinese leaders—to show the other nonindustrialized countries of the world that the Communist Chinese system is
the best. In any case, the Chinese have asserted that they are going to
take a "great leap forward" so as to industrialize with great speed. What
this amounts to is a denial of consumers' goods to the public so as to
provide capital as a basis for heavy industry. Implementation of this
policy has necessitated extraordinary controls over the Chinese people.

Resources. Communist China is a land of great, but often unex-
ploited, mineral resources. Manchuria in particular has the iron ore
and coal needed for heavy industry. Other parts of China contain yet
more coal, but not very much iron ore. Additional minerals include tungsten, antimony, tin, mercury, molybdenum, manganese, and copper. So
far, China has not shown many deposits of petroleum, but it does have
oil shale. Doubtless there are many sources of minerals that are still
undiscovered; at present it does seem that in order to become a very
large steel-producing country, China will have to import both iron ore
and manganese. Mining is very inefficient, and mineral output has been
much below the announced goals.

Agriculture. Agriculture today in Communist China is carried out
largely through huge farm communes that may include thousands of
people, tilling government-owned land. The communes also have a role
in national defense; each is intended to be self-sufficient in terms of
food, so as to preserve the lives of its members in case of nuclear war.
Agriculture in China is very intensive and in the past has yielded enormous crops; however, under the commune system the farms all together
have not grown their quotas. Partly for this reason, in 1961 the government started breaking up some of the communes and permitted the private ownership of some lands. The chief crops are grains, mainly wheat
in the north and rice in the south. Other important grains are barley,
millet, and kaoliang (a type of sorghum). The Chinese also grow such
foods as soy beans and sugar, as well as large quantities of tea. They
have such industrial crops as cotton and flax; silk has diminished in
importance. Farmers have usually had some poultry and a hog or two,
and the nomads of the arid, grassy western areas pasture a great deal
of livestock. China does have to import grains, notably rice from the
countries to the south. In 1960 and 1961 it was buying wheat and barley
from Canada and Australia. Nevertheless, famine in China is more often
caused by transportation failure than by crop failure.

Industry and Transportation. Although primarily agricultural,
China has for many years had a few rather well established industries—
especially domestic industry, involving such goods as textiles and proc-

essed foods, and some rather large-scale industries, such as cotton textiles. Also, after the Japanese seized Manchuria, they built steel mills there. When the Communists secured power, the government came into possession of all these facilities. Since that time, under its plans the government has striven to erect new industries, mostly heavy, in an effort to make Communist China a great manufacturing center. In some cases the workers were organized into urban communes. In general these efforts have not been very successful. Among other things, the Communist Chinese have erected some impressive plants that have not yet gone into operation either because of lack of raw or semifinished materials or because of shortages of skilled workmen. In an attempt to increase steel output the government encouraged hosts of families to erect "back-yard" blast furnaces and steel mills. Almost all of the metal so produced was of such poor quality as to be useless, and the government discarded the program. As of 1961, the government has had to make drastic downward revisions of its manufacturing quotas. Although Communist China has increased its manufacturing output, it is still far from being a great industrial power. The chief means of transportation in Communist China are human beings, pack animals, and animals drawing primitive carts over unpaved roads and trails. Since they came to power, the Communist Chinese have worked toward the extension of their railroad and highway systems. Still, there are very few highway vehicles in Communist China. The Hwang is generally not navigable, but the Yangtze is a very important avenue for freight. Furthermore, coastal waters carry thousands of small ships. Nevertheless, the significant point is that in the still very localized Chinese economy there is comparatively little long-distance traffic.

Foreign Trade. Foreign trade is not very important for the mass of the Chinese people, and for that reason a blockade of China would not have very much economic effect. Furthermore, the foreign trade of Communist China is almost entirely with the countries of the Soviet Bloc and is carried by rail. In the late 1950's the Communist Chinese began putting certain manufactured goods on the world market. Their aim in doing so, however, was almost entirely political; that is, these goods were offered at very low prices with the goal of damaging the industries of other countries, especially those of Japan. Also, in 1960 and 1961, when government officials were admitting the existence of severe famine conditions, they nevertheless signed an agreement with Cuba obligating them to sell the Castro government thousands of tons of rice. In fact, at least some of the wheat it was buying at this time from Canada was shipped directly to Albania. In the past its exports have included some foodstuffs of which it produced a surplus, such as beans and tea, and some textiles; it has imported other foodstuffs, raw materials and semifinished goods for its industries, and finished goods such as machinery.

GOVERNMENT

Although there is a camouflage of a parliamentary government in Communist China, as in the Soviet Union, actual political power resides in the leaders of the Chinese Communist Party.

The Communist Party. The Communist Party is the actual government of Communist China and is probably more pre-eminent there in relation to the formal structure of the government than it is in the Soviet Union. The Communist Party of China has several million members, but it is not so large in proportion to population as is that of the USSR. The head of the Chinese Communist Party is Mao Tse-tung, who, like Joseph Stalin for some years, is dictator of his country without occupying any government post. (He was, however, Chairman of the People's Republic until 1959.) The Chinese Communist Party was much more experienced and strong when it occupied all of the mainland than the Russian Communist Party when it seized power. Since 1949 the Chinese Communists have assured and strengthened their control by such means as the ruthless extermination of their opponents; Mao himself has admitted that several million anti-Communist Chinese have been killed. The Party also subjects the populace to extraordinary amounts of propaganda. Mao argues that he has devised a new interpretation and application of Marxism, for use in nonindustrial countries. Furthermore, since Stalin's death, he has occasionally given indications of a belief that he, and not the master of the Kremlin, should be viewed as the leader of world communism. An outstanding feature of this belief is that the Party should be not just a civilian political organization but an army that is skilled in the use of not only military weapons but also every type of psychological persuasion. These tactics have had considerable success when employed in the small countries formed out of Indochina.

Government Structure. The structure of the Communist Chinese government is somewhat like that of the Soviet Union at the national level; it also makes a pretense of being federal. Officially the chief organ of the national government is the National People's Congress, a unicameral legislative body of 1,027 members (in 1962) popularly elected for four-year terms. This body has no real power; it meets for a few days every year to give formal approval to proposed laws submitted to it. There is a titular executive, the Chairman of the People's Republic of China, elected by the Congress. The only government organ with any real power is the State Council, a sort of cabinet comprising the heads of the various administrative offices. Its members are appointed by the Chairman of the Republic. It is composed entirely of leading Communists; in 1961 the principal figure in the State Council, the premier, was Chou En-lai, one of the half dozen most important Party members. Local governments have legislative and executive officials who are directly or indirectly chosen by the voters. They are officially as well as actually subordinate to the national government. The constitution of the People's Republic guarantees a variety of freedoms, but they do not really exist. This fact was made clear in the late 1950's. First, Mao proclaimed official toleration of dissenting opinions; but, when the quantity of dissent far surpassed official expectations, many individuals were sentenced to death or to long prison terms, and dissent was forbidden. Nevertheless, this regime has ended the power of local war lords and brought China its first genuine political unity.

POWER AND STRATEGIC SITUATION

Communist China can supply millions of men for its armed forces, but must still rely upon the USSR for a large part of its armaments. China possesses a fortunate geographic situation for the conduct of either an aggressive or a defensive foreign policy.

Armed Forces. Communist China has the second-largest army in the world, containing 3,000,000 men, recruited by conscription. Potentially, it could summon 50,000,000 to the colors. In the Korean War these soldiers proved themselves tough and able. Communist Chinese military leaders do not hesitate to expend them in huge numbers; their casualties in Korea were several times as large as those of the UN forces, but their morale remained high. Communist China also has a large air force and a modest naval fleet that apparently includes some submarines. The greatest weakness of the Communist Chinese armed forces is the lack of an armament industry to supply them; they must depend on the USSR for most of their weapons, especially their aircraft.

Geographic Situation. Communist China occupies what is in many ways a very favorable geographic situation for implementing its foreign policy. In the first place, the country is so large that its conquest, even with modern equipment, would be very difficult against determined military resistance. In the second place, it borders directly on certain countries, notably Vietnam, Laos, Thailand, and Burma, that are very attractive to it. In the third place, it has a long common border with its chief ally, the USSR, so that it can readily secure needed goods. In the fourth place, its populous area and manufacturing heart are separated by the mountains of Tibet from India and Pakistan—two potentially hostile Asiatic countries that together nearly equal it in manpower. In the fifth place, its coastline facilitates attack on Japan, provided that China controls the East China Sea, yet does not permit ready invasion by an enemy even if he controls that sea. Thus Communist China is in an excellent geographic position both defensively and offensively.

FOREIGN POLICY

Two main factors underlie the foreign policy of Communist China. First, it is a country that has just thrown off a quasi-colonial status and assumed, for the first time in many years, the standing of a fully independent country, with the brash ambitions that typify most newly emerged sovereignties. Second, China is a country with a centuries-old tradition of conquest and domination in the Far East. It has had this tradition interrupted for several decades and has now fallen under the control of a group whose ideology demands world-wide power and who have clearly indicated their plan to resume the Chinese tradition. The main elements in Communist Chinese foreign policy are:

1. Maintaining its alliance with the USSR, whose manufactured goods are essential for the conduct of any aggressive foreign policy by Communist China.

2. Conquering Formosa, seat of the Nationalist Chinese regime, not simply to regain formerly Chinese territory but also to destroy the threat of the Nationalist Chinese and to break United States Pacific defense lines.

3. Extending Communist Chinese influence into Southeast Asia, both by supporting local Communist movements and by winning the support of the millions of "overseas Chinese" in these countries who often hold positions of importance there.

4. Unifying North and South Korea under a single Communist regime, again to penetrate United States defenses.

5. Extending its influence to Europe, as it has already begun to do by having an observer present at the signing of the Warsaw Pact, by sending Chou En-lai as an "adviser" to the Eastern European countries, and by apparently acquiring a satellite in Albania.

6. Destroying the power of Japan in the Far East, at present by the commercial device of underpricing Japanese goods in Asiatic markets.

7. Helping foment hostility to the United States in Latin America, as it has done by sending "advisers" to the Castro regime in Cuba and

distributing propaganda materials among Latin American Communist Parties.

8. Securing world "respectability" through diplomatic recognition by the United States government, and supplanting Nationalist China in the United Nations.

Review Questions

1. Compare the structure of the government and the organization of the national economy in Communist China with those in the Soviet Union.

2. Describe the nature and purposes of Communist Chinese foreign trade. What might be the results if the United States government removed all barriers to trade with Communist China?

3. Compare the foreign policy of Communist China with the foreign policy of China under the Kuomintang in about 1930. If Chiang Kai-shek regained control of mainland China, what kind of foreign policy might he conduct?

4. Taking all the elements of national power into consideration, how great a role in world politics can the Communist Chinese government really claim?

19 JAPAN, SOUTH KOREA, AND NATIONALIST CHINA

Japan, South Korea, and Nationalist China are interrelated inasmuch as all are significant elements in the United States Far Eastern defenses against Communist China and the USSR. At the same time, there are marked differences among these three states. For one thing, the governments of South Korea and of Nationalist China make sweeping claims to dominion over other areas and conduct aggressive foreign policies in efforts to secure these areas. The government of Japan, by contrast, at least currently makes no claims of ownership on any external regions and wages a rather passive foreign policy. Also, Japan is a highly industrialized power. Nationalist China, on the other hand, even in control of the Chinese mainland would still be a mainly agricultural country with aspirations to the status of a great power; and South Korea, even if united with North Korea, would still be a secondary country that had just emerged from the status of a colony. Furthermore, these countries have had serious conflicts with one another. In recent times, for instance, the Japanese held South Korea as a colony and occupied large parts of China that were then under the Nationalist Chinese government. Thus these countries have some clashing goals and traditions, but they are likely to remain subordinated as long as the countries share a common enmity toward the Soviet Union and Communist China, and feel similarly threatened by them. (See map, p. 210.)

JAPAN

Japan is the industrial and commercial heart of the Far East and, for the time being, the pivot of American foreign policy in the whole area.

Population. The population of Japan in 1960 was about 93,600,000 —a little more than half that of the United States. Japan is the fifth most populous country in the world and one of the most densely populated.

This population until recently was increasing at a fast pace, because of both a high birth rate and a low death rate. In the past few years, however, the Japanese government has actively promoted birth control. An important part, but a minority, of the population of Japan is rural. At the same time there are such cities as Tokyo, whose population exceeds 9,000,000 and which is the largest city in the world; Osaka, with more than 3,000,000 people; and Kobe, Kyoto, Nagoya, and Yokohama, each with more than 1,000,000. The people racially and nationally are rather homogeneous, being of mixed Malay-Manchu-Mongol stock. There is one important national minority group, the Koreans. There are no outstanding regional linguistic variations among the Japanese. The growth of Japanese industry and the rise in Japanese personal incomes have brought a heightened number of people from agriculture into industrial, commercial, and service professions and trades. The one-time rigid class system has at least legally been abolished, and many restrictions once imposed upon women have been outlawed. Japan has an extensive tax-supported school system and almost no illiteracy. Its chief religions are Buddhism and Shinto.

Geography. Japan is a comparatively small country. It now comprises four main islands—Hokkaido, Honshu, Shikoku, and Kyushu—and many smaller islands. Honshu is by far the largest and contains the most people and the principal cities. Japan is very mountainous, but on Honshu there are several important although small plains. There are no large rivers. The coast facing the Pacific is much more indented than that facing the Sea of Japan and has most of the chief harbors. The weather varies considerably from north to south, but in general it is marked by hot summers and cold winters; rainfall is copious.

Economic Life. The economic life of Japan is based chiefly on a high concentration of industry, both light and heavy, producing great quantities of goods for export purposes and being able to survive only through imports of essential raw materials.

NATURAL RESOURCES. Japan contains many natural resources; but they are in small quantities, especially by comparison with the size of its industrial plant. Japan does produce considerable amounts of coal, fluorspar, copper, chrome, manganese, sulfur, graphite, pyrites, and iodine. It must import most of its iron, bauxite, zinc, tin, lead, phosphates, and petroleum; and all its mercury, platinum, antimony, tungsten, and nickel. Also, its coal is of poor quality for use in iron- and steel-making, a fact contributing to Japanese interest in exploiting Alaskan coal fields. Finally, Japan is fairly well forested but still imports timber.

AGRICULTURE. Since only about one-sixth to one-fifth of the Japanese land area is suited to cultivation, Japanese agriculture is very intensive. Japan is more nearly self-sufficient in food than the United Kingdom. Farms are small, and many are tilled by tenants. The principal crop is rice, but the Japanese still have to import some to satisfy their needs. They raise other grains, potatoes, some vegetables, a variety of fruits, tea, and tobacco. The shortage of land makes it difficult to pasture livestock, but the protein content of Japanese diets is increased by huge quantities of fish.

INDUSTRY AND TRANSPORTATION. At the beginning of World War II, Japan was already a highly industrialized country; since the end of the war, in spite of wartime losses, Japanese industry has been producing at a far higher level than ever before. The first important Japanese industries were founded by the government, then sold to nongovernmental individuals and groups. At first, cotton and silk textiles were the chief commodities. By the 1930's, however, especially under the stimulus of military demands, the Japanese had begun erecting a good deal of heavy industry. Today Japanese steel output has surpassed that of France and ranks fifth in the world. The Japanese lead the world in the production of ocean-going ships. They also produce railroad and electronic equipment, cameras, office machinery, and automobiles. One other significant feature of industry in Japan is that much of it comprises branch factories established by manufacturers in the United States who want, among other things, to employ less-costly Japanese labor, to avoid Japanese tariffs, and to be close to the market for the goods. For transportation, Japan has an excellent railroad system, mainly owned by the government and to a great extent electrified. Automobiles and trucks have gained importance since 1945. Coastal waters furnish another main avenue for freight traffic.

FOREIGN TRADE. Foreign trade has a position in the Japanese economy much like that it has traditionally held in the British economy. That is, the Japanese import mostly raw and semifinished materials and export mostly finished goods. The chief goods for export are textiles, but the Japanese have been increasing the proportion of their machinery exports. They also ship large quantities of processed fish. Since 1945 the Japanese have met growing difficulties in their sale of goods to both Southeast Asia and the United States, two areas with which they customarily have had a large trade. The difficulties in Southeast Asia have arisen from the competition of the Communist Chinese, who for political reasons are trying to drive the Japanese from these markets. The difficulties in the United States have arisen from the low prices of Japanese goods, whose quality now rivals or even surpasses that of goods made in the United States. The United States government has hesitated to levy protective tariffs on imports from Japan, lest such an act alienate Japanese leaders. However, because of many complaints from American manufacturers the Japanese have voluntarily agreed to limit their exports to the United States, especially of cotton goods and canned tuna. The Japanese by 1958 had the fifth largest merchant fleet in the world, plying even the St. Lawrence Seaway to Chicago; thus they are partly compensated for their unfavorable balance of trade by their income from shipping fees.

Government. The national government of Japan is a limited hereditary monarchy. The titular executive is the emperor. The chief organ of the government is the Diet, a bicameral legislature composed of a House of Councilors and a House of Representatives. Each house is elected by universal adult suffrage; the members of each are apportioned according to population. The actual chief executive is the premier, who is generally the leader of the majority party and who, as in a typical parliamentary government, is responsible to the legislature. Japan today has a two-party system, and a large percentage of the potential electorate usually votes. Japan has a unitary government similar to that of France. The freedoms of speech and of the press are guaranteed by the government and are widely exercised, so that private citizens and organizations can have, and doubtless do have, influence over the making of foreign policy.

Power and Strategic Situation. Japan today possesses very little immediate military power. In fact, its present constitution denies the government the power to wage war, and there is a powerful, widespread antiwar sentiment in Japan. Nevertheless, an act of the Diet in 1954 re-established the Japanese armed forces. Even so, in terms of its population and economic structure, Japan has a very small army, navy, and air force. On the other hand, the strong and efficient Japanese industrial plant could furnish large quantities of war equipment. The most important elements in the defense of Japan today are its alliance with the United States and the huge United States military base on Okinawa just a few hundred miles southwest of Japan. Japan is well situated geographically for the conduct of both offense and defense— with the important proviso that the Japanese, or their backers, control the sea and air about Japan. From their island center the Japanese can readily launch attacks upon the mainland of Asia, as they have done in the past. Furthermore, in the first years of World War II they were able to extend their power far to the east in the Pacific by establishing bases on the many islands that are not far from Japan. Finally, so far as the defense of Japan proper is concerned, it should be remembered that although the Japanese Navy and Air Force had been practically destroyed and the Japanese had been cut off from most of their sources of supply, Allied military commanders anticipated hundreds of thousands of casualties for their troops in an invasion of Japan.

Foreign Policy. The foreign policy of Japan today is rather passive. It is concerned mainly with defending Japan from possible attack by either the Soviet Union or Communist China. The Japanese in this respect are not deviating very far from their policy before 1941, since they have for many years looked upon the USSR as a main competitor in the Far East, and China as the country that would be the prey. The most important change is the aggressiveness the new Communist Chinese regime is showing, with a long-term threat of an invasion of Japan. The Japanese policy of relative dependence on the United States appears certain to change as the Japanese become stronger economically and as they recover from the shock of defeat. A proud, able, and ambitious people such as the Japanese are not apt to content themselves for long with a secondary role, especially when they see their one-time allies, the West Germans, winning economic supremacy in Western Europe. Some leaders in Japan are already counseling a more autonomous foreign policy, at least to the extent of widening commercial relations with Communist China. Such proposals will not fail to gain backing from some Japanese business interests.

SOUTH KOREA

South Korea is the southern half of a peninsula that for centuries was a buffer state among the clashing imperial drives of China, Russia, and Japan. South Korea is an independent country, but in effect it is a ward of the United States.

Population and Geography. The population of South Korea in 1960 was about 25,000,000. The population is chiefly rural, but there are two cities that are quite large: Seoul, with 2,100,000; and Pusan, with 1,100,000. The Koreans are a homogeneous Mongolian people; their language is akin to Japanese, but their alphabet resembles that of India. In the past most Koreans have been farmers, especially in South Korea; today, however, growing numbers have entered industry, commerce, and the service trades and professions. Confucianism is the most common faith in South Korea, but there has been a good deal of Christian missionary activity. The country is extremely mountainous; much less than half is arable. It has a long and irregular coastline; its only land border is purely artificial—the 38th parallel of latitude, which the participants at the Potsdam Conference agreed would separate the Soviet and United States occupation zones. The rainfall is plentiful. Summers are hot, but in spite of the latitude—almost all of South Korea is south of San Francisco—winters may be bitterly cold.

Economic Life. Although all Korea has important deposits of certain minerals such as coal and iron, these are chiefly in North Korea. The economic life of South Korea is dominated by agriculture, carried out by intensive means on a multitude of small farms. The chief crop is rice, but Koreans plant other grains and beans as well. There is little livestock, since arable land is too valuable for use as pasture. Industry on a wide scale has come into being only since 1945; under the Japanese, it was concentrated in northern Korea, near the mines. Of course, for centuries there have been such domestic undertakings as the spinning and weaving of cotton. In recent years, plants have been erected for the commercial production of textiles, flour, glass, cement, and electrical equipment. There is also some shipbuilding. Under the Japanese, a considerable railway network was constructed, and this has been expanded. Highways have been improved, but there are few automobiles and trucks. Many of these accomplishments are due partly or entirely to financial aid from the United States government and the International Bank for Reconstruction and Development. Korean foreign trade is not very brisk; exports include tungsten and some foods, and imports include other foods, raw cotton, and manufactured goods. A considerable portion of Korean trade is with the United States.

Government. The government of South Korea, based on a constitution amended in 1960, is a parliamentary republic. Under the constitution adopted in 1948, the president, Syngman Rhee, exercised near-dictatorial powers. In 1960, however, Rhee's political opponents, aroused by apparent corruption in the presidential elections of that year, compelled him to leave office and flee to Hawaii. New elections were held, and the legislature, a unicameral body called the Assembly, elected John M. Chang premier. In 1961, however, Chang in turn was overthrown by a strongly anti-Communist military junta. This political instability appears to result not only from the Koreans' inexperience at self-government but also from the profound dissatisfaction of urban workers with Rhee's program and with the slowness of Chang's reforms.

Power and Foreign Policy. South Korea has a fairly large army, which has been trained and equipped by the United States. Geographically, South Korea is hard to defend. Its long coastline makes it apt for invasion, unless it or its allies command the surrounding waters; General MacArthur proved this by his invasion at Inchon, at a time when the North Koreans did not command the adjacent waters. Moreover, the 38th parallel offers no natural defense line; the nearest such border is a few miles to the north. The chief ally of South Korea is the United States; control of South Korea by either the Communist Chinese or the Soviet Union would break the United States Far Eastern defense line and pose an immediate threat to Japan. At the outset of the Korean War, the United States denied South Korea the help of another potential ally—the Nationalist Chinese; however, in case of another North Korean or Communist Chinese assault on South Korea, the United States government would probably allow the Nationalist Chinese to participate in the defense of South Korea. The foreign policy of South Korea is directed almost solely toward the annexation of North Korea. The South Korean government also works to assure continued support from the United States. Finally, under Rhee the South Korean government was very hostile to Japan, doubtless because of the years during which Korea was a colony of Japan and Rhee himself had to live in exile. Rhee's successors may be less inimical toward Japan.

NATIONALIST CHINA

Nationalist China, like South Korea, is fundamentally a ward of the United States. However, the Nationalist Chinese government leaders regard themselves as heirs to the centuries-old Chinese political tradition of national independence and Far Eastern predominance.

Population and Geography. The population of Nationalist China —that is, Formosa (Taiwan) and the neighboring islands—in 1960 was about 10,500,000. The population is chiefly rural, but the capital city, Taipeh, has about 900,000 inhabitants. The population is mainly Chinese, large numbers of whom are not natives but refugees from the mainland; the chief tongues consequently are also Chinese. Formosa consists in part of a long, high mountain range extending from north to south. On the west there is a wide, fertile lowland. Rainfall is copious, and the climate on the western plain is subtropical.

Economic Life. Formosa has some mineral wealth, such as coal, copper, and sulfur. Its agriculture is very productive, since Formosa can yield two harvests annually, and Formosans have worked successfully to raise output. Its chief crop is rice; Formosan farms also raise tea, sugar, and sweet potatoes. There is considerable industry, notably sugar refining but also cotton textiles, chemicals, and drugs. The government encourages investment by foreigners. While the Japanese held Formosa as a colony, they built a considerable railroad mileage. Recently, a number of highways have been constructed, chiefly for military purposes. The overseas trade of Formosa, especially with Japan, is fairly significant. It exports mainly sugar and rice, and imports manufactured goods.

Government. The government of Nationalist China today is primarily that of a military base under siege, tempered by a few constitutional and legal restrictions. Officially Nationalist China is a republic, functioning under a constitution that was promulgated for all China in 1947. Political authority supposedly stems from the voters, but actually the Kuomintang, still headed by Chiang Kai-shek, is still supreme. Chiang is aging, and the fate of the government on his departure is hard to predict. One point does seem incontestable: the Nationalist Chinese government on Formosa is much more efficient, upright, and tolerant than it was on the mainland when the Communists swept over China.

Power and Foreign Policy. Like that of South Korea, much of the military power of Nationalist China results from assistance given by the United States government. Under a conscription law, Nationalist China has an army of about 500,000, which is extremely large in proportion to its population and its national income. Most of the weapons for this army come from the United States. Nationalist China also has a navy and an air force, similarly equipped by the United States. The Nationalist Chinese Navy is supported by major units of the United States fleet. Nationalist Chinese foreign policy is directed almost solely to the reconquest of mainland China. Even though the Nationalist Chinese have some supporters on the mainland, it is now generally agreed that the achievement of Chiang's purposes would require United States backing—unless the Communist Chinese government should be near collapse. However, unless this occurs there seems no likelihood that Chiang would get United States backing for an invasion of China proper.

Review Questions

1. In what way is the national power of Japan greater today than it was in 1941, and in what way is it less?

2. What is the role of foreign trade in the Japanese national economy? How does it affect the status of Japan in world politics?

3. For what reasons might it be said that the national economies of both South Korea and Nationalist China are at least partly "artificial"?

4. In your opinion, is it more important to the United States that South Korea

be anti-Communist, or to the Soviet Union that North Korea be Communist?
Explain your conclusion.

5. Nationalist China not only is a "ward" of the United States today but also
has been a "ward" of the United States for many years. Why should this be so,
considering, among other things, their geographic separation and their cultural and
ideological differences?

20 SOUTH AND SOUTHEAST ASIA

South and Southeast Asia include, for the purposes of this text, all the countries from Pakistan and Afghanistan to Indonesia and the Philippines. From their location these countries have a sort of geographic and climatic unity. They also have a certain strategic unity, inasmuch as all are actual or potential victims of Chinese Communist aggression. Perhaps their most important bond lies in the fact that all, with the single exception of Thailand, have recently been colonial possessions; all have, therefore, just gained national independence and have similar political, economic, social, and military weaknesses. All of these countries are technologically more or less backward, and the people in a number of them are very conservative of traditional ways for doing things. It is significant that despite their recent colonial status the peoples of all these countries save the Republic of the Philippines had achieved a high level of civilization centuries before Europeans began establishing colonies in this area during the sixteenth century. There are numerous important differences among these countries. This chapter gives some attention to most of them. (See map, p. 210).

INDIA

Because of its population, its area, its expanding industry, and the respect that Prime Minister Jawaharlal Nehru commands in many other countries, India is by far the most important country of South and Southeast Asia.

Population. The population of India in 1960 was about 440,000,000, more than double that of the United States; India is the second most populous country in the world. This population is increasing very rapidly, inasmuch as the birth rate is high and the death rate is being

227

reduced. The government is very concerned about the problems raised by a speedy increase in the population and maintains numerous centers for the dissemination of birth-control information. Great numbers of the people are rural, living in the estimated 500,000 villages that dot the countryside. Yet there are some large cities. According to official statistics, both Calcutta and Bombay have 3,000,000 inhabitants, and New Delhi has 2,000,000; two other cities have more than 1,000,000 each. These figures almost certainly are too low; Calcutta may have as many as 9,000,000. It is important to realize that, unlike the situation in technologically advanced countries, this growth in the cities in India is not necessarily a sign of industrial development; millions of city-dwellers in India are simply people who have left their farms in hopes of finding work in a city, and a large percentage are unemployed. The people of India stem mainly from the Aryan race, mixed with aboriginal inhabitants. There are several major languages, and hundreds of dialects; the chief, and official, tongue is Hindi, and English is the second tongue. The hereditary caste system of India has been legally abolished. The new government of India has begun establishing a far-flung tax-supported school system, but most adults are illiterate. The religion of most Indians is Hindu. There are also about 30,000,000 Moslems, although the boundaries of India were supposedly drawn to exclude them. Besides these there are several million Christians and Sikhs. The Indian people in general are intensely religious and often confuse religious with political issues.

Geography. India occupies most of a huge subcontinent extending south from the land mass of Asia into the Indian Ocean. It can be divided into three large regions. Northernmost is the lofty range of the Himalayas, which divides the subcontinent from the rest of Asia. Farther south is the great river valley of the Ganges, which drains the southern slopes of the mountains, along with the lower reaches of the Brahmaputra, which drains the northern slopes. These valleys are by far the most densely settled parts of India. The third region, comprising mainly the triangle of land that projects into the ocean, is primarily a large, elevated tableland with a number of mountain ranges, along with coastal plains. The coastline provides very few natural harbors. The climate of India is varied. In the higher ranges of the northern mountains there is perpetual snow. On the other hand, the valleys are hot, with heavy rainfall; this condition also prevails in the coastal plains. The weather in the tableland is also hot, but rainfall is moderate or even scanty. India generally is dependent on monsoons, the winds that bring heavy summer rains from the Indian Ocean.

Resources and Economic Life. India is an outstanding example
of a technologically backward country whose government is striving to
improve agriculture, industry, and transportation under a socialist
economy.

THE SOCIALIST ECONOMY. The government of India lays down plans
for the entire economy and owns a significant and growing fraction of
the productive facilities of the country. India thus ranks with Communist China in its importance as an area for demonstrating the efficacy of
one type of national economy. The success or failure of the socialist
economy in India may have a great impact upon leaders in other underdeveloped states that have not definitely sided with either the Communist or the non-Communist Bloc. The success of industrialization in
India under government planning has been mixed. It must be noted that,
as of 1961, about ninety per cent of industry was still in nongovernmental hands, although output and prices are set by law. Many of the
new nongovernmental undertakings have been successful; some of the
governmental ones have been also. Other governmental enterprises have
been failures. Furthermore, the economy has revealed a trend toward
"giantism" and is in some respects unbalanced; for instance, the capacity of its mills to produce steel is several times as great as the capacity of its other industries to consume steel.

RESOURCES. India possesses numerous important resources. It has
large and workable deposits of coal and iron ore. It also produces significant quantities of limestone, mica, silver, manganese, and tungsten.
However, it does not have much petroleum or good coking coal. Still,
India has sufficient resources for a major industrial country. The land
of the Ganges Valley and along the coasts is very fertile. About one-
fifth of India is forested.

AGRICULTURE. Agriculture is still the basis of the Indian economy. It
is practiced intensively, on a myriad of small farms many of which are
cultivated by tenants. Output per acre is low, and today the population
is increasing more rapidly than the food supply. There is an enormous
irrigation system that the government is planning to extend. The principal crops are grains, especially rice, wheat, and corn. Other important
farm products are coffee, tea, sugar cane, spices, cotton, jute, and lin-
seed. Despite a comparatively large total yield, there is still not enough
food for the people of India, so that some foodstuffs are imported.
Shortages result in part from the insufficiency of arable land and from
the employment of primitive tools and methods. Their religion also con-
demns most Indian people to a vegetarian diet so deficient in proteins
that many of them lack the energy to sow and harvest two crops annu-

ally, a practice for which India is excellently suited. Farming in India is to be contrasted with that in China and Japan, where the people labor under many of the same natural handicaps but usually raise enough food to eat comparatively well. The government of India is trying to increase farm output by encouraging the establishment of cooperative agricultural societies of various sorts.

INDUSTRY AND TRANSPORTATION. India has considerable industry, which is increasing at a fairly rapid pace. As in the typical underdeveloped country, there is a great deal of domestic industry, devoted mainly to textiles. At the same time, there is a very large commercial textile industry. India also has a rather important steel industry; the Tata works have for some time been the largest in Asia. Yet the steel output of India is still exceeded by that of many cities in the United States. Under government plans, India has acquired a variety of new industries, such as those devoted to machine tools and electronic equipment. Nevertheless, industrial growth is still dependent upon continued gifts of money from the United States government. Industry is favored in one major respect, at the expense of agriculture: intelligent young people are much readier to be educated as industrial technicians than as agricultural technicians, if only to live in a city instead of in a village. There is a considerable government-owned railroad network, although it is small in terms of the area of the country. There is also a considerable airline network, likewise government-owned. There is, however, relatively so little domestic commerce that means of freight transportation are not very important.

FOREIGN TRADE. The foreign trade of India is not very large, for the people in general do not have the means to buy imported goods and the industrial structure is comparatively so small that it does not produce much for export. Still, foreign trade is growing. India has more trade with the United States than with any other country. Its principal exports include textiles, tea, and manganese ore. Its imports include foodstuffs, raw cotton, metals, and machinery. Most Indian trade is carried in British ships and provides considerable income for the British.

Government. The government of India is essentially a parliamentary republic within the British Commonwealth. The legislative branch is the bicameral Parliament, composed of the House of the People, apportioned according to population, and the Council of States, apportioned among the fifteen states contained in India. Both are popularly elected. The titular executive is the president, indirectly chosen by an electoral college. The actual executive is the prime minister, who is the leader of the majority party in Parliament and who heads the cabinet.

The states are semiautonomous; the voters elect members of state legislatures, but the national government appoints governors as executives. The national constitution contains also the constitutions for the state governments. The power of making foreign policy is centered in the national government. Political matters have been colored not merely by the newness of the government—it was established in 1947—but also by the dominating personality of the prime minister, Nehru. Nehru has been quite impatient with opposition, and for a time restricted freedom of the press. Also, India has undergone some of the political limitations that seem always to accompany a socialist economy. The fact that most voters are illiterate complicates choosing government officials. The chief political organization is the Congress Party, which for many years led the movement for Indian self-rule. There is a fairly influential Communist Party, but it is strongly opposed by Nehru. It was elected to power in the state of Kerala but was later ousted by the national government; it is noteworthy that Kerala is in the most prosperous and most literate part of India.

Power and Military Forces. India is still only potentially a great power. Furthermore, unlike the leaders of Communist China, the leaders of India do not seem intent upon making India a great power at the expense of all other considerations. In terms of geography India is ill-situated for either offense or defense. The mountains to the north prevent any landward expansion of the Indian state; however, their configuration is such that they readily admit a determined invader—as Communist Chinese incursions show. Also, the Indian coastline is long and, in light of the poor land transportation facilities in India, hard to defend. India has no real allies; in fact, the present government of India seems to have concluded that it is preferable, and morally stronger, to have none. In relation to the population of the country, the Indian armed forces are very small; there is no conscription. It must be emphasized that the policy of the Indian government toward defense is greatly influenced by the precepts of Mohandas Gandhi, who stressed the virtues of "passive resistance" and whose ideas are closely followed by Prime Minister Nehru. At the same time, the whole country is so impoverished that it would be difficult for the Indian government to recruit a vigorous armed force of large size.

Foreign Policy. In its foreign policy the Indian government has been the outstanding supporter of the principle of neutralism. That is, the government of India has led those that have refused to make any distinction between the United States and the Soviet Union. The government of India has welcomed economic assistance from both the Communist and the non-Communist Blocs. Also, it has been among the chief supporters of the admission of Communist China to the United Nations; Indian delegates to the United Nations have often taken the Soviet side in votes. By 1959, however, it appeared that there was developing a slow shift in the attitude of Indian leaders, because for the first time there was Communist aggression on their doorstep. Communist Chinese armies had invaded Tibet, had forced the Tibetan head of state to take refuge in India, and had then started encroaching on land the Indians claimed as their own. Finally, in 1961, Nehru declared publicly that India must be ready to go to war in defense of its frontiers. Nevertheless, the foreign policy of India seems to aim at isolating India from external disputes and to count on the United Nations for the prevention of major warfare. In December, 1961, the Indian government captured three Portuguese enclaves by military invasion and incorporated them. Nehru rejected all criticism of this act. He has also been quite aggressive toward Pakistan regarding the disputed province of Kashmir.

PAKISTAN

Pakistan comprises two separate areas once included in British India that are populated chiefly by Moslems and that were united into a country outside Hindu India so as to stop religious warfare between the members of the two faiths.

Population and Geography. The population of Pakistan in 1961 was somewhat more than 93,800,000—roughly comparable with that of Japan. It is increasing fairly rapidly, and government officials have expressed some alarm at the rise. Most of the population is rural. The largest city is the former capital, Karachi, with about 1,100,000 people; the second is Lahore, with about 850,000. Many languages are spoken, but only Urdu, English, and Bengali are official. Most Pakistanis pursue agricultural occupations. There is a tax-supported school system, and schooling is compulsory; but most Pakistanis are illiterate. The principal religion is Islam; indeed, the chief reason for erecting the state of Pakistan was to provide a country for the Moslems of the Indian subcontinent, who for centuries had tense relations with the more numerous Hindu peoples. In order to include as many Moslems as possible, yet contain few Hindus, the boundary lines of Pakistan were drawn so that the country consists of two parts, West Pakistan and East Pakistan, separated by about 1,000 miles of India. West Pakistan is much the larger; it includes most of the valley of the Indus River extending down to the sea. Much of this region has comparatively little rainfall and is very hot. East Pakistan also reaches to the sea; it includes the delta of the Brahmaputra-Ganges. Its climate is hot and humid.

Economic Life. Pakistan has various important natural resources, such as petroleum, gas, coal, salt, sulfur, and antimony; however, it lacks iron ore. The basis of the national economy is farming. Pakistan produces more jute than any other country in the world. Its farmers also harvest large quantities of rice, wheat, cotton, sugar, and tea. A good part of the Indus Valley is irrigated. Much Pakistani industry is domestic. However, there are commercial cotton-spinning and weaving plants and flour mills, along with steelworks and shipbuilding. The government does not have a doctrinaire economic policy as does that of India, but it does encourage industry through such means as tax advanages. Most transportation is primitive, but there are some railroads and everal airlines.

Government. The government of Pakistan, which is based on a constitution promulgated in 1962, is a presidential federal republic. The chief executive is the president, who has wide powers including that of a suspensive veto over all acts of the legislature. The legislature is a unicameral body. Both the president and the legislature are indirectly elected by the voters; the actual elections are carried out by an 80,000-member electoral college whose members compose the "local democracy councils" that are the fundamental units of organized Pakistani political life. The new constitution bans political parties. The constitution also establishes two capital cities, several hundred miles apart, one as the seat of the executive and the other as the seat of the legislature.

Power and Foreign Policy. Pakistan today is not a very strong country. It is seriously handicapped by being divided into two parts; this is particularly true because the country that divides it, India, is one with which it has a major dispute. East Pakistan is especially vulnerable, since it is small and has no defensible borders; moreover, its fertile soil makes it very attractive. Unlike India, Pakistan has several allies, through its membership in SEATO and CENTO. It also has separate defense agreements with Turkey and the United States. Being Moslem, Pakistani leaders also have amicable relations with the Arab states. Pakistan has an army, navy, and air force; but they are small in relation to the population. The foreign policy of Pakistan is strongly anti-Communist. The Communist Chinese have threatened the Pakistan border just as they have threatened that of India, and the Pakistanis seem more belligerent in the face of this threat than the Indians are. The chief quarrel of the Pakistani government, however, is that with India over Kashmir, although the common threat of Communist China ap-

pears to be drawing the two governments together. In 1961 President
Mohammed Ayub Khan announced, perhaps to get into a stronger position in the Afro-Asian bloc, that Pakistan would vote for the admission
of Communist China to the United Nations.

AFGHANISTAN

Afghanistan according to the latest estimate has a population of approximately 13,000,000. Most of the population subsists on agriculture,
the chief form being sheepherding. The country is mostly quite mountainous, yet it is geographically strategic because of its position between
the Soviet Union and India. Its economy is very backward. It is the target of a concentrated Soviet drive; the Soviet Union is, among other
projects, building a railroad to the country and supplying it with technicians who are attempting to industrialize the national economy. Although the country is not hostile to the United States—its people gave
President Eisenhower a rousing welcome on his visit there in 1959—it
may slip into the Soviet orbit because of the lack of attention from the
anti-Soviet bloc.

BURMA

Like India and Pakistan, Burma is a former British colony that became independent after World War II. Burma, however, does not have
the potential power of either of the other two countries, nor the imperial tradition of India.

Population and Geography. Burma in 1960 had about 20,500,000
people. The country could support far more people. The population is
chiefly rural; the only large city is Rangoon, with 750,000 people. The
Burmese are mainly of Mongolian stock and are related to such other
nations as the Chinese. There are also thousands of Indians who serve
as laborers in the rice fields. The principal tongues are Burmese and
English. There is a tax-supported school system, and elementary education is compulsory; although the illiteracy rate is high, the Burmese
are the best-educated people in Southeast Asia. Most Burmese adhere
to the Buddhist faith. The northern part of the country is mountainous,
but in the south there are large fertile valleys. Since these valleys and
the intervening mountain ranges run along north-south axes, east-west
travel in Burma is very limited. The chief river, the Irrawaddy, is navigable upstream for almost 1,000 miles.

Economic Life. The Burmese national economy is principally agricultural, with rice as the main crop. National prosperity to a large degree rests on the overseas market for rice. Other crops include corn, cot-

ton, and tobacco. Burma is well forested, especially with teakwood, and is the largest exporter of that product in the world. Although it has such mineral resources as tin, silver, and petroleum, it has relatively little commercial industry. Considerable freight is transported by river and by coastal waters. The national economy is currently subject to government planning that aims at great increases in manufacturing, transportation, and power generation.

Government, Power, and Foreign Policy. According to its constitution, Burma is a republic that has now severed all ties with the British Commonwealth. The government is a typical parliamentary structure with a bicameral legislature, a figurehead president, and a prime minister and cabinet responsible to the legislature. Officially Burma is a federal union, but the component political units have little autonomy. The Burmese constitutional government was replaced in 1958 by a military dictatorship, by actual agreement with civilian government chiefs. The stimulus for this change was the presence of thousands of Chinese Communist guerrillas in the Burmese jungles and the fact that the government of Prime Minister U Nu received part of its support from pro-Communist organizations. Certainly factional struggles and agitation over corruption added to the confusion of this and subsequent strife. Anti-Communist military leaders arranged with U Nu that General Ne Win, who had won fame fighting Communist jungle bands, should become prime minister. In February, 1960, civilian government was restored when U Nu's party won a large parliamentary majority in an election. In 1962 Ne Win headed a group that ousted U Nu from power once more. Burma can be easily invaded from the north, as the Communist Chinese have shown, and is an important target for Communist China. Burma has few armed forces to resist an attack and evidently has no aggressive aims. The Burmese government has tended to cling to neutralism and has no military allies. It has often showed hostility toward India. Recent Communist Chinese moves against India may alter Burmese foreign policy.

CEYLON

Ceylon is another former British colony that secured national independence after World War II.

Population, Geography, and Economic Life. The population of Ceylon in 1959 was about 9,600,000. Most of the population is rural; the largest city is Colombo, with 425,000 inhabitants. The Ceylonese people are related to the aboriginal and Aryan stocks of India. There are two main language groups, the Sinhalese and the Tamil; the government order in 1957 that made Sinhalese, which is the more common, the official tongue instead of Tamil led to riots. There are also two main religious bodies, which follow linguistic lines: most Sinhalese are Buddhists, and most Tamils are Hindus. Geographically, Ceylon comprises an island off the southeast coast of India. Some of the island is mountainous, but there are important arable and fertile lowlands. The basis of the Ceylonese economy is agriculture; the island produces enough tea to export large quantities, and also grows such crops as rice, tobacco, spices, and rubber. There is some mining, especially for mica, precious stones, and graphite. Since 1945 the government has encouraged new enterprises, some of which have been completed and some of which are still under construction. They include flour mills, sugar refineries, brick and cement plants, textile factories, and steel works.

Government, Power, and Foreign Policy. Ceylon is a republic within the British Commonwealth. It has a bicameral legislature and a responsible prime minister and cabinet. It has a vigorous two-party system. Ceylon has some armed forces but is relatively powerless; its defense relies upon the control of the surrounding waters by friendly navies. The government of Ceylon has no allies, and it has kept a fairly neutralist position. Solomon Bandaranaike, head of the People's United Front, argued in 1956 that the extremes of both the United States and the USSR would disappear and that the "middle" neutralist path was best.

THAILAND

Thailand is the one country in this area with a continuous history of independence, a condition its diplomats achieved by astute bargaining with the French in Indochina to the east and the British in Burma and India to the west.

Population, Geography, and Economic Life. The population of Thailand in 1960 was about 25,500,000. Its agriculture could support a much greater population. Most of the people live in the countryside or in villages; there is one quite large city, Bangkok, with about 1,800,000 inhabitants. The Thais resemble both the Mongol and the Malay peoples; they speak a tongue akin to that of the Indochinese peoples. There are also considerable numbers of Chinese in Thailand, especially in commercial occupations. Despite a tax-supported school system and laws compelling schooling, many Thais are illiterate. Most of the people are Buddhists. The bulk of the country consists of lowlands and rolling hills, with an extensive river system and copious rainfall. There are magnificent forests of teakwood. Thailand has various mineral resources, such as coal, iron, tin, tungsten, manganese, and mercury. Nevertheless, most of the people are engaged in agriculture. Thai farms produce large exportable surpluses of rice, along with rubber, tobacco, cotton, spices, and coconuts. Most industry is domestic.

Government and Foreign Policy. Thailand is the only country of Southeast Asia with a long recent history of national independence. Its government is a limited monarchy. The king has but ceremonial powers; the actual executive is the prime minister, who with his cabinet is responsible to a unicameral legislature, the National Assembly, whose members are either elected or appointed. In 1958 this government was peaceably set aside in favor of a military dictatorship. The reasons for this change were the apparent threat of Communist agents, both native and Chinese, the paralyzing factionalism of politics, and the widespread corruption in the government. Thailand has some armed forces but can exercise little power. Unlike their neighbors, the Thais do not have a common frontier with Communist China, but they still must guard themselves against infiltration by Communist agents. The Thai government officially is not neutralist; for Thailand is a member of SEATO, and the leaders of the present government are anti-Communist. At the same time, Thai leaders describe their country as "neutral," in the special sense of a policy requiring that a country be ready and able to defend itself. For this reason, Thai leaders say, Thailand joined SEATO.

THE INDOCHINESE COUNTRIES

The Indochinese countries include Laos, Cambodia, and Vietnam, all carved from the one-time French colony of Indochina. In 1954 Vietnam was divided into a Communist northern zone and a non-Communist southern zone. Of the two, this section deals mainly with South Vietnam.

Population and Geography. According to recent estimates, the approximate populations of the three non-Communist Indochinese countries were: South Vietnam, 14,500,000; Laos, 3,000,000; Cambodia, 5,000,000. In all three the population is generally rural; the chief cities are Saigon, South Vietnam (1,800,000); Phnom-Penh, Cambodia (550,-000); and Vientiane, Laos (140,000). Most of the people are of Mongolian stock, more or less closely related to the Chinese. There are also a number of Chinese who have immigrated in comparatively recent times and who have a disproportionately large role in commercial affairs. The various nations speak distinctive but related tongues, similar to Chinese. Almost all the natives are employed in agriculture; the

Chinese dominate much of the commercial activities in these countries. Many of the people of these countries are illiterate, although efforts have been made to establish tax-supported school systems. The chief religious faith is Buddhism. Laos is quite mountainous, with some heavy forests. South Vietnam is also mountainous, although less so than Laos; it has a long, irregular coastline. The south comprises the delta of the Mekong River. Cambodia contains much fairly level land, since it occupies the lower valley of the lengthy Mekong.

Economic Life. The economies of these countries are fundamentally agricultural. The chief crop is rice, which is produced in exportable quantities. Other crops include tea, coffee, sugar cane, tobacco, cotton, and rubber. There are some mineral resources, such as iron, copper, tin, lead, and gold. (The economy of South Vietnam was weakened by the loss of North Vietnam, where there is coal.) There are also valuable timber stands. Most industries are concerned with food processing. Despite large infusions of monetary and technical aid from the United States, the industries, transportation systems, and power-generating facilities are all backward.

Government and Foreign Policy. All three countries have governments patterned after those of Western Europe. Cambodia and Laos are limited monarchies in which the kings have few powers and the true executives are prime ministers and cabinets responsible to unicameral legislatures. South Vietnam is a parliamentary republic, with a president and a responsible prime minister. These governments have all tended to be inefficient and corrupt. None of these countries has large armed forces, although all have received military aid from the United States. All three countries are constantly being infiltrated by Communists from Communist China, and these Communists have received some material aid from the USSR. By 1961 matters in Laos had degenerated to the point that three different groups—pro-Communist, anti-Communist, and neutralist—were contending for power. Finally, in the same year the United States, the USSR, the United Kingdom, and France agreed that there should be a cease-fire, so that negotiators could work toward ending the war. The United States government, which at first had backed the anti-Communist group, now seemed ready to settle for the neutralist group. Meanwhile the refusal of the British and the French governments to help the United States repulse the pro-Communist faction significantly weakened SEATO. At the same time, the United States government greatly increased its aid to South Vietnam. By 1962 the governments of both Laos and Cambodia were neutralist, but the regime of South Vietnam was anti-Soviet.

THE FEDERATION OF MALAYA

The Federation of Malaya is yet another one-time British colony that is independent today.

Population and Geography. The population of Malaya in 1960 was about 6,900,000. The majority of the people live in the countryside or in small towns. While Malaya was a British colony, the chief city and port was Singapore; however, it has been separated from Malaya and is itself autonomous. Now the capital and leading city is Kuala Lumpur (325,000); the main port is Penang (250,000). About half the people are Malays; the great majority of the remainder are Chinese. The Chinese have a dominant role in the commercial life of the country and furnish most of the industrial workers. There are considerable numbers of Indians. Malaya occupies the southern part of the Malay Peninsula together with the island of Penang off the western coast. Much of the country is mountainous and covered with jungles. Elsewhere there is arable, fertile soil. The climate is hot and humid, with a good deal of rain.

Economic Life. Malaya is the greatest producer of tin in the world. Other minerals include iron ore, bauxite, and manganese; much of the iron ore feeds Japanese mills. Malaya also grows large amounts of rubber. Still, most of the people derive their income from small farms, where they harvest rice, coconuts, sugar, and pepper. Since a great part of Malayan agriculture is commercial, the country is not self-sufficient in foods, but must depend on imports. There are some light industries, producing such goods as cement, bricks, tile, pottery, furniture, and soap.

Government and Foreign Policy. The national government of Malaya is a limited monarchy within the British Commonwealth. The titular monarch is called the Supreme Head of State. The actual executive is the prime minister, who with his cabinet is responsible to a bicameral national legislature. Malaya is a federation composed of nine Malay states, each with its ruler, and the two former British colonies of Penang and Malacca. The rulers of the Malay states elect the Supreme Head of State from their own number for a five-year term. After World War II, while Malaya was still a British colony, there was a protracted struggle between the British and the Communists, who were almost all Chinese. When Malaya achieved independence, its government had to assume the burden of this struggle, which ended only in 1960. By itself, Malaya has little power, but as a member of the British Commonwealth it can count on some support from the United Kingdom. Otherwise it has no allies, and its long coastline makes it rather easy to invade. The Malayan government now tends quite strongly toward anti-Communism.

INDONESIA

Indonesia comprises most of the former Dutch East Indies, which were overrun by Japan during World War II and then granted autonomy under the Netherlands crown after the war. In 1954 the two governments reached an agreement severing their union.

Population and Geography. Indonesia in 1960 had a population of about 92,600,000, roughly the same as that of Japan and Pakistan. Most of this population lives on the island of Java, which is very densely populated. The bulk of the population is rural; yet the capital, Djakarta, contains more than 3,300,000 inhabitants, and Surabaja about 1,300,000. The people are descended chiefly from two major stocks, the Malay and the Melanesian. As in some other Southeast Asian countries, the Chinese play an important part in commercial life. There is an extensive tax-supported school system, and illiteracy is being reduced. The great majority of the people are Moslems. Indonesia comprises a vast archipelago straddling the Equator. Out of the approximately 3,000 islands in the group, the four largest are Borneo (the Indonesian part of which is called West Borneo), Sumatra, Celebes, and Java. There are numerous mountains, some of them volcanic. Elsewhere are major areas of very fertile land. The climate is generally hot and rainy.

Economic Life. The economic life of Indonesia, which President Achmed Sukarno terms a "guided economy," operates under rather stringent government controls. Government planning has done little to raise the standard of living of the Indonesian people. Actually, the country is so fertile that rural dwellers need exert themselves very little in order to grow the food needed for survival. By contrast, the urban residents, who have become far more numerous since Indonesia won political independence, experience important economic shortages. To worsen matters, slums in the cities have greatly expanded. Furthermore, Indonesian money is inflated, and government policies have reduced investments from abroad. Indonesia is rich in certain natural resources, particularly oil, iron ore, tin, and coal. It has lesser deposits of copper, nickel, bauxite, and manganese. It is also a leading producer of natural rubber, although production has fallen under the "guided economy." There are vast hardwood forests. Indonesian farmers grow rice, corn, tea, coffee, sugar, spices, tobacco, quinine, and various other crops. Commercial farming is largely based on patterns introduced by Europeans. Indonesian leaders are striving to increase manufacturing and electric-power generating facilities. A considerable portion of whatever well-being Indonesians do enjoy is due to the government's seizure of the property (and income) of Dutch citizens and corporations.

Government. Indonesia is officially a unitary parliamentary republic. The president, although he is granted little authority constitutionally, actually has considerable powers. The prime minister, who with his cabinet is constitutionally the true chief executive, can be ousted by the president. The legislature is unicameral, with its membership apportioned according to population. Such political freedoms as those of speech and of the press are limited. There has been great political unrest in Indonesia for several years. President Sukarno appears to be supported by the mass of poorer voters and opposed by the educated and urban upper classes. He has shown little resistance to the strong Communist movement in Indonesia. In 1957 he dismissed an anti-Communist prime minister and became in effect dictator, in a personally dominated regime he called "guided democracy." Subsequently he was faced by a large-scale uprising of anti-Communist army officers, during which the Chinese Communists offered him their support. He did not accept the proffered aid but by 1959 seemed in control of the situation. In 1960 Sukarno dissolved the legislature, making the government an open dictatorship. Indonesia has received military equipment from both the United States and the Soviet Union.

Foreign Policy. Over the years, President Sukarno has been about as ardent a neutralist as Nehru. In 1959 he gravely offended Communist China by imposing limitations on the commercial privileges of the Chinese merchants in Indonesia, especially those outside the cities. This action was perhaps more economic than political; that is, its chief goal was probably to give Indonesian natives more economic power. In 1960 the Indonesian government received a loan of $250 million from the USSR; in return, Sukarno promised to maintain a policy of neutrality. Indonesia is not well situated for self-defense unless it controls the waters surrounding it; but it has only a small navy and no allies. Recent Communist Chinese advances on territory claimed by India may lead Sukarno to shift his policy to one of greater resistance to communism. Perhaps the chief immediate goal of Indonesian foreign policy is to secure the remaining Dutch possession in this area, West New Guinea. The Indonesians argue that this area, which they call West Irian, is a "natural" part of their country. The Dutch reply that the area and people have nothing in common with Indonesia. Soviet-Bloc governments back Indonesia in this dispute. The United States government in 1962 proposed that the area be turned over to Indonesia but that the administration of the area be supervised by UN officials for two years.

THE REPUBLIC OF THE PHILIPPINES

The Republic of the Philippines comprises a former colony of the United States whose people received their national independence in 1946.

Population and Geography. The population of the Philippines in 1960 was over 27,500,000. The bulk of the population is rural; yet Greater Manila contains more than 2,000,000 people. The majority of the people are of Malay descent, and they are primarily occupied with agriculture. A numerous Chinese colony has a major hand in trade, and a smaller but important Japanese group furnishes many skilled farm workers. As a colony of the United States, the Philippines acquired a considerable number of both tax-supported and church-supported schools; the school system has been even further extended since the achievement of national independence. There are three official tongues: Tagalog, English, and Spanish. Most of the people are Christian, owing to centuries of Spanish rule. The Philippines comprises an archipelago of over 7,000 islands, most of them tiny. Much of the country is mountainous; yet there are important arable lowlands. Rainfall ranges from adequate to excessive.

Economic Life. The country is rich in natural resources, which belong to the government. They include coal, petroleum, iron, chromite, manganese, copper, zinc, lead, gold, and silver. Over half the country is forested; some of the stands are worthless, but others contain excellent hardwood. Farmers raise important quantities of such crops as rice, corn, sugar cane, tropical fruits, coconuts, tobacco, and hemp. Yet plantation agriculture is so widespread that food must be imported. There is considerable domestic industry, but the government is encouraging the development of commercial manufacturing in such fields as metal products, electrical equipment, and paper. Internal transportation comprises mainly an interisland ship service. The Philippines has a flourishing overseas trade, especially with the United States.

Government and Foreign Policy. The Philippines has a republican government patterned after that of the United States, except that it is unitary. The chief executive is a popularly elected president. The legislature consists of a bicameral Congress whose Senate is elected at large and whose House is apportioned according to population. Until 1961 the government tended to be dominated by one party, the Nationalists. In that year, however, a Liberal, Diosdado Macapagal, won the presidency. After World War II there was a strong Communist movement in the Philippines composed of guerrillas known as "Huks." By 1960, however, their threat had been practically eliminated. The Philippines has considerable armed forces, largely equipped by the United States; it also has a military treaty with the United States that permits maintenance of United States bases on the islands. The Philippines is also a member of SEATO, but by 1961 Filipino leaders had become quite open about their conviction that SEATO was meaningless. The Philippines can be easily invaded by the country whose navy dominates the western Pacific, as both Japan and the United States proved in World War II. The Philippines has followed a consistent anti-Communist policy since winning national independence; the government was probably fortified in this stand by the attacks of the Huks.

Review Questions

1. Compare India with Communist China in terms of population, geography, and economic capabilities. Does either country seem especially qualified to dominate this part of the world? Or is the area so large that there is room for two huge states?

2. Compare the organization of the national economy in India with that in Communist China. Which type is more likely to depend upon outside assistance? Are other matters, such as resources, the determining factors?

3. Name several factors that will make it difficult for the government of Pakistan, despite the population of the country, to conduct an aggressive, great-power foreign policy.

4. Why are such countries as Burma, Thailand, and South Vietnam the targets of Communist Chinese imperialism? What are the interests of the United States in this region? Compare the interests and the activities of the United States in this region today with its interests and activities in 1941 that were a main factor in bringing on war with Japan.

5. Name several factors that will make it difficult for the government of Indonesia, despite the population of the country, to conduct an aggressive, great-power foreign policy.

21

THE MIDDLE EAST AND AFRICA SOUTH OF THE SAHARA

This chapter deals with a huge area composed of all Asia west of Pakistan along with the whole continent of Africa. The countries of this area have great differences in the racial and national backgrounds of their peoples and in their political and economic structures. Yet there are some elements of unity. For one thing, the Moslem faith predominates from northwestern Africa to Iran. Furthermore, many of these countries, like those of South and Southeast Asia, have only recently obtained national independence. Other areas in Africa are on the verge of becoming independent. Finally, these countries in general are technologically underdeveloped, and they furnish areas for economic competition between the United States and the Soviet Union. It should be noted at the outset that although some parts of Africa are discussed in previous chapters, this chapter—at the risk of some repetition—deals with the whole continent.

THE MIDDLE EAST

The Middle East, a term that has had various definitions, is used here to include Africa north of the Sahara and the part of Asia reaching from Suez to Pakistan. This section deals with Algeria, the United Arab Republic (Egypt), Syria, Israel, Lebanon, Jordan, Saudi Arabia, Iraq, and Iran. One other important country of the Middle East, Turkey, is described in the chapter on Eastern Europe.

Algeria. Algeria is the newest state in the Middle East, having acquired national independence in 1962. Prior to this date, Algeria was politically integrated with France, having the same sort of connection with the government at Paris that Alaska has with the government at

Washington, D.C. For some time before 1962 a sense of nationalism had been developing among the native peoples of Algeria, and from 1954 guerrilla war raged between irregular native troops and large units of the French army. This war was very costly for the French, militarily and financially, and it diminished their ability to conduct a forceful policy elsewhere in the world. Besides, it earned the French a good deal of ill will from the other Arab states of North Africa, from Soviet-Bloc governments, and from the enemies of colonialism all over the world. Finally, a large majority of the French and Algerian voters together agreed in a plebiscite that Algeria should become a separate and independent state.

POPULATION, GEOGRAPHY, AND ECONOMIC LIFE. The population of Algeria is about 10,000,000, nine-tenths of whom are native Arabs and Berbers. The approximately one million Europeans, who are chiefly of French ancestry, comprise an important national and political minority; they opposed national independence, arguing instead that Algeria should remain politically united with France; for a time they had considerable support in France itself. Only a very small number of the Europeans in Algeria are wealthy; most of the land in Algeria is owned by natives. The future of these Europeans is uncertain, although native leaders have promised to guarantee their personal safety and property. Algeria contains about 850,000 square miles, much of it in the Sahara. The coastal area is quite fruitful, yielding a number of crops whose chief market has been France. The most important economic activity is the production of oil from the enormous reserves that have only recently been discovered in the Sahara. According to the present agreement, the profits from the sale of this oil are to be divided between the French and the Algerians.

GOVERNMENT AND FOREIGN POLICY. Having just become independent, Algeria is currently ruled by a provisional government; the plans for its permanent regime call for a typical parliamentary republican structure. The leaders of the forces that secured national independence received a great deal of material assistance from the United Arab Republic, Tunisia, and Morocco; they also had at least the open sympathy of the Soviet Bloc. Some of these Algerian leaders have expressed views that reveal considerable Marxist influences. Yet the new country is economically dependent on France in so many ways that its leaders almost surely will approach no closer to Moscow than a neutralist position.

The United Arab Republic (Egypt). The United Arab Republic (UAR) is the ambitious though impoverished state traditionally called Egypt.

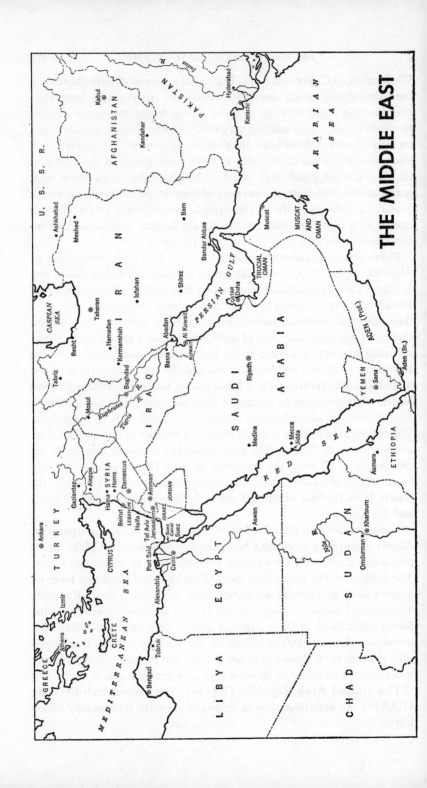

THE MIDDLE EAST

POPULATION AND GEOGRAPHY. The population of Egypt in 1960 was over 25,000,000. It is increasing very rapidly, a fact of major concern to the government, since the per capita income is extremely low and the amount of arable land is limited. A large portion of this population is rural; however, there are 3,100,000 people in Cairo, 1,600,000 in Alexandria, and 100,000 or more in several other cities. Such concentrations, as in India, result in large part from the influx of one-time farmers who have hoped in vain for urban employment. The largest racial and national group comprises people of Semitic extraction. In spite of tax-supported school systems, with compulsory attendance, illiteracy among adults is still high. The chief religion is Islam. The most notable feature of the geography of Egypt is the Nile River, in whose valley almost all the people of the country live. Another feature is that Egypt is athwart the Suez Canal. In recent years, however, oil firms have been acquiring tankers so large that they can economically bypass the canal by sailing around the Cape of Good Hope.

ECONOMIC LIFE. The government of the UAR exercises almost dictatorial powers over the national economy. There are not many mineral resources in Egypt: petroleum and phosphate rock, and smaller quantities of such metals as iron, copper, manganese, and gold. Agriculture is the basis of the national economy. That in the Nile Valley is extremely productive, yielding grains, cotton, fruits, and sugar cane. The government has introduced a sweeping land-redistribution program. The country has some industry, such as food processing, textiles, tobacco, and cement.

GOVERNMENT AND FOREIGN POLICY. The UAR is a presidential republic, with a popularly elected president and a unicameral legislature. Actually it is a dictatorship, under President Gamel Abdel Nasser. This government is supported to a considerable extent by the revenue from the Suez Canal, which it seized in 1956 and for which it is paying its former stockholders. This seizure led to a brief armed clash between Egypt and Israel, France, and the United Kingdom. It halted after the governments of the United States and the Soviet Union brought pressure on the United Kingdom and France, and after the UN Assembly by an almost unanimous vote appealed for a cease-fire agreement. The Suez area is currently being policed by troops under the supervision of the United Nations. Despite predictions to the contrary, the UAR government is managing the canal efficiently. The country is not very well situated for defense or offense. It maintains substantial armed forces that are supplied with arms partly by the Soviet government. The foreign policy of the country has undergone certain shifts in recent years.

At one time it appeared that Nasser was completely pro-Soviet and that he would lead his country into the Soviet Bloc. He reached an agreement with the USSR for Soviet aid in building a multipurpose high dam across the Nile at Aswan. Nevertheless, he has since veered toward neutralism and has been very friendly with Nehru. Nasser seems to feel himself the head of the entire Arab world and would like to make a political union of all Arab countries under the United Arab Republic. He has been one of the foremost opponents of Israel.

Syria. Syria contains about 4,600,000 people, chiefly impoverished Moslems. The country is largely rural with typical Mediterranean landscape and crops—grain, tobacco, cotton, fruits, and nuts. Oil pipelines cross Syria and terminate at its Mediterranean ports, from which the oil is shipped to the industrialized western countries. Its principal cities are Aleppo and Damascus. Its government broke off its union with Egypt in 1961 and resumed its course as a parliamentary regime, with strong military influences. The new government apparently rejected Nasser's practice of land distribution. In 1962 the new regime was overthrown by a group of military leaders who favored at least some land distribution. The rupture of the tie with the UAR did not, however, apparently mitigate the Syrians' implacable attitude to the Israelis.

Israel. Israel is a section of the former territory of Palestine, a part of the Ottoman Empire that was mandated to the United Kingdom after World War I and that received national independence in 1948.

POPULATION AND GEOGRAPHY. The population of Israel in 1960 was about 2,100,000. It is growing constantly from immigration, which Israeli officials encourage. A large percentage of the people are refugees from persecution in Europe; another sizable group consists of enthusiasts for the "Jewish National Homeland." A large part of the population lives in farm communities, or collectives. The largest metropolitan center is Tel Aviv-Jaffa, with about 380,000 inhabitants. The population of Israel is chiefly Jewish; about ten per cent is Arab. Many of the people are farmers, but there are numerous tradesmen and factory operatives as well. It must be stressed that the borders of Israel have not yet been drawn exactly; the country is still disputing with the UAR the ownership of the "Gaza Strip," on the southwest corner of the country. The part of the country along the Mediterranean is fertile and well watered, but much of the interior is a desert. The Israeli government is devoting great efforts to irrigating this region to restore the Biblical "land of milk and honey."

ECONOMIC LIFE. The whole national economy is under strict government regulation. Farming is important; among the crops are citrus fruits, grains, and grapes. There are a number of mineral resources, such as limestone, sandstone, gypsum, salt, iron, and copper. The Israeli government is seeking more industry; that at present includes automobiles and automobile parts, oil refining, and textiles. The government is also erecting several hydroelectric power stations, and it has built a functioning nuclear reactor. Much of the Israeli national income comprises gifts from sympathizers all over the world and reparations from the West German government. Still, the country is now prosperous enough to export both investment capital and technical aid.

GOVERNMENT AND FOREIGN POLICY. Israel is a parliamentary republic. The titular executive is the president, chosen by the legislature. The actual executive is the premier, who is responsible to the legislature. The legislative branch is the unicameral Knesset, popularly elected under a system of proportional representation. The Israeli people enjoy numerous political rights and freedoms; the Communist Party is legal and is represented in the Knesset. Israel is a very heavily armed country; every adult, male and female, who is physically fit is a member of the armed forces to an advanced age. Israel is in effect at war with all its neighbors, who commenced war when the country came into existence in 1948 and who have gone no farther than to make armistices with it by agreements reached under the supervision of the United Nations. The various Arab countries argue that the Israelis have stolen land that is rightfully Arab, and many Arab leaders have vowed to destroy Israel. Israeli foreign policy is thus one chiefly of defense. Israel generally can enjoy the support of the United States, although the United States was opposed in 1956 when the Israeli Army invaded Egypt. It has a great deal of support from individuals and nongovernmental organizations in the United States, whose financial gifts have enabled the country to maintain its existence.

Lebanon. The population of Lebanon in 1960 was a little greater than 1,600,000. The people are almost equally divided between Christian churches and Moslem sects. Lebanon has economic significance in being the terminus for two of the oil pipelines from the Persian Gulf and the Arabian oil fields. Lebanon is a parliamentary republic, with a president, a responsible premier, and a unicameral Chamber of Deputies. Militarily, Lebanon is very weak. In 1958, when Egypt and the Soviet Union were on very friendly terms, and when Lebanon had a strongly anti-Communist government, a revolution appeared so likely to overthrow the Lebanese government that the president of Lebanon asked the United States government for help. In a short time, United States Marines landed, but later that year they were withdrawn.

Jordan. Jordan, previously known as Trans-Jordan, is the largest part of Biblical Palestine and in 1960 had a population slightly smaller than 1,700,000. The largest city is Amman, with about 70,000 people. The people are almost all Moslems. Some of the western half of the country is very fertile, but much of the rest is arid desert. Jordan is a limited, parliamentary monarchy much like the United Kingdom. Jordanian foreign policy has been generally anti-Communist and pro-British. At present the relations between Jordan and both Iraq and the UAR are poor. Meanwhile the Jordanians are carrying on a running battle with the Israelis in the form of numerous frontier skirmishes. The Jordanian government enjoys some influence through its potential control over oil pipelines passing through Jordanian territory.

Saudi Arabia. Saudi Arabia according to the most recent estimate has a population of approximately 6,500,000. Much of the population is nomadic; yet Mecca has 300,000 people. Almost all Arabians are Moslems. The country is primarily a desert. The government of Saudi Arabia is a nearly absolute monarchy. In 1958 King Saud did grant considerable powers to a prime minister, his brother Feisal; apparently Saud did so only under pressure. Feisal used his office to reduce government spending. He evidently had strong sympathies for the Soviet Union, and in 1961 the king dismissed him from office. The Saudi Arabian government is supported largely by the royalties it receives from the Arabian-American Oil Company (Aramco), which is owned by four major United States petroleum corporations. The country possesses one of the largest reserves of crude oil in the world, the exploitation of which is its principal economic activity. Saudi Arabia is very hostile to Israel. Saud apparently believes that he is destined to unite all Arabs under the flag of Saudi Arabia, especially since his country was the homeland of Mohammed; Saud has sometimes shown resentment toward Nasser of Egypt, who has been much more successful in setting himself up as a leader of the Arabs. Today, however, Saudi Arabia has a defense agreement with the UAR. It is also the seat of a major United States air base, at Dharan. Saudi Arabia can bring influence upon Western European governments by cutting off, or threatening to cut off, supplies of oil.

Iraq. Iraq, the ancient Mesopotamia, was a part of the Ottoman Empire that was mandated to the United Kingdom after World War I and that was recognized as sovereign in 1932.

POPULATION, GEOGRAPHY, AND ECONOMIC LIFE. The population of Iraq in 1959 was about 7,000,000. A considerable fraction of the people dwell in the countryside. Nevertheless, there are such large cities as

Baghdad (550,000), Basra (200,000), and Mosul (350,000). Almost all the people are Moslems. The country lies chiefly between the Tigris and the Euphrates Rivers, in the "Fertile Crescent" of antiquity. Hence much of it is extremely productive; irrigation systems built thousands of years ago and later destroyed during invasions are being restored. The chief crops are dates, grains, tobacco, and cotton; some are produced in exportable quantities. The most crucial economic activity in Iraq is the production of crude oil, by both domestic and foreign concerns. Royalties from these wells provide the Iraqi government with a large part of its revenue. Because of its petroleum output, Iraq has a substantial trade with Western Europe. Iraq contains the western terminus of the Berlin-to-Baghdad railroad, and the government is expanding the highway system.

GOVERNMENT AND FOREIGN POLICY. The government of Iraq since July, 1958, has been a republic, at least on paper; to a considerable degree it is actually a dictatorship under the premier, General Abdul Karim el-Kassem. This republic was established through a successful revolution that overthrew a limited monarchy. The revolution had a major effect upon Iraqi foreign policy and the alignment of the Arab countries in this area. Iraq under the monarchy had been anti-Soviet, and its government had combined with that of Jordan to form the Arab Union, a counterweight to the United Arab Republic. At this time, Iraq was also a member of METO. The leaders of the revolution against the monarchy, by contrast, were either neutralist or pro-Soviet. They at first stated that they would attach themselves to the policies of the UAR; however, as Nasser became increasingly nationalistic instead of pro-Soviet, relations between Iraq and the UAR cooled. The new Iraqi government withdrew from METO, and King Hussein of Jordan dissolved the Arab Union. In 1961, the Iraqi government still seemed friendly toward the USSR. During the same year the Iraqi government attempted to seize Kuwait, a tiny but very oil-rich sheikdom over which the British had just relinquished a protectorate. At the request of the sheik of Kuwait, the British government sent both troops and aircraft to the area, after which the Iraqis suspended their preparations to absorb the sheikdom. In 1962, however, the Iraqis once more began voicing claims to Kuwait. In the UN discussions over this quarrel, the Iraqis were supported only by the UAR and the USSR.

Iran. Iran, traditionally called Persia, has long enjoyed formal independence while in fact occupying a more or less semicolonial status.

POPULATION, GEOGRAPHY, AND ECONOMIC LIFE. The population of Iran in 1960 was about 20,500,000. Many of the people are farmers, but

Tehran contains 2,000,000 residents and three other cities each contain more than 300,000. Almost all Iranians are Moslems; however, they belong to a sect that has frequently been at odds with the predominant sect in other Moslem states. The northern part of the country has some high mountains, and the central section includes a vast plateau intersected by mountain ranges. There are few true lowlands. Agriculture is quite important, with large yields of grains, fruits, tea, tobacco, cotton, and wool. The monarch has begun selling land from his estates to his tenants and has tried to compel other great landlords to do likewise. Iran has considerable mineral resources, such as coal, iron, lead, copper, nickel, manganese, cobalt, and precious stones. Among industries, Iranian carpet-weaving is world-famed. There are also other light industries, and some heavy industry as well. The most significant economic activity, however, is the production and refining of crude oil. As in other countries of the Middle East, the Iranian oil industry is owned and operated by foreign companies and supplies a large part of the Iranian government revenues. An attempt by the Iranian government to nationalize the industry in 1951 led to economic disaster for the country. There is a major rail line uniting the Persian Gulf with the Caspian Sea, and other routes provide links with Soviet railroads.

GOVERNMENT AND FOREIGN POLICY. The government of Iran is a limited monarchy, with a king, a prime minister and cabinet, and a bicameral legislature. It is parliamentary in structure. Iran for many years was a target of both British and Russian—later Soviet—imperialism. With the almost total disappearance of British imperialism after 1945, Iranian leaders have come to look upon the USSR as their chief menace. This feeling was reinforced by the refusal of the USSR to withdraw its occupation troops from Iran after World War II, until subjected to pressure by the United States and the United Kingdom. Altogether, Iran has followed a consistently anti-Soviet policy, but by 1961 its ruler, Shah Reza Pahlavi, was voicing strong suspicions as to how much protection the United States government was willing to provide against the USSR. Iran has compulsory military service and is a member of CENTO. Finally, the situation of Iran is rather precarious, since its only friend on its frontiers is Pakistan.

AFRICA SOUTH OF THE SAHARA

Africa south of the Sahara today is an area of vast political, economic, social, and psychological change, as the European countries have given up one after another of their colonial possessions and allowed the native peoples to work out their own destinies. The resulting insecurity, disorder, and deprivation have made Africa a prime target for the contestants in the "Cold War."

Population. The nearly 200,000,000 people of Africa south of the Sahara display tremendous cultural variety, but with comparatively few exceptions they exist at a very low level of civilization. Today, and for many years to come, their leaders are and will be trained in a European, and therefore alien and even hostile, tradition. This fact makes the path of development even rougher than it generally is everywhere.

NUMBERS AND RACES. The population of Africa south of the Sahara is almost 200,000,000, roughly the same as that of the United States. In the tropics, on both sides of the equator, the people are largely Negroid and Bantu, of a great variety of stocks. Among these black peoples there are approximately 1,000,000 permanent white settlers, scattered on individual farms or in small communities. At the southern tip of the continent is a large transplanted European group, of mingled British and Dutch origins. The great majority of the population is occupied with agriculture and stock raising, but their techniques are so primitive that little of the continent may be described as underpopulated. There are very few cities, except in the Republic of South Africa.

CULTURAL TRAITS. There are numerous religious faiths. The native peoples are attached to various religious bodies, most of which tend toward primitive animism. However, Islam is very strong among some native groups, especially those living near the Sahara. The Caucasians in the south are largely Protestant Christian. Throughout this area are Christian missions, both Catholic and Protestant, which have had some impact on the natives and have won some converts. No great civilization has ever had its center in any area of Africa south of the Sahara. Most African natives today can neither read nor write; however, the rate of illiteracy is dropping, and it appears that as the people achieve national independence they tend to establish tax-supported school systems. Some of the colonial powers are also trying to establish such systems. There is a dangerous shortage of persons with training in industrial and administrative techniques. It should be emphasized that a huge gulf separates the few intellectuals from the illiterate masses. These intellectuals, it is also significant, feel more than most of the people the urges of nationalism.

Geography. Africa south of the Sahara has an area more than twice as large as that of the United States. Classified according to vegetation, its surface can be divided into two regions. Immediately south of the Sahara and along both sides of the Equator is a belt of dense tropical forests and savannas, much of it nearly impenetrable. The southern-

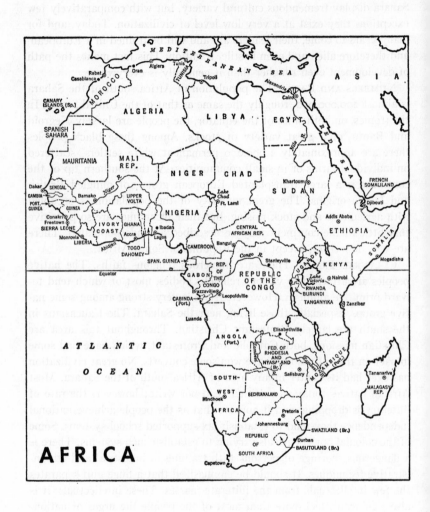

most part of Africa consists of both plains and smaller deserts. There are considerable mountains, the tallest being in Tanganyika, Kenya, and Ethiopia. Much of Africa, especially in the south, is plateau. There are several important rivers, such as the Congo, Niger, and Zambesi; most of them do not provide routes from the sea into the interior because of waterfalls near the coast. The coasts of Africa do not contain many harbors; the few that there are have until recently been the sites of European colonies. Most of the continent has a very oppressive climate. This feature contributes to the fact that many African natives have not risen far above the food-gathering stage of life. Some parts of Africa, however, can support highly productive farming.

Economic Life. Economically Africa is the most retarded of all continents, yet it contains vast potentialities. It is here that investments of foreign capital, governmental and nongovernmental, can be and are being extremely valuable. In general there is apt to be a great deal of government ownership, because of the shortage of capital in Africa. The new governments are almost the sole African agencies that can obtain, either through taxing or borrowing, the amount of capital needed for the rapid and large-scale economic advances planned.

NATURAL RESOURCES. Africa south of the Sahara is very rich in mineral resources; furthermore, because the civilization of this area is comparatively backward and because much of the area is difficult to reach, there probably are many more resources than are now known. There are large quantities of usable bauxite near the western coast, especially in Guinea. The Congo has a variety of minerals, among them cobalt, manganese, and uranium. South Africa has been producing gold and diamonds since before 1900. Another important ore is copper, in Rhodesia and elsewhere. There is some good iron ore; Liberia contains immense deposits of very high grade ore, currently being developed by United States firms. There is, however, little coal or oil. One important difficulty is that some countries are well endowed whereas others have few minerals. Such inequalities may contribute to producing international tensions unless the officials of the states concerned agree on a policy of relative free trade.

AGRICULTURE, INDUSTRY, AND TRANSPORTATION. Agriculture south of the Sahara is very extensive. Much of it, of course, is purely for subsistence. On the other hand, there is considerable commercial farming that includes grains, fruits, coffee, cocoa, cotton, and plantation rubber. Most of the large and prosperous commercial farms are owned and managed by Europeans. As the nations of Africa achieve statehood and as the European farmers resident there are forced out, the agricultural output of these new states will fall. Moreover, at least for the uninitiated, the dense tropical forests disguise the fact that the tropical soils generally are very poor. Finally, it is a major handicap that the typical African male despises tilling the soil—it is "women's work." There is yet comparatively little industry in Africa, except in the Republic of South Africa. However, the governments of the newly independent states are encouraging the development of factories; in Ghana, for instance, there is a project under way for the basis of a substantial aluminum industry. Some Soviet-Bloc technicians, especially Czechoslovakians, have come to Guinea and to other areas. A few Chinese technicians also are present. Transportation and power facilities are also lacking in many places. The British for many years planned a "Cape-to-Cairo" railroad but never managed to complete it. In more recent times governments have concentrated on building highways, so that much of Africa can now be reached by truck. Owing to the dearth of speedy land transportation, airlines are extremely important.

FOREIGN TRADE. The foreign trade of the African countries is important, and its importance to both Africa and the world will increase. The main pattern of this trade is the export from Africa of foodstuffs and raw materials, and the import into Africa of finished goods. The chief participants in this trade, outside of Africa, are the European countries that own or formerly owned colonies in Africa. Even where the African participant is a newly independent state, the old currents of foreign trade have been very little disturbed. Then, the United States is importing larger quantities of goods from Africa, as various African states such as Liberia become major suppliers of raw materials. One very significant aspect of African foreign trade is that the exports from any given African country tend to be predominantly of a single commodity. For instance, in 1957 peanuts made up 95 per cent of the value of the exports of Gambia; cloves and their oil, 83 per cent of the value of the exports of Zanzibar; copper, 92 per cent of the value of the exports of Northern Rhodesia. Neither the percentages nor the nature of the commodities themselves is static. This condition does illustrate the dependence of the peoples of these countries on specialized world markets. It also illustrates the fact that in some cases the African peoples devote so much energy and capital to the production of exportable goods that they depend upon imports for staples that they could easily raise for themselves.

Government. The most important feature of government in Africa south of the Sahara is that in the past two decades this area has changed from almost total colonialism to almost total national independence.

When World War II started, there were only two actually sovereign states south of the Sahara: Liberia and the Union of South Africa. Ethiopia also had a long tradition of sovereignty, but at this time it was an Italian colony. By 1960, most of the continent was self-governing, and the majority of the remaining colonies were being prepared for self-government. This change came about partly because the European countries were no longer capable of sustaining their rule and partly because of a widespread conviction in the non-Communist world that colonialism was improper. The governmental structures that African leaders have erected, or tried to erect, have been considerably influenced by the colonial policies of the European governments. It is important, therefore, to survey these policies before looking at the African governments themselves.

THE COLONIAL POLICIES OF THE EUROPEAN GOVERNMENTS. The five main European powers with possessions in Africa after World War II— the United Kingdom, France, Belgium, Portugal, and Spain—had varying policies toward these possessions. The policy of the United Kingdom centered about preparing the African peoples as quickly as possible for self-government within the Commonwealth, letting them maintain their own traditions. This policy encouraged the development of native self-government, first at the local level and later at the colonial, or "national," level. The policy of France centered about an effort to transform the Africans into Frenchmen, to give them French citizenship, and to ready them for self-government according to French principles. The policy of Belgium was concerned almost exclusively with the economic welfare of the Africans, on the theory that the Africans would not be ready for self-government until they were self-supporting. Thus the Belgian government allowed the Congolese almost no practice in self-government. The policy of both Portugal and Spain involves assimilating the Africans into the nationality of the mother country, with the intention of keeping the African possessions politically integrated with the mother country. In keeping with this principle, the Portuguese in particular avoid racial discrimination, and in 1961 the Portuguese government enfranchised all adult residents of the Portuguese African territories.

GENERAL TRAITS OF THE NEW AFRICAN GOVERNMENTS. The new African governments are commonly republican in form; however, a number of them have denied the people a substantial number of political liberties. This trend toward dictatorship is partly a result of the fact that despite enthusiasm for national liberty many of the new leaders do not insure individuals their political freedoms and judicial rights to the extent guaranteed by the old colonial governments. Moreover, the economies of these countries are apt to be at least partly socialistic, entailing the denial of certain freedoms. Several political leaders in Africa are strongly influenced by Marxist teachings, and at least some of them are persuaded that the swiftest way to secure an industrial economy—which most consider a major goal—is to adopt some of the principles of the Soviet economy.

THE GOVERNMENTS OF CERTAIN AFRICAN STATES. The governments of certain African states illustrate the varying political attitudes and institutions of the continent. This section describes the governments, and certain other pertinent features, of the Republic of South Africa, a former member of the British Commonwealth, dominated by whites; Liberia, a Negro state with a long history of self-government; Ghana, a new Negro state with a doctrinaire view of politics and economics; and Nigeria, a new Negro state with a more or less pragmatic view of politics and economics.

The Republic of South Africa. The national government of South Africa is a republic, established after the voters in 1960 indicated their desire to end their ties with the British crown. This vote in effect removed South Africa from the British Commonwealth, a step carried out in 1961 when the republican government was founded. The British residents showed their unwillingness to leave the Commonwealth by voting almost unanimously against adopting the republican form of government. They were, however, outnumbered by the Dutch voters. South Africa has a federal government for its four states. It also controls South-West Africa, a one-time German colony for which it has refused to accept a UN trusteeship. All life, political and otherwise, is substantially influenced by the fact that the white minority deliberately keeps the nonwhite majority in a subordinate position. Practically all inhabitants of South Africa, whether Bantu, Dutch, or English, are either immigrants or the descendants of immigrants, for the Bantu and English first came into the area after the Dutch had settled the Cape Colony. Far from adopting a "melting pot" policy, however, the dominant group has pursued a forcible segregationist policy with respect to the Bantus and mixed races. The government of South Africa has almost severed connections with the United Nations, takes almost no part in the "Cold War," and has a far more "isolationist" foreign policy than that of any other important state.

Liberia. The government of Liberia is a republic, established over a century ago by freed Negroes who were transported from the United States to Africa by a philanthropic organization so that they could enjoy self-rule. It is modeled after the government of the United States, with a president and a bicameral legislature. Liberia has two important characteristics. First, until the last few years its economy was more retarded than that of most colonial areas in Africa. Although Liberia possesses such resources as a fertile soil, dense and valuable forests, and high-grade iron ore, the European powers made no investments there, and without investment capital there was no way for the natives to exploit their resources. Consequently the natives were extremely impoverished. Second, until recent times the very small number of Negroes who were descended from the immigrant stock discriminated vigorously against the original African tribes; for one thing, they monopolized government offices. Hence discrimination against natives in Africa is not necessarily a racial problem. It must be noted that in recent years the Liberian government has placed curbs on this sort of discrimination, so that the Americo-Liberians are beginning to accept the Afro-Liberians on a more nearly equal plane.

Ghana. The government of Ghana, which consists of the former Gold Coast colony and Togoland trusteeship, is a republic within the British Commonwealth, established in 1957. To a major degree it is the creature of its present leader, Prime Minister Kwame Nkrumah, a graduate of a Protestant church-controlled university in the United States who later became associated with Marxist groups in the United Kingdom. He has consistently denied being a Communist but seems to favor certain Communist principles of government. Despite constitutional guarantees, there are very few political liberties in Ghana. Ghanaian laws require every worker to belong to a union, and forbid strikes. Nkrumah himself is the founder of a quasi-religious political cult with himself as chief divinity. Nkrumah has a very aggressive foreign policy. Because members of a certain tribe, the Ewe, live in both Ghana and neighboring Togo, Nkrumah has demanded cession of the Ewe lands in Togo. Nkrumah also appears to envision himself as the leader of a movement to unify Negro Africa; Ghana has already joined Guinea and Mali in a federation. Nkrumah has expressed friendliness toward the Soviet government and admiration for the Soviet economy. Nevertheless, the American and British governments and the World Bank are financing the establishment of an aluminum industry in Ghana.

Nigeria. Nigeria is a republic within the British Commonwealth formed from the former colony of the same name. With 35,000,000 inhabitants, it is the most populous state in Africa. Nigeria contains a great number of distinct tribes; there are many Moslems, and many Christians. The state is divided into three Regions—North, East, and

West—each of which enjoys considerable autonomy. At least among the Moslems of the North, the British found it possible to confer local administrative, fiscal, and judicial powers upon already existing native authorities a number of years before granting the whole colony its independence. After Nigeria had obtained national independence, these local authorities kept most of their powers. Thus Nigeria is a federation, with a rather weak national government. The people of Nigeria in the recent past seem to have had anticolonialism as their chief bond, and it remains to be seen whether they will remain united. The government has a titular executive, the governor general named by the British crown; a true executive, the responsible prime minister; and a bicameral legislature. The first prime minister was a Moslem from the North, Abubakar Tafawa Balewa. In the first year of his rule, Balewa indicated a preference for nongovernmental business enterprise and strong ties with the non-Soviet world.

Foreign Policies. The foreign policies of the African countries are generally either anti-Soviet or neutralist. The degree to which a government may adopt a neutralist policy seems related to the feeling among its leaders about Western Europe. For instance, when the voters of the former French colonies were given the opportunity to choose between complete independence and membership in the French Community, the government of Guinea, whose voters opted for independence, was headed by an outspoken Marxist-neutralist. By contrast, the governments of other areas, whose voters chose to remain with France, included some of the most important anti-Communists in Africa. Another feature of the new African governments is that, notwithstanding the amount of political power that has been conferred upon the bulk of the people, illiteracy and indifference are so widespread that the framing of foreign policy is almost entirely the task of a few leaders.

Review Questions

1. What factors tend to unify the states of the Middle East? What factors tend to divide them?

2. What are the respective interests of the United States, of the Soviet Union, and of Western Europe in the Middle East?

3. To whom is national independence for the African peoples advantageous? To whom is it disadvantageous? Does national independence for the African peoples increase or decrease the likelihood of war?

4. What is the nature of African foreign trade?

5. Describe the governments in some of the new African countries. What are some of the factors that have shaped governmental structures, practices, and beliefs?

22 *LATIN AMERICA*

Latin America, for the purposes of this text, includes all of the Americas south of the United States, together with the islands of the Caribbean. Most of this area is occupied by twenty politically independent countries. A small part consists of British, French, and Dutch possessions, dependencies, and outposts. The area is termed Latin America because in most of these countries a Latin tongue—Spanish, Portuguese, or French—is the official language. This linguistic similarity provides a considerable bond among the Latin American peoples. There are a number of other similarities, such as those of religion, stage of technological development, and attitude toward the United States, that furnish additional bonds. Yet there are important differences and rivalries among the Latin American governments and peoples. Hence these countries possess some significant national contrasts, so that despite their many similarities they are far from establishing a unified government. Nevertheless, this chapter discusses Latin America more or less as a unit, pointing out important distinctions among the various countries. It deals chiefly with the independent areas; the British, French, and Dutch regions are described elsewhere, along with the mother country.

POPULATION

The approximately 200,000,000 people of Latin America show considerable diversity. Yet the diversity is far less than in Africa. The whole vast area has been fashioned into a European culture, with fewer major cultural differences from Europe than the United States has. Still there occur fierce nationalistic feelings.

Numbers and Location of the People. The total population of Latin America is about 200,000,000. About one-third, or 68,000,000, of these people live in Brazil; about one-sixth, or 35,000,000, live in Mexico. On the other hand, there are barely 1,000,000 people in Pan-

SOUTH AND CENTRAL AMERICA

ama. The population of Latin America is increasing more rapidly than that of any other continent, primarily through natural increase; still, the governments of some of these countries actively promote immigration from Europe. A large part of the population is rural. At the same time, Latin America is undergoing a swift process of urbanization, a considerable part of which is linked with a genuine pattern of industrialization. The largest cities include Mexico City (4,800,000); Buenos Aires (4,500,000); São Paulo (3,800,000); Rio de Janeiro (3,300,000); and Santiago de Chile (1,650,000). The Brazilian government in 1961 was finishing construction of a new capital city in the interior, Brasilia, which could become another great center.

Races and Nationalities. The races and nationalities of the Latin American peoples show a great admixture, which varies greatly from one country to another. This admixture is partly a result of the Spanish-Portuguese treatment of the native Indians centuries ago: that is, unlike the British of North America, they did not—except in the West Indies— exterminate the Indians, but rather intermarried with them or, at worst, tried to enslave them. Furthermore, there were several times as many Indians in what became Latin America as there were in what became the United States and Canada. Also, Negro slaves were brought to some, but not all, of the Latin American states. At the same time, there were some parts of Latin America that had a very scanty native population. Hence in Argentina and Uruguay most of the people are whites; in Paraguay, most are Indian-whites; in Bolivia, most are Indians; and in Haiti, most are Negroes. Then, owing to immigration from Europe, there is considerable national admixture as well. Besides the Spanish and Portuguese, Italian and German elements are prominent, and English, French, and other influences are noticeable.

Other Traits of the People. In the past, most people have followed agricultural pursuits. Recently, however, with the rise of cities and of industry, there has been an increasing percentage of engineers, factory operatives, and other technicians. This trend has led to the emergence in some of these countries, notably Mexico, of a relatively strong and growing middle class that bridges the once yawning political, economic, social, and cultural gap between farmers and landlords. Though there are some flourishing Protestant communities in Latin America, most of the people are Roman Catholics. The Catholic Church has some political influence; one reason for the fall of Perón in Argentina was his final open aggression against the Church. Latin American countries generally have tax-supported school systems, but their impact differs from one country to another. For example, Paraguay is culturally very retarded, whereas Argentina is comparatively advanced. Urban intellectuals in Latin America generally maintain a high cultural level; it is noteworthy that they tend to regard Latin Europe, and not the United States, as their spiritual home.

GEOGRAPHY

The total area of Latin America is somewhat greater than 7,500,000 square miles, more than double that of the United States. Most of this area, about 6,800,000 square miles, is in South America. The surface of Latin America has great diversity. Along the Pacific coast from Mexico to Cape Horn is an almost uninterrupted range of lofty mountains, called the Andes in South America. There are a number of other lesser, but still important, ranges, in such countries as Mexico and Brazil. These two countries along with Argentina also contain extensive plateau regions. The areas most nearly resembling the southeastern United States are in Uruguay and the pampas district of Argentina. There are several major rivers, notably the Amazon, the Paraná-Plata, and the Orinoco. The Amazon Valley is mainly a vast and almost uninhabitable tropical forest and savanna. The coasts do not furnish many good harbors; perhaps the best are those of Argentina and Uruguay along the inlet of the Plata. The climate of most of Latin America is hot and wet; only Argentina and Uruguay compare with much of the United States. No part of Latin America has a climate like that of the Corn Belt.

ECONOMIC LIFE

The economic life of Latin America, with great variations from one country to another, is in general undergoing rapid industrialization.

The Bases of Latin American Economic Life. Latin American economic life has two bases: a dependence upon foreign investments and a program of government intervention.

THE DEPENDENCE UPON FOREIGN INVESTMENTS. Like all areas that experience a shortage of capital, Latin America has long been dependent upon foreign investments for the expansion of its national economies. For many years the United States has been the principal source for investments in Latin America. Before World War II, Great Britain and Germany also were major sources of funds, but the losses they suffered during the war removed them from this activity for some time. By 1960, however, these two countries, along with France, Italy, and Japan, once more were supplying capital to Latin American countries. The total of investments from the United States, both governmental and nongovernmental, surpasses $10 billion; most of them are nongovernmental. They are distributed quite unevenly through the area. The country with the largest investments is Venezuela; other major recipients are Mexico and Brazil. Cuba, until the Castro regime, was also a major recipient. On the other hand, United States investments in Bolivia and Uruguay are small. These investments, both large and small, have been profitable not only for stockholders in the United States but also for the governments and citizens of the countries involved. Some firms have devoted considerable attention to the welfare of their employees and of the areas in which they operate. Nevertheless, such financial activities have earned the United States a large amount of resentment in some Latin American circles. At the same time, investors always face the possible confiscation of their properties, as most recently in Cuba.

THE PROGRAM OF GOVERNMENT INTERVENTION. The program of government intervention in Latin American national economies has two principal and interrelated aspects: the government ownership of business enterprises and the enactment of social welfare laws.

Government Ownership of Business Enterprises. Government ownership of business enterprises may itself be divided into two types: the business enterprises that the government inaugurated and operated from the beginning; and the business enterprises that were first owned by private companies and were subsequently nationalized by the government. Nationalization has often been principally a means whereby governments have sought to enrich themselves and to curry favor with the voters. In fact, there have been outstanding cases of failures among the enterprises after their nationalization; neither the Mexican oil industry nor the Bolivian tin industry is as productive today as it was under nongovernmental ownership. The seizure of the Cuban sugar plantations in 1960 by the Castro government drastically reduced income from the sugar harvests. In the late 1950's the government of Argentina, after the failure of the government-owned oil industry, opened the field to nongovernmental investors.

Social Welfare Laws. Social welfare laws have been another type of instrument designed to win popular support for governments, and they also have brought troubles. In Argentina, Juan Perón created a dictatorship from an alliance of the army with labor unions and in ten years bankrupted the government. The tremendous inflation suffered by many Latin American states such as Brazil derives from expensive social-welfare programs, without a level of industrial production adequate to sustain them. These policies reduce the willingness of foreigners to invest their funds in these countries.

Natural Resources. Latin America is extremely rich in natural resources, some of which are just entering exploitation. There are enormous quantities of high-grade iron ore in such countries as Cuba, Venezuela, and Brazil. Venezuela, where the wells are owned by private companies, ranks second only to the United States in its output of crude oil; however, in the late 1950's the government adopted some antibusiness policies that may slow exploration and drilling. Other important producers of crude oil include Mexico, Colombia, and Argentina; there seem to be vast untapped reservoirs in many places near the Andes. Peru and Chile both contain large amounts of copper, and Chile is also a leading source of nitrates. Cuba has valuable supplies of nickel, and Brazil of manganese. Bolivia has in the past been a principal supplier of tin. Other significant minerals include sulfur, bauxite, lead, chromite, tungsten, platinum, vanadium, zinc, gold, and silver. Latin America does not have very large stocks of coal; ships that bring iron ore from Brazil to the United States may return with a load of coal. The continent appears otherwise capable of supporting an industrial economy. Also, some of the waters off Latin America are excellent for fishing. A further important resources is timber. Though Latin America was the first source of natural rubber, it has few rubber plantations today. The only country that has few resources is Uruguay.

Agriculture. Agriculture has been very important in the Latin American economy, but this importance is declining rapidly in relation to that of industry. Yet in spite of the apparently favorable conditions for agriculture, farming generally is rather unbalanced. Only a small percentage of the total land area is cultivated; of the ten countries in South America, Uruguay and Argentina alone produce enough food to supply their populations. This distortion results partly from the fact that in most of the Amazon Valley, which seems eminently suited for agriculture, the soil tends to wash away if the jungle is cleared for tillage. Latin America is the site of huge commercial farming operations: sugar in the West Indies, bananas and coffee in Central America, coffee in Colombia and Brazil, and cattle and wheat in Argentina and Uruguay. Smaller yet important commercial crops include tobacco in Cuba, fruits in various countries, and cotton and rice in Brazil. So much capital and manpower are devoted to commercial farming that there is a great shortcoming in subsistence agriculture. A related problem is the great number of large estates much of whose land lies fallow; government purchase or expropriation of these estates, followed by a redistribution of the land so that it would be owned by individual families, would probably increase agricultural output.

Industry. Industry has been growing rapidly in Latin America. Here also, the growth has been uneven, depending upon such factors as the presence of mineral resources and the attitude of government officials toward foreign investors. There is not much new industry in Bolivia, Paraguay, or Uruguay. Two countries undergoing rapid industrialization are Mexico and Brazil; in Brazil, industry now contributes at least twice as much to the national income as does agriculture. Brazil today has a considerable steel industry and manufactures such other products as automobiles, aluminum, cement, petrochemicals, and drugs. Still, the government-owned oil industry satisfies only one-fourth of the national demand for oil, but the government bars any investment by foreign oil companies. Other countries that have, or probably will have, steel mills include Argentina, Colombia, Peru, and Venezuela. Mexican industry is quite diversified. Food processing is widespread in Latin America, especially in Argentina and Uruguay. Petrochemicals are increasingly important in Venezuela. Many countries have textile factories. Cuba is famous for its cigars.

Transportation and Internal Trade. Transportation facilities are generally backward in Latin America. The whole area has fewer than 100,000 miles of railroad, less than half the trackage of the United States in more than double the area. Moreover, under government ownership service is extremely inefficient; also, passenger fares and freight rates are kept so low, for political reasons, that the systems cannot afford to replace worn-out and obsolete rolling stock. There are also comparatively few highways; there are fewer miles of paved roads in Brazil than in Vermont. Buses supply transportation for passengers in some areas. Airlines from the United States and Europe are extending service into Latin America. Some of the rivers, especially the Amazon, do furnish avenues for commerce far into the interior. Coastal shipping is also very important. Still, the movement of both persons and goods is in many places hampered by transportation shortages. Trade among the Latin American countries has been limited also by the tariff laws of the various governments. In 1960, however, the governments of Argentina, Brazil, Chile, Mexico, Paraguay, Peru, and Uruguay formed the Latin American Free Trade Association. The governments of Colombia and Ecuador later announced that they would join this group. The governments concerned are to negotiate a series of agreements among themselves that at the end of twelve years will yield free trade.

Foreign Trade. The foreign trade of Latin America is important, but during the 1950's the overall value of the export trade dropped.

NATURE OF THE GOODS IN FOREIGN TRADE. Generally speaking, Latin America exports agricultural goods and raw materials, and imports finished goods. Some very important minerals that the United States needs come from these countries, such as iron ore from Chile, tin from Bolivia, and manganese from Brazil. Leading agricultural goods shipped to the United States include coffee, bananas, sugar, and sisal. United States commercial policies can have a profound effect not only upon trade patterns but also upon a national economy and even a foreign policy in Latin America. This is especially true since Latin American states, like African countries, tend to export a predominance of a single commodity. For instance, the ban laid on imports of Latin American cattle contributed to Argentinian hostility toward the United States and oriented Argentinian trade to Europe. Large rises in the price of coffee may turn North Americans to tea drinking and wreck the economy of Colombia. One very serious problem for Latin American governments today is the fall in the world prices of the goods their countries export, which is leading to an unfavorable balance of trade—a very disadvantageous situation for countries that are receiving investment capital.

DIRECTION AND VEHICLES OF FOREIGN TRADE. The largest amount of Latin American trade is with the United States. By the late 1950's, however, Great Britain and Germany were again important Latin American markets; they can buy such goods as wheat and beef that the United States does not need to import. Soviet-Bloc governments have sent trade missions to various Latin American countries, but by 1961 still had little trade with the area. A significant fact is that Soviet-Bloc governments, for political reasons, will buy such items as coffee and copper that are in surplus in Latin America and for much of which the United States and Western European countries have no immediate economic use. Latin American commerce is transported in the ships of many countries. Argentina and Brazil have fairly large merchant marines.

GOVERNMENT

In every Latin American country the government is formally a republic. Such large states as Argentina, Brazil, and Mexico are federal; the component political units have fairly wide powers. Generally, however, the government is unitary. In imitation of the United States, the governments tend to be presidential, with an official separation of powers. Usually the legislature is bicameral; the "upper" house may have exceptional qualifications for members. In some smaller countries, such as El Salvador and Honduras, however, the legislature is unicameral. Voting power is generally conferred upon all adults. In a few countries, such as Costa Rica, voting is compulsory. With important exceptions, Latin American countries have a long tradition of political unrest and dictatorship. Costa Rica and Uruguay are two countries that have had rather stable governments. On the other hand, such states as Haiti and Colombia have often suffered revolutions. In the recent past, almost every Latin American state has had a period of dictatorship. Still, in the last ten years Latin American leaders have shown more self-restraint; two major dictators overthrown in the 1950's were Perón in Argentina and Getulio Vargas in Brazil, and in 1961 Rafael Trujillo of the Dominican Republic was assassinated. Latin American dictators have tended to pattern themselves not so much after Hitler or Mussolini as after Franco; that is, they are not totalitarian, but authoritarian. Fidel Castro is the outstanding exception. Today in a number of countries there is genuine competition among political parties for office and power, through legal elections.

MILITARY FORCES AND STRATEGIC SITUATION

Every Latin American state has armed forces of some type, their size and nature depending upon both the foreign policy and the domestic stability of the government. The strategic situation of all Latin America is based on its geographic location and upon the attitudes adopted toward it by the governments of the United States and the Soviet Union.

Military Forces. All the Latin American countries have some sort of armed forces. There are, however, considerable differences among these armed forces, depending largely on their purposes. In Haiti and Costa Rica, for instance, there is solely an armed police force to maintain civil order. That in Costa Rica has only 500 members, doubtless because the country has a tradition of stable government. Other countries, including one as small as the Dominican Republic, have distinct armies, navies, and air forces. In some countries, where the government is a military dictatorship and there seems to be a threat of revolution, these are fairly large. Most of these countries have conscription. Still, these forces are not as large in proportion to population as are those of the United States. What is in 1962 unique among Latin American military forces is that of Cuba, where almost the entire able-bodied population has been organized into a mass militia, doubtless for the ends of propaganda and of combatting any domestic "counterrevolutionary" forces. Many Latin American governments receive some military aid and equipment from the United States; Cuba has received such large quantities of weapons from the Soviet-Bloc countries that many authorities rank the Cuban armed forces as second only to those of the United States in the New World.

Strategic Situation. The most important factor in the strategic situation of Latin American countries is their nearness to the United States. For this reason they may expect assistance from the United States in case of attack upon them, or intervention by the United States in case of hostile action by them toward the United States. At the same time, they may be used as bases for Soviet attacks upon the United States.

THE POSSIBILITIES OF ASSISTANCE FROM, AND INTERVENTION BY, THE UNITED STATES. In case they are attacked by a non-American country, Latin American states may look to the United States for immediate assistance; this is assured to them by United States adherence to the Monroe Doctrine. On the other hand, in case any Latin American government carries on activities that officials in the United States regard as hostile, United States armed forces are in a position to intervene in the country involved. However, since Presidents Coolidge and Hoover laid the basis for the Good Neighbor Policy and since the United States abrogated the Platt Amendment, United States armed forces have not interfered in any Latin American state. Nevertheless, by using various sorts of pressure, the United States government contributed to the fall of a Communist regime in Guatemala in 1954. Then, in 1960 and 1961, it brought commercial and diplomatic pressure on the Castro government in Cuba. However, after organizing an invasion force of anti-Castro Cubans and promising to furnish air support, it withheld this support. Primarily for this reason, it appears, the invasion attempt was smashed by Cuban troops.

THE USE OF LATIN AMERICA AS A BASE FOR SOVIET OPERATIONS. Soviet officials regard Latin America as a principal base for their operations against the United States. Soviet agents appeal to various sentiments and groups for backing; nationalism, anti-Yankeeism, students, intellectuals, and union leaders are among their chief targets. Communist Parties are outlawed in some countries. Yet there are strong Communist Parties, or Communist-dominated parties, in such countries as Brazil, Argentina, Bolivia, and Venezuela. Early in 1960 it was estimated that there were 240,000 Communist Party members in Latin America. Mexico City and Montevideo are important centers for the distribution of Communist literature and gathering places for Communist functionaries. The Castro government of Cuba is a Communist regime, as shown by its economic policies, its violent anti-Americanism, its fomenting of anti-American riots in Panama, its sympathetic ties with the Soviet and the Communist Chinese governments, and Castro's statement to this effect.

FOREIGN POLICY

There is no one foreign policy for all Latin American governments. Indeed, as can be seen from the foregoing, the foreign policy of any individual Latin American country may depend upon which group or party is in control. Cuba provides an outstanding illustration of this principle: the government of Fulgencio Batista, which preceded that of Castro, was little less dictatorial than the Castro government, but it was pro-United States. In general, in 1962 the governments of Latin America except that of Cuba are friendly toward the United States. Their chief complaints are that they are too dependent upon nongovernmental investments from the United States and that the United States government has granted them a disproportionately small share of its overseas economic aid. This complaint may be at least partly stopped by the establishment, in 1960, of the Inter-American Development Bank, which is designed to stimulate economic growth in Latin America; and by the drafting, in 1961, of a ten-year plan to give Latin American governments $20 billion in aid from the United States and other countries. Meanwhile, among themselves the Latin-American countries have far fewer disputes than they once had. The unseating of Perón and the assassination of Trujillo have removed two men whom leaders in several other countries viewed as threats to their security. Perhaps the most serious tensions today are those between Castro and the heads of the other Caribbean nations, particularly Venezuela, which have accused Castro of trying to foment pro-Communist revolutions. The Organization of American States (OAS) including the governments of all Latin American countries along with that of the United States, furnishes machinery that can probably halt any inter-American dispute short of war, provided that the governments concerned are willing to use this machinery. In 1962 the Council of the OAS excluded Cuba from participation in OAS affairs, on the ground that the political system of Cuba was "incompatible" with the principles of the inter-American community.

Review Questions

1. What factors in the population, geography, and natural resources of Latin America may add to the future role of this area in world politics, and what factors in these elements may detract from this future role?

2. Except for the presence or absence of natural resources, what factors in Latin America may contribute to a rise in the general standard of living, and what factors may impede such a rise? What advice should the governments of the United States and Western Europe furnish to Latin American officials seeking to raise the standard of living in their countries?

3. What are the principal interests of the Soviet Bloc powers concerning Latin America? Compare Latin America, Africa south of the Sahara, and South and Southeast Asia, in terms of their importance to the Soviet Bloc.

4. What are the future possibilities of peace among the Latin American states? What means are available for the prevention of war among these countries?

PART 3 INSTRUMENTS OF WORLD POLITICS

23 THE ELEMENTS OF INTERNATIONAL LAW

International law comprises essentially the body of rules according to which governments are expected to conduct their relations with one another. The term *international law* itself includes two somewhat confusing ideas. First, the word *international* may lead to the inference that these are rules affecting *nations* viewed simply as peoples; to the contrary, these rules concern *governments,* as representatives or agents of nations, and the word *nation* here must be equated with *state.* Second, in various ways the word *law* here has a sense different from that when the word is used in connection with the enactments of a legislature; one of the most obvious differences is that there is no executive agency possessing by common consent the authority to enforce international law. Yet the term *international law* has the strength of custom behind it, and in a great number of ways the rules that it contains are viewed as law. Apart from the rules that affect the relations among governments, there have been—especially in recent years—attempts to institute a code of international law under which individual government officials may be prosecuted for certain acts. The trials of wartime German and Japanese leaders after World War II illustrated these efforts. This text, however, is concerned chiefly with intergovernmental relations. This chapter deals mainly with the historical origins and presently accepted sources of international law and with the position of states under international law.

HISTORICAL ORIGINS OF INTERNATIONAL LAW

Most of the historical origins of current international law reach back only a few centuries. It is true that, as noted in a previous chapter, there was a rudimentary sort of international law among the Greek city-states. Almost certainly there were comparable rules, now lost,

275

governing the interrelations in even older city-state systems, such as that of Sumeria. However, these codes have had almost no impact upon the development of modern international law. The succession of the Greek city-state system by the empires of Alexander the Great and of Rome in effect abolished the very objects to which international law applies—independent, equal states. Then, the fall of the Roman Empire eventually brought such a disruption of law and such a scattering of political authority that not only the objects of international law but also any sense of a moral obligation to strive for law and order vanished. Hence the real beginnings of present-day international law date from the time when this moral obligation was reborn through the Christian Church and when objects for international law reappeared in the form of nation-states.

The Spanish Theologians. A group of Spanish theologians in the sixteenth and early seventeenth centuries was responsible for the first studies of what might be termed international law. One of these thinkers, Francisco de Vitoria (1480–1546), attempted to make a legal system out of certain medieval rules and practices governing such matters as war and commerce. Another Spanish theologian, the Jesuit Francisco Suarez (1548–1617), tried to base this kind of system upon natural law, or the law of reason.

Gentili. Alberico Gentili (1552–1608), an Italian jurist, applied the precedents of Roman law to problems of contemporary international relations. At the same time he was prone to balance these precedents of *actual* practice against the principles of natural law, which were as much hope as reality. Gentili also distinguished between international law and the authority of the Roman Catholic Church. A few writers consider him to be the founder of international law.

Grotius. Hugo Grotius (1583–1645) is viewed by most writers as the "father of international law" through his chief work, *De jure belli ac pacis (On the Law of War and Peace)*. This work shows that Grotius was considerably influenced by both Suarez and Gentili. A Dutchman with military and diplomatic experience, Grotius had witnessed some of the ravages brought to Europe by the religious wars of his times. His principal aim was to write a textbook on the laws and rules governing the conduct of states toward one another similar to existing books on national laws, with the hope that his work would encourage governments and rulers to observe these laws and rules. In pursuing this aim, Grotius united two great currents of law stemming from Rome, the *jus gentium* (law of nations) and the *jus naturale* (natural law). The *jus gentium* was a system of imperial law compiled from the laws of the many peoples in the Roman Empire. The *jus naturale,* which embodied reason, was a code of ethical behavior applicable to all men. Grotius visualized as the objects of his legal system a group of independent, equal states. Although he was not especially concerned with preventing all wars, he did seek to assure that all wars be "just"—that is, that their goal be the achievement of justice. He also aimed at lessening the cruelties of warfare. One other noteworthy interest was his insistence on the principle of the *open sea*—the doctrine that the oceans, save for coastal waters, are open to the ships of all countries.

Schools of Theorists. With the appearance of *De jure belli ac pacis,* three important schools of international-law theorists emerged.

THE NATURALIST SCHOOL. The Naturalist School based international law chiefly on the *jus naturale.* For instance, Samuel Pufendorf (1632–1697), a German jurist, argued that international law is applicable to all governments, whether or not they are Christian.

THE POSITIVIST SCHOOL. The Positivist School held that the *jus gentium,* or practice, was the prime source of international law. Gentili was a forerunner of this school. One leading member of the school, John Selden (1584–1654), an English jurist, denied Grotius' principle of the open sea. To set these two men in their contexts, Grotius was writing in behalf of Dutch efforts to break the long-standing Portuguese monopoly of trade in the East Indies. Selden, by contrast, was writing to attack Dutch fishermen operating in waters claimed by the English.

THE GROTIAN OR ECLECTIC SCHOOL. The Grotian, or Eclectic, School drew its inspiration from Grotius' combination of the *jus naturale* with the *jus gentium.* Christian de Wolff (1679–1754) expanded Grotius' principles by using the greater knowledge of historical events available by his time. Emeric de Vattel (1714–67), whose works followed but added little to those of Wolff, was the first popularizer of international law.

International Conferences and Agreements. Although these theorists created a framework for, and aroused interest in, international law, they did not contribute much to its subject matter or codification. These have accumulated largely since 1800, through the processes and machinery of international conferences and agreements. This work, it must be emphasized, rests to a very large degree upon prior customs, habits, traditions, and understandings.

POST-NAPOLEONIC AGREEMENTS. The representatives who gathered at two of the great conferences during the post-Napoleonic years, the Congresses of Vienna (1815) and Aix-la-Chapelle (1818), reached agreements on various subjects. For one thing, they agreed on the status and classification of diplomatic agents, such as ambassadors and ministers. The representatives also agreed that the slave trade should be abolished. They could not, however, agree on the specific means to be used in accomplishing this goal. Still another point in which the representatives concurred was the principle that international rivers should be open to the ships of all countries.

THE DECLARATION OF PARIS. The Declaration of Paris, drafted in 1856 at the Congress of Paris after the Crimean War, was designed mainly to lessen barriers to international trade during wartime. It was connected with the efforts to secure universal peacetime free trade then current in many European countries. The Declaration affirmed the principle that enemy-owned goods on a neutral ship, except contraband of war, are exempt from seizure in time of war, and the rule that warring countries should respect neutral noncontraband property on enemy ships. The Declaration furthermore asserted the doctrine that a blockade is legal only when effective. Finally, the Declaration forbade the issuance of letters of marque and reprisal, for converting merchant ships into privateers. Most of the great powers afterward agreed to the Declaration.

THE HAGUE CONFERENCES. The Hague Conferences of 1899 and 1907 perhaps more than any other international gatherings assembled a body of existing principles and practices into a code of international law. The delegates at the Conferences also relied upon certain earlier declarations of policy and agreements. They were particularly concerned with the laws of warfare. Here they used as precedents the "Instructions for the Government of Armies of the United States in the Field" (1863), the *Geneva Convention for the Amelioration of the Condition of the Wounded in War* (1864), and the *Code of Land Warfare* (Brussels Conference of 1874). The delegates concerned themselves with, among other things, the rights of neutral countries in naval warfare; the status of enemy property in land warfare; the treatment of prisoners of war; and the naval bombardment of undefended towns. Finally, as discussed in a preceding chapter, the delegates deliberated the pacific settlement of international disputes and in 1899 created the Permanent Court of Arbitration.

THE LONDON CONFERENCE. The London Conference of 1908–9 met partly to deal with questions left unsettled by the Hague Conference of 1907. Its delegates reached agreements mainly in the area of naval warfare. They adopted rules concerning such matters as blockades, contraband, and convoys.

ROOTS OF INTERNATIONAL LAW

The roots of international law, for the purposes of this discussion, lie in four areas: its purposes, or aims; its sources; its evidences, or documents proving the existence of the law; and its sanctions, or instruments for enforcement.

Purposes. The traditional purposes of international law, as seen by its practitioners, are to prevent suffering in international conflicts and to uphold national rights. Such purposes show a general aim of lessening the hardships of war upon individuals, national groups, and governments. In recent times, when many political leaders have sought to outlaw war entirely or to establish means for blocking its occurrence, international law has acquired the added and perhaps most important purpose of keeping the peace.

Sources. The sources of international law, to contrast them with its causes or its evidences, are the authorities giving rise to law. Today it is generally accepted that there are two sources of international law—custom and treaties. These are the "historical facts" that give international law its force. Some writers add reason as a third source of international law. Custom includes general usages among governments that are based on implied consent and widespread imitation. Ideally, at least, the custom eventually reaches all governments. Treaties may here be defined as express agreements of any sort among governments, comprising, for example, conventions and protocols as well. Treaties officially involve only the countries that are parties to the agreements; however, other countries may voluntarily abide by their terms. For instance, neither the United States nor Spain was a party to the Declaration of Paris of 1856; nevertheless, each complied with its terms during the Spanish-American War of 1898.

Evidences. The evidences of international law are the documents that give authority to the law and that may be cited in court to prove the existence of the law. The statute that organizes and empowers the International Court of Justice directs its members to use as evidences of international law: (1) conventions and treaties binding upon the parties in the case at issue; (2) international customs; (3) general principles of public law accepted in the domestic court systems of states; and (4) the writings of jurists and the precedents set by court decisions. It must be emphasized that as a general rule international courts are not bound by precedents and that this trait marks one of the principal differences between national law and international law. Nevertheless, the Court often respects prior decisions rendered by such bodies as courts of arbitration, international commissions of inquiry, and prize courts. Yet it must be noted that the interrelations among all these judicial agencies are not the same as those among the courts in the United States: there is no prescription of "supreme law" in international relations like the one in the United States Constitution.

Sanctions. The sanctions of international law are very weak by comparison with those of national law. Under national law, a national government imposes the sanctions of the law over the individuals and groups that are the subjects of the law. Under international law, since there is no international government to impose the sanctions of the law upon the national governments that are the subjects of the law, these national governments impose the sanctions of the law themselves. In other words, national governments interpret and enforce international law upon themselves. Still, notwithstanding such glaring violations of international law as the 1939 Soviet attack upon Finland despite Soviet obligations under the League of Nations Covenant, international law is much more often obeyed than it is disregarded. Among the factors that may be termed sanctions are (1) good faith and world public opinion; (2) habits and inertia, making the obedience of governments to international law often routine and mechanical; and (3) self-interest, inasmuch as governments may benefit by observing a given law and may thus protect themselves from reprisals and retaliation. These factors underlie the common respect paid the immunity of diplomatic agents and the general adherence to commercial treaties. In recent years, world leaders have also striven to institute sanctions against governments breaking international law by waging aggressive warfare, through (1) the Kellogg-Briand Pact, which renounced recourse to war; (2) the League of Nations Covenant, which provided for economic sanctions; (3) the United Nations Charter, which authorizes the Security Council to use force against an aggressor; and (4) the Nuremberg Trials, at which some German leaders were found guilty of, and punished for, planning aggression and committing crimes against humanity.

STATES UNDER INTERNATIONAL LAW

States are the fundamental units and subjects of international law. A state (not to be confused with a State in the United States) consists of a definite territory with a settled population under a stable government that possesses *sovereignty*. Sovereignty is the power to make final decisions over a territory and people. Sovereignty has several aspects, which are described below, that are concerned with international law.

Areas that do not have sovereign governments are dependencies of various sorts.

Some Important Aspects of Sovereignty. Some important aspects of sovereignty include the right of a sovereign state to existence, the right of a sovereign state to independence, and the equality of sovereign states.

THE RIGHT TO EXISTENCE. Every sovereign state has the right to existence, or, in other terms, the right of self-preservation. It is inherently entitled to take any steps its leaders deem necessary, within the bounds of international law, to oppose any attack that threatens its existence. The chief grounds for dispute over this right stem from the questions as to how immediate a threat is and as to whether there is a threat at all. This right of sovereign states to existence is one of the bases for the inherent authority of the President of the United States to conduct foreign relations without reference to the Constitution.

THE RIGHT TO INDEPENDENCE. Every sovereign state has the right to independence in the conduct of both its domestic and its foreign policies, subject to the restraints of international law. As a corollary of this right, every state has the obligation not to intervene in the affairs of other states. Presumably intervention can be justified by authority given in a treaty agreed to by both countries involved; thus by its own consent one state may empower another to interfere in its governmental actions. The impact of international law upon the conduct of domestic policies is shown in the following case: Officials of the city of Chicago sought permission from Congress to draw more water out of Lake Michigan, for use in the city sewage disposal system. However, the government of Canada protested to the United States Department of State, on the ground that this action might dangerously lower the water level in the Great Lakes, an international waterway; the State Department honored these protests, and notified Congress about them.

EQUALITY. Every sovereign state has equality of legal status under international law. However, this does not mean that every state has an equality of rights and obligations under international law; for instance, after its 1947 peace treaty with the Allies, Italy had particular obligations concerning reparations that the Allies did not have. Of course, states do not have equality with respect to power, population, wealth, or territory; they even accept such forms of inequality as that existing in the UN Security Council, where five countries have permanent seats and the others have temporary seats. Thus this sense of equality means only, for example, that the USSR and Bulgaria are legal equals as members of the Warsaw Pact, or as petitioners before the World Court.

Dependencies. Dependencies—or dependent states, a somewhat contradictory term—are political units that are not sovereign. Essentially, they are political units that do not have native governments free to conduct their own affairs. In recent years, as discussed in a previous chapter, the number of dependencies has been falling, as their leaders and peoples have either assumed or been granted political independence. Yet, as indicated in the analysis of sovereignty above, new sovereign states are not necessarily equal in the factors that underlie national power and consequently may be so subject to influence over the conduct of their affairs that in fact they are little more than dependencies. There are several types of dependencies.

COLONY. A colony is a completely dependent area under the title of the possessor. The Falkland Islands are a colony of the United Kingdom.

CONDOMINIUM. A condominium is a colony possessed by two or more powers. The New Hebrides is a condominium of the United Kingdom and France.

PROTECTORATE. A protectorate has a government that is comparatively independent in domestic affairs but that conducts foreign relations under the supervision of some other country, which may be termed the suzerain. Bhutan is a protectorate of India.

LEASED TERRITORY. A leased territory is an area in one sovereign state that by terms of a treaty is leased from it by another sovereign state. Guantánamo Bay is a leased territory in Cuba held by the United States.

TRUST TERRITORY. A trust territory is any one of several sorts of areas administered by a sovereign state under the supervision of the United Nations. The Caroline Islands is a trust territory administered by the United States.

DIPLOMATIC RECOGNITION

Diplomatic recognition is an act that is elemental for international law since it involves the decision of whether a political unit is sovereign and whether, consequently, it has become a subject of international law. Recognition also is important as being often the decision by government officials in one country that the government of another country respects international law and may be dealt with under the principles of international law.

The Process of Diplomatic Recognition. Officially, the process of diplomatic recognition is a legal act by which the officials of the government in one country accept the government in another country as sovereign and as the legitimate agent of the people in that country to administer their relations with other peoples and governments. The act of recognition is customarily performed by the executive branch of the government and is symbolized by the exchange of diplomatic representatives. However, recognition may be inferred from some act such as the willingness of one government to negotiate concerning a disputed matter with the representatives of another government. The foregoing indicates that recognition is generally a bilateral process, involving the recognizing state and the state to be recognized. Sometimes, however, a government may grant recognition only after consultation with other governments. Also, recognition may be formally collective, as through admission into the United Nations. The refusal to extend recognition generally prevents the two governments from communicating with one another officially except through a third government that recognizes both of them. Finally, it should be noted that recognition may involve either the acceptance of a new government within an existing state or the acceptance of the government of an entirely new state. In recent years the United States government has extended recognition to the rule of Karim el-Kassem in Iraq, an already existing state, and to the government of Ghana, a new state.

The Practice of Diplomatic Recognition. The practice of diplomatic recognition is essentially political rather than legal. Traditionally most governments have extended recognition to any new government that appeared capable of maintaining domestic order and honoring its foreign obligations. In 1913, however, President Wilson of the United States denied recognition to a new government in Mexico, because he thought its leaders had secured power only through bloodshed and treachery. Partly because of Wilson's policy, the Mexican government soon collapsed. Since then the governments of the United States and of some other countries have withheld recognition of new governments to indicate their opposition to them. Hence today the United States does not recognize the government of Communist China. By extending recognition, government leaders can give an inkling of their orientation; thus the new country of Guinea showed where its sympathies lay by recognizing, in 1960, the government of East Germany, which no other government outside the Soviet Bloc had yet recognized. Recognition, moreover, may be continued for a government even when its country has been absorbed by another; the United States continues to recognize Lithuania, although Lithuania has been incorporated into the Soviet Union, to show United States rejection of Soviet claims to this territory. A speedy tender of recognition, such as that of the United

States to Israel in 1948 and that of the USSR to Guinea in 1959, in itself is an indication of the desire to win a friend. Finally, one government may show its hostility to another by withdrawing recognition, as the United States government did with respect to Cuba in 1961.

Review Questions

1. Describe the historical origins of international law. Show how the stages in the codification of international law often comprised responses to specific needs or demands, either general or on the part of one government.

2. What types of evidence are sought in cases at international law? If possible, give an example of each. In terms of evidence, how does international law differ from national law?

3. What are three traditional sanctions of international law? Name four recent documents or actions designed to institute sanctions? How do the sanctions of international law differ from those of national law?

4. What are three important aspects of sovereignty?

5. What is the main difference between a dependency and a state? Name the different kinds of dependencies.

6. How does the government of one country acknowledge the sovereignty of the government of another country? What complications may be involved?

24 APPLICATIONS OF INTERNATIONAL LAW

International law can be, and is, applied to the interrelations among governments in a number of ways. This chapter describes certain phases of world politics in the context of international law. First, it describes diplomacy, which is the machinery and techniques for the conduct of international relations. Diplomacy itself is subject to limits imposed by international law and involves negotiations over, among other things, disputes concerning international law. Next, the chapter discusses two leading fields over which states exercise jurisdiction: persons and places. The exercise of such jurisdiction and the efforts to assure the authority for exercising it are among the commonest grounds for international disputes. Governments have striven through agreements over international law either to eliminate or to lessen the number and severity of these disputes. Finally, the chapter deals with some of the processes, conditions, and instruments involved in the resolution of these disputes: pacific means for settling disputes; the interrelations of belligerents and neutrals during war; the interrelations of belligerents during war; and certain aspects of treaties that may mark the conclusion of a dispute or provide grounds for a new dispute. The importance of international law can be seen in the facts that at any given time there may be a dispute between two or more governments and that almost any such dispute can be argued in terms of international law.

DIPLOMACY

Diplomacy is the conduct of negotiations between governments by a special, formal hierarchy of government personnel.

The Hierarchy of Diplomatic Personnel. The diplomatic personnel of any country actually begins with the executive head of the government, who officially bears the chief responsibility for the international relations of his country. Subordinate to the executive head is an office for conducting these relations, bearing some such title as Department of State or Ministry of Foreign Affairs. The head of this office —the Secretary of State or Foreign Minister—is the principal subordinate of the executive head in the area of foreign relations. Under him are two main groups of officials and employees: those who serve in the country and those who serve abroad. In 1961 the United States Department of State had almost 39,000 officials and employees, 10,000 in the United States and 29,000 overseas. These overseas employees are the ones loosely termed *diplomats*. In most countries they are career personnel, selected according to professional capabilities. These overseas personnel may be divided specifically into two groups: *diplomatic* and *consular*. The diplomatic personnel is concerned mainly with political affairs; the consular, with economic. The overseas diplomatic personnel is assigned to offices maintained by its government abroad. There are two levels of such offices: embassies, which have the greatest prestige, and legations. The heads of these offices, or "chiefs of mission," are called ambassadors in embassies and ministers in legations.

Privileges and Immunities of Diplomatic Personnel. Diplomatic personnel enjoy numerous and distinctive privileges and immunities. The most important of these stem largely from the principle, established in international law, that an embassy or a legation constitutes an enclave of foreign territory and consequently may not be invaded by the forces of the host country. In other words, governments may not enter the embassies or legations of other governments to investigate or seize papers, property, or persons. This is the rule that makes it possible for a political refugee to obtain asylum in an embassy or legation. Diplomatic personnel themselves are immune from arrest, even for trivial offenses; however, the host country may declare such an individual *persona non grata*, after which his government is expected to call him home. Consular personnel have similar, but fewer, immunities. Diplomatic and consular personnel have regular salaries, which in the lower ranks compare favorably with those paid in nongovernmental posts. The chiefs of mission, however, those of the United States in particular, are often not paid salaries commensurate with the ordinary expenses of their posts. This is one of the reasons for which the United States ambassador to a country such as Great Britain is likely to be chosen from among the wealthy contributors to the President's political party.

Functions of Diplomacy and Diplomats. The essential function of diplomacy and diplomats is to safeguard and advance the interests of their country in time of peace, by peaceful means. Ideally, the diplomat may be said to strive for peace through accommodation, that is, by working with diplomats from other countries to balance and compromise their respective national interests with a minimum of dissatisfaction for their governments. To be more specific, diplomats have three leading tasks. First, they represent their government in negotiations with other governments. For instance, they submit the views of their government in preliminary discussions regarding a treaty. Second, they gather information about the country in which they are stationed, for transmission to their government. Here their role is somewhat akin to that of the spy; but the information they send is generally available to the public, so that the diplomats' value lies in their sifting the important from the immaterial and in the interpretations they give to the information they send. Finally, the diplomat is a symbol of his country; hence the apparent need for the sumptuous banquets that he provides for the representatives of other governments. Consular personnel seek to further the economic well-being of their country through its business ties with other countries. For example, they assemble and transmit manufacturing data for the country in which they are posted. Moreover, consular personnel are more likely than diplomats to handle the personal concerns and difficulties of individuals from their countries.

Past Achievements of Diplomacy and Diplomats. In the past, diplomacy and diplomats could claim many achievements in their efforts to advance the interests of their country without recourse to war. These achievements fell mainly in the time between the Thirty Years' War and the outbreak of World War I—from 1648 until 1914—a period that is sometimes called the "Golden Age of Diplomacy." For example, the Congress of Berlin in 1878 probably prevented a war between Great Britain and Russia. By his adroit dealings, Benjamin Franklin persuaded the French to come to the aid of the young United States in 1778. The French, although inherently much weaker than the Germans in respect to power, through their diplomacy from 1890 on formed a series of alliances that by 1914 made them feel equal to challenging Germany. Talleyrand at the Congress of Vienna in 1814–15 kept France from losing much of the territory that its conquerors thought it should surrender. Count Wenzel Kaunitz-Rietburg, Chancellor of Austria, in 1756 effected a "diplomatic revolution" that made France an ally of Austria instead of its enemy; the ultimate failure of this "revolution" came from the defeat of Austrian armies by Prussian troops, and not from diplomacy. Yet diplomats in these years sometimes not only failed to prevent war but even shared responsibility for bringing it on; the fumbling of the French ambassador to Prussia in 1870 contributed to the outbreak of the Franco-Prussian War.

The Present Eclipse of Diplomacy and Diplomats. Both diplomacy and diplomats have gone into eclipse in recent years, especially since 1945. Diplomacy suffers from the handicaps indicated in Chapter 11. Specifically, the two superpowers in general have adopted positions from which they rarely if ever withdraw, so that diplomacy suffocates from deprivation of its essential atmosphere of compromise. Moreover, thanks in part to Woodrow Wilson's demand for "open covenants, openly arrived at," efforts at diplomacy today are conducted in a glare of publicity that forbids government officials to retreat from an assumed position lest they incur public disfavor at home. Efforts at diplomacy through the United Nations are especially hampered by public attention and information. The veto power in the Security Council imposes another difficulty upon diplomacy: the refusal of one government to accept a multilateral treaty means only that this government will not adhere to an agreement accepted by other governments; the exercise of the veto, however, forbids the establishing of any agreement at all. As for diplomats themselves, the airplane and radio have permitted executive chiefs and heads of foreign offices to conduct direct negotiations among themselves and thus supersede their diplomats. Executive chiefs, moreover, use these negotiations to strengthen their political standing at home.

JURISDICTION OVER CITIZENS AND ALIENS

The jurisdiction of a state over citizens and aliens—which two groups include all persons—revolves about such questions as the determination of a person's citizenship and the protection that a government owes its citizens abroad.

Citizenship. Citizenship is a constitutional and legal status involving the allegiance that an individual owes and pays to a particular government; it is established by the laws of that government and respected by international law. Possession of citizenship today, at least among adults, is commonly accompanied by the power to vote.

THE ACQUISITION OF CITIZENSHIP. Citizenship may be acquired either by birth or by naturalization.

By Birth. Individuals may acquire citizenship by birth, according to either the *jus soli* (right of the soil) or the *jus sanguinis* (right of the blood). According to the *jus soli*, a person is a citizen of the country that has jurisdiction over the place where he was born. Every person born in the United States, with a few exceptions, has United States citizenship, notwithstanding the citizenship, or the national or racial origins, of his parents. According to the *jus sanguinis,* a person is a citizen of the same country as his parents are. A child born in a foreign country to parents both of whom are United States citizens and at least one of whom has previously resided in the United States is a United States citizen. There is no international law regarding acquisition of citizenship by birth. The two methods for acquiring citizenship by birth may so conflict that two different governments may claim the same person as their citizen. That is, an individual might be born in country A of parents who were citizens of country B. Country A, according to the *jus soli,* as well as country B, according to the *jus sanguinis,* might claim him as its citizen.

By Naturalization. Individuals, either singly or in groups, may acquire citizenship by naturalization, a legal process controlled by national law. This process almost always involves exchanging citizenship of one country for citizenship of another. Naturalization by group may occur through treaty, as when the United States government assured United States citizenship to all residents of the Louisiana Purchase area; or by legislation, as when Congress made all residents of Puerto Rico United States citizens. Naturalization singly may take place through association or relation with another person; a minor may change citizenship when his parents do, and a wife may change her citizenship to that of her husband. Finally, naturalization may be a purely individual act, by means of petition or application. A person who satisfies a number of standards such as residence, literacy, and allegiance, may secure United States citizenship. Other governments similarly grant citizenship but often have standards lower than those of the United States.

Loss of Citizenship. Persons may lose their citizenship, whether acquired by birth or by naturalization, either by deliberate act on their part or by governmental legislation or decree. Any United States citizen may give up his citizenship by renouncing it, an act termed *expatriation.* In the eyes of the United States government, every naturalized United States citizen has expatriated himself from the country of his birth. Governments in some countries, however, do not acknowledge such acts of expatriation; natives of such countries found within their borders after becoming naturalized citizens of another country may be charged with evading compulsory military service. The country that has granted them naturalization has no way of protecting them. The government of the United States may take naturalized citizenship away from persons who have, among other things, committed fraud to secure citizenship; this process is called *denaturalization*. Some governments have tried to remove citizenship from native-born citizens, by *denationalization*; the Nazi German government tried to do this to the Jews. Nevertheless, the governments of many countries regard such *stateless persons* as citizens of the country of their birth.

Authority over Citizens Abroad. A government has little authority over its citizens abroad, except for those in military or diplomatic service. It may demand that the government of another country extend to its citizens the full protection of the laws, but it has no way under international law for enforcing this demand. Since 1945 the stationing of troops in foreign countries, especially by the United States and the USSR, has brought a new problem. That is, it is particularly to the interest of the governments to which these troops belong that the troops do not by their acts offend the people of the country in which they are stationed. Hence the United States government has negotiated with the governments of many countries what are termed *status-of-forces* treaties. These treaties generally provide that military personnel charged with criminal offenses while on duty be tried in United States military courts, and that those charged with criminal offenses while off duty be tried in the civilian courts of the host country. A government does retain some authority over a citizen who has fled his country after apparently committing a crime. Most governments have signed with most other governments so-called *treaties of extradition,* under which they may ask officials of the country to which the suspected person has fled to have him arrested and sent home for trial. However, a government will generally not honor such a request for a person charged with a political crime; it may, however, deny permanent asylum to the political refugee.

Authority over Aliens. Every government has full authority over aliens—that is, citizens of other countries—who are resident or transient within its borders. The only exceptions to this are the diplomatic and military personnel indicated above. Otherwise a government may require aliens to abide by the same laws as those for citizens and may impose upon them the same penalties for violations. Furthermore, a government may place special requirements upon aliens, such as that they register yearly with the government. It may also to some degree handicap them, as by demanding exceptional qualifications in order to secure a license for a trade or profession. In recent times, in keeping with the world-wide trend toward economic nationalism, some governments have forbidden aliens to own property of certain sorts in the country, particularly land. Occasionally a government has seized the property of aliens within its borders; it may then be the task of the aliens' governments to seek redress for their citizens. Still, in spite of the distinctions a government may make between its citizens and aliens, it owes aliens the full protection of the laws, and the government of a weak country that mistreats the citizens of a strong country may find itself in serious trouble.

JURISDICTION OVER TERRITORY

A government has full jurisdiction over the territory of its country and over the persons and things in it. The only exceptions to this principle are diplomatic and military personnel and property. This jurisdiction enjoyed by a government is one of the hallmarks of its sovereign status.

Acquisitions of Territory. According to international law, a state, under its government, may acquire territory in any one of several ways: occupation, prescription, cession, conquest, and accretion.

OCCUPATION AND PRESCRIPTION. *Occupation* is the effective possession of a territory not owned by any other state, with the desire and ability to hold it permanently. The absence of competing claims, the establishing of a settlement in the territory, official proclamations affecting the territory, and the recognition of title to the territory by other governments are good evidences of legal occupation. Occupation may or may not have been preceded by discovery; discovery alone is not now respected, as it was to some degree centuries ago, as a valid claim to ownership. The only area on earth not yet "owned" by some state is Antarctica, although several governments have claimed portions of it. In the absence of settlement, these claims have relatively little meaning. The principal significance of this rule today involves extraterrestrial bodies—the moon and the planets. In the absence of some new "space law," the moon, or any part of it, will belong not to the country that first lands a man upon it but to the country that first colonizes it. *Prescription,* which is similar to occupation, is the long-continued possession of territory, which in itself gives title without benefit of other proof.

CESSION, CONQUEST, AND ACCRETION. *Cession* is the transfer of title to land from one state to another. It may be achieved through war, threat of war, sale, exchange for some other territory, or the granting of some other privilege. It is usually expressed in a treaty. *Conquest* is the seizure of territory from another state by force of arms, followed by a declaration of annexation. Such physical acquisition is not always followed by a treaty. The Kellogg-Briand Pact was, among other things, an effort to end the practice of acquisition by conquest. *Accretion* results from the natural changes in territory such as the formation of a delta.

Types of Territory Subject to Disputes. Certain types of territory are especially subject to disputes over jurisdiction, and a considerable body of international law has been created in efforts to prevent or resolve such disputes.

TERRITORIAL WATERS. Territorial waters are the waters touching or close to the land of a given state that are under the jurisdiction of that state. Any body of water completely surrounded by a state is territorial; moreover, a gulf or estuary opening into the ocean comprises territorial waters from headland to headland, provided that the opening is no more than ten miles wide. Along the coast itself, the width of territorial waters has been contested. The traditional width has been three miles, which long ago was the range of coast artillery. In recent years, however, countries have been claiming jurisdiction over waters farther from shore, not only for military purposes but also for fishing, exploiting oil resources, and pursuing smugglers. In 1960 most governments sent representatives to a conference where they debated establishing a six-mile policing limit with an additional six-mile fishing limit, but they achieved no agreement. The state generally grants the *right of innocent passage* to privately owned ships from other states. The state concerned may inspect and regulate these foreign vessels, but it cannot take action respecting crimes committed on these ships unless the crimes have effects ashore. Under the *doctrine of hot pursuit,* a ship suspected of association with some crime may be followed and captured outside territorial waters. Local government authorities may not under any conditions board a *public vessel,* such as a warship, owned by a sovereign government.

PORTS. Ports are under the jurisdiction of the country in which they are situated unless they have been leased by some other power. According to international usage, however, foreign ships have certain privileges. Government-owned ships such as war vessels have complete immunity in the ports of other countries, but government-owned merchant ships may be subject to almost the same rules as privately owned ships. With respect to foreign merchant ships, the United States assumes jurisdiction over any serious crime that may occur on board.

RIVERS. Rivers that flow between or through two or more countries, such as the St. Lawrence, the Rhine, the Danube, and the Jordan, are international rivers. Where these rivers are boundaries, the boundary line follows the deepest navigation channel. If the channel moves slowly, by *accretion,* the line moves with it. However, if the channel moves rapidly or erratically, by *avulsion,* the line is constant; this is the situation concerning the Rio Grande between the United States and Mexico. Specialists in international law agree widely, but not universally, that an international river is not necessarily open to the ships of all countries. The questions of navigation rights and of the use of water for irrigation or power generation are usually settled by specific treaties.

CANALS. Canals are under the jurisdiction of the country that owns them, subject to limitations by treaty or statute. The Panama Canal is open to all ships, and the same rates of fees are imposed upon vessels of the United States as upon those of other countries. The Suez Canal has belonged to Egypt since 1956 and is open to the ships of all countries except Israel.

THE HIGH SEAS. The high seas—the waters outside the territorial jurisdiction of any state—are open to the ships of all countries. Every country has full jurisdiction over any ship flying its flag. The chief crime that may occur on the high seas is piracy. Piracy is defined by both national and international law. Under national law it is generally viewed as robbery on the high seas. Under international law it is viewed as any act of violence committed from a ship that does not have the authority of some sovereign state. Every government is empowered to punish acts of piracy; however, a government may seize a foreign ship only for acts defined as piracy under international law.

THE AIR. The air traditionally has been subject to the jurisdiction of the state beneath. Governments generally grant freedom of passage to all civilian aircraft of friendly countries provided they satisfy local regulations. Governments usually require special permits for military planes. International law regarding the air is little developed, since there was little apparent need for it until this century.

SPACE. Proposals for an international law of space are currently being discussed. Such proposals must take into account certain unique features of space and space vehicles. An object such as an artificial satellite when launched has a constant orbit beyond human control; owing to the rotation of the earth, it may pass over many countries, or—to be exact—many countries may pass under it. Also, because of the rotation of the earth the sector of space directly over any one country is always changing. These and other features make it possible that a space law of the future may have a rough analogy to present international law regarding the sea; in other words, up to a specified altitude there may be a "territorial space," beyond which there may be an "open space" or a "high space." The greatest present barrier to the adoption of such a law is that the governments of the chief countries do not yet find any advantage in such a law.

PACIFIC MEANS FOR SETTLING DISPUTES

There are various pacific means for settling international disputes. Such means involve, it must be emphasized, the decision by officials in at least one of the states concerned that the dispute does not merit a war. One fundamental distinction among these means is that some are unilateral whereas others are bilateral or multilateral.

Unilateral Means. Unilateral means are those used by a government that may be said to "take the law into its own hands." They are "measures just short of war." Sometimes, but not always, the state using such methods is far larger than the state subjected to them, so that any resulting settlement is almost the product of coercion. One such method is a *boycott*—a refusal to buy goods from another country. The Chinese imposed a boycott on goods from Japan in 1931–32, as a reaction to the occupation of Manchuria. Another such method is the *embargo*—a ban on all trade with another country. The United States imposed an embargo on trade with France and Great Britain in the early nineteenth century, trying to secure guarantees of neutral rights. A third method is the recall of diplomatic representatives; in 1960 the United States recalled its ambassador to Cuba in an effort to punish the Castro government for its hostile assertions about the United States. A fourth method is the severing of diplomatic relations; the United States severed relations with Cuba in 1961 when the Castro government continued its hostile assertions about, and actions toward, the United States. These methods, and similar ones, do not have much effect except when used by a strong country against a weak one. In other cases, they may lead to war.

Bilateral and Multilateral Means. The bilateral and multilateral pacific means for settling disputes include negotiations, good offices and mediation, inquiry and conciliation, arbitration, and adjudication.

NEGOTIATION. *Negotiation* through bilateral diplomatic communications is the primary and usually effectual method for settling disputes. It may take place by meetings between heads of governments or their representatives, by exchange of notes, or by congress or conference. It may result in full agreement, or it may lead to some other means for achieving a settlement. Sometimes the reasons, or the apparent reasons, for a dispute vanish in the "cooling-off" period that occurs during negotiations. Hence the very continuance of negotiations over a seemingly hopeless situation may result in the easing of the crisis. This seemed to be the attitude of many leaders in the United States during the 1950's, when repeated discussions with Soviet officials brought no important consequences.

GOOD OFFICES AND MEDIATION. When the governments of two countries appear unable to resolve a dispute through negotiation, or when war has actually broken out, leaders in a third country may tender *good offices* in an attempt to advise or induce a settlement. If the tender is accepted, the third country begins *mediation,* or intervention as middleman in bringing the disputants together. The mediating country is an instrument of communication or even an advisor, but not a judge. Rules of mediation were drafted at the Hague Conferences of 1899 and 1907, and in many particular cases afterward.

INQUIRY AND CONCILIATION. *Inquiry* and *conciliation* are viewed as the steps that follow mediation. Inquiry, or investigation, may be conducted either by *mixed commissions* or by *commissions of inquiry,* which include representatives of other states who are empowered to look into the causes of the dispute. Commissions of inquiry have an odd number of members, and only seek facts. Mixed commissions have an even number of members, and not only seek facts but also make recommendations. In 1913 and 1914 United States Secretary of State William J. Bryan negotiated so-called *cooling-off* treaties with a number of countries, which included provisions for permanent *commissions of conciliation.* These bodies were to contain an odd number of members, an equal number being chosen by each party and the odd member being chosen by the other members. Though a number of such commissions were established, none was ever used to settle a dispute. It must be stressed that in all these cases neither party is bound to accept the findings or the decision of the commission.

ARBITRATION. *Arbitration* is a quasi-judicial method for settlement of disputes that includes (1) the voluntary application of the disputing states for an arbitral settlement, (2) their selection of judges for the purpose, (3) their allowing the decision to be based on special facts as well as on points of law, and (4) their agreement to accept the decision as binding on them. Arbitration thus differs from regular judicial procedure in that the court is temporary and that the judges are chosen by the disputants. In earlier times, parties to a dispute who wanted to settle it by arbitration first negotiated a treaty called a *compromise,* in which they agreed upon the question to be dealt with and the procedures to be followed. Later, governments began inserting in other treaties promises to submit all questions, or all questions of certain types, to arbitration. Eventually the governments represented at the Hague Conference of 1899 established the Permanent Court of Arbitration. Governments often refuse to arbitrate questions dealing with "national honor," "vital interests," and "independence." A noteworthy dispute settled by arbitration was that between the United States and Great Britain over the damages inflicted by the "Alabama," a warship supplied by the British to the Confederacy during the Civil War.

ADJUDICATION. *Adjudication* is the settlement of a dispute by a permanent judicial body dealing with international law. Presumably the court is free from dictation or pressure; its decisions are binding and final. As a permanent court it can establish a set of legal traditions and therefore a body of precedents. The first successful international court was the Central American Court of Justice, with members from every Central American country except Panama. It operated usefully for ten years (1907–17), then dissolved because of a quarrel over Nicaraguan canal rights. Subsequently more comprehensive agencies—the Permanent Court of International Justice and the International Court of Justice—were established; they are described elsewhere in the text.

THE INTERRELATIONS OF BELLIGERENTS DURING WAR

International law governing the interrelations among belligerents during war has been developed over several centuries. In the past century it has been codified in several documents, some of the most recent being the Genocide Convention of 1948—not yet ratified by the United States—and the Geneva Conventions of 1949. Despite such efforts, however, the laws of war were frequently violated in both World War I and World War II.

Declarations of War. Supposedly a declaration of war precedes the opening of military action. In 1914, for instance, Germany made formal declarations of war upon Russia and France, and Great Britain upon Germany. By contrast, Germany went to war against Poland in 1939 without a declaration of war. Japan first attacked Pearl Harbor, then declared war, in 1941. In the future, declarations of war seem improbable for at least two reasons. First, the government that declares war may be in effect labeling itself as the aggressor, and, if it loses, its leaders may afterward be charged with "war crimes" and brought to trial. Second, the technology of war has become such that a declaration against one of the superpowers could lead to severe countermeasures within hours or even minutes. In fact, if radar signals had been correctly interpreted on the morning of December 7, 1941, United States planes might have attacked Japanese aircraft before the ships moored in Pearl Harbor were bombed.

Combatants and Noncombatants. Combatants and noncombatants are the two groups into which people are classed for the purposes of the rules of war. Such a distinction was comparatively easy at the time that armaments were fairly simple and soldiers "lived off the land." Today, however, when an entire population may contribute in one way or another to the conduct of hostilities, it is much more difficult to make this distinction. Combatants include not only the members of the regular armed forces but also the personnel of merchant ships that resist capture and groups of civilians organized and functioning under government authority as regular military bodies. All combatants may be fired upon and, if captured, treated as prisoners of war. It is also legal to take noncombatants as hostages to enforce the performance of the laws of war; but it is only for such military necessity that it is legal to interfere with noncombatants. Resident or transient enemy aliens may be deported, interned, or left alone. Persons offering armed resistance without the authority of any government are guerrillas and have no protection from the laws of war. Persons who assume disguises and seek information behind enemy lines are spies; they are entitled to a trial but may be executed. The use of certain weapons and the destruction of unfortified towns have been outlawed. The general purpose of these rules has been to lessen the cruelty of war. It has been presumed that they would be observed if only because of the fear of retaliation, especially against prisoners of war. However, a government such as that of the USSR or Communist China, which does not hesitate to treat almost any of its own citizens with the utmost severity, is not apt to concern itself much with their welfare should they become prisoners of war.

Property. For the purposes of the rules of war, property has been classified in two different ways: (1) governmental and nongovernmental; (2) on land and on sea. Governmental real property in enemy-occupied territory may be used but not confiscated; most other governmental property may be confiscated. Property owned by a citizen of one country located in a country with which his country is at war is generally put under government control for the duration of the war, then may be returned to its owner. Nongovernmental property on land occupied by enemy forces may be taken, but only with compensation. Government-owned enemy ships and other property at sea may be captured, with a few exceptions. Likewise, privately owned enemy ships, except fishing craft and small vessels engaged in coastal trade, may be taken. A partial reason for the harsher treatment of property on sea than that on

land is that loss of property on land, such as a farm, may threaten the
very life of the owner; but loss of property on sea, such as a ship, is not
apt to threaten the very life of the merchant who owns it. This reason
accounts for the exception of fishing craft from the general rule.

THE INTERRELATIONS OF BELLIGERENTS
AND NEUTRALS DURING WAR

In the past two centuries there has developed an important body of
rules distinguishing between belligerents and neutrals. Such rules have
aimed not only at protecting the "innocent bystander" but also at limiting the spread of war. Violations by belligerents of these rules have
been cited as grounds for a declaration of war. In recent years, however, such rules have been less and less observed. Belligerents have become increasingly dependent on products from neutral countries for
waging war; leaders in belligerent countries have intensified their efforts to draw neutrals into the war on their side; leaders in neutral
countries have, willingly or not, tended to favor one belligerent over another; and modern techniques of war, especially nuclear devices, may
by their effects involve the peoples of neutral countries.

Governments of Neutral Countries. Once a war has commenced,
one of the prime necessities for a country seeking to remain neutral is
that the government proclaim its neutrality. Such was the action of
Washington in 1794, which was paralleled by those of Wilson in 1914
and Roosevelt in 1939. A belligerent may demand a declaration of neutrality from another country, as Germany did of France in 1914, then
declare war after the rejection of its demand. After a government has
declared its neutrality, its territory, citizens, and property may not be
attacked by a belligerent save under particular conditions. Meanwhile
the neutral government must not show favors to any of the belligerents.
It cannot permit its territory to be used for the recruiting of troops by a
belligerent, or lend money or sell war materials to a belligerent, or allow
private citizens to fit out vessels for war in its ports. It may, however,
permit its private citizens to lend money or sell munitions to belligerents. Violations of any of the above rules, and of many others, may be
interpreted by a belligerent as an act of war under international law.
The Axis powers held that the execution of the Lend-Lease Act of 1941
was an act of war by the United States government.

Trade of Neutral Countries. The trade of neutral countries enjoys
a number of legal protections, but these protections have often been disregarded by belligerents. Actually, the rules that are meant to protect
neutral trade are a matter of debate, since during a war belligerents and

neutrals interpret them according to their own interests. Supposedly neutral commerce is to be free from interference by belligerents. However, *contraband goods*—that is, goods that may be used for military purposes—may be confiscated from neutral ships by one belligerent if being transported to another belligerent. If more than half the cargo of a neutral ship is contraband, the whole ship may be confiscated. There is no generally accepted definition of contraband, but in recent years belligerents have expanded the term to include almost everything. Under the "doctrine of the continuous voyage," such goods have been confiscated even when their immediate destination was a neutral country, on the suspicion that their final destination was an enemy belligerent. Neutral commerce may also be restricted by an actual blockade of enemy ports, by which one belligerent has on hand the effective military force that can regulate shipping in and out of the ports of another belligerent. With such a blockade, a belligerent is authorized to capture neutral ships.

TREATIES

Treaties in general are written agreements between governments that create international law by specifying a series of relations between these governments. A treaty that involves two countries is *bilateral;* one that involves three or more is *multilateral.* In its effect a treaty is binding upon governments as sovereign entities. It thus differs from an *executive agreement,* which is binding only upon the executive chiefs that agreed to it. In content, treaties differ from *protocols,* which are, among other things, multilateral agreements concerned with general principles of law; *armistices,* which are agreements to terminate hostilities; and *compromises,* defined above (see p. 295). Treaties deal with such matters as alliances, mutual guarantees, consular status, commerce, monetary standards, copyrights, extradition, and the like. A treaty amounts, in international law, to a contract between or among sovereign governments.

Validity. The validity of a treaty depends largely upon the procedure through which it was reached. It must be first negotiated by duly accredited representatives of recognized governments. Once signed, it must be ratified by the government of each of the participating countries according to constitutional methods. In the United States, a treaty after being signed by United States representatives is transmitted to the Senate. If the Senate concurs to the treaty, the President signs it. It is at the ratification stage that a government may demand the inclusion of amendments or reservations that it deems essential or advantageous for its well-being. Such changes need not be accepted by other countries signing the treaty and are binding only upon those that do accept them. A treaty is valid even though one of the governments signing it has been subject to coercion, but not if the ruler or the diplomatic agents of that government have been so subject. Finally, the treaty must comply with established international law and not aim at subverting the law.

Countries Affected. A treaty is immediately binding only upon the countries that have signed it. Sometimes a treaty provides for the adherence of other countries; if they sign it, it becomes binding on them as well. A treaty may affect other countries by giving them advantages; for instance, it may extend to all countries the right to use the waterways of a given state. Moreover, all countries are obliged to respect bilateral boundary and sphere-of-influence agreements. A commercial treaty may include a *most-favored-nation* clause, which assures the nationals of the signatory countries whatever privileges are granted by each state to any third, "most-favored" country.

Interpretation. The authoritative interpretation of a treaty must be international. Unilateral interpretation would lead to mistrust and, in many cases, uncertainty. In interpreting a treaty, an international court accepts first any interpretation agreed upon by the parties. If this does not resolve the issue, the court next examines the history of the treaty— the negotiations with their preparatory work and related correspondence. Then it turns to the actual implementation of the treaty before the particular issue arose. At length it analyzes the meaning of the treaty terms themselves. The court strives to get at the real intentions of the parties in the beginning and tries to interpret the treaty as a whole rather than as a group of unrelated parts.

Observance. Concerning the observance of treaties, the general doctrine is *pacta sunt servanda*—treaties must be adhered to. Such a doctrine is in keeping with the principle that a treaty amounts to a contract. There is, however, little to prevent a government that wants to break a treaty from doing so. In practice, governments tend to observe treaties as long as observance coincides with what their leaders deem their chief interests. Ultimately, a political consideration may override apparent legal obligations. Sometimes a government in breaking a treaty will do so in rather callous fashion, as Germany did with its invasion of Belgium in 1914. On other occasions a government will rely upon the battery of international lawyers that is attached to its foreign office to produce a legal justification for the departure from the terms of the treaty, so as to avoid outraging foreign governments and publics.

Duration and Termination. Legally the duration of a treaty may be viewed as indefinite unless the treaty itself specifies a period of duration or a termination date, as did the ten-year Italo-German alliance treaty signed in 1939. It is legal, however, to terminate a treaty by consent of both parties or to amend it for its extension. Sometimes, also, a treaty may include a provision allowing one country to withdraw from its terms upon notice to the other party or parties. Treaties cease to have effect when one country is conquered and absorbed by another. When war breaks out between two countries, their commercial treaties are no longer applicable but certain other treaties may remain in effect. When a government seeks unilaterally to declare a treaty at an end, it may resort to the argument of *rebus sic stantibus*—conditions remaining the same. That is, this government may hold that a treaty is effective only so long as the conditions prevailing at the time of its negotiation still exist and that a change in them justifies ending the treaty. One other legal argument for ending a treaty is that the other party to the treaty has not complied with its obligations. Finally, a treaty may lapse when the particular task it provided for has been completed.

Review Questions

1. Describe the hierarchy and status of diplomatic personnel.

2. What have been the traditional functions of diplomats and diplomacy? How have these functions evolved recently?

3. What are the two means whereby an individual may acquire citizenship and the variations of each of these means?

4. What authority does a government have over its citizens when they are abroad? over aliens within its borders?

5. What are the various ways in which a state may acquire territory? Which of these ways was probably most important in the year 1600? Which seems most important today? What may be the most important in the future?

6. What kinds of jurisdiction prevail over the various bodies and streams of water in the world? What disputes have arisen over these kinds of jurisdiction?

7. What are the various bilateral and multilateral pacific means for settling disputes? What connection, if any, do these means have with the UN organization?

8. How are the people and property of belligerent states to be treated, according to the rules of war? What is one inherent weakness of these rules today—a weakness quite apart from the absence of an enforcing agency?

9. In what ways, according to international law, are the governments and peoples of neutral countries restricted during a war? In what ways are they protected? What has been the status of international law regarding neutrals in the recent past? How does this aspect of international law particularly show the difference between international law and national law?

10. What characteristics determine the validity of a treaty?

11. What determines which countries are affected by a treaty? how long a treaty lasts?

25 NUCLEAR POWER, MISSILES, AND DISARMAMENT

Nuclear weapons and modern missiles were first used near the end of World War II, and they had comparatively little effect upon the outcome of the war. Since 1945, however, developments in nuclear weapons, sources of nuclear power, and missiles have so expanded their potentiality that their use and their control constitute two of the chief problems in world politics today. At the same time, the application of some of these developments to nonmilitary uses offers immense possibilities for beneficial change in the life of mankind. The "Cold War," however, has led to a concentration of effort on expanding the military uses of nuclear power and missiles, and on establishing a system of international controls primarily for the sake of disarmament.

THE USES OF NUCLEAR POWER

Nuclear power comprises the energy released either in the splitting of atoms through the process termed *fission* or in the combining of atoms through the process termed *fusion*. In the natural world, fission is represented by radioactivity, and fusion by the solar process of transforming hydrogen into helium. In the laboratory, controlled nuclear power was released for the first time in the United States in 1942, at a project administered by an international group of scientists.

Uses in Defense and War. Devices based on nuclear power have been used only twice in war, but they play a major part in the planning and equipping of the military forces of both the United States and the Soviet Union today.

PAST USES. Devices based on nuclear power have been used only by the United States, against the Japanese in the closing days of World War II, when United States aircraft dropped atomic bombs on the Japanese cities of Hiroshima and Nagasaki. These two raids exhausted the existing stock of nuclear weapons, but United States officials had both the materials and the facilities to manufacture more bombs within a few days or weeks. Since that time the United States armed forces have acquired a stockpile of many thousands of these devices, but government officials have rarely used them as a threat for tactical purposes. For example, the United States government did not threaten their use against the USSR at the time of the blockade of Berlin in 1948, nor against Communist China when Communist Chinese troops invaded Korea in 1950. But, in 1954, Secretary of State Dulles announced, mainly for the benefit of the Communist Chinese, who were interfering in Vietnam, that the United States would counter aggression with instant and massive retaliation, which suggested the use of nuclear weapons. These words evoked a great deal of hostility in the United States, and ever since that time United States officials have been asserting that they do not plan to initiate a nuclear war. In 1962, however, President Kennedy expressed a more flexible policy, for he was quoted as saying that "in some circumstances we might have to take the initiative" in using nuclear weapons. He at the same time denied that the United States would ever start a "preventive" war. By contrast, Soviet officials have often threatened to use their nuclear devices, and these threats have induced people in the United States, the United Kingdom, and elsewhere to demand unilateral disarmament or withdrawal from co-operation with the United States on the part of their governments.

PRESENT DISTRIBUTION OF NUCLEAR-POWERED DEVICES. In considering the present distribution of nuclear devices, it is essential to bear in mind that for the purposes of war and defense nuclear energy may be used in at least two different ways: as a source of propulsive power and as an explosive. As a source of propulsive power nuclear energy so far has been applied widely only to submarines. The United States Navy has commissioned several nuclear-powered submarines; Soviet officials claim to have one or more of such craft. No other country has such a vessel. The United States Navy has also launched a nuclear-powered aircraft carrier and has plans for a nuclear-powered cruiser. For explosive devices both the United States and the Soviet armed forces have stockpiles of nuclear weapons to be transported by aircraft or missiles. According to available information, the United States Air Force has a much greater carrying capacity than that of the USSR, and the United States total missile stock is now larger than that of the USSR. Besides, some United States submarines are equipped to fire missiles from beneath the surface; no Soviet submarine is known to be so equipped. Early in 1961 it was calculated that the United States could drop about 3,600 nuclear bombs on the USSR whereas the Soviet Union could drop a few more than 250 on the United States. Where they would fall, and with what force, are, of course, important questions whose answers are not so available. Moreover, the United States Army possesses artillery that fires nuclear devices for battlefield use. Among other nations, the British have a modest stockpile of nuclear explosives, and the French have detonated nuclear devices in tests. Scientists in other countries, especially Communist China, are known to be experimenting with these mechanisms.

FUTURE USES. In the United States, at least, there are some problems connected with just what may be the future uses of nuclear power in warfare. Some officials point out that the United States already controls a stockpile of nuclear explosives sufficient to destroy the Soviet Union several times over, and they are concerned at this "overkill" capacity. In 1961, President Kennedy and his advisers apparently adopted the policy of increasing the strength of the nonnuclear military forces of the United States, under the belief that there might never be a nuclear war and that significant fighting in the future was more and more likely to be of the "brushfire" sort then going on in Laos. Some United States officials have urged studying the possibility of nuclear-powered aircraft, but in 1961 the President asked Congress to abandon the plane as a military project. Some scientists are contemplating the use of nuclear power for missile propulsion, either as an aid to a conventional power system or as a missile propellant by itself. This use of nuclear power could be most important for peaceful interplanetary flight, but it might be significant in the establishment of orbiting military bases.

Present and Potential Nonmilitary Uses. The main potential nonmilitary use for nuclear power is probably for the generation of electricity in thermal power stations. Nuclear power has not been adapted for this purpose as quickly as was predicted, for the electricity so produced has turned out to be much more expensive than that generated at coal-fired stations. There are a few nuclear stations now functioning in the United States and the United Kingdom, and they could be very valuable in countries with a shortage both of coal and of hydroelectric-power sites. One other problem is that the fission method of releasing nuclear power, which is the only one to be applied so far, yields large amounts of radioactive wastes; the fusion method, which does not yield these wastes, is much more difficult to apply because of the tremendous heat involved. Finally, some scientists are working at the task of transforming nuclear energy directly into electricity, with no steam-turbine mechanism; the discovery and application of this process would make thermal stations unnecessary. Another possible use of nuclear power is for marine transportation; the Soviet government already has a nuclear-powered icebreaker, and United States officials are observing tests on a nuclear-powered merchant vessel. Perhaps the most important present nonmilitary use of nuclear power is that of the isotopes of certain elements yielded in the process of releasing nuclear energy through fission. These isotopes have various uses in industrial research and testing, and they are being used in medicine for the detection and cure of cancer.

MISSILES

Missiles, in the modern sense, are unmanned projectiles carrying their own power source. They thus differ from aircraft, which are manned, and from bullets and shells, which have an external power source. Missiles fall into two general categories, ballistic and guided. A ballistic missile is one that receives all its velocity and direction at its original firing and that cannot be controlled during its flight. A guided missile is one that receives its velocity and its general direction at its initial firing, but that may afterward be steered by external "stimuli," such as its intended target, by means of radar or an infrared detector. Missiles are also classified according to their point of launching and the nature of their target; for instance, they may be "air-to-air," "ground-to-air," or "air-to-ground." In a broad military sense, missiles constitute the most advanced form of long-range heavy artillery and are in the process of superseding aircraft in that function.

Present State of Development. Missiles attained their present importance when scientists so reduced the size of nuclear-explosive devices that they could be used as warheads. From this point, American scientists and engineers created a variety of intercontinental ballistic missiles (ICBM's) and intermediate-range ballistic missiles (IRBM's). These missiles are primarily for ground-to-ground and sea-to-ground use. Meanwhile scientists and engineers also devised effective air-to-air and ground-to-air guided missiles with conventional-explosive warheads, for downing enemy aircraft. The greatest present need appears to be for a ground-to-air missile that can bring down enemy missiles; exploratory work on such an "anti-missile missile" is considerably advanced.

The "Missile Race." The so-called "missile race" is the contest between the United States and the Soviet armed forces to maintain at least equality in the capacity to deliver missiles equipped with nuclear warheads and if possible to obtain a preponderance. In May, 1962, estimates showed the USSR about equal in terms of ICBM's, with from 50 to 75 as against 63 for the United States. The Soviet Navy was also believed to have missile-equipped submarines, but unlike United States submarines Soviet vessels can deliver their missiles only from the surface and thus would be easier to detect. One great advantage of the United States in terms of missiles lies in the approximately 90 IRBM's based in Great Britain and Italy. The Soviet Union has comparable missiles but can use them only against such targets as Western Europe and United States overseas bases. Both the United States and the Soviet armed forces are acquiring more missiles. As protection against a missile attack, the United States maintains along the Arctic Ocean a series of radar outposts known as the Ballistic Missile Early Warning System (BMEWS); however, its functioning can be impeded by Soviet radar jamming. Introduction of an "anti-missile missile" would also add to the security of the United States, but its functioning might similarly be impeded. Inasmuch as Soviet authorities confront the same problem, the current situation comprises essentially a stalemate.

SPACE ACTIVITIES

Space activities—primarily the placing of man-made objects into orbit around the earth and the hurling of man-made objects outside the gravitational field of the earth—have been significant only since World War II. From 1957 on, reports of successes in various types of these activities have been an important part in the propaganda phase of the "Cold War." Space activities are conducted chiefly under government auspices, for they are very costly and are deeply indebted for their very existence to their potential military applications and to the techniques developed in conjunction with missiles.

Uses for War and Defense. The principal anticipated use for space devices in war and for defense is espionage—the securing of military intelligence, especially about the location of the enemy's missile sites. A group of orbiting satellites equipped with television cameras, now at least, cannot be shot down. One other military use for space vehicles that has been suggested is the establishment of extraterrestrial missile bases, perhaps on a huge man-made satellite or even on the moon. However, some people find it hard to discover an advantage in taking a missile to the moon just to fire it back at the earth.

Nonmilitary Uses. United States technicians are now experimenting with three possible nonmilitary uses for space devices. One is forecasting the weather by photographing cloud formations that may indicate storms. A second is a world-wide communications network; space devices might either reflect high-frequency signals or amplify and re-broadcast them. A third is for aids for navigation, such as satellites in known orbits to fix locations for maritime and airborne navigators. Then, in the more remote future, space devices may be used for exploration. Already scientists using such devices have found a hitherto unknown belt of radiation fairly close to the earth and by employing the same techniques could determine the feasibility of maintaining existence on the moon and the planets. Finally, scientists are testing devices that may carry one man or more to the moon or a planet.

The "Space Race." The "space race" is the present competition between the United States and the Soviet Union to be the first to achieve certain successes with space devices. The "space race" became public in October, 1957, when Soviet technicians placed a man-made satellite, a "sputnik," in orbit around the earth. United States scientists did not accomplish the same feat until early the following year. Between October, 1957, and March, 1961, Soviet authorities reported putting 11 objects into space, whereas United States technicians put 38. Then, in April, 1961, Soviet authorities announced that their technicians had sent a space vehicle containing a man into a single orbit around the earth; in August they stated that their technicians had sent a similar vehicle into seventeen consecutive orbits. In the same months, United States technicians succeeded only in sending two manned space vehicles into test, "suborbital" flights. Then, in February, 1962, the United States placed a man-carrying vehicle into three orbits around the earth and, unlike the Soviets, broadcast the feat for people all over the world to see and hear. However, there remain almost countless possibilities for innovation in manned space travel. Only the United States has attempted to use artificial satellites for weather-forecasting, for navigation and communication aids, and for espionage, as far as is known. Soviet authorities apparently concentrated from the beginning on putting a man into space.

THE PROBLEM OF DISARMAMENT

Under the stimulus of nuclear weapons, missiles, and the "space race," disarmament has become one of the most widely discussed of all international issues. It is well here to note certain problems connected with disarmament projects in general, in terms of certain commonplace misconceptions. Three of these misconceptions are: military leaders are desirous of war; the possession of heavy armaments is the leading cause for war; and disarmament can be viewed, and even accomplished, in isolation from other political and strategic considerations. The final paragraphs discuss some efforts to achieve disarmament since World War II.

The Asserted Desires of Military Leaders for War. One argument offered in behalf of disarmament is that military leaders consistently desire war and that disarmament would deny them the ability to wage the wars they desire. But military leaders have not consistently sought war; some wars have broken out in spite of the military leaders' views rather than because of them. The Austro-Hungarian general staff wanted war against Serbia in 1914; Japanese generals were very aggressive in the 1930's. On the other hand, in 1939, the German generals were appalled at the idea of war against Great Britain and France, and in 1941 they opposed war against the Soviet Union; United States military chiefs were not seeking war against Japan in 1941. Furthermore, it is not always the generals who want to prosecute a war to the bitter end. Allied civilian heads, and not military officers, made the "unconditional surrender" policy of World War II; a number of German generals were apparently willing to surrender long before May, 1945. Thus absolute statements about military leaders' views concerning the desirability of war defy proof.

Heavy Armaments as an Asserted Cause for War. A corollary misconception is that the possession of heavy armaments induces a nation to wage war; therefore, according to those who hold this misconception, disarmament will remove this cause for war. It is true that some countries with a relative advantage in armaments have gone to war against their neighbors, as Germany against Poland and the Soviet Union against Finland, both in 1939. On the other hand, a country with a huge relative advantage of armaments may refuse to go to war, even after severe provocation; France did not go to war against Germany in 1936, and the United States did not go to war against the Soviet Union in 1948 or Communist China in 1950–51. Then, "heavy armaments" is always a relative term. The destruction of all mechanical armaments would leave Communist China "heavily armed," since it would contain over 400 million highly organized adults, with fists. Perhaps the most important aspect of the entire question is that the possession of large quantities of armaments may often be a symptom rather than a cause—the indication that the government of the country involved fears the possibility of war. Thus the French in the 1920's maintained powerful armed forces to prevent a resurgence of German military power, and the Nazis rebuilt German military power in the 1930's partly out of fear of some future attack by the French.

The Possibility of Isolating Disarmament from Other Problems. The third misconception revolves about the notion that governments may undertake the task of disarmament, or will urge or have in the past urged a policy of disarmament, in isolation from other factors. On the contrary, government officials must view disarmament in the context of other factors, on pain of national suicide. When Tsar Nicholas II in the 1890's was urging disarmament, he was doing so largely because the Germans were acquiring a powerful army and at the same time no longer showed the friendliness toward Russia that they had manifested before 1890. When the United States government in the 1920's recommended naval disarmament, it did so partly because United States officials saw no need for a large navy and wanted to reduce government costs. United States proposals for disarmament today stem partly from the fact that United States authorities intend to implement United States foreign policy mainly with economic instruments. At the same time, Soviet proposals for the abolition of nuclear weapons, which were probably sincere at least before they developed their own atomic bomb, are aimed partially at improving the relative strategic position of the USSR, since Soviet land forces are several times those of the United States or even of the NATO countries combined. Moreover, government officials in both countries mean these calls for disarmament to indicate that they are the champions of peace, in order to win public support from the nations of Africa and Asia. Ultimately, then, nongovernmental organizations may recommend disarmament for its own sake, but responsible government officials will usually do so only to further the political and military interests of their government.

Disarmament Negotiations since World War II. Disarmament negotiations since World War II have been concerned chiefly with nuclear weapons, but there have also been some efforts to reduce conventional armaments.

NUCLEAR WEAPONS. After World War II the United States government made the first comprehensive proposal for disarmament of nuclear weapons, in the Baruch Plan, named for its sponsor, the financier and statesman Bernard Baruch. The plan called first for the control of all nuclear materials by an International Atomic Development Authority in the UN. Then, according to the plan, all nuclear weapons were to be destroyed and no more were to be produced. In response, the Soviet government urged a disarmament program under which the first step would be the outlawing and destruction of nuclear weapons. These two plans, submitted in 1946, reflected the fact that the United States then had nuclear weapons whereas the Soviet Union did not. Even after the

Soviet government had detonated its first nuclear weapon, in 1949, it still rejected the Baruch Plan. The chief asserted barrier to Soviet acceptance was the intensive inspection system that the Baruch Plan called for, a system that Soviet authorities charged would permit spying. During negotiations that lasted for years afterward and in 1962 were still going on, United States officials lowered their demands for strict inspection methods, but never enough to satisfy the Soviet government. In 1958 the two superpowers halted the testing of nuclear explosives, and representatives of their governments negotiated regarding a permanent ban on such testing. In 1961, however, Soviet technicians resumed their testing; and shortly afterward United States technicians also exploded some nuclear devices, although they were smaller and fewer in number than the Soviet explosions.

CONVENTIONAL ARMAMENTS. Negotiations for the reduction of conventional armaments began in the UN, where in 1946 the Security Council established a Commission on Conventional Armaments. Here the spokesmen of the superpowers again revealed fundamental differences of approach. According to the Soviet view, the essential first step was the reduction of armaments, to provide a basis for "world confidence." According to the United States view, the first requirement was the achieving of "world confidence," as a foundation for disarmament. Subsequently the United States government proposed that the armed forces of all countries be drastically reduced to specified quotas, but the Soviet government rejected this proposal. More than once the Soviet government has announced a unilateral reduction of its armed forces, as it did, for example, in January, 1960. It is almost impossible for anyone outside the Soviet Bloc to know whether Soviet figures on such asserted reductions have been accurate. Some people have suggested that if there was a reduction in 1960, it was ordered with the aim of securing more workers for Soviet factories and farms. Finally, non-Soviet observers generally agree that such announcements are at least partially propagandistic.

Review Questions

1. What military uses have been made of nuclear devices in the past, and by what countries? What military uses could be made of them today, and by what countries?

2. Show how certain elements of the national power of the United States and the USSR contribute to determining which type of missile or missiles may be most advantageous to each.

3. What are the various military and nonmilitary uses for space activities? Is the

value of these activities for a given country related to any of the elements of national power?

4. Outline the three misconceptions associated with the problem of disarmament. Is any of these misconceptions particularly common among the members of any group or groups?

5. Show how the disarmament programs suggested by the governments of the two superpowers since 1945 reflect or do not reflect the national interests of the two countries.

26 POPULATION INCREASES AND ECONOMIC DEVELOPMENT

Population increases and economic development are two problems confronting almost every nation and government in the world today. Combined, they form a unique problem. That is, government leaders in the past have concerned themselves with the economic development of their countries, but usually for simple economic or strategic reasons. Today they are faced with questions such as whether the national economy of their country can furnish enough necessities for the increasing population; whether the national economy can offer enough employment opportunities; and what government measures, if any, can be desirable and effective means for assisting the development of the national economy. Moreover, economic development itself has become a device of propaganda warfare; governments in both Communist and anti-Communist countries strive to demonstrate that their form of national economy is best suited for achieving a high rate of increase and compete with one another in efforts to improve the national economies of economically retarded, neutralist countries. The situation is complicated by the fact that all over the world, and especially in economically retarded countries, the population is increasing at a rate higher than ever before in history and that this population increase, by stimulating expenditures on consumers' goods, hampers the capital formation that is the basis for economic development.

THE PATTERN OF POPULATION GROWTH

Today the population of the world is evidently increasing at a faster rate than ever before, but the rate of population growth and the reasons for it vary from one country or region to another.

World-Wide Population Growth. Today the population of the world is about three billion, and it is now increasing at a rate that will double it in about 40 years. The great problem of the moment is not so much the absolute number of people as the rate at which this number is growing. For example, it has been estimated that in the year 1650 there were about 500 million people in the world, a large number in terms of existing productive techniques; however, this population was increasing at a rate of only about 0.5 per cent a year. That is, for every 1,000 persons in one year there would be 1,005 in the following year. The three billion people now inhabiting the earth could be, as is shown below, well supplied with their necessities by modern productive facilities, but their numbers are increasing at a rate of 1.6 per cent yearly; hence for every 1,000 persons this year there will be 1,016 next year. At this rate the population of the world will exceed six billion by the year 2000. Mathematically, at this rate of increase there will be, sometime before the year 3000, only one square yard of land space for each inhabitant of the globe.

Variations in Population Growth. There are great variations from one region of the world to another in the rate of population growth. Today the region with the highest rate of population increase is Latin America; the population of Mexico, for example, is growing by three per cent every year and is expected to rise from 36,000,000 today to 123 million 40 years hence. Another region with a high rate of population increase is Asia, although at least in Japan the rate has been considerably reduced in the last ten years. In the United States, Canada, and Western Europe the rate of increase is a good deal lower. The rate in some countries, however, notably the United States and France, is much higher than it was a generation ago. Also, the rate of increase may vary greatly even between neighboring countries; it is far higher in the Netherlands than in Belgium. Furthermore, it can vary from one section to another in a given country; in Canada it is higher in French-speaking Quebec than in the English-speaking remainder of the country. It can also vary from one income level to another in the same country; in the United States the people of the lower-income group are increasing more rapidly than those of the upper-income group, although the difference is not so great today as it was 30 years ago. The effect of this trend is lessened in the United States by the comparative ease with which an individual may rise out of the lower-income group. The fact is that impoverished nations around the world tend to have a higher rate of increase than wealthier nations, and it is far more difficult for a nation than an individual to secure a higher standard of living. (See graphs on page 314.)

Causes for Recent Population Increases. There are several causes for population increases during the past century, but by far the

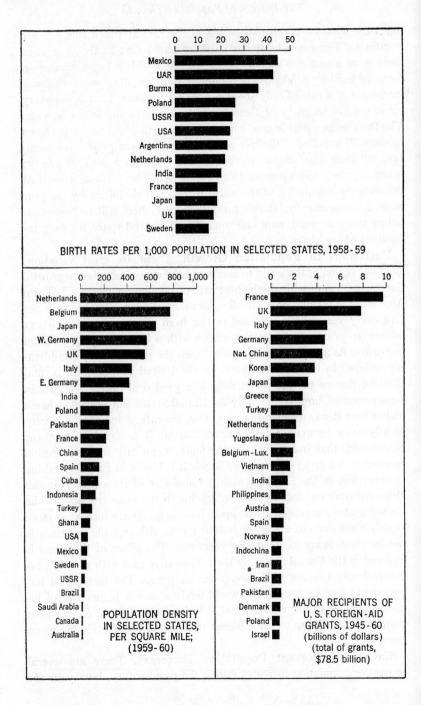

BIRTH RATES PER 1,000 POPULATION IN SELECTED STATES, 1958-59

POPULATION DENSITY IN SELECTED STATES, PER SQUARE MILE; (1959-60)

MAJOR RECIPIENTS OF U.S. FOREIGN-AID GRANTS, 1945-60 (billions of dollars) (total of grants, $78.5 billion)

most important has been the reduction in death rates. In a more advanced country such as the United States this reduction began decades ago; the life expectancy of a newborn American baby was only about 40 years in 1900 whereas it is about 70 years today. In less advanced countries this reduction has taken place chiefly in the past 20 years; in Ceylon, for instance, life expectancy rose from about 46 years in 1946 to 60 years in 1954. The lowered death rate is mainly the consequence of public health measures concerned with the reduction of infant mortality, the control of epidemic diseases such as malaria, and the provision of pure water supplies and modern sewerage systems. A second, far less important cause for the population increase in a few advanced countries, particularly the United States and France, has been a somewhat higher birth rate. It is not clear just what have been the reasons for this situation; in fact, there is no scientifically demonstrable and universal bond between any level of birth rate and any other feature of national life. One contributing factor in the United States today appears to be the great social pressure upon single persons to get married and to have children, a series of acts comprising an end in itself.

PROBLEMS OF POPULATION INCREASES

These population increases have raised, either directly or indirectly, problems for government leaders in almost every country. There are four categories of especially urgent problems: food, schooling, geographical crowding, and political power.

The Problem of Food. The problem of food in relation to current population increases is rather complex, not so much because of the general situation as because of local conditions. In general, the earth could produce immensely more food than it now does and support a much larger population. The author of one recent study maintains that the available farm land of the world today, cultivated by the methods used in the Netherlands, could furnish an adequate, grain-based diet for ninety billion people. However, such agricultural productivity exists in few places outside the Netherlands. In many countries, especially those of Africa and Asia, the mass of the people have a diet deficient in calories or vitamins, or both. What is even more significant is that since World War II the production of food has lagged behind the growth of population in most areas; during the period from 1949 to 1951, only in North and Central America, Africa, and Oceania was the annual per capita food production higher than it had been in 1939. An especially critical situation existed in the Far East, where the total output of rice was less than it had been before the war although the population had

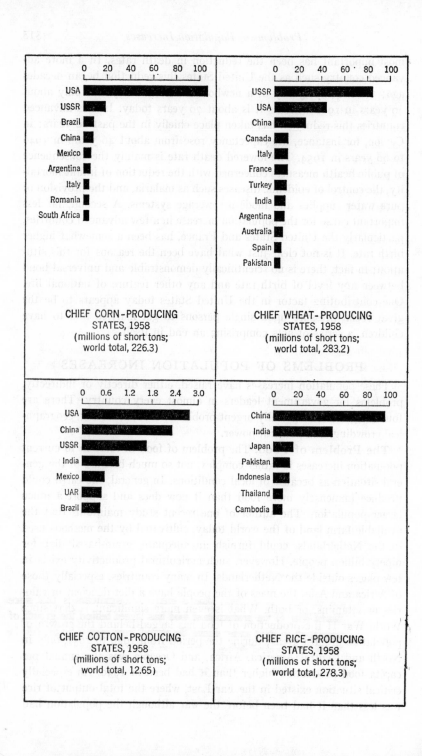

CHIEF CORN-PRODUCING
STATES, 1958
(millions of short tons;
world total, 226.3)

CHIEF WHEAT-PRODUCING
STATES, 1958
(millions of short tons;
world total, 283.2)

CHIEF COTTON-PRODUCING
STATES, 1958
(millions of short tons;
world total, 12.65)

CHIEF RICE-PRODUCING
STATES, 1958
(millions of short tons;
world total, 278.3)

risen ten per cent. Government policies themselves may contribute to such a condition, as when, for instance, government planning calls for an industrial crop such as cotton on land previously used for food.

The Problem of Schooling. The problem of schooling with relation to the increase in population also has more than one aspect. It is true that in some countries, such as the USSR, there are reportedly severe shortages in teaching personnel; by contrast, in the United States the ratio of students to teachers in tax-supported elementary and secondary schools is lower now than it was in 1940. What is much more significant is that in socially and economically retarded areas, especially Africa, the growth in population is reflected to a great degree by an urbanization of the population. This process has broken down the tribal system that once provided an extensive education for children and adolescents. Moreover, the urbanization of countries in Asia, Africa, and Latin America has brought demands for new kinds of schooling, in industrial and technical subjects. All together, the pressures for tax-supported schooling have raised enormous new fiscal burdens for the governments in these countries, many of which have just attained national self-government and are suffering from many other difficulties.

The Problem of Crowding. The problem of crowding that has resulted from population increases is reflected mainly by a phenomenon referred to above—the swift urbanization of economically retarded states. As noted in Chapter 20, the growth of a city such as Calcutta is not connected with industrialization alone; it is connected also with a degree of rural overpopulation that has induced many members of agrarian families and communities to come to the cities simply because the land could not support them. This process inflicts two related hardships upon such cities. First, the city governments have an exceptional burden of charity and welfare. Second, this great number of unemployed and therefore non-tax-paying inhabitants imposes an extreme fiscal burden on the city governments. Even in advanced countries such as the United States, the crowding of people into cities leads to unusual demands for new governmental services, notably transportation facilities.

The Problem of Political Power. The speedy growth of population has brought or accentuated a host of political problems, especially in retarded states. The most important reason for these problems is probably the simple fact that the farmer, even though impoverished, has land that can produce some food and provide him with some kind of dwelling place, whereas the unemployed urban inhabitant has neither; hence the farmer is more nearly self-sufficient and less apt to call upon government officials for aid. The unemployed city dweller, by contrast, is apt to view some government, eventually the national government, as the one institution that can help him. In many of the new countries this is true, if only because the national government alone has access to capital and resources that can generate the wealth needed to feed, clothe, and house these people. Government leaders may or may not be willing to inaugurate programs for the relief of such people; there may be a great deal of resistance from rural areas to these costly and nontraditional programs. The final consequence may be a sharp political division between city and country, such as that in South Korea, and the establishment of an authoritarian regime to discourage urban uprisings.

PAST LIMITATIONS AND PROPOSED FUTURE REMEDIES

In the past, population increases and the problems resulting from them have been limited by certain cataclysms such as famine, war, and disease. Today governments are trying such methods as birth control, increased food supplies, the redistribution of goods, an increase in the standard of living, and emigration.

Famine, War, and Disease. Throughout history, famine, war, and disease have led to reductions in surplus populations. Indeed, famine may be actually no more than an indication that a given area is populated beyond its capacity. These means for reducing excess population can be very effective, but they are so harsh that no government today is apt to prescribe them for its own people.

Birth Control. Birth control is an ancient and effective means for dealing with surplus population. However, each of the various methods suffers from some sort of limitation.

METHODS. Probably the oldest method of birth control is infanticide, which has been practiced widely. As a postnatal rather than prenatal arrangement, it had the "advantage" of providing selectivity; the usual victims were female and defective babies. Deliberate abortion, too, is very old. Emphasis in recent times has been upon the initial prevention of pregnancy, through such means as mechanical devices and the "rhythm" or "period" method. Chemists and pharmaceutical firms around the world are working to devise an inexpensive, effective medicine that will prevent pregnancy. These modern methods are practiced widely, but until recent times their use has been promoted chiefly by individuals. Since World War II, however, government leaders in countries threatened by inordinate growth of population have encouraged birth control. In India, for example, the state maintains birth control clinics in numerous cities and towns. As yet, however, Japan appears to be the only country in which state-subsidized birth control has had a significant impact upon population growth; the population of India increased by 80 million in just the decade between 1951 and 1961.

PRACTICAL LIMITATIONS. The practical limitations to birth control fall into three categories: individual, social, and religious. The chief problem involving individuals is simple lack of information; this is the reason for the many governmental and nongovernmental clinics and for the "planned parenthood leagues" around the world. The social limitations are especially evident among African tribes, where parents consider large families desirable to insure their own support in their old age. A different kind of social limitation, existing, for example, in the United States, is reflected in the vague disapproval or deprecation that many childless couples experience, particularly in middle-income suburban neighborhoods. The chief source of religious opposition has been the Catholic Church, whose doctrine maintains that sexual relations were intended for procreation; hence the only form of birth control that Catholic leaders sanction is the "rhythm" method, except for reasons of health. Also, many persons hold that the spreading of birth-control information promotes extramarital sexual relations and is therefore harmful to public morals.

Increased Food Production. Increased food production has been employed since prehistoric times as a means for coping with population growth. The introduction of agriculture itself in place of food gathering and herding demonstrates the antiquity of this practice. Today, as noted above, the application of Dutch farming techniques to all the arable land in the world could produce enough food for thirty times the present population of the world. The greatest problem is that of educating farmers in backward areas. Sometimes traditions run counter to better farming methods; for instance, in parts of Africa the measure of social status is the sheer number of cattle owned, regardless of their quality; reduction in the number of cattle to the capacity of the grazing land would lower some men's prestige, a fate they might consider worse than starvation. On the other hand, simple improvements in techniques may have exceptionally rewarding consequences, as in the change from hill-cultivation to row-cultivation of corn in Ethiopia, which resulted in far larger harvests. Another problem is the shortage of capital in some areas, even when the question is no more than the substitution of plows for pointed sticks. This shortage of capital also hampers wider application of chemicals to the soil, particularly in countries where animal dung is viewed as more valuable for fuel than for fertilizer. More remote yet conceivable projects include the cultivation of marine waters and the irrigation of desert areas with desalted sea water.

The Redistribution of Goods. The redistribution of goods, either through voluntary nongovernmental means or through compulsory government agencies, has sometimes been suggested. That is, some people and groups have argued that certain nations are so well supplied with goods that they could afford to give away a great deal of what they possess to the impoverished areas of the world. Actually, such a process has been in effect for centuries, first through religious missionary work, and later through foreign-aid programs. If carried out on a very large scale, however, any program of this kind would diminish the capacity of the wealthier nations to produce a surplus, since the capital needed to create and expand productive facilities comes from the surplus that would be given away. Furthermore, a nation compelled to give away a large part of its wealth might soon lose the desire to produce great quantities of goods.

Emigration. Emigration, too, is a method for relieving the difficulties produced by a high rate of population increase. Surplus population, after all, is relative to environment, so that the migration of tribes from grazed-out lands to new lands was simply an answer to surplus population difficulties. The emigration of Europeans to the United States in the nineteenth century was in part the same phenomenon. Governments since ancient times have sought colonies to settle their surplus populations, with varying results. The number of people in a given country who are willing and able to emigrate fluctuates widely; moreover, emigrants often shun colonies in favor of other countries. Today the Soviet government is trying, without much success, to colonize the "virgin lands" of its Asiatic territories; some observers foresee the day when millions of Chinese will burst northward into sparsely settled Siberia. Today the most important form of emigration is that of capital, which both secures goods needed for the larger populations of more advanced countries and helps the people of retarded nations acquire a higher standard of living.

ECONOMIC DEVELOPMENT

Almost every national government in the world, including those in the most advanced countries, has some sort of plan for the economic development of its country. Such plans may have economic, social, political, or strategic aims, or a combination of them. In every country, however, those who strive to execute these plans must cope with scarcities of one kind or another.

Scarcities in the World. The scarcities, actual or potential, that face the governments of the world in their efforts to carry out economic development plans include those of raw materials, of water, of power, of capital, of individual skills, and of orderly and receptive social organization.

SCARCITIES OF RAW MATERIALS. The world as a whole does not suffer from present or impending shortages of raw materials. Within the top mile of the crust of the earth whose surface is above sea level there are enough aluminum, iron, copper, lead, zinc, and tin to supply a much larger population, at present per capita consumption rates, for thousands or even millions of years. The extraction of these minerals in some cases would require a heavy but not insupportable capital investment. The main difficulty is that these minerals are distributed unevenly about the earth, so that some countries possess a surplus of them whereas others have a deficiency. For example, there is not enough iron ore in either Japan or Germany to supply a high level of steel construction. On the other hand, there is a great deal of iron ore, but almost no industry, in Liberia and Gabon. One other point is that scarcities may be relative, in terms of costs of extraction, especially labor. Thus in terms of cost iron ore is becoming scarce in the United States, in comparison with that in Canada and Venezuela. Governments have shared in the task of acquiring raw materials in at least two ways. First, they have stockpiled raw materials that might become scarce in time of war—a practice that amounts to a subsidy for extractive businesses and that doubtless keeps some marginal firms in operation. Second, they have offered awards for the discovery of new raw material sources, as the United States government did for uranium.

SCARCITIES OF WATER. Although most of the surface of the earth is covered with water and although there is generally enough water for the uses of mankind, many parts of the world suffer from an existing or threatening scarcity of water. Some areas, such as the Sahara, adjacent Middle Eastern countries, the Gobi desert, western Australia, and the southwestern United States, receive little or no rain; other areas, including much of Siberia and the High Plains in the United States, have insufficient or only periodical rainfall. Irrigation projects have made a small fraction of this land arable, but most of it is still waste. Efforts to increase rainfall by cloud-seeding have thus far enjoyed indifferent success. Water for agriculture is, of course, a very old problem. A much newer problem is the increasing need for water in industries such as steel and chemicals; this need helps account for the industrial concentrations on and near such water sources as Lake Erie and the Ohio River.

Finally, water supplies for many urban areas are contaminated. Even in pre-Christian times, water was so important for human survival that, according to one school of historians, the need for its control by the state in the arid Middle Eastern countries led to the establishment of "hydraulic civilizations" there under consciously despotic governments.

SCARCITIES OF POWER. Although the world as a whole does not suffer a present or immediately threatening scarcity of power, many countries do have such a scarcity. Today the per capita quantity of power consumed by the people of a country is an infallible index to the level of economic development that the people of that country have achieved. At present the people of the United States consume almost half of all the power used in the world, most of it for manufacturing and transportation. In a highly industrialized country the chief sources of power are petroleum, coal, and natural gas; in an underdeveloped country they are men and animals. Today, at least in the United States, petroleum is the chief source. On the other hand, reserves of coal in the United States are sufficient for over a thousand years, whereas reserves of oil are not. Consequently the United States government and American corporations are deeply involved in the problem of finding and exploiting new sources of oil. The existence of a power source within a country does not assure economic advancement to that country; either the government or the people must have access to capital as well, to develop the source. The oil reserves of the Middle East do not directly benefit Middle Eastern peoples very much, and they make the whole area a target for intense competition among the more advanced nations. It is possible that within a century the exploitation of nuclear and solar energy as sources of power for industrial and household uses will drastically reduce such competition. The continent of Africa has a greater hydroelectric power potential than any other continent, but for various reasons almost none of this potential has been harnessed. (See graphs, p. 129.)

SCARCITIES OF CAPITAL. Scarcities of capital, which afflict the people of most countries in the world, are among the principal hindrances to economic development. As noted above, capital comprises essentially the excess of production over consumption; in effect, it is the result of saving. For the purposes of economic development, capital takes the form of instruments of production, or the money that can buy such instruments. Capital formation can occur at a very simple level; the African farmer who makes a hoe out of a stick, a piece of discarded metal, and a piece of twine has created capital. There are significant barriers to capital formation in economically retarded countries. Doubtless the most important is that most production is needed for immediate consumption, in order for the people to survive. The current high rate of population increase only magnifies this barrier. A second, sometimes overlooked, barrier is the absence of incentive to save. This is well illustrated by the practices of some Middle Eastern rulers who devote their enormous incomes from oil royalties to buying Cadillacs instead of to building local textile mills. For several centuries the governments and peoples of economically advanced countries in Western Europe, and more recently of the United States and Japan, have alleviated these scarcities of capital in underdeveloped countries through investments and loans. Since World War II the government of the United States has assumed the burden of lessening these scarcities all over the world through foreign aid.

SCARCITIES OF INDIVIDUAL SKILLS. Scarcities of individual skills are another major problem for economically retarded nations. Actually the scarcity of manufacturing skills is not a very important aspect of this problem. A greater difficulty is the scarcity of agricultural skills, simply because agriculture is, and for a long time will remain, the chief element in the national economy of these countries. This is another realm in which the improvement of skills may be resisted by traditions. Another scarcity is that of bookkeeping and secretarial skills, which are essential for operating a modern government. They are particularly required in the new governments whose leaders plan to take a major part in the economic development of their countries. Then, there are great scarcities of skills that demand more training, notably those connected with public health facilities and economic management. One of the greatest difficulties for these new governments has been the failure or refusal of their leaders to understand that these tasks are complicated and that learning how to perform them is a lengthy process. Almost every government that has expropriated foreign properties has afterward either operated them at a loss or else rehired European or American managerial personnel—the Egyptian government and the Suez Canal being a remarkable exception; yet leaders of new governments in some cases still appear to feel that large enterprises can be managed by unskilled and even illiterate workers. Planning and creating new enterprises is still more difficult. The reduction of these scarcities will actually take two stages. The first will be that in which the leaders and peoples of economically retarded countries come to accept these skills as essential for realizing their economic plans. The second will be that in which individuals acquire the skills.

SCARCITIES OF ORDERLY AND RECEPTIVE SOCIAL ORGANIZATION. Almost every economically backward country lacks the orderly social organization that is receptive to economic development projects. A disorderly society, of course, is a massive hindrance to economic development; if theft is rampant, there is little reason for saving. This is especially a problem among government officials; that is, if they regard holding government posts simply as a means to self-enrichment—and this is a very common view among officials of the new Asiatic and African countries—the natives will be disinclined to create capital, and foreigners will be disinclined to invest it. Perhaps even more important, however, is the existence of a society that values economic development. Not every society respects the "acquisitive instinct"; some analysts of tribal societies in Africa and Latin America have concluded that among certain groups a doubling of hourly pay rates would simply lead workers to halve their working time. Then, in tropical and subtropical Asiatic countries where climate and soil make it easy to secure a living, the whole tenor of the people's philosophy and religion is apt to emphasize attaining harmony with nature, not mastering nature as in the more rigorous climates of Europe and North America. Thus the European or American who tries to introduce a program of economic development may arouse the hostility of the native people rather than evoke their appreciation and friendship.

Principal Government Plans and Programs. In most, though not all, economically backward countries, government leaders have drafted plans and programs for economic advancement. These plans and programs have depended in varying degrees upon outside sources for their initiation, their content, and their realization. The most extensive and ambitious of these plans and programs have been those of the Communist Chinese. These projects were initiated almost entirely by the Chinese, and, although they have benefited from Soviet contributions of money and technical advice, their chief source of capital has been the forced labor of millions of Chinese peasants. These plans and programs were intended to produce a "great leap forward" for the entire Chinese national economy, but by 1961 it was clear that in the main they had been a costly failure. Another major set of plans and programs was that of the Indian government, whose leaders expected a considerable amount of financial aid from both the Soviet and the non-Soviet Blocs. Some of the projects were to be government-owned, and others privately owned. Today it seems that a few of these projects have been successful but that others will be successful only with the help of more foreign investment. Leaders in many of the new African governments are busy drafting plans and programs, and many of them are apparently willing to accept outside aid from any source. Perhaps the greatest problem for most of these leaders is their failure, or refusal, to understand that domestic capital investments are far more important than foreign capital grants and loans, and that domestic capital can be acquired only through individual and governmental self-denial.

FOREIGN AID

Foreign aid—the granting or lending of money by the people or government of a comparatively wealthy country to the people or government of a comparatively impoverished country—is a very old practice. A pre-Christian illustration is Phoenician assistance to Carthage. In relatively modern times, the countries of Europe sent such aid to the United States. They also conducted vast foreign aid programs for their African and Asiatic colonies. The people and the government of the United States have only in the past few decades engaged in large-scale foreign aid programs. Since World War II, however, the United States government has been making foreign aid grants and loans on an unprecedented scale. During the late 1950's the Soviet government inaugurated its own foreign aid program, but on a far smaller scale. Meanwhile the governments of Western Europe, having recovered from World War II, resumed their own programs. Finally, the governments of a number of countries conducted foreign aid projects through agencies of the United Nations.

Motives for Foreign Aid Programs. There are at least three distinctive types of motives for foreign aid programs for backward areas. One is the conviction that economically advanced peoples have a "moral obligation" to help economically retarded peoples advance themselves. A second is the belief that by extending foreign aid to a retarded area the people of an advanced country may profit economically, through such means as exploiting new sources of raw materials and establishing new markets for goods. A third is the hope that by making foreign aid grants and loans an advanced country can secure a strategic advantage through winning the alliance, or at least the friendship, of the people and the government of a retarded country.

United States Foreign Aid Programs. United States foreign aid programs have been conducted by both the government and a host of nongovernmental agencies.

GOVERNMENTAL PROGRAMS. United States governmental foreign aid programs really began during the war, with Lend-Lease assistance and United States participation in UNRRA. The first programs after the war stemmed mainly from the desire to help the peoples of Europe achieve economic recovery. Such were the aims of the large loans made just after the war to Western European governments, and also of the Marshall Plan at its outset. Next, the United States government began dispensing aid on the theory that a prosperous people would shun communism. This was the ultimate basis of the Marshall Plan and the funds managed by the International Co-operation Administration (ICA), merged in 1961 into a new Agency for International Development (AID). At about the same time the United States government began extending military assistance, first to Greece and Turkey and later to other countries that appeared threatened by Soviet armed forces or that entered a military alliance with the United States. Finally, the United States government began making grants and loans to less advanced countries, beginning with the Point Four Program of 1949, for humanitarian, economic, and strategic reasons. At first American aid was conducted on a bilateral basis, but by the end of the 1950's the United States government was encouraging European leaders to form multilateral agreements for administering aid programs. In 1961 the United States joined the Organization for Economic Co-operation and Development (OECD), whose members included also Canada and 18 European countries; the OECD was, among its other functions, to administer aid programs for underdeveloped countries. Between the end of World War II and March 31, 1962, United States aid expenditures totaled $84.1 billion, about two-thirds of it in the form of economic assistance and most of the remainder in that of military assistance. The principal results of these foreign aid programs have been to help rebuild strong national economies in Western Europe and Japan and to strengthen the economies in some of the less advanced countries.

NONGOVERNMENTAL PROGRAMS. United States nongovernmental foreign aid programs have a much longer history. The earliest of these programs were those carried out by religious groups among the Indian tribes. Ever since, religious groups have performed a variety of tasks among foreign peoples, bringing them literacy, sanitation, medicine, and new farming techniques, among other things. Later, nonreligious groups such as educational and charitable foundations started carrying out various projects abroad, having aims similar to those of the religious organizations but sometimes equipped with far greater financial resources. The nonreligious groups have also dealt a good deal more with the problems of economic development. A third kind of nongovernmental program has been overseas investing by business corporations, simply to earn profits. A large part of these investments has been in Canada and Western Europe, but a considerable fraction has gone to less advanced areas such as Latin America, Liberia, and the Middle

East. In just the decade of the 1950's, American businesses sent $12.2 billion abroad. Although business investors have had profits as their chief goal, they have incidentally—if only to raise output per worker—contributed a great deal toward improving living conditions in the countries of their operations. These nongovernmental foreign aid programs have had a great impact abroad; far more than governmental programs, they have contributed to establishing amicable person-to-person bonds in foreign countries.

Soviet Foreign Aid Programs. Soviet foreign aid programs—which are, of course, governmental only—were first introduced on a large scale in the 1950's. For one thing, it was not until this time that the Soviet government had sufficient capital for major investments abroad. Perhaps even more important, the Soviet policy of using poverty to stimulate unrest abroad militated against such activities, and the Soviet government seems to have discarded this policy in favor of foreign aid programs only in order to oppose the United States. Thus Soviet programs aim almost entirely at strategic advantages. Soviet aid may come not only from the USSR but also from such other Communist-Bloc states as Czechoslovakia and China. Soviet aid programs have involved much smaller sums than those of United States programs. In the four years from 1956 through 1959, when total United States governmental and nongovernmental aid to underdeveloped countries was about $14 billion, the total of Soviet aid was only $560 million. It is generally in the form of long-term loans arranged on a bilateral basis. It also has included, in a number of countries, the establishment of technical schools. Such programs may be instituted side by side with those of the United States, as in India; or they may have the field almost completely to themselves, as in Guinea. Up to the present, Soviet aid programs seem to have yielded more strategic advantage per unit of investment than United States programs have.

Foreign Aid Programs of Other Non-Communist States. Other non-Communist states—primarily Canada, Japan, and the Western European countries—have substantial foreign aid programs. In fact, during the four years from 1956 though 1959, the total of aid, governmental and private, that went from these countries to underdeveloped areas was almost exactly equal to that from the United States—about $14 billion. The motives for this aid have been similar to those of the United States, but with a lesser anti-Communist bent; in countries such as Great Britain and France government officials had in mind also the problems of colonies and former colonies. Today, leaders in the United States hope that these officials will also realize that their aid programs can lessen the pressure on the dollar, which by 1960 was showing signs of weakness because of a constantly unfavorable balance of payments. The forms and relative quantities of aid have varied considerably from one country to another. The largest quantity of aid has come from France, about half of it in government money, going mainly to colonial areas that are now segments of the French Community. In once poverty-stricken Italy, business corporations have become substantial investors. The West German government is sending money to Israel as reparations for Nazi treatment of the Jews. With the creation of the OECD, all these programs supposedly will be co-ordinated by this single agency, and it is presumed that the United States representatives to the agency will encourage the other member governments to contribute proportionately more of the costs in order to reduce the burden of the assistance programs for which the United States government has taken responsibility.

United Nations Foreign Aid Programs. United Nations foreign aid programs comprise programs financed by some, but not necessarily all, members of the UN and administered by specialized agencies of the UN. They are, then, multilateral projects that are distinguished simply by the fact that they are conducted under the auspices of the UN. The principal agencies involved, such as the FAO, the WHO, UNESCO, and others, are described in a later chapter. Such activities differ from the over-all foreign aid programs of the United States, and to a lesser degree from those of other countries as well, in that they are concerned primarily with aid for retarded areas and in that they do not include military assistance. Moreover, they are supposedly divorced from the economic and strategic advantages of any country. In many countries, UN workers are more respected than nationals of a particular aiding country. These activities have been financed much more heavily by the government of the United States than by that of any other country; in fact, the Soviet government has contributed nothing to some of these projects. Soviet policy here may well stem from the conviction of Soviet leaders that foreign aid projects are valuable for the Soviet Union only insofar as they are clearly identifiable with the Soviet Union. These UN agencies have conducted a great deal of research, showing the way for governments and nongovernmental organizations to fulfill specific needs. The agencies have also worked toward solving a number of problems throughout the world, including malnutrition and epidemic diseases.

Review Questions

1. Describe the characteristics of the growth of population around the world today. How does this growth vary among nations, regions, and groups? What seem to be its principal causes?

2. What problems has the present rate of population growth brought on? Which of these problems do you think will be the most difficult to solve, and why?

3. What solutions have been tried for population growth? Which solution seems likely to bring the smallest amount of government interference into the individual's life? Or does population growth appear certain to result in a disproportionate increase in government functions?

4. What are the principal economic scarcities in the world? Which one of these scarcities do you think can be most easily dealt with by nongovernmental institutions and undertakings?

5. Describe the nongovernmental foreign aid programs carried on by American and foreign individuals and groups.

6. What kinds of foreign aid programs have been conducted under the auspices of the UN organization?

27 PSYCHOLOGICAL FORCES AND PROPAGANDA

Certain psychological forces can and do have as powerful an impact upon world politics as questions of overpopulation and economic underdevelopment. These psychological forces work upon both individuals and groups. Today the most significant of all these forces is a group attitude called nationalism, a form of mass thinking that in numerous ways resembles a religion and whose doctrines exercise enormous power on men's minds and actions. To promote the sense of nationalism in their own country and to counteract the workings of unfriendly foreign nationalisms, governments today devote vast efforts and expenditures to propaganda undertakings.

PSYCHOLOGICAL PROBLEMS AND INTERNATIONAL TENSIONS

Psychological problems of one sort or another may contribute significantly to the origin or the strengthening of international tensions. Sometimes these problems, such as aggressiveness, comprise what a clinician would term a neurosis or psychosis. On other occasions, as with cultural barriers, they are no more than distortions of views, or intellectual "blind spots."

Aggressiveness. Aggressiveness among individuals and groups is a leading cause of war. Over the years, some thinkers and political leaders have argued that aggressiveness is an innate characteristic and that war is its natural expression. Today, however, the bulk of informed opinion holds that this argument is erroneous if not self-serving, that aggressiveness is an acquired or learned characteristic, and that war is not necessarily "natural." Aggressiveness toward the government or the people of another country may stem from feelings of persecution or of racial inferiority. It is difficult to know the degree to which an entire people, or a large percentage of it, may have these feelings at the outset and, on the other hand, the degree to which the political leader or leaders may experience them and then arouse them in the people. For example, it appears that in 1870 a great number of Frenchmen reacted spontaneously to the seeming insult delivered by the Prussian king to the French emperor. On the other hand, whatever aggressiveness the Russian people today manifest toward the United States seems to be mainly induced by the Soviet government; Soviet leaders themselves are very aggressive toward the United States and according to their doctrine maintain that the governments of the United States and of every other non-Soviet country are persecuting the government and people of the USSR.

Cultural Barriers. Cultural barriers—that is, impediments between peoples arising from cultural differences, which prevent them from correctly appraising the attitudes and values of other peoples—are also factors in producing international tensions and may help bring on war. The simplest basis for such cultural barriers is difference in language. Other, more complex bases involve differences in values. Every difference of this sort hampers international communication, a situation that is especially critical today with the emergence of new sovereignties in Asia and Africa in which even the leaders have no more than a veneer of European culture. Every member of a society that has lasting cultural values is apt to esteem these values and to scoff at, or even revile, conflicting values of other cultures. Furthermore, people of one culture often analyze the values of other cultures in terms of stereotypes, which frequently are distorted as well as oversimplified. People at every level of civilization are likely to feel and show some degree of contempt for attitudes and values of other cultures. For instance, in the 1950's when the king of Saudi Arabia paid an official visit to the United States, some American newspapers published disparaging remarks about the king's having more than one wife. This sort of view toward the values of other peoples, and the resulting failures in comprehension and communication, tend to increase rather than lessen international tensions and may lay the groundwork for the outbreak of war.

NATIONALISM

Nationalism is the most important of all individual and group psychological forces as far as world politics is concerned. Nationalism is not only a psychological force in its own right; it tends to strengthen, or at least modify, such other psychological forces as aggressiveness and cultural values, and it provides a cement for individuals having a common possession of these other forces.

The Nature of Nationalism. Nationalism is the feeling among a number of people that, because they have a common language, some common cultural traditions, a history of common experiences, or some other attribute or attributes in common, they comprise a unit. Nationalism provides the sense of "belongingness" that, at least according to many students of the subject, most people want and need. This is especially important today, when such institutions as the rural community and the tribe in Africa are disintegrating before the agencies of industrial society. Nationalism has many of the traits of a religion, with its gods, its martyrs, its holy places, and its sacred writings. It has been described as the one set of beliefs for which modern man will fight and die.

The Factors in the Emergence of Nationalism. There are various factors in the emergence of nationalism, and they vary from one people to another. It should be emphasized at the outset that a sense of nationalism does not necessarily emerge naturally in the presence of these factors; instead, it can and does happen that political leaders and intellectuals use these factors to implant this feeling among the mass of the people. Probably the most important factor is a common language. A common language involves not only the ability to "understand" some people and the inability to "understand" others; it includes the fundamental ways of thinking that vary from one language or language system to another. A second factor is common cultural traditions, such as Gothic cathedrals among the French, Wagnerian opera among the Germans, and Elizabethan drama among the English. A third factor is common historical experiences. It is noteworthy that the threat of attack or the presence of military invaders on the soil may be far more important than a history of military triumphs. The feelings of nationalism in Spain and Switzerland owe a great deal, respectively, to Moslem and Hapsburg aggression; nationalism surged up in Central Europe in response to Napoleonic invasions. Still another factor is the government itself; government leaders are apt to promote the sense of nationalism, as they do in the United States, for example, by means of tax-supported schools. The recent emergence of nationalism in Africa has been affected by such factors as colonialism, racial distinctions, and poverty. This nationalism, and that in Asia, is sometimes credited to, or charged to, the Communists. Actually, whereas the Communists have both promoted and exploited it, they are not responsible for its origins.

The History of the Emergence of Nationalism. Nationalism of the modern type dates back somewhat more than five centuries. Its emergence has often accompanied other factors in the development of a people.

THE CHRONOLOGICAL EMERGENCE OF NATIONALISM. Nationalism in its present form is usually dated from the uprising of the French against the English at the time of Joan of Arc. As noted in a previous chapter, nationalism then and for more than three centuries to come was generally identified with the dynasty and was confined to a handful of European states along the Atlantic. Then, with the French Revolution, nationalism came to be identified with an entire people. It also spread east from the Atlantic to infect the Germans and the Italians. It reached across the Atlantic as well; the rise of nationalism in the United States is commonly placed from the period just after the War of 1812. Later in the nineteenth century it developed among the peoples of Eastern Europe. Only in the twentieth century has it appeared among Asiatic and African peoples.

THE EMERGENCE OF NATIONALISM AND OTHER DEVELOPMENTS. The emergence of nationalism among a people is apt to accompany other developments, such as the extension of literacy and the establishment of modern systems of communication and transportation. Among economically retarded peoples, however, nationalism may be an exotic and premature growth planted and watered by Western-educated political leaders. It is noteworthy that in recent years nationalism in some countries has been identified not so much with the people as with a particular leader, for such reasons as the modern trend toward subordinating the legislative branch and exalting the executive branch. Illustrations of this trend include the *Führerprinzip* of Adolf Hitler and the quasi-religious cult that has developed around President Nkrumah of Ghana.

The Impact of Nationalism on Politics. The impact of nationalism on politics for the past two centuries is a result of the historical accident whereby the concept of nationalism was combined with the institution of the state. According to the resultant doctrine of the right of national self-determination, every group that feels itself to be, or whose leaders proclaim it to be, a nation is entitled to political independence and a state of its own. The last great peace settlement that was *not* based on this doctrine was that reached at the Congress of Vienna in 1814–15, and the ensuing 35 years of uprisings in Europe constituted efforts to amend this settlement in the direction of national self-determination. The wars fought, and the peace settlements reached, since about the year 1850 have almost without exception been based on this doctrine. Efforts to actualize this doctrine have brought great international unrest. Lines of nationality in Europe are so blurred that treaties such as those of St. Germain and Trianon could not help leaving some people dissatisfied. Furthermore, the achievement of national self-determination may be but the opening wedge for imperialistic ventures, as illustrated by Serbian policies after 1878. Also, the little countries born out of this doctrine are apt to be no more than pawns of the great powers. Finally, many of the peoples in Africa and Asia that have just achieved national self-determination now enjoy fewer political freedoms than they did under colonial governments. Nevertheless, the theory that all nations should achieve national self-determination remains a categorical imperative for many leaders not only in Africa and Asia but also in the United States and Western Europe.

PROPAGANDA

Propaganda in a political sense is an instrument deliberately employed by governments and by politically oriented nongovernmental bodies for the purpose of altering psychological forces that affect politics; it may be aimed at either domestic or foreign audiences.

The Content and Emergence of Propaganda. Political propaganda consists of statements, either true or false, that are intended to influence the opinions of those at whom they are directed. For centuries, politicians and military leaders have realized that governing and fighting involve men's minds as well as their bodies and have resorted to propaganda as a psychological instrument. For example, King Henry V (1413–22) of England employed psychological tactics against the French prior to the Battle of Agincourt, and the colonial militiamen distributed subversive tracts among the English soldiers before the Battle of Bunker Hill. Today, probably for the first time in history, propaganda is directed against whole nations; the conditions that make such practices worthwhile include higher literacy rates, modern techniques of communication through the press, radio, and television, and mass public involvement in both government and political ideologies. The statements contained in modern propaganda include, in part, promises of rewards; threats of violence and punishment; claims of political, economic, social, and technological superiority; and charges of the enemy's inferiority.

Propaganda for Domestic Consumption. Propaganda for domestic consumption is concerned chiefly with strengthening the regime in power and with convincing the people that the policies adopted by this regime are the most desirable. In the United States government there is no central propaganda office for domestic consumption, although the Office of War Information (OWI) assumed this task as one of its functions during World War II. This lack can be attributed to the simple fact that the United States government is not menaced with immediate overthrow by any effective subversive body. Nevertheless, agencies connected with framing and administering the foreign policy of the United States, such as the State Department, have "press officers" whose task it is to present and defend the activities of their agencies to the public. Also, there are a host of nongovernmental organizations carrying on propaganda activities in behalf of these agencies and of United States policies. There are also a handful of organizations that emit propaganda against these agencies and policies. The domestic propaganda operations of British Commonwealth and Western European governments are fairly similar to those of the United States government. By contrast, in Soviet-Bloc countries and in other totalitarian and authoritarian states, just as in Nazi Germany and Fascist Italy, there are central government propaganda agencies constantly working to infuse the native population with respect for its government and with hatred and fear of the governments of countries that are to be regarded as potential or actual enemies. Hence, like the Berlin resident in 1939, the Moscow resident of today may be expected to ask the American tourist why the United States government is "plotting aggression."

Propaganda for Foreign Consumption. Propaganda intended for foreign consumption requires many instruments and appeals, and varies according to its targets.

FOREIGN TARGETS OF PROPAGANDA. Propaganda for foreign consumption varies, first of all, according to whether the government and people of the target country are regarded as friendly, hostile, or uncommitted. Propaganda aimed at friendly countries is designed to confirm and strengthen the ties of amity. That aimed at hostile countries is designed to reduce the ability of the governments in these countries to carry out acts of aggression; such propaganda is in effect a substitute for war. That aimed at uncommitted countries is designed to shift their policies toward friendship. The targets of propaganda may also differ according to whether the propaganda is aimed at government leaders or simply at the general public of the country involved. United States propaganda efforts do not appear to be directed very often toward the leaders of hostile countries, probably out of conviction among United States propaganda administrators that little can be done to change leaders' attitudes about the United States; for instance, Premier Khrushchev's tour of the United States in 1959 made little if any evident change in his views. Governments of foreign countries, by contrast, especially those of the Soviet Bloc, work hard at influencing the leaders of other countries.

Many foreign governments, for example, maintain lobbyists in Washington, to discuss matters with United States government officials; and these governments entertain visiting foreign leaders in regal fashion.

INSTRUMENTS. The chief instruments of propaganda directed abroad are the various mass communications media. Today the most important is radio; the effectiveness of television is limited not only by the cost of transmitters and receivers but also by the fact that television waves with present techniques do not follow the curvature of the earth and therefore have a short range. Radio broadcasts, unlike printed matter, easily cross international frontiers and can be stopped only by jamming devices. Furthermore, they can carry messages to the illiterate. The use of radio is hampered by the fact that in some parts of the world, notably tropical Africa, atmospheric conditions produce very large amounts of static. In the United States, the main governmental radio propaganda activities are conducted by the Voice of America (VOA), in the United States Information Agency (USIA). Its operations are supplemented by those of Radio Free Europe, a privately supported body. These groups together have a number of stations abroad to transmit programs of news and entertainment. The Soviet government, too, spreads propaganda by radio; its stations operate far more hours per week than those of the VOA. Other governments particularly active in this regard include those of the United Kingdom, Communist China, and the United Arab Republic. Apart from the VOA, the USIA maintains information centers and libraries abroad and distributes huge quantities of printed matter. Other governments have comparable offices and activities, often conducted at their embassies. The Soviet government far more than any other has enlisted the citizens of foreign countries into its propaganda operations through such organizations as the Partisans of Peace.

TYPES OF APPEALS. Propaganda directed abroad is based on various types of appeals. One generally accepted psychological rule is that people will believe, and act upon, what they *want* to believe and act upon. So far, the Soviet and Communist Chinese governments have followed this rule more closely than the United States government has.

Soviet-Bloc Appeals. Soviet-Bloc leaders appeal especially to the desires for peace that most people have. Actually, according to Marxist theory there can be no peace so long as capitalism exists, and "peaceful coexistence" really means the conduct of war by other than military means. Nevertheless, this appeal is very effective, even in the United States. Soviet-Bloc propaganda also appeals to the nationalist sentiments of Asiatic and African intellectuals and denounces colonialism, racism, and the asserted greed of the wealthy.

United States Appeals. In its propaganda activities, by contrast, the United States government tends to emphasize the personal well-being that can be achieved in a society patterned after that of the United States. It also plays upon its efforts for peace, its large programs of foreign aid, and its support of the United Nations. United States propaganda efforts are handicapped by old charges that the interests of the United States are linked with those of the colonial powers. (There is little truth to this allegation in the last generation. For instance, in 1961 the United States UN delegate joined the Soviet delegate in voting for an investigation of affairs in Portuguese Angola.) American interests are, with more truth, often identified with those of the wealthy in many countries. Furthermore, since World War II leaders in the United States have relied almost entirely upon economic instruments, such as the Marshall Plan, without exploiting their full propaganda value. Then it is important to realize that the Soviet government appears before the world with one authoritative ideological position, whereas the United States government reflects in its actions the fact that America is a pluralistic country, with a number of viewpoints that freely express themselves throughout the world.

Review Questions

1. Describe two particular psychological problems that affect world politics. Would you say that either of these problems, or any other, is particularly typical of any one country or group of countries today? Would you say that either of these problems, or any other, is apt to develop when the people of any country reach a particular economic, social, or political level?

2. Describe the factors involved in the emergence of nationalism. Show how the factors connected with the recent emergence of nationalism in Turkey and Communist China differ from the factors connected with its emergence in Ghana and Kenya.

3. Compare the organization of propaganda for domestic consumption in the United States with that in the USSR. How do you account for the differences?

4. Compare the content of the propaganda for foreign consumption emitted by the United States with that emitted by the USSR. How do you account for the differences?

28 REGIONALISM

Regionalism comprises a movement, which has been very prominent since World War II, toward the voluntary integration of groups of countries for the purpose of achieving certain easily defined and clearly visible goals. Usually the countries involved have some sort of geographical propinquity; the governments share common interests; and the peoples have certain cultural similarities. Regionalism thus signifies the willingness of certain national leaders to subordinate some of the claims of national sovereignty to a supranational authority. The various regional arrangements that have emerged from this movement constitute both supplements to the United Nations and potential nuclei for larger full-fledged political units in the future. This movement—or, perhaps better, the recognition and study of this movement—is such a recent phenomenon that the term *regional arrangement* does not yet have a generally accepted definition. This chapter follows an *exclusive* rather than an *inclusive* definition. That is, it describes certain associations of countries. It does not, however, except for NATO, deal with those that are primarily military, such as CENTO; nor with those that constitute fundamentally a new set of interrelations among a former colonial empire, such as the French Community; nor with those that are obviously involuntary, such as the bonds among the Eastern European countries forced upon them in their role as Soviet satellites.

THE ORGANIZATION OF AMERICAN STATES

The Organization of American States (OAS), created in 1948, is based upon a considerable tradition that the countries of the New World have a community of interests and that their governments should co-operate in efforts to realize these interests.

Structure of the OAS. The structure of the OAS is based on the Charter of the OAS, adopted at the Bogotá Conference in 1948. This structure has some similarities to that of the UN. The "supreme organ" of the OAS is the Inter-American Conference, which resembles the UN General Assembly except that its regular sessions occur only once every five years. The principal functioning body of the OAS is the Council, which has one delegate from each of the 21 member governments. Thus each government has one vote; there is no veto. Depending upon the nature of the question, the Council reaches its decisions by either a simple majority or a two-thirds majority. The Council does not have as much power as the UN Security Council. It does concern itself with disputes between or among American states, and in efforts to secure a peaceful solution it may summon a Meeting of Consultation of Ministers of Foreign Affairs. The Council also supervises the technical organs of the OAS: the Inter-American Economic and Social Council, the Inter-American Council of Jurists, and the Inter-American Cultural Council. Finally, the Council chooses the Secretary General of the OAS; he is also the Director of the Pan American Union, which is the secretariat of the OAS. As in the case of the UN, there are various specialized agencies, such as the Pan American Sanitary Bureau, that are integrated into the OAS.

Achievements and Prospects. During the existence of the OAS there have not been many serious threats to the peace in the Americas, so that the political agencies of the OAS have had little opportunity to demonstrate their effectiveness. Units of the organization have, however, taken a few steps to halt threats of aggression. For instance, the Council of the OAS interceded in 1955 when troops invaded Costa Rica from Nicaragua. Then, in 1960, the Foreign Ministers of the OAS urged all member governments to sever diplomatic ties with the Trujillo regime in the Dominican Republic, because of its plotting against other American governments; the Foreign Ministers also implicitly censured the Castro regime in Cuba for its attachments to the USSR. By refusing to break completely with the Castro regime, an act urged by the United States government, Latin American officials showed their continued suspicions of the motives of the United States, and their persistent conviction that the Castro regime represented a "good" revolution. At length, as noted previously, in 1962 the Foreign Ministers voted to exclude Cuba from hemisphere affairs. It was noteworthy that the representatives of six countries, containing over two-thirds of the people in Latin America, did not agree with this vote. The structure of the OAS, which makes each Latin American state the legal equal of the United States, has the capability of lessening the anti-"Yankee" sentiments that condition the foreign policies of almost all Latin American governments. The organization appears to have good prospects of bringing the governments of the New World closer together.

WESTERN EUROPEAN REGIONAL ARRANGEMENTS

Since the end of World War II, leaders in Western Europe have devised and instituted a number of regional arrangements. These arrangements appear motivated by such goals as establishing defenses against the USSR, improving standards of living, achieving political integration, and creating a "third force" that is a mediating and independent party in the struggle between the United States and the Soviet Union. These arrangements in general have had the encouragement and support of the United States government.

The Council of Europe. The Council of Europe was formed in 1949, in conjunction with the inauguration of the Marshall Plan. It included some, but not all, of the countries that had established the Organization for European Economic Co-operation (OEEC), a primarily economic group whose chief task was the implementation of the Marshall Plan. The aims of the Council are chiefly to seek agreements among its members on social, legal, administrative, and cultural matters. It has two main bodies. One, the Consultative Assembly, is composed of representatives from the member countries; it might be the forerunner of a "parliament of Europe," though at present it has no authority to pass binding enactments. The other body, the Committee of Ministers, comprises the foreign ministers of the member countries; it is the more powerful, for among other things it has the formal power to draft the agenda for the Assembly. Discussions in the Committee and the Assembly have revealed the principal division among the European governments over the question of European political unity: spokesmen for the United Kingdom and the Scandinavian countries have tended to urge confederative arrangements under which the individual governments would keep almost all of their sovereign powers, whereas the spokesmen for the main continental states have recommended a more federal grouping.

The European Coal and Steel Community. The European Coal and Steel Community (CSC) was organized in 1952 to place a federal type of authority over the coal, iron, and steel industries of France, West Germany, Italy, and the Benelux countries. The principal agencies of the CSC are the High Authority, which is the actual governing body; the Consultative Committee, a technical group that advises the Authority; the Council of Ministers, which with one representative from each country links the Authority with the member governments; and the Common Assembly, which serves as a check on the Authority. The main function of the CSC is to establish a free market for coal, iron, and steel in the six-nation area. The operations of the CSC have led to the abolition of most restraints on the trade of the three specified items among the member countries, and they have made French and German industry much more dependent upon one another—thus helping to reduce the possibility of political disputes between the two countries.

The European Economic Community. The European Economic Community, often called the European Common Market, was formed in 1957 by the members of the CSC to serve largely as an extension of the CSC. As time has gone on, however, the Community has acquired an organization much larger than necessary for the mere regulation of economic activities; in 1960 the Community was estimated to have more than 2,000 officials. The approaching affiliation of Great Britain and other countries promises a new growth besides. The largest unit in the Community structure is the Assembly, with over 100 delegates chosen by the parliaments of the member countries. More important is the Council of Ministers, in which each country has one representative but whose representatives have different numbers of votes roughly apportioned according to the population of their countries. The Council exercises the main powers of decision in the Community. Besides these two bodies there are a Commission, to oversee the application of the treaty; a Court of Justice, to interpret the treaty; and an Economic and Social Committee, to advise the Community. The Community is designed largely to facilitate commerce in all items, as well as the travel of persons, among the six countries. It also establishes a single tariff schedule for goods imported from countries outside the Community. The establishment of the Community indicated, moreover, a conviction among the leaders of these countries that their national economies were interdependent. In addition, the organs of the Community have substantial political power to carry out their economic ends.

The European Atomic Energy Community. The European Atomic Energy Community, also called Euratom, was established at the same time as the European Economic Community and by the same countries. Euratom has the same Assembly and Court of Justice as the Community. It has a separate Council of Ministers, but with the same structure, which establishes the programs of research, and a Commission, which promotes research. The general goal of Euratom is to raise the standards of living in the member countries through the peaceful application of atomic energy. Among other things, it guides atomic research and secures materials for the production of atomic energy. Euratom itself owns the nuclear materials used by the member countries, and it also owns patents on any discoveries made by its scientists. In 1958 the United States government promised to furnish both nuclear materials and technical information to Euratom.

The European Free Trade Area. The European Free Trade Area was established in 1959 by the governments of Portugal, the United Kingdom, Norway, Sweden, Denmark, Austria, and Switzerland. The Finnish government received permission from Soviet authorities to join the Free Trade Area provided that it maintain present Soviet commercial privileges; subsequently, Finland became a member of this group. By contrast with the European Economic Community, the Free Trade Area has few officials; the member governments apparently intended to make the Area self-liquidating. Its main function was to establish free trade among its members; unlike the states of the Community, the countries of the Free Trade Area were all expected to establish their own tariff rates for goods imported from any other country. All members of the Free Trade Area except perhaps Finland evidently wanted at some future time to enter the Community; the chief promoters of the Free Trade Area seem to have been the British, who hesitated to enter the Community because of their low-tariff "imperial preference" arrangements. Initially it seemed that the two regional groups might compete with one another. By mid-1961, however, the Free Trade Area seemed about to dissolve since the British, the Danes, and the Austrians had announced publicly their intention to seek admission into the Community.

THE NORTH ATLANTIC TREATY ORGANIZATION

The North Atlantic Treaty Organization (NATO) is described in a previous chapter as fundamentally a military alliance that includes the United States, Canada, and 13 countries of Europe. However, in structure, function, and goals, NATO exceeds a simple military alliance. First, it has a sizable central organization, headed by the North Atlantic Council. Subordinate to the Council are not only the military organizations but also several boards that deal with nonmilitary problems. The NATO Council occupies itself not only with mustering armed forces but also with strengthening the national economies of the member countries; Council officers often co-operate with agencies working toward the economic integration of Western Europe. Then, the government of the United States has been using NATO as a prod to hasten European unification. Finally, many people who feel that the Atlantic is not a barrier separating Europe from America but an avenue linking the two conti-nents regard NATO as the first step in the establishment of a federal Atlantic community.

THE ARAB LEAGUE

The Arab League, formed in 1945 with a great deal of encouragement from the British government, by 1961 consisted of eleven Arab states: Tunisia, Libya, the UAR, Sudan, Syria, Saudi Arabia, Yemen, Lebanon, Jordan, Kuwait, and Iraq. Its headquarters are in Cairo. The League possesses a council called the Majlis, made up of the prime ministers of the member countries or their representatives. It also has a secretariat, headed by a Secretary General. Finally, it contains several functional departments and committees. The asserted aims of the League are to safeguard the national independence of the Arab states and to advance the well-being of the Arab peoples. Besides these aims, Arab leaders wanted to prevent the establishment of a Jewish state in Palestine, which had been peopled chiefly by Arabs for over a thousand years. For themselves, the British sought the unified friendship of all the Arab governments partly as a safeguard for British oil investments in the Middle East. The League has shown little strength in its functioning. Its principal military undertaking, the attempt to wipe out Israel, was a failure. The League has done almost nothing to implement the various economic and social projects that its officials have studied. Actually, these countries are very impoverished, so that they lack the resources for creating powerful military forces or supporting broad projects for economic and social change. Also, the League has been rent by competi-tion among some of its members, especially the UAR and Saudi Arabia, for leadership. Nevertheless, the League has drawn the attention of other governments to the fact that Arab leaders are extremely conscious of their newly won national independence and that they insist on being treated as the heads of equal, sovereign states.

Review Questions

1. Compare the structure and functions of the OAS with those of the UN or-ganization. Why would the United States government adopt a firmer stand about excluding Communist Cuba from OAS affairs than about continuing to exclude Communist China from the UN?

2. Describe the organization and functions of the European Coal and Steel Com-munity. Why was the agency based on these commodities? Can you imagine an arrangement involving these or any other commodities that might include two or more other countries elsewhere in the world?

3. How does the European Economic Community differ from the Coal and Steel Community? Which contains the greater promise of being the base for a political union?

4. What are the main differences between the Arab League and the various European regional arrangements? Do the European or the Arab national governments seem more likely to establish a political union? Why?

29 *CONTEMPORARY INTER-NATIONAL ORGANIZATIONS*

The numerous contemporary international organizations may be classified in various ways. They may be classified according to whether they are intended to be permanent, or whether they are designed to carry out certain tasks over a limited period. They may also be classified according to whether they are world-wide or are regional. Moreover, they may be classified according to whether they are governmental or are composed of nongovernmental individuals or groups. Finally, they may be classified according to whether they are concerned chiefly with political matters, or with such nonpolitical affairs as economic activities and social welfare. This chapter deals primarily with the chief contemporary permanent, world-wide, governmental, political international organization—the United Nations. The remainder of the chapter is devoted almost entirely to international organizations that are affiliated with the UN. The previous chapter discusses some major regional bodies, such as the OAS and the European Economic Community. Furthermore, it should be noted here that some nongovernmental international organizations, such as the Catholic Church and the World Federation of Trade Unions, may have considerable roles in world politics.

THE UNITED NATIONS

The United Nations is an international organization composed of representatives from most of the governments in the world that are generally regarded as sovereign. By 1961 there were 104 member governments. These governments retain their sovereignty; the UN is not their superior. Thus the UN is not a kind of "supergovernment"; instead, it comprises machinery through which the member governments may try to settle problems among themselves. Hence in a way there is no

justification for attributing "successes" to the UN, or imputing "failures" to it. Just as with the League of Nations, "successes" and "failures" result from the willingness or refusal of UN members to use UN
machinery in handling their problems.

Asserted Purposes. According to its Charter, the United Nations
has four purposes: (1) the maintenance of international peace and security, by means of effective collective measures toward that end;
(2) the development of friendly relations among nations based on the
principles of equal rights and self-determination of peoples; (3) the
achievement of international co-operation for the solution of international economic, social, cultural, and humanitarian problems; and
(4) the provision of a center for unifying the actions of governments in
attaining these purposes.

Structure. The structure of the UN organization comprises six major
bodies, which are listed and described below. It is important to stress
here that the observer should not seek a separation of powers in this organization and that he should be cautious in trying to establish a parallel between any of these bodies, except the International Court of Justice, and either the legislative, the executive, or the judicial branch of a
typical national government.

THE GENERAL ASSEMBLY. The General Assembly, which at the time
the UN organization was created seemed primarily a kind of world
forum, has since revealed itself to be potentially the most effective part
of the UN machinery, because no one country can veto action by the
General Assembly. The Assembly membership today reflects the postwar emergence of new sovereignties, since by 1961 there was an "Afro-
Asian Bloc" of 50 countries. This "Bloc," however, is a potentiality
rather than an actuality, for its members do not always vote as a unit.

Composition and Procedure. The General Assembly is the largest
body in the UN organization. It consists of as many as five delegates,
and their alternates, from each member country. Each country, however, has but one vote, with one exception: the governments of Byelo-
russia and the Ukraine, both of which are republics within the USSR,
are recognized as sovereign states for the purposes of the UN, and each
has a vote in the Assembly, so that for practical purposes the Soviet
government has three votes. On certain major issues, which are specified in the Charter, a two-thirds majority is necessary to reach a decision
in the Assembly. On other issues, a simple majority suffices. The chief
officers are the President and a number of Vice Presidents, elected by
the Assembly. The Assembly meets in annual sessions, and in special
sessions if deemed necessary.

Committees. The General Assembly includes several committees, much like those of Congress, to conduct the preparatory work for Assembly proceedings. These committees, whose functions are fairly evident in their titles, are (1) Political and Security; (2) Special Political; (3) Economic and Financial; (4) Social, Humanitarian, and Cultural; (5) Trusteeship; (6) Administrative and Budgetary; and (7) Legal. In administrative terms, the first five committees perform line functions, and the last two perform staff functions.

Functions. The Assembly is empowered to deal with any question in the jurisdiction of the UN, save those on the agenda of the Security Council. Moreover, at any time when the Security Council fails to perform its duty of maintaining peace during an actual threat to or breach of the peace or during an act of war, the Assembly may examine the situation and recommend steps, including the use of armed force. In general, however, the authority of the Assembly is confined to discussion; furthermore, it is barred from probing the internal affairs of any country. It is to call the attention of the Security Council to any situation that endangers peace. It is also to scrutinize the reports that must be sent to it annually by every organ of the UN. It adopts amendments to the UN Charter, which become effective when ratified by governments of two-thirds of the members. It votes on the admission of new members to the UN, following a recommendation by the Security Council. Finally, it elects a number of the officials in other UN bodies and agencies.

THE SECURITY COUNCIL. The Security Council was intended to be the organ that would execute the policy of the UN membership. However, chiefly because it has a voting procedure that confers upon each of its five principal member countries what amounts to a veto on important actions, the Council has become less and less important as an executive instrument.

Composition and Procedure. The Security Council consists of individual representatives from each of 11 member countries. Five of these countries—the United States, the United Kingdom, the USSR, France, and (Nationalist) China—have permanent seats. Representatives from the other six countries are elected by the General Assembly for overlapping two-year terms, with three seats becoming vacant each year. Supposedly the seats are filled with an eye to equitable representation for the several regions of the world. Each member has one vote. Any proposal submitted to the Council can be passed by seven affirmative votes. Proposals concerning procedural matters can be passed by affirmative votes from any seven members. Proposals on other matters require affirmative votes from seven members, including all those with permanent seats. Thus through its power to cast a negative vote, each great power has in effect a "veto" in Security Council voting. When one of the Council members is party to a dispute that the Council is trying to settle by peaceful means, the member loses its vote on that issue; however, it retains its vote on any proposal to apply economic or military sanctions. The Council is continuously in session.

Subordinate Bodies. The Security Council has two subordinate bodies to assist in performing Council functions. These bodies differ from the committees of the Assembly in that the committees are made up of Assembly members whereas the subordinate bodies of the Council are made up of distinct personnel not in the Council. One is the Military Staff Committee, which consists of the Chief of Staff, or his representative, from each permanent member of the Council. Its functions are to advise the Council on military needs for keeping peace and to supervise any international police force that may be established under UN auspices. The other body is the Disarmament Commission, which is occupied with the reduction of national armed forces and stocks of weapons.

Functions. The wide functions of the Security Council make it potentially the most powerful body in the UN. Specifically, it has the authority to determine what measures shall be imposed in efforts to effect the peaceful settlement of a dispute. It may investigate any dispute to determine whether it threatens to break the peace. It may call upon the parties to a dispute to attempt a settlement through such means as negotiation, mediation, or arbitration. If the parties to the dispute refuse to employ such methods or if such methods fail to resolve the dispute, the Council may refer the dispute to some international group such as a regional association of countries or the International Court of Justice. If these methods likewise fail to settle the dispute and war commences, the Council is authorized to declare which of the parties is the aggressor and what measures the other UN members should take against it. Such measures can be rather moderate, such as the breaking of diplomatic relations, the imposition of economic sanctions, and the severing of telephone and telegraph links. Finally, the Council may prescribe the use of armed force against the aggressor, under the supervision of the Military Staff Committee.

THE ECONOMIC AND SOCIAL COUNCIL. The Economic and Social Council (ECOSOC) comprises 18 members; they are elected by the General Assembly for three-year overlapping terms, with six members retiring each year. ECOSOC also includes a number of commissions—

11 in 1960. Seven are functional: Statistical; Social; Population; Narcotic Drugs; Human Rights; Status of Women; and International Commodity Trade. There are four Regional-Economic Commissions: for Europe; for Asia and the Far East; for Latin America; and for Africa. Moreover, ECOSOC supervises the various specialized agencies that are affiliated with the UN, which are described later in this chapter. Through these groups ECOSOC performs, or sees to the performance of, such tasks as making studies and reports on economic, social, and related matters. Then, on the basis of these studies and reports, it makes recommendations to the General Assembly for actions to promote human rights and freedoms. It carries out its tasks in co-operation with not only the specialized agencies but also any pertinent nongovernmental agency.

THE TRUSTEESHIP COUNCIL. The Trusteeship Council was designed to place the colonial, or "non-self-governing," areas in the world under international supervision. The Council actually has custody over only a few areas, but these include all the former Japanese and Italian possessions that are not self-governing. The widespread process of granting political independence to colonies since 1945 has drastically reduced the number of regions over which the Council might exercise authority. Moreover, the governments of some countries, such as Australia and the Republic of South Africa, have refused to give up their control of areas over which the Trusteeship Council might wield its jurisdiction.

Composition and Procedure. The Trusteeship Council includes all countries that administer non-self-governing territories under the international trusteeship system; all remaining permanent members of the Security Council; and enough additional countries to give the Trusteeship Council an equal number of countries administering such territories and of countries not administering such territories. In 1962 the Council had ten members. Five—Australia, Belgium, New Zealand, the United Kingdom, and the United States—were administering territories. Three others—France, the USSR, and China—belonged by virtue of their seats on the Security Council. The last two—Bolivia and India—were nonadministering countries elected by the General Assembly for three-year terms. In voting on proposals, the Council reaches a decision by a simple majority.

Functions. The functions of the Trusteeship Council involve the supervision of the international trusteeship system. This system includes all non-self-governing territories assigned as mandates after World War I; all colonies of the defeated countries in World War II; and all non-self-governing territories that other countries may wish to place under the system. The administering countries are to ready the peoples of these territories for self-government and to provide for their economic, social, and cultural self-betterment. The Trusteeship Council is to oversee these activities, to receive and examine reports sent to it by the administering countries, and to investigate any charges that the administering countries are performing their tasks in an improper manner. Finally, any part or all of a trust territory may be designated "strategic" and for that reason placed under the supervision of the Security Council.

THE INTERNATIONAL COURT OF JUSTICE. The International Court of Justice consists of 15 judges, each from a different country. They are elected by the General Assembly and the Security Council, voting separately, for overlapping nine-year terms. The Court reaches its decisions by a simple majority vote. Every member country of the UN is automatically a party to the Court, and a nonmember country may become a party under specific rules fixed by the General Assembly and the Security Council. Each country may submit to the Court such cases as its government may permit. Some countries have agreed to turn over to the Court all cases falling within its general province; others have placed limits on the sorts of cases they will surrender to the Court. For example, the government of the United States, according to the so-called Connally Amendment, denies the Court the power to hear cases involving matters that bear upon the internal affairs of the United States. In general, the Court handles such cases as those involving boundary disputes, the meaning of treaties, and violations of international law or international obligations. Decisions of the Court are final. If one party to a dispute disregards a Court decision, the other party may ask the Security Council to enforce it.

THE SECRETARIAT. The Secretariat is headed by the Secretary General of the United Nations, who is appointed by the General Assembly on the recommendation of the Security Council. There are numerous subordinate officers. Some, such as the Legal Counsel, the Controller, and the Director of Personnel, carry out staff functions. Others, among them the Under-Secretaries for Special Political Affairs, for Political and Security Council Affairs, and for Economic and Social Affairs, perform line functions. Essentially the Secretariat is the permanent civil service of the UN organization, and the Secretary General is its chief administrative official. In theory, in the performance of their duties the members of the Secretariat owe allegiance only to the UN. The main special tasks of the Secretary General and his subordinates are to prepare an annual report for submission to the General Assembly and to draw the attention of the Security Council to any situation that may seem to threaten world peace. In 1960 Secretary General Dag Hammarskjold added greatly to the real power of his office. During the uprising in the Congo, Hammarskjold exploited powers assigned by the Charter to his office, but previously unused, to direct the UN effort to restore order to the Congo.

Some Disputes Submitted for Action through the United Nations. There have been many international disputes submitted for action through the United Nations organization. This section deals only with some of the most important. The dispute over Korea and the war there are discussed in a previous chapter (see pages 112–113).

IRAN. The dispute involving Iran stemmed from the fact that during World War II British and Soviet troops had occupied the country, both to prevent its capture by Nazi agents and to supervise transportation of Lend-Lease goods from the Persian Gulf to the USSR. After the war, the British withdrew their troops but the Soviets did not. In 1946 the Iranian government complained to the UN that the USSR was attempting to interfere in Iranian internal concerns through these troops. The Soviet government denied the charge and temporarily vacated its seat in the Security Council. Later in the same year, however, the Soviet government summoned its troops home.

GREECE. The dispute over Greece lasted for a number of years. It resulted both from the role of Greece during World War II and from the efforts of the USSR to incorporate the country into the Soviet Bloc after the war. Early in 1946 the Soviet government charged in the UN that the British troops in Greece were interfering with Greek internal matters and were therefore a threat to peace. The Security Council heard some discussion of the issue, then laid it aside. Later in the same year, the Ukrainian government accused the Greeks of violating their frontier with Albania. In return the Greeks charged not only Albania but also Yugoslavia and Bulgaria—all Soviet-Bloc countries—with interference in Greek affairs. The subsequent debate resolved nothing. At length the Greeks asked the Security Council to investigate conditions along the northern Greek border. The Council appointed a committee of investigation with representatives from each Council member. In 1947 this committee published its findings. According to a majority of the committee members, the Soviet-Bloc countries were guilty of assisting Communist guerrillas in a war against the Greek government. According to a minority of the members—Poland and the USSR—the Greeks were responsible for all the difficulties. When these two groups could not reach an agreement over what should be done next, the question was passed on to the General Assembly. Here the members established a Special Balkan Committee to seek establishment of better relations and to prevent border violations. Only the Greeks would co-operate with this body. The end of the dispute came when Greece began receiving military aid under the Truman Doctrine and when Yugoslavia was expelled from the Soviet Bloc.

INDONESIA. The dispute concerning Indonesia arose from the efforts of certain Indonesian leaders to win national independence and the ensuing conflict with the Netherlands. It, too, lasted for several years. In 1946, the Ukrainian government maintained before the UN that British and Japanese troops were being used to repress an independence movement in Indonesia. In the debates that followed, the Netherlands government asserted that these troops were really being used to restore order to the islands and that, since the islands were a Dutch colony, any UN action would be an interference with Dutch internal affairs. Thereupon the Security Council terminated the discussions. Later in 1946, the Netherlands government reached an agreement with Indonesian leaders that in many quarters was interpreted as making Indonesia an equal partner in a Netherlands-Indonesian Union under the Dutch crown. In July, 1947, however, the governments of Australia and India asked Security Council action against Dutch military activities in Indonesia. The Netherlands government still held the situation to be a domestic affair, but other countries argued that the 1946 agreement had given Indonesia autonomy so that the situation fell within the jurisdiction of the UN. The Council then set up a Committee of Three, with one member chosen by each party and one chosen by both, to reach a settlement. On recommendation of the Committee, in 1948 both parties agreed to a cease-fire, but in fact the fighting did not stop. After still more negotiations, Indonesia became officially a partner of the Netherlands in 1949, and entirely independent in 1954.

ISRAEL. The dispute over Israel, which is not yet settled, initially concerned Palestine, once a part of the Ottoman Empire but a British mandate since World War I. It was, at the beginning of the mandate, inhabited chiefly by Arabs, but, largely because of the Zionist movement, it became the area for a projected Jewish national home. In spite of Arab objections, large numbers of Jews immigrated. With the close of World War II, the situation in Palestine became much more serious. Great numbers of Jews from Europe now wanted to enter the area, but the British had imposed limits on immigration. Furthermore, the Arabian peoples had much stronger feelings of nationalism than ever before. In 1947, largely because of a British request, the UN chose a special committee to examine the situation. Later that year a majority of the committee proposed, among other things, that Palestine be partitioned so as to make a Jewish and an Arab state, which would be independent with the end of the British mandate. The Jews and the governments of the United States and the USSR accepted this proposal, but the Arabs rejected it. The Assembly voted to adopt a partition arrangement similar to that proposed. It also named a commission that, among other things, would draw the boundaries and see to the establishment of the new governments. In May, 1948, when the British laid down their mandate over Palestine, Jewish leaders proclaimed the new and independent republic of Israel, which immediately received diplomatic recognition from the governments of the United States and the USSR. Subsequently the Arab countries unsuccessfully waged war upon Israel in an effort to destroy the Jewish state. In 1949 they reached separate armistices with Israel on terms suggested by a UN mediator. There is still no Arab state of Palestine; the areas assigned to the Arabs are in general occupied by the United Arab Republic and Jordan.

EGYPT AND THE SUEZ CANAL. The dispute over Egypt and the Suez Canal was the consequence of such factors as the unresolved struggle between Israel and the Arab countries, the growth of Arab nationalism, and the determination of the USSR to have more influence in the Middle East.

Immediate Background. The immediate background of the dispute lay in the refusal of the United States and British governments, in 1956, to help the Egyptian government build a dam across the Nile at Aswan. Evidently in reprisal for this act, the Egyptian government nationalized the Suez Canal. According to an international agreement of 1888, the Canal, owned by a private corporation, was to be open to merchant vessels of all countries although it was on Egyptian soil. British troops, which had been stationed there for many years, had been withdrawn earlier in 1956; and the Egyptian government had been authorized to take possession of the Canal in 1968, when the privileges of the corporation were to expire. One asserted reason for Egyptian seizure of the Canal was to use the tolls for financing the Aswan Dam. The chief users of the Canal, notably Great Britain and France, protested against nationalization; and in September, 1956, the Security Council began considering the dispute. In October the Council drafted a set of principles for operation of the Canal that were transmitted to the governments of the interested countries.

Military Operations and UN Action. The military operations in Egypt in 1956 were first simply an extension of hostilities between Israel and the Arab states. For years there had been continual skirmishes and border raids involving Israeli and Arab troops. In October, 1956, the armed forces of Egypt, Syria, and Jordan were placed under a single commander. Soon afterward, Israeli troops attacked Egyptian forces and invaded Egypt. The British and French governments then called for a cessation of fighting and demanded the authority to occupy places in Egypt along the Suez Canal. The Israelis accepted these demands, but the Egyptians rejected them. Consequently the British and the French attacked and invaded Egypt. It now seemed that the USSR might intervene in behalf of Egypt. On October 30, after the Israeli attack but before the Anglo-French invasion, the Security Council took up a United States proposal for a cease-fire call; the British and the French vetoed it. On November 1, after the Anglo-French invasion, the General Assembly voted for a cease-fire and for the establishment of a United Nations Emergency Force (UNEF) to police the Canal area. In the face of this vote, on November 6 the British, French, and Israelis ceased hostilities, and the UNEF assumed the task of policing the area. Subsequently the British, the French, and the Israelis withdrew their troops from most of the districts they had been occupying. The Israelis completed their withdrawal only after UN pressure. United Nations salvage crews also cleared the Suez Canal of ships sunk there by the Egyptians to block traffic, and the Canal was reopened in March, 1957, under the supervision of the UAR.

HUNGARY. The dispute over Hungary arose from efforts by Hungarian nationalists and patriots late in 1956 to end Soviet rule in Hungary. Soviet troops with artillery and tanks attacked these Hungarians but after a few days apparently halted operations. Two days later, however, Soviet forces once more advanced on Budapest; the Hungarians appealed to the UN. In less than a week these Soviet forces crushed the uprising. Meanwhile, an effort in the Security Council for UN action was vetoed by the USSR. In the following month the General Assembly called for a withdrawal of Soviet troops and for a UN investigation in Hungary, but the USSR and the new pro-Soviet Hungarian regime disregarded these protests. Afterward, the General Assembly voted to create a special investigating committee and to debate the execution of the Hungarian nationalist leaders. The governments of the USSR and Hungary denounced these actions on the ground that they constituted interference into Hungarian domestic affairs.

THE CONGO. The difficulties in the Congo that led to UN action there started in July, 1960, when the Belgian government gave the Congolese their national independence. The Congo comprises an area of more than

900,000 square miles whose 14,000,000 people come from various often hostile tribes with little sense of nationhood. The Belgians had made progress in satisfying the physical needs of the Congolese but had given them almost no training in self-government. Disorders broke out immediately after the achievement of independence, as tribes attacked one another and natives killed or abused whites. Moreover, Moise Tshombe, the leader of the richest province, Katanga, proclaimed his intention to secede from the central government. In a few days Patrice Lumumba, the Congolese prime minister, asked for help from the UN to restore order and, apparently, to get the remaining Belgians out of the country. Secretary General Hammarskjold led the movement to install a UN Emergency Force in the Congo. Meanwhile the Soviet government began charging the Western countries with interfering in the Congo; Lumumba was pro-Soviet and was expected possibly to pave the way for the new state to enter the Soviet Bloc. By 1961, however, an anti-Soviet politician was head of the Congolese central government and in February Lumumba was assassinated. Meanwhile the economic life of the country had practically halted except in Katanga, the only province in which the Belgian administrators and managers were encouraged to stay. Furthermore, the central government was almost powerless. Late in 1961 a UN army invaded Katanga with the announced aim of forcing it to unite with the rest of the Congo. This project was endorsed by the United States, the Soviet Union, and most of the states in Africa and Asia; it was opposed particularly by the British and the French. Finally, in December, 1961, after the UN forces had made further resistance almost impossible, Tshombe made a personal agreement with Congolese Premier Cyrille Adoula to end the secession of Katanga from the central Congolese government. By this time, even the productive Katanga mining enterprises had ceased operating. It appeared that the Congo for many years would be the ward of the UN.

Differences between the UN and the League of Nations. Although there are important similarities between the UN and the League of Nations, there are some important differences as well. Two historical differences are pointed out in an earlier chapter: (1) Whereas the League of Nations was established at a single conference, the UN organization was produced through various conferences and agreements over a number of years. (2) The Covenant for the League of Nations was a section in the peace treaties after World War I, but the Charter for the UN organization was a separate document written at an international meeting called for that one purpose. There are at least two more significant differences. One is the specific authority conferred upon the

Security Council to employ force against a given country. No branch of, or agency in, the League of Nations had such authority. The second is the concession in the UN Charter that international disputes may arise from other than political causes and the accompanying provision of such bodies as ECOSOC to handle the nonpolitical causes of war. This concession involves also the belief that a cause for war may develop at any time. The League of Nations, by contrast, was organized and operated on the premise that with the end of World War I and the drawing of "satisfactory" international boundaries the causes for war had disappeared.

THE SPECIALIZED AGENCIES

The so-called specialized agencies are international organizations whose functions are mainly economic, social, or cultural. Each has a link with the UN organization through an agreement with ECOSOC (see pp. 348–349). Yet some were established without the prompting of the UN, and some even antedate the UN. Each has substantial autonomy in administering personnel and finances and in determining policy. They are discussed below in alphabetical order.

The Food and Agriculture Organization. The Food and Agriculture Organization (FAO), which has 81 member countries, operates through a conference that meets at least biennially and that contains one delegate, with one vote, from each member. The stated purposes of the FAO are to raise the levels of nutrition and standards of living of the peoples in the member countries, to improve the efficiency of the production of food and agricultural goods, to better the condition of rural populations, and thus to contribute to an expanding world economy. Through regional offices in North America, Latin America, the Near East, and the Far East, as well as through its headquarters at Rome, it deals with five technical fields: agriculture, fisheries, forestry and forest products, nutrition, and economics and statistics. It has served as an agency for the international exchange of information, recommended certain national and international activities, supplied a variety of technical assistance, and organized special missions.

The Intergovernmental Maritime Consultative Organization. The Intergovernmental Maritime Consultative Organization (IMCO), which has 43 member countries, functions through an Assembly, with representatives from all members; a Council, representing mainly the states with the greatest interest in international shipping services and international seaborne trade; a Maritime Safety Committee, representing mainly the members with the greatest interest in maritime safety;

and a Secretariat, to keep the records of the organization and inform the members of the activities of the organization. The chief functions of the IMCO are to promote international co-operation respecting governmental regulation of shipping in international trade; to seek the lessening of discriminatory restrictions; and to consider unfair restrictive practices by shipping concerns.

The International Bank for Reconstruction and Development. The International Bank for Reconstruction and Development, with 68 member countries, is managed by a Board of Governors, with one delegate from each of the countries. The operations of the Bank are conducted by 18 Executive Directors, selected by the member countries. These Directors have voting power approximately in proportion to the amount of capital subscribed by the country each represents. The Bank is mainly a lending agency, with funds based upon the approximately $20 billion of capital stock subscribed by the member countries. The bulk of the money the bank lends is derived from the sale of its bonds to the public. The Bank is empowered to lend money to member governments; if the loans are guaranteed by the member governments, the Bank can lend money to nongovernmental organizations. The first loans were made chiefly to such countries as France and Belgium, which needed funds in order to achieve economic recovery from the war. Subsequent loans have been made to economically backward countries such as Brazil and India, for the development of industry, transportation, power, and agriculture. The Bank also extends technical aid, not only in connection with specific loans but also for the purpose of drafting comprehensive economic plans. By March 31, 1961, the Bank had made loans of over $5.5 billion to 55 countries and territories.

The International Civil Aviation Organization. The International Civil Aviation Organization (ICAO), which has 84 member countries, operates through a number of bodies; the principal of these is a Council of 21 persons. The ICAO aims to establish standardization and uniformity in international air navigation, with especial regard to such matters as navigational aid, airports, rules of the air, the licensing of personnel, and weather information. It amasses economic statistics, conducts studies of pertinent economic matters, and issues recommendations based on these studies. Finally, it supervises a fleet of weather observation ships in the Atlantic.

The International Finance Corporation. The International Finance Corporation (IFC), with 58 member countries, is affiliated with the International Bank. The Corporation is similarly interested in improving the economic conditions of underdeveloped countries. The Corporation, however, is an investing agency; and it places its funds only in private enterprise, without government guarantees. These investments take the form of loans that carry interest and that give the Corporation some voice in the management of the receiving enterprise. Presumably the IFC will sell its investment in a firm to nongovernmental individuals and groups as soon as the enterprise concerned has become an attractive business risk.

The International Labor Organization. The International Labor Organization (ILO), which comprises 97 member countries, includes the International Labor Conference, the Governing Body, and the International Labor Office. The chief functions of the ILO are to better the conditions of labor, raise living standards, and foster economic and social stability. The Conference is an international discussion center for social problems. It also drafts recommendations for various aspects of working conditions, such as the hours of work, the freedom to organize labor unions, and workmen's compensation. The Governing Body, elected by the Conference, supervises the work of the Conference Committees. The International Labor Office both serves as a secretariat for the ILO and provides technical assistance for member countries in such matters as vocational training. It is also a world center for information on social questions.

The International Monetary Fund. The International Monetary Fund, with 68 member countries, is controlled fundamentally by its Board of Governors, with two representatives from each country. The Fund is administered chiefly by its Board of Executive Directors, which has five members each chosen by one of the countries with the largest financial stake in the Fund, and 13 members chosen by other countries. The chief purpose of the Fund is to help stabilize the value of moneys in international exchange, so as to expand international trade and the benefits it provides for national economies. The Fund is thus designed to forestall practices that occurred before World War II, when certain governments deliberately inflated their money with the goal of increasing exports and curtailing imports. The Fund was created also to prevent governments from placing restrictions on the international movements of their money and from installing discriminatory exchange arrangements. The Fund operates on the basis of a stock of money contributed by the member countries, each of which is assigned a quota roughly proportionate to its national wealth. The total of these quotas is just under $15 billion. The money of each member country has been assigned a certain value in international exchange that the government of the country may alter only within narrow limits. If the balance of payments of a given country in international trade makes it difficult for the government to maintain this value, the Fund may provide a loan for stabilization purposes. In making this loan, the Directors of the Fund may impose certain requirements concerning the policies of the government toward the national economy, particularly with an eye to reducing domestic expenditures and imports.

The International Telecommunication Union. The International Telecommunication Union (ITU), with 106 member countries, conducts its activities largely by means of international conferences meeting every five years. For its day-by-day functions it has an Administrative Council of 18 member governments and a secretariat. The functions of the ITU are to bring about the best possible systems of international communication by means of telegraph, telephone, and radio; and to carry out studies aimed at improving these means of communication. One special task of the ITU is to register the frequency of radio transmitting stations throughout the world in an effort to avoid confusion and conflict in the use of the limited number of wave bands available.

The United Nations Educational, Scientific and Cultural Organization. The United Nations Educational, Scientific and Cultural Organization (UNESCO), with 82 member countries, operates according to policies drafted by its biennial General Conference and administered by its Executive Board. It also functions through co-operating national agencies in the member countries. The premise of UNESCO is that the chances for world peace will be increased if the peoples of the world have a greater understanding of, and appreciation for, each other's cultures. Hence it participates in, and promotes, international exchanges of educational, scientific, and cultural information, and encourages governments and peoples to initiate co-operative international undertakings in these fields. These undertakings are also intended to increase respect for justice, the rule of law, and human rights and freedoms.

The Universal Postal Union. The Universal Postal Union (UPU), with 102 member countries and many dependent areas, includes a Postal Congress that sets policies and an Executive and Liaison Committee that administers them. The UPU also contains a permanent secretariat, the International Bureau, to distribute information to the member governments. The main purpose of the UPU is to unite all countries belonging to it into a single postal territory. The UPU is concerned with such specific matters as the handling of international mail, the classification of mail articles, and the uniformity of mailing rates.

The World Health Organization. The World Health Organization (WHO), which has 87 members, contains a World Health Assembly that drafts policies, an Executive Board to furnish advice, and a Secretariat to carry out the policies. These programs are conducted not only through the main office in Switzerland, but also through regional offices in India, Egypt, the Philippines, French Equatorial Africa, Denmark, and the United States. The WHO helps governments to improve public sanitation systems, seeks to bring communicable diseases under control, recommends standard names for drugs, and contributes to establishing a uniform method for gathering health statistics.

The World Meteorological Organization. The World Meteorological Organization (WMO), which has 107 member countries, functions through a quadrennial World Congress, an executive committee, various regional associations, and a number of technical commissions. Among the functions of the WMO are promoting the establishment of a worldwide network of weather stations; encouraging the development of services for the swift exchange of weather information; helping standardize weather statistics; advancing the use of weather data for transportation, farming, and other activities; and stimulating research in meteorology. The WMO through its secretariat publishes a variety of items, such as lists of weather stations and schedules of radio weather broadcasts.

THE INTERNATIONAL ATOMIC ENERGY AGENCY

The International Atomic Energy Agency (IAEA) was an outgrowth of a proposal by President Eisenhower in 1953 for the creation of an international stockpile of atomic materials for peaceful purposes.

The IAEA, with 70 members, resembles in many ways a specialized agency of the UN but has no formal ties with ECOSOC. However, it makes regular annual reports to the UN. The IAEA is headed by a General Conference, made up of one delegate, with one vote, from each member country. The executive body is the Board of Governors, which names a Director General for the IAEA. The general purpose of the IAEA is to "enlarge the contribution of atomic energy to peace, health, and prosperity throughout the world." In pursuance of this goal, the IAEA promotes and conducts research into the problems of atomic energy; seeks out necessary materials for the generating of atomic energy; arranges for the international exchange of both information about atomic energy and persons schooled in the techniques associated with atomic energy; works for safeguards against the military use of atomic energy; and acquires facilities for the study of atomic energy.

CONCLUSION

Today the world is organized *as a world* more than ever before. Nearly every part of the world has almost instantaneous communication links with every other part. Hundreds of international organizations, inside and outside the UN, governmental and nongovernmental, concern themselves with the problems of mankind. If, as is always possible, men fail to prevent war in our time, their failure will not be due to the lack of mechanisms and structures for peaceful collaboration. Yet the presence of such mechanisms and structures does not guarantee the prevention of war; World War II broke out in 1939 notwithstanding the existence of the League of Nations and various lesser international bodies. Moreover, the absence of such mechanisms and structures does not condemn mankind to the waging of incessant warfare; for 99 years, from 1815 until 1914, there was no general war among any of the great powers, but there was no worldwide political organization. There are a number of factors that threaten war today and that make it a more perilous undertaking than ever before. Three of them deserve especial note: (1) Much of the world is divided into two consciously hostile armed camps. (2) Each of these camps possesses a stock of the most efficient weapons of death and destruction ever created. (3) Throughout the world, men show an increased willingness to use extremes of force in the solution of political disputes. What is critical for the world is the development of the will to prevent recourse to war for the solution of international disputes. These international mechanisms and structures may encourage the development of such a will among political leaders, and can provide these leaders with the means by which they can implement this will.

Review Questions

1. Describe the organization and functions of the UN General Assembly. Might the UN be a more effective agency to deal with threats of war if it contained a second "house" with seats apportioned according to the population of the member countries?

2. Describe the organization and functions of the UN Security Council. Explain why the question of accepting Communist China into the UN especially involves the Security Council.

3. What kind of future may one predict for the Economic and Social Council?

4. What kind of future may one predict for the Trusteeship Council?

5. Have there been any common traits among the disputes, or most of the disputes, submitted for action through the UN? Could any of these disputes have been solved without recourse to war if the UN had not existed?

6. What are the principal differences between the UN and the League of Nations? What factors have caused these differences?

7. To what extent do the various specialized agencies depend upon the UN organization for their functioning?

8. Describe the differences among the specialized agencies whose functions are chiefly monetary and financial. To what extent does the functioning of each of these agencies involve probable interference in the internal affairs of the beneficiary country?

SELECTED REFERENCES

For the purpose of saving space, this bibliography lists the title of any given book only once. Therefore the reader may profit by consulting the references for more than one chapter.

1—Introduction: The Study of World Politics

Barber, Bernard. *Science and the Social Order,* 1952.

Deutsch, K. W. *Political Community at the International Level: Problems of Definition and Measurement,* 1953.

Goodwin, G. L., ed. *The University Teaching of International Relations,* 1951.

Gross, Feliks. *Foreign Policy Analysis,* 1954.

Herz, J. H. *Political Realism and Political Idealism: A Study in Theories and Realities,* 1951.

Kaplan, Morton. *System and Process in International Politics,* 1957.

Lasswell, H. D., and Daniel Lerner, eds. *The Policy Sciences,* 1952.

McDonald, John. *Strategy in Poker, Business, and War,* 1950.

Manning, C. A. W. *The University Teaching of Social Sciences: International Relations,* 1954.

Salvadori, Massimo, ed. *Contemporary Political Science: A Survey of Methods, Research, and Teaching,* 1950.

Schelling, T. C. *The Strategy of Conflict,* 1960.

Snyder, W. C., H. W. Bruck, and Burton Sapin. *Decision-Making as an Approach to the Study of International Politics,* 1954.

Van Dyke, Vernon, ed. *The Teaching of International Politics,* 1955.

Van Wagenen, R. W. *Research in the International Organization Field,* 1952.

Voegelin, Eric. *The New Science of Politics, an Introduction,* 1952.

Wright, Quincy. *The Study of International Relations,* 1954.

2—The Beginnings of the Modern State System

Abbott, W. C. *The Expansion of Europe,* 1938.

Bryce, James. *The Holy Roman Empire,* 1914.

364 *Selected References*

Buck, P. W. *The Politics of Mercantilism*, 1942.
Dorn, W. L. *Competition for Empire, 1740–1763*, 1940.
Frank, Tenney. *Roman Imperialism*, 1914.
Gulick, E. V. *Europe's Classical Balance of Power*, 1955.
Hayes, C. J. H. *The Evolution of Modern Nationalism*, 1931.
Hrozny, Bedrich. *Ancient History of Western Asia, India, and Crete*, 1954.
Larsen, J. A. O. *Representative Government in Greek and Roman History*, 1954.
Numelin, Ragnar. *The Beginnings of Diplomacy*, 1950.
Packard, L. B. *The Commercial Revolution*, 1927.
Parry, J. H. *Europe and a Wider World, 1415–1715*, 1949.
Waddy, Lawrence. *Pax Romana and World Peace*, 1951.

3—*World Politics from 1789 to 1900*

Artz, F. B. *Reaction and Revolution, 1814–1832*, 1934.
Ashton, T. S. *The Industrial Revolution, 1760–1830*, 1948.
Binkley, R. C. *Realism and Nationalism, 1852–1871*, 1935.
Bruun, Geoffrey. *Europe and the French Imperium, 1799–1814*, 1938.
Clough, S. B., and C. W. Cole. *Economic History of Europe*, 1946.
Clyde, P. H. *The Far East*, 1948.
Ferrero, Guglielmo. *The Reconstruction of Europe*, 1941.
Gottschalk, L. R. *The Era of the French Revolution, 1715–1815*, 1940.
Hayes, C. J. H. *A Generation of Materialism, 1871–1900*, 1941.
Kohn, Hans. *Panslavism: Its History and Ideology*, 1953.
Lockwood, W. W. *The Economic Development of Japan: Growth and Structural Change, 1868–1938*, 1954.
Schenk, H. G. *The Aftermath of the Napoleonic Years: The Concert of Europe—an Experiment*, 1948.
Taylor, A. J. P. *The Struggle for Mastery in Europe, 1848–1918*, 1955.
Townsend, M. E. *European Colonial Expansion since 1871*, 1941.

4—*The Growth of the United States, 1789–1917*

Bailey, T. A. *A Diplomatic History of the American People*, 1958.
Bemis, S. F. *A Diplomatic History of the United States*, 1955.
——. *The Latin American Policy of the United States*, 1943.
Dennett, Tyler. *Americans in Eastern Asia*, 1922.
Griswold, A. W. *The Far Eastern Policy of the United States*, 1938.
Perkins, Dexter. *History of the Monroe Doctrine*, 1955.
——. *The United States and the Caribbean*, 1947.
Pratt, J. W. *America's Colonial Experiment*, 1950.
——. *A History of United States Foreign Policy*, 1955.
Rippy, J. F. *The United States and Mexico*, 1931.
Williams, B. H. *Economic Foreign Policy of the United States*, 1929.

5—*The Background and Campaigns of World War I*

Albertini, Luigi. *The Origins of the War of 1914,* 1952.
Buehrig, E. H. *Woodrow Wilson and the Balance of Power,* 1955.
Bunyan, James, and H. H. Fisher, comps. *The Bolshevik Revolution, 1917–1918,* 1961.
Chamberlin, W. H. *The Russian Revolution,* 1952.
Curtiss, J. S. *The Russian Revolutions of 1917,* 1957.
Edmonds, J. E. *A Short History of World War I,* 1951.
Fay, S. B. *The Origins of the World War,* 1929.
Kennan, G. F. *Russia Leaves the War,* 1952.
Langer, W. L. *The Diplomacy of Imperialism, 1890–1902,* 1951.
Schmitt, B. E. *The Coming of the War,* 1930.
Seymour, Charles. *American Diplomacy during the World War,* 1934.
Slosson, P. W. *The Great Crusade and After, 1914–1928,* 1930.
Tansill, C. C. *America Goes to War,* 1938.
Tate, Merze. *The Disarmament Illusion: The Movement for a Limitation of Armaments to 1907,* 1942.
Wolff, Theodor. *The Eve of 1914,* 1936.

6—*The Peace Settlement after World War I*

Bailey, T. A. *Woodrow Wilson and the Great Betrayal,* 1945.
———. *Woodrow Wilson and the Lost Peace,* 1944.
Birdsall, Paul. *Versailles Twenty Years After,* 1941.
Fleming, D. F. *The United States and the League of Nations,* 1932.
Garraty, John. *Henry Cabot Lodge,* 1953.
Howard-Ellis, Charles. *The Origin, Structure, and Working of the League of Nations,* 1928.
Mangone, J. G. *A Short History of International Organization,* 1954.
Marston, F. S. *The Peace Conference of 1919,* 1944.
Miller, D. H. *The Drafting of the Covenant,* 1928.
Nicolson, Harold. *Peacemaking, 1919,* 1938.
Walters, F. P. *A History of the League of Nations,* 1952.
Wright, Quincy. *Mandates under the League of Nations,* 1930.
Zimmern, Alfred. *The League of Nations and the Rule of Law,* 1936.

7—*The Period of False Stability, 1919 to 1929*

Baykov, A. M. *The Development of the Soviet Economic System,* 1947.
Carr, E. H. *The Bolshevik Revolution, 1917–1923,* 1950–54.
———. *International Relations between the Two World Wars,* 1948.
Churchill, Winston S. *World Crisis, 1918–1928; the Aftermath,* 1929.
Craig, C. A., and Felix Gilbert, eds. *The Diplomats: 1919–1939,* 1953.
Ebenstein, William. *Fascist Italy,* 1938.

Ferrell, R. H. *Peace in Their Time: The Origins of the Kellogg-Briand Pact,* 1952.

Fleming, D. F. *The United States and World Organization, 1920–1933,* 1938.

Kennan, G. F. *Russia and the West under Lenin and Stalin,* 1961.

Knapton, E. J. *France since Versailles,* 1952.

Mowat, C. L. *Britain between the Wars, 1918–1940,* 1955.

Nevins, Allan. *The United States in a Chaotic World: A Chronicle of International Affairs, 1918–1933,* 1950.

Reischauer, E. O. *Japan Past and Present,* 1946.

Vinacke, H. M. *A History of the Far East in Modern Times,* 1941.

Vinson, J. C. *The Parchment Peace,* 1950.

Wheare, K. C. *The Statute of Westminster and Dominion Status,* 1938.

Wheeler-Bennett, J. W. *The Pipe-Dream of Peace: A Study of the Collapse of Disarmament,* 1935.

8—*The Background of World War II, 1929 to 1939*

Baumont, Marice, J. H. E. Fried, and Edmond Vermeil, eds. *The Third Reich,* 1955.

Carr, E. H. *Britain: A Study of Foreign Policy from the Versailles Treaty to the Outbreak of the War,* 1939.

———. *The Twenty Years' Crisis, 1919–1939,* 1939.

Causton, E. E. N. *Militarism and Foreign Policy in Japan,* 1936.

Feis, Herbert. *The Spanish Story,* 1948.

Highley, A. E. *The First Sanctions Experiment,* 1938.

Jarman, T. L. *The Rise and Fall of Nazi Germany,* 1956.

Langer, W. L., and S. E. Gleason. *The Challenge to Isolation, 1937–1940,* 1952.

Lee, D. E. *Ten Years: The World on the Way to War, 1930–1940,* 1942.

Rossi, Angelo. *The Russo-German Alliance,* 1951.

Seton-Watson, Hugh. *Eastern Europe between the Wars, 1914–1941,* 1945.

Smith, S. R. *The Manchurian Crisis, 1931–32,* 1947.

Wecter, Dixon. *The Age of the Great Depression, 1929–1941,* 1948.

Wheeler-Bennett, J. W., *Munich: Prologue to Tragedy,* 1948.

Wiskemann, Elizabeth. *The Rome-Berlin Axis,* 1949.

Wolfers, Arnold. *Britain and France between Two Wars,* 1940.

9—*The Campaigns of World War II*

Beard, C. A. *President Roosevelt and the Coming of the War, 1941,* 1948.

Churchill, Winston S. *The Second World War,* 1948–53.

Drummond, D. F. *The Passing of American Neutrality, 1937–1941,* 1955.

Feis, Herbert. *Churchill, Roosevelt, Stalin,* 1957.

Friedin, Seymour, and William Richardson, eds. *The Fatal Decisions,* 1956.

Fuller, J. F. C. *The Second World War: A Strategical and Tactical History,* 1948.

Gordon, D. L., and R. J. Dengerfield. *The Hidden Weapon: The Story of Economic Warfare,* 1947.

Hinsley, F. H. *Hitler's Strategy,* 1951.

Jones, F. C. *Japan's New Order in East Asia: Its Rise and Fall, 1937–1945,* 1954.

Langer, W. L., and S. E. Gleason. *Undeclared War, 1940–41,* 1953.

McNeill, W. H. *America, Britain, and Russia: Their Co-operation and Conflict, 1941–1946,* 1953.

O'Neill, H. C. *A Short History of the Second World War and Its Social and Political Significance,* 1953.

Pratt, Fletcher, *War for the World,* 1951.

Puleston, W. D. *The Influence of Sea Power in World War II,* 1947.

10—The Peace Settlement after World War II

Arne, Sigrid. *United Nations Primer,* 1948.

Dean, V. M. *The Four Cornerstones of Peace,* 1946.

Dennett, Raymond, and A. C. Leiss. *European Peace Treaties after World War II,* 1954.

Fearey, R. A. *The Occupation of Japan,* 1950.

Feis, Herbert. *Between War and Peace: The Potsdam Conference,* 1960.

Friedmann, W. G. *The Allied Military Government of Germany,* 1947.

Litchfield, E. H., *et al. Governing Postwar Germany,* 1953.

Sherwood, Robert. *Roosevelt and Hopkins,* 1950.

Snell, John, ed. *The Meaning of Yalta,* 1956.

11—The Postwar Conflict, 1945 to 1962

Appleman, J. A. *Military Tribunals and International Crimes,* 1954.

Arnold, G. L. *The Pattern of World Conflict,* 1955.

Aron, Raymond. *The Century of Total War,* 1954.

Barber, Joseph, ed. *The Marshall Plan as American Policy,* 1948.

Beloff, Max. *Soviet Policy in the Far East, 1944–1951,* 1953.

Bingham, J. B. *Shirt-Sleeve Diplomacy: Point 4 in Action,* 1954.

Boorman, H. L., *et al. Moscow-Peking Axis: Strengths and Strains,* 1957.

Brown, W. A., and Redvers Opie. *American Foreign Assistance,* 1953.

Caldwell, J. C., and Lesley Frost. *The Korea Story,* 1952.

Curti, Merle, and Kendall Birr. *Prelude to Point Four,* 1954.

Dulles, F. R. *America's Rise to World Power, 1898–1954,* 1955.

Feis, Herbert. *The China Tangle,* 1953.

Fitzsimons, M. A. *The Foreign Policy of the British Labour Government: 1945–1951,* 1952.

Gaitskell, Hugh. *The Challenge of Coexistence,* 1957.
Goodrich, L. M. *Korea: A Study of U.S. Policy in the United Nations,* 1956.
Herz, J. H. *International Politics in the Atomic Age,* 1959.
Hodgkin, Thomas. *Nationalism in Colonial Africa,* 1956.
Holborn, Hajo. *The Political Collapse of Europe,* 1951.
Holland, W. L., ed. *Asian Nationalism and the West,* 1953.
Ingram, Kenneth. *The History of the Cold War,* 1955.
Jackson, J. H. *The World in the Postwar Decade: 1945–1955,* 1956.
Kahin, G. M. *The Asian-African Conference, Bandung, Indonesia, April 1955,* 1956.
Latourette, K. S. *The American Record in the Far East, 1945–1951,* 1952.
Price, H. B. *The Marshall Plan and Its Meaning,* 1955.
Reitzel, William, *et al. United States Foreign Policy, 1945–1955,* 1956.
Roberts, H. L. *Russia and America: Dangers and Prospects,* 1956.
Romulo, C. P. *The Meaning of Bandung,* 1956.
Scott, John. *Political Warfare: A Guide to Competitive Coexistence,* 1955.
Seton-Watson, Hugh. *Neither War nor Peace,* 1960.
Strausz-Hupé, Robert, A. J. Cottrell, and J. E. Daugherty. *American-Asian Tensions,* 1956.
Thayer, P. W., and W. T. Phillips, eds. *Nationalism and Progress in Free Asia,* 1956.
Toynbee, Arnold, and V. M. Toynbee. *The Realignment of Europe,* 1955.
Vinacke, H. M. *Far Eastern Politics in the Postwar Period,* 1956.
Wilmot, Chester. *The Struggle for Europe,* 1952.
Woodbridge, George. *United Nations Relief and Rehabilitation Administration,* 1950.

12—Fundamental Principles of National Power

Aitken, H. G., ed. *The State and Economic Growth,* 1959.
Ayres, Eugene, and C. A. Scarlott. *Energy Sources—the Wealth of the World,* 1952.
Cottrell, Fred. *Energy and Society,* 1955.
Ekirch, A. A., Jr. *The Civilian and the Military,* 1956.
Emme, E. M. *The Impact of Air Power: National Security and World Politics,* 1959.
Fifield, R. H., and G. E. Pearcy. *Geopolitics in Principle and Practice,* 1950.
Gyorgy, Andrew. *Geopolitics,* 1944.
Hart, B. H. L. *Strategy: The Indirect Approach,* 1954.
Hilsman, Roger. *Strategic Intelligence and National Decisions,* 1956.
Kaufman, W. W., ed. *Military Policy and National Security,* 1956.
Knorr, Klaus. *The War Potential of Nations,* 1956.
Lasswell, H. D., and Abraham Kaplan. *Power and Society,* 1950.
Lincoln, G. A., *et al. Economics of National Security,* 1954.
Mackinder, H. J. *Democratic Ideals and Reality,* 1942.

Mattern, Johannes. *Geopolitik: Doctrine of National Self-Sufficiency,* 1942.
Mouzon, O. T. *International Resources and National Policy,* 1959.
Ogburn, W. F., ed. *Technology and International Relations,* 1949.
Organski, K. F., and A. F. K. Organski. *Population and World Power,* 1961.
Pratt, W. E., and Dorothy Good. *World Geography of Petroleum,* 1950.
Puleston, W. D. *The Influence of Force in Foreign Relations,* 1955.
Scitovsky, Tibor, *et al. Mobilizing Resources for War,* 1951.
Sprout, Harold, and Margaret Sprout. *Foundations of National Power,* 1951.
Stamp, L. D. *Land for Tomorrow,* 1952.
Stoessinger, J. G. *The Might of Nations,* 1962.
Strausz-Hupé, Robert. *The Balance of Tomorrow,* 1945.
———. *Geopolitics: The Struggle for Space and Power,* 1942.
———. *Power and Community,* 1956.
Van Royen, William, *et al. The Mineral Resources of the World,* 1952.

13—The United States

Almond, G. A. *The American People and Foreign Policy,* 1950.
Arciniegas, Germán. *America and the New World,* 1955.
Bailey, T. A. *America Faces Russia: Russian-American Relations from Early Times to Our Day,* 1950.
Barber, H. M. *Foreign Policies of the United States,* 1953.
Battistini, L. H. *The United States and Asia,* 1956.
Bemis, S. F. *The Latin American Policy of the United States,* 1943.
Berle, A. A., Jr. *Tides of Crisis: A Primer of Foreign Relations,* 1957.
Bernardo, C. J., and E. H. Bacon. *American Military Policy,* 1955.
Bidwell, P. W. *Raw Materials: A Study of American Policy,* 1958.
Bloomfield, L. P. *The United Nations and U.S. Foreign Policy,* 1960.
Brown, W. N. *The United States and India and Pakistan,* 1953.
Burdett, F. L., ed. *Conduct of American Diplomacy,* 1951.
Cheever, D. S., and H. F. Haviland, Jr. *American Foreign Policy and the Separation of Powers,* 1952.
Colegrove, Kenneth. *The American Senate and World Peace,* 1944.
Crabb, C. V., Jr. *American Foreign Policy in the Nuclear Age,* 1960.
DeConde, Alexander, ed. *Isolation and Security,* 1957.
Dewhurst, J. F., *et al. America's Needs and Resources,* 1955.
Dizard, W. P. *The Strategy of Truth: The Story of the U.S. Information Service,* 1961.
Elder, R. E. *The Policy Machine: The Department of State and American Foreign Policy,* 1960.
Elliott, W. Y., *et al. United States Foreign Policy: Its Organization and Control,* 1952.
Finletter, T. K. *Power and Policy: US Foreign Policy and Military Power in the Hydrogen Age,* 1954.

Furniss, E. S., Jr. *American Military Policy: Strategic Aspects of World Political Geography,* 1957.

———, and R. C. Snyder. *An Introduction to American Foreign Policy,* 1955.

Gordon, Morton, and K. N. Vines. *Theory and Practice of American Foreign Policy,* 1955.

Gorter, Wytze. *United States Shipping Policy,* 1956.

Graebner, N. A., ed. *An Uncertain Tradition: American Secretaries of State in the Twentieth Century,* 1961.

Hammond, P. Y. *Organizing for Defense: The American Military Establishment in the Twentieth Century,* 1961.

Hitch, C. J., and R. N. McKean. *The Economics of Defense in the Nuclear Age,* 1960.

Holt, R. T., and R. W. Van de Velde. *Strategic Psychological Operations and American Foreign Policy,* 1960.

Hughes, J. J. *The United States and Italy,* 1953.

Hurewitz, J. C. *Middle East Dilemma: The Background of United States Policy,* 1953.

Kaufmann, W. W., ed. *Military Policy and National Security,* 1956.

Kennan, G. F. *Realities of American Foreign Policy,* 1954.

Kertesz, S. D., ed. *American Diplomacy in a New Era,* 1961.

Knappen, Marshall. *An Introduction to American Foreign Policy,* 1956.

Knorr, Klaus. *NATO and American Security,* 1959.

Kohn, Hans. *American Nationalism: An Interpretative Essay,* 1957.

Leonard, L. L. *Elements of American Foreign Policy,* 1954.

Lerche, C. O. *Foreign Policy of the American People,* 1961.

Liska, George. *The New Statecraft,* 1960.

Logan, J. A., Jr. *No Transfer: An American Security Principle,* 1961.

McCamy, J. L. *The Administration of American Foreign Affairs,* 1950.

McKay, Donald. *The United States and France,* 1951.

Marshall, C. B. *The Limits of Foreign Policy,* 1954.

Mikesell, R. F. *United States Economic Policy and International Relations,* 1952.

Milliken, M. F., and D. L. M. Blackmer. *The Emerging Nations: Their Growth and United States Policy,* 1961.

Morley, Felix. *The Foreign Policy of the United States,* 1951.

Morris, B. R. *Problems of American Economic Growth,* 1961.

Osgood, R. E. *Ideals and Self-Interest in America's Foreign Relations,* 1953.

———. *Limited War: The Challenge to American Security,* 1957.

Patterson, Gardner, and E. S. Furniss, Jr. *NATO: A Critical Appraisal,* 1957.

Perkins, Dexter. *The American Approach to Foreign Policy,* 1952.

Potter, E. B., and J. R. Fredland, eds. *The United States and World Sea Power,* 1955.

Slessor, J. C. *What Price Coexistence?* 1961.

Smith, D. O. *U.S. Military Doctrine: A Study and Appraisal,* 1955.

Smith, Louis. *American Democracy and Military Power,* 1951.

Stillman, E. O., and William Pfaff. *The New Politics*, 1962.

Strausz-Hupé, Robert, W. R. Kintner, and S. T. Possony. *A Forward Strategy for America*, 1961.

Tannenbaum, Frank. *The American Tradition in Foreign Policy*, 1955.

Thomas, L. V., and R. N. Frye. *The United States and Turkey and Iran*, 1951.

Tucher, R. W. *The Just War: A Study in Contemporary American Doctrine*, 1960.

Warne, W. E. *Mission for Peace: Point 4 in Iran*, 1956.

Whitaker, A. P. *The United States and Argentina*, 1955.

Wolf, Charles, Jr. *Foreign Aid: Theory and Practice in Southern Asia*, 1960.

Wolfers, Arnold, ed. *Alliance Policy in the Cold War*, 1959.

Lucian Pye

14—The Soviet Union

Allen, R. L. *Soviet Economic Warfare*, 1960.

Barghoorn, F. C. *The Soviet Cultural Offensive*, 1960.

———. *The Soviet Image of the United States: A Study in Distortion*, 1950.

———. *Soviet Russian Nationalism*, 1956.

Bauer, R. A., Alex Inkeles, and Clyde Kluckhorn. *How the Soviet System Works*, 1956.

Beloff, Max. *The Foreign Policy of Soviet Russia, 1929–1941*, 1947.

Bergson, Abram, ed. *Soviet Economic Growth*, 1953.

Berliner, J. S. *Soviet Economic Aid: The New Aid and Trade Policy in Underdeveloped Countries*, 1958.

Brzezinski, Z. K. *Ideology and Power in Soviet Politics*, 1962.

Campbell, R. W. *Soviet Economic Power*, 1960.

Christman, R. C., ed. *Soviet Science, a Symposium*, 1952.

Conquest, Robert. *Power and Policy in the USSR*, 1961.

Crankshaw, Edward. *Russia without Stalin: The Emerging Pattern*, 1956.

Dallin, D. J. *The Changing World of Soviet Russia*, 1956.

Fainsod, Merle. *How Russia Is Ruled*, 1953.

Fischer, Louis. *The Soviets in World Affairs*, 1951.

Fisher, H. H. *The Communist Revolution: An Outline of Strategy and Tactics*, 1955.

Galenson, Walter. *Labor Productivity in Soviet and American Industry*, 1955.

Garthoff, R. L. *Soviet Strategy in the Nuclear Age*, 1958.

Goldwin, R. A., Gerald Stourzh, and Marvin Zetterbaum. *Readings in Russian Foreign Policy*, 1959.

Goodman, E. R. *The Soviet Design for a World State*, 1960.

Gruliow, Leo, ed. *Current Soviet Policies*, 1953.

———, ed. *Current Soviet Policies: II*, 1957.

Gurian, Waldemar. *Bolshevism: An Introduction to Soviet Communism*, 1952.

Haines, C. G., ed. *The Threat of Soviet Imperialism*, 1954.

Hardt, J. P., *et al*. *The Cold War Economic Gap*, 1961.

Hart, B. H. L., ed. *The Red Army*, 1956.

372 *Selected References*

Hazard, J. N. *The Soviet System of Government,* 1957.
Hunt, R. N. C. *The Theory and Practice of Communism,* 1957.
Huszar, G. B. de, *et al. Soviet Power and Policy,* 1955.
Inkeles, Alex. *Public Opinion in Soviet Russia,* 1950.
Jasny, Naum. *The Soviet Economy during the Plan Era,* 1951.
Kovner, Milton. *The Challenge of Coexistence: A Study of Soviet Economic Diplomacy,* 1961.
Kulski, W. W. *The Soviet Regime: Communism in Practice,* 1954.
Lee, Asher, ed. *The Soviet Air Force,* 1961.
Leites, Nathan. *A Study of Bolshevism,* 1953.
Moore, Barrington. *Soviet Politics: The Dilemma of Power,* 1950.
Nogee, J. L. *Soviet Policy toward International Control of Atomic Energy,* 1961.
North, R. C. *Moscow and Chinese Communists,* 1953.
Nove, Alec. *The Soviet Economy,* 1961.
Nutter, G. W. *The Growth of Industrial Production in the Soviet Union,* 1962.
Possony, S. T. *A Century of Conflict; Communist Techniques of World Revolution,* 1953.
Roberts, H. L. *Russia and America,* 1956.
Russian Institute, eds. *The Anti-Stalin Campaign and International Communism,* 1957.
Schwartz, Harry. *Russia's Soviet Economy,* 1950.
Schwarz, S. M. *Labor in the Soviet Union,* 1952.
Scott, D. J. R. *Russian Political Institutions,* 1961.
Selznick, Philip. *The Organizational Weapon: A Study of Bolshevik Strategy and Tactics,* 1952.
Seton-Watson, Hugh. *From Lenin to Malenkov: The History of World Communism,* 1954.
Shimkin, D. B. *Minerals: A Key to Soviet Power,* 1953.
Simmons, E. J., ed. *Continuity and Change in Russian and Soviet Thought,* 1955.
Smal-Stocki, Roman. *The National Problem of the Soviet Union and Russian Communist Imperialism,* 1952.
Stupp, J. I., ed. *Soviet Russia Today,* 1957.
Towster, Julian. *Political Power in the USSR,* 1949.
Walsh, E. J. *Total Empire: The Roots and Progress of World Communism,* 1952.
Wolfe, B. D. *Communist Totalitarianism,* 1961.

15—The British Commonwealth of Nations

Allen, H. C. *Great Britain and the United States,* 1955.
Bell, P. W. *The Sterling Area in the Postwar World,* 1956.
Brady, Alexander. *Democracy in the Dominions,* 1947.
Brady, Robert. *Crisis in Britain,* 1950.

Bull, Hedley. *Britain in Western Europe: WEU and the Atlantic Alliance,* 1956.

Bullard, Reader. *Britain and the Middle East,* 1951.

Cole, G. D. H., and Raymond Postgate. *The Post-War Condition of Britain,* 1957.

Crisp, L. F. *The Parliamentary Government of the Commonwealth of Australia,* 1961.

Deutsch, J. J., et al., eds. *The Canadian Economy,* 1961.

Franks, Oliver. *Britain and the Tide of World Affairs,* 1955.

Gardner, R. N. *Sterling-Dollar Diplomacy,* 1956.

Glazerbrook, G. P. de T. *A History of Canadian External Relations,* 1951.

Jennings, W. I. *Problems of the New Coammonwealth,* 1958.

Keenleyside, H. L., et al. *The Growth of Canadian Policies in External Affairs,* 1960.

Knaplund, Paul. *Britain, Commonwealth and Empire, 1901–1955,* 1956.

McKittrick, T. E. M. *Conditions of British Foreign Policy,* 1951.

Marshall, Geoffrey. *Parliamentary Sovereignty and the Commonwealth,* 1957.

Plant, G. F. *Oversea Settlement: Migration from the United Kingdom to the Dominions,* 1951.

Roberts, Henry, and H. G. Wilson. *Britain and the United States: Problems in Cooperation,* 1953.

Somervell, D. C., and Heather Harvey. *The British Empire and Commonwealth,* 1954.

Soward, F. H. *The Changing Commonwealth,* 1950.

Thomas, I. B. *The Socialist Tragedy,* 1951.

Tunstall, W. C. B. *The Commonwealth and Regional Defence,* 1959.

16—Western Europe

Aron, Raymond, and David Lerner, eds. *France Defeats EDC: Studies in an International Controversy,* 1956.

Bathurst, M. E., and J. L. Simpson. *Germany and the North Atlantic Community,* 1956.

Dewhurst, J. F., et al. *Europe's Needs and Resources,* 1961.

Einaudi, Mario, et al. *Communism in Western Europe,* 1951.

Freund, Gerald. *Germany between Two Worlds,* 1961.

Friis, Henning, ed. *Scandinavia: Between East and West,* 1950.

Furniss, E. S. *Weaknesses in French Foreign Policy-making,* 1954.

Godfrey, E. D. *The Government of France,* 1961.

Goguel, François. *France under the Fourth Republic,* 1952.

Grindrod, Muriel. *The Rebuilding of Italy,* 1955.

Grosser, Alfred. *The Colossus Again: Western Germany from Defeat to Rearmament,* 1955.

Hinterhoff, Eugène. *Disengagement,* 1959.

Horne, Alistair. *Return to Power: A Report on the New Germany,* 1956.

Laponce, J. A. *The Government of the Fifth Republic,* 1961.

Liddell Hart, B. H. *Deterrent or Defense,* 1960.

Luethy, Herbert. *France against Herself,* 1955.

Matthews, Ronald. *The Death of the Fourth Republic,* 1955.

Meade, E. M., ed. *Modern France: Problems of the Third and Fourth Republics,* 1951.

Morgenthau, H. J., ed. *Germany and the Future of Europe,* 1951.

Pickles, Dorothy. *The Fifth French Republic,* 1960.

——. *The Fourth Republic,* 1955.

Scott, F. D. *The United States and Scandinavia,* 1950.

Wallich, H. C. *Mainsprings of the German Revival,* 1955.

Werth, Alexander. *France, 1940–1955,* 1956.

Whitaker, A. P. *Spain and the Defense of the West,* 1961.

Williams, Philip. *Politics in Post-War France,* 1954.

——, and Martin Harrison. *De Gaulle's Republic,* 1961.

17—Eastern Europe

Armstrong, H. F. *Tito and Goliath,* 1951.

Black, C. E., ed. *Challenge in Eastern Europe,* 1954.

Brzezinski, Z. K. *The Soviet Bloc: Unity and Conflict,* 1960.

Cretzianu, Alexandre, ed. *Captive Rumania: A Decade of Soviet Rule,* 1956.

Dedijer, Vladimir. *Tito,* 1953.

Djilas, Milovan. *The New Class: An Analysis of the Communist System,* 1957.

Dragnich, A. N. *Tito's Promised Land,* 1954.

Gluckstein, Ygael. *Stalin's Satellites in Europe,* 1952.

Herling, A. K. *The Soviet Slave Empire,* 1951.

Kertesz, S. D., ed. *The Fate of East Central Europe,* 1956.

Kolarz, Walter. *Russia and Her Colonies,* 1953.

Lasky, M. J., ed. *The Hungarian Revolution: The Story of the October Uprising,* 1957.

Lukacs, J. A. *The Great Powers and Eastern Europe,* 1953.

Mazour, A. G. *Finland between East and West,* 1956.

Milosz, Czeslaw. *The Captive Mind,* 1953.

Ripka, Hubert. *Czechoslovakia Enslaved: The Story of the Communist Coup d'État,* 1951.

——. *Eastern Europe in the Postwar World,* 1961.

Roberts, Henry L. *Rumania,* 1951.

Seton-Watson, Hugh. *The East European Revolution,* 1961.

Shepherd, Gordon. *Russia's Danubian Empire,* 1954.

Taborsky, Edward. *Communism in Czechoslovakia, 1948–1960,* 1961.

Wolfe, R. L. *The Balkans in Our Time,* 1956.

Zinner, P. E., ed. *National Communism and Popular Revolt in Eastern Europe,* 1956.

18—Communist China

Adler, Solomon. *The Chinese Economy*, 1957.

Barnett, A. D. *Communist China and Asia: Challenge to American Policy*, 1960.

Chandra-Sekhar, Sripati. *Communist China Today*, 1961.

Cressey, G. B. *Land of the 500 Million: A Geography of China*, 1955.

Fitzgerald, C. P. *Revolution in China*, 1952.

Hudson, G. F., *et al.*, eds. *The Sino-Soviet Dispute*, 1961.

Isaacs, H. R. *Tragedy of the Chinese Revolution*, 1952.

Kahin, G. M., ed. *Major Governments of Asia*, 1958.

Kennedy, Malcolm. *A History of Communism in East Asia*, 1957.

Kirby, E. S., ed. *Contemporary China, 1959–1960*, 1961.

Levi, Werner. *Modern China's Foreign Policy*, 1953.

Lindsay, Michael. *China and the Cold War*, 1955.

MacNair, H. F., and Donald Lach. *Modern Far Eastern International Relations*, 1955.

North, R. C. *Kuomintang and Communist Chinese Elites*, 1952.

Rostow, W. W., *et al. The Prospects for Communist China*, 1954.

Schwartz, B. I. *Chinese Communism and the Rise of Mao*, 1951.

Tang, Peter S. H. *Communist China Today: Domestic and Foreign Policies*, 1956.

Walker, R. L. *China under Communism: The First Five Years*, 1955.

Wei, Henry. *China and Soviet Russia*, 1956.

Wittfogel, K. A. *Oriental Despotism: A Comparative Study of Total Power*, 1957.

Wu Yuan-li. *An Economic Survey of Communist China*, 1956.

19—Japan, South Korea, and Nationalist China

Ball, W. M. *Nationalism and Communism in East Asia*, 1956.

Bisson, T. A. *Zaibatsu Dissolution in Japan*, 1955.

Borton, Hugh. *Japan's Modern Century*, 1955.

Brown, D. M. *Nationalism in Japan: An Introductory Historical Analysis*, 1955.

Burks, A. W. *The Government of Japan*, 1961.

Buss, C. A. *The Far East*, 1955.

Ike, Nobutaka. *Japanese Politics: An Introductory Survey*, 1957.

Linebarger, P. M. A., Djang Chu, and A. W. Burks. *Far Eastern Governments and Politics: China and Japan*, 1956.

Mendel, D. H. *The Japanese People and Foreign Policy*, 1961.

Quigley, H. S., and J. E. Turner. *The New Japan: Government and Politics*, 1956.

Sansom, George. *The Western World and Japan*, 1950.

20—South and Southeast Asia

Bauer, P. T. *Indian Economic Policy and Development,* 1961.

Boeke, J. H. *Economic and Economic Policy of Dual Societies as Exemplified by Indonesia,* 1953.

Brecher, Michael. *The Struggle for Kashmir,* 1953.

Brown, Norman, ed. *India, Pakistan, and Ceylon,* 1951.

Davis, Kingsley. *The Population of India and Pakistan,* 1951.

Emerson, Rupert. *Representative Government in Southeast Asia,* 1955.

Golay, F. H. *The Philippines: Public Policy and National Economic Development,* 1961.

Hall, D. G. E. *A History of South-East Asia,* 1955.

Hammer, E. J. *The Struggle for Indochina,* 1954.

Higgins, B. H. *Indonesia's Economic Stabilization and Development,* 1957.

Jennings, W. I. *Constitutional Problems in Pakistan,* 1957.

Kahin, G. M. *Nationalism and Revolution in Indonesia,* 1952.

King, J. K. *Southeast Asia in Perspective,* 1956.

Korbel, Josef. *Danger in Kashmir,* 1954.

Kundra, J. C. *Indian Foreign Policy 1947–1954,* 1955.

Levi, Werner. *Free India in Asia,* 1952.

Low, Francis. *Struggle for Asia,* 1956.

Mende, Tibor. *South-East Asia between Two Worlds,* 1955.

Panikkar, K. M. *Asia and Western Dominance,* 1954.

Schiller, A. A. *The Formation of Federal Indonesia, 1945–1949,* 1955.

Spear, Percival. *India, Pakistan, and the West,* 1953.

Thayer, P. W. *Southeast Asia in the Coming World,* 1955.

Vandenbosch, Amry, and R. A. Butwell. *Southeast Asia among the World Powers,* 1957.

Wertheim, W. F. *Indonesian Society in Transition,* 1956.

Woodman, Dorothy. *The Republic of Indonesia,* 1956.

Woytinsky, W. S. *India: The Awakening Giant,* 1957.

21—The Middle East and Africa South of the Sahara

a. The Middle East

Anshen, R. N., ed. *Mid-East: World Center,* 1956.

Campbell, J. C. *Defense of the Middle East: Problems of American Policy,* 1960.

Cooke, H. V. *Challenge and Response in the Middle East,* 1952.

Eytan, Walter. *The First Ten Years: A Diplomatic History of Israel,* 1958.

Fisher, C. A., and Fred Krinsky. *Middle East in Crisis: Historical and Documentary Review,* 1959.

Fisher, S. N., ed. *Social Forces in the Middle East,* 1955.

Fisher, W. B. *The Middle East,* 1961.

Gibb, H. A. R., and Harold Bowen. *Islamic Society and the West,* 1950.

Gillespie, John. *Algeria: Rebellion and Revolution,* 1960.

Hollingsworth, Claire. *The Arabs and the West,* 1952.

Hoskins, H. L. *The Middle East: Problem Area in World Politics,* 1954.

Hurewitz, J. C. *The Struggle for Palestine,* 1950.

Izzeddin, Nejla. *The Arab World,* 1953.

Kerekes, Tibor, ed. *The Arab Middle East and Muslim Africa,* 1961.

Kimche, Jon. *Seven Fallen Pillars,* 1953.

Kirk, G. E. *Contemporary Arab Politics: A Concise History,* 1961.

Landau, Rom. *Moroccan Drama, 1900–1955,* 1956.

Laqueur, W. Z. *Communism and Nationalism in the Middle East,* 1956.

Lenczowski, George. *The Middle East in World Affairs,* 1956.

Sanger, R. H. *The Arabian Peninsula,* 1956.

Shwadran, Benjamin. *The Middle East, Oil, and the Great Powers,* 1955.

Spiro, M. E. *Kibbutz: Venture in Utopia,* 1956.

Thayer, P. W., ed. *Tensions in the Middle East,* 1958.

Villard, H. S. *Libya: The New Arab Kingdom of North Africa,* 1956.

Warriner, Doreen. *Land Reform and Development in the Middle East: A Study of Egypt, Syria, and Iraq,* 1957.

b. Africa South of the Sahara

American Assembly. *The United States and Africa,* 1958.

Apter, David. *The Gold Coast in Transition,* 1955.

Bartlett, Vernon. *Struggle for Africa,* 1953.

Carter, G. M. *The Politics of Inequality: South Africa since 1948,* 1958.

Davidson, Basil. *The African Awakening,* 1955.

Haines, C. G., ed. *Africa Today,* 1955.

Hance, W. A. *African Economic Development,* 1958.

Hatch, J. C. *Africa Today—and Tomorrow: An Outline of Basic Facts and Major Problems,* 1960.

———. *The Dilemma of South Africa,* 1952.

Kimble, G. H. T. *Tropical Africa,* 1960.

Marquard, Leo. *The Peoples and Policies of South Africa,* 1952.

Oakes, J. B. *The Edge of Freedom,* 1961.

Robertson, H. M. *South Africa: Economic and Political Aspects,* 1957.

Spiro, Herbert J. *Politics in Africa: Prospects South of the Sahara,* 1962.

Stamp, L. D. *Africa: A Study in Tropical Development,* 1953.

Stillman, C. W., ed. *Africa in the Modern World,* 1955.

Wallbank, T. W. *Contemporary Africa,* 1956.

Welsh, Anne, ed. *Africa South of the Sahara: An Assessment of Human and Material Resources,* 1951.

22—Latin America

Adams, R. N., *et al. Social Change in Latin America Today: Its Implications for United States Policy,* 1960.

Alexander, R. J. *Communism in Latin America,* 1957.

Arciniegas, Germán. *The State of Latin America,* 1952.

Benham, Frederic, and H. A. Holley. *A Short Introduction to the Economy of Latin America,* 1960.

Blanksten, G. F. *Ecuador,* 1951.

Butland, G. J. *Chile,* 1952.

Daniels, W. M., ed. *Latin America in the Cold War,* 1952.

Gomez, R. A. *Government and Politics in Latin America,* 1960.

Houston, J. A. *Latin America in the United Nations,* 1956.

Jorrin, Miguel. *Governments of Latin America,* 1953.

Keen, Benjamin, ed. *Readings in Latin-American Civilization,* 1955.

Lieuwen, Edwin. *Arms and Politics in Latin America,* 1962.

MacDonald, A. F. *Latin American Politics and Government,* 1954.

Perkins, Dexter. *The United States and Latin America,* 1961.

Smith, T. Lynn. *Brazil,* 1956.

Stuart, Graham H. *Latin America and the United States,* 1956.

Wilgus, A. C. *The Caribbean: Peoples, Problems, and Prospects,* 1952.

23—The Elements of International Law
24—Applications of International Law

Acheson, D. G. *Meetings at the Summit: A Study of Diplomatic Method,* 1958.

Bishop, W. W. *International Law, Cases and Materials,* 1962.

Brierly, J. L. *The Law of Nations,* 1949.

Briggs, H. W. *The Law of Nations,* 1952.

Burdett, F. L., ed. *Conduct of American Diplomacy,* 1951.

Butterfield, Herbert. *Christianity, Diplomacy, and War,* 1954.

Chen, T. C. *The International Law of Recognition,* 1951.

Corbett, P. E. *Law and Society in the Relations of States,* 1951.

———. *Morals, Law and Power in International Relations,* 1956.

———. *The Study of International Law,* 1955.

De Visscher, Charles. *Theory and Reality in Public International Law,* 1957.

Dickinson, E. D. *Law and Peace,* 1951.

Garcia-Mora, M. R. *International Law and Asylum as a Human Right,* 1956.

Green, L. C. *International Law through the Cases,* 1951.

Greenspan, Morris. *The Modern Law of Land Warfare,* 1960.

Huddleston, Sisley. *Popular Diplomacy and War,* 1954.

Jackson, Elmore. *Meeting of Minds: A Blueprint for Peace through Mediation,* 1952.

Jessup, P. C. *Transnational Law,* 1956.

Jouvenel, Bertrand de. *Sovereignty: An Inquiry into the Political Good,* 1957.

Kaplan, M. A., and N. D. Katzenbach. *The Political Foundations of International Law,* 1961.

Kelsen, Hans. *Principles of International Law,* 1952.

Falk
Lissitzyn

Kertesz, S. D., and M. A. Fitzsimons, eds. *Diplomacy in a Changing World,* 1959.

Lauterpacht, Hersch. *International Law and Human Rights,* 1950.

Liska, George. *International Equilibrium: A Theoretical Essay on the Politics and Organization of Security,* 1957.

Lissitzyn, O. J. *The International Court of Justice,* 1951.

Marek, Krystyna. *Identity and Continuity of States in Public International Law,* 1954.

Morgenthau, H. J. *In Defense of the National Interest,* 1951.

Nicolson, Harold. *Diplomacy,* 1950.

———. *The Evolution of Diplomatic Method,* 1954.

O'Connell, D. P. *The Law of State Succession,* 1956.

Oppenheim, L. F. L. *International Law,* 1952–55.

Panikkar, K. M. *The Principles and Practice of Diplomacy,* 1952.

Pearson, L. B. *Diplomacy in the Nuclear Age,* 1959.

Plischke, Elmer. *Conduct of American Diplomacy,* 1961.

Pompe, C. A. *Aggressive War, an International Crime,* 1953.

Schiffer, Walter. *The Legal Community of Mankind,* 1954.

Schwarzenberger, Georg. *Manual of International Law,* 1952.

Stone, Julius. *Legal Controls of International Conflict,* 1954.

Stuart, Graham H. *American Diplomatic and Consular Practice,* 1952.

Svarlien, Oscar. *An Introduction to the Law of Nations,* 1955.

Thomas, Ann V. W. *Communism versus International Law: Today's Clash of Ideals,* 1953.

———, and A. J. Thomas, Jr. *Non-Intervention,* 1956.

Vagts, Alfred. *Defense and Diplomacy: The Soldier and the Conduct of Foreign Relations,* 1956.

Verplaetse, J. G. *International Law in Vertical Space: Air, Outer Space, Ether,* 1961.

Webster, Charles. *The Art and Practice of Diplomacy,* 1952.

Weis, Paul. *Nationality and Statelessness in International Law,* 1956.

Wilson, Robert R. *International Law Standard in Treaties of the United States,* 1955.

Wright, Quincy. *Contemporary International Law: A Balance Sheet,* 1955.

———. *International Law and the United Nations,* 1961.

———. *Problems of Stability and Progress in International Relations,* 1954.

———. *The Role of International Law in the Elimination of War,* 1962.

25—*Nuclear Power, Missiles, and Disarmament*

Bechhoefer, B. G. *Postwar Negotiations for Arms Control,* 1961.

Biorklund, Elis. *Atomic Policies, 1945–1954,* 1955.

Blackett, P. M. S. *Atomic Weapons and East-West Relations,* 1956.

Brennan, D. G., ed. *Arms Control, Disarmament, and National Security,* 1961.

Bull, Hedley. *The Control of the Arms Race,* 1961.

Clarke, A. C. *The Exploration of Space,* 1952.

Claude, I. L., Jr. *Swords into Plowshares,* 1956.

Compton, A. H. *Atomic Quest,* 1956.

Dean, Gordon. *Report on the Atom,* 1957.

Isard, Walter, and Vincent Whitney. *Atomic Power,* 1955.

Kahn, Herman. *On Thermonuclear War,* 1961.

Kissinger, H. A. *Nuclear Weapons and Foreign Policy,* 1957.

Leyson, B. W. *Atomic Energy in War and Peace,* 1951.

McClelland, C. A. *Nuclear Weapons, Missiles, and Future War: Problem for the Sixties,* 1960.

Mann, Martin. *Peacetime Uses of Atomic Energy,* 1961.

Marshack, Alexander. *The World in Space: The Story of the International Geophysical Year,* 1958.

Mezerik, A. G. *Disarmament: Impact on Underdeveloped Countries,* 1961.

Miksche, F. O. *Atomic Weapons and Armies,* 1955.

Oberth, Hermann. *Man into Space: New Projects for Rockets and Space Travel,* 1957.

Parson, N. A., Jr. *Guided Missiles in War and Peace,* 1956.

Preston, R. A., *et al. Men in Arms,* 1956.

Schelling, T. C., and M. H. Halperin. *Strategy and Arms Control,* 1961.

Shepley, J. R., and Clay Blair, Jr. *The Hydrogen Bomb,* 1954.

Strausz-Hupé, Robert, ed. *Air Power in the Nuclear Age,* 1956.

Turner, G. B., and R. D. Challener, eds. *National Security in the Nuclear Age,* 1960.

US Atomic Energy Commission. *The Effects of Nuclear Weapons,* 1957.

Woodbury, D. O. *Atoms for Peace,* 1955.

Wright, Quincy. *A Study of War,* 1942.

26—Population Increases and Economic Development

Aitken, H. G., ed. *The State and Economic Growth,* 1959.

Asher, R. E. *Grants, Loans, and Local Currencies: Their Role in Foreign Aid,* 1961.

Belshaw, Horace. *Population Growth and Levels of Consumption,* 1956.

Black, E. R. *The Diplomacy of Economic Development,* 1960.

Braibanti, Ralph, and J. S. Spengler, eds. *Traditions, Values, and Socio-Economic Development,* 1961.

Brown, Harrison. *The Challenge of Man's Future,* 1954.

Buchanan, N. S., and H. S. Ellis. *Approaches to Economic Development,* 1955.

Carey, J. N. *The Pattern of a Dependent Economy,* 1953.

Chandra-Sekhar, Sripati. *Hungry People and Empty Lands,* 1952.

Clark, Colin. *The Conditions of Economic Progress,* 1951.

Cook, R. C. *Human Fertility: The Modern Dilemma,* 1951.

De Castro, Josue. *The Geography of Hunger,* 1952.

Diebold, William. *Trade and Payments in Western Europe,* 1952.
Frankel, H. S. *The Economic Impact on Underdeveloped Societies,* 1953.
Froehlich, Walter, ed. *Land Tenure, Industrialization, and Social Stability,* 1961.
Hatt, P. K., ed. *World Population and Future Resources,* 1952.
Hertzler, J. C. *The Crisis in World Population,* 1956.
Hoselitz, B. F., ed. *The Advancement of Underdeveloped Areas,* 1952.
Krause, Walter. *Economic Development: The Underdeveloped World and the American Interest,* 1961.
Kuznets, Simon, *et al. Economic Growth: Brazil, India, Japan,* 1955.
Lorimer, Frank, *et al. Culture and Human Fertility,* 1954.
Mead, Margaret, ed. *Cultural Patterns and Technical Change,* 1953.
Meade, J. E. *Trade and Welfare,* 1955.
Millikan, Max F., and W. W. Rostow. *A Proposal: Key to an Effective Foreign Policy,* 1957.
Nurkse, Ragnar. *Problems of Capital Formation in Underdeveloped Countries,* 1953.
Pentony, D. E., ed. *United States Foreign Aid: Readings in the Problem Area of Wealth,* 1960.
Pepelasis, Adamantios, *et al. Economic Development: Analysis and Case Studies,* 1961.
Piquet, H. S. *Aid, Trade, and the Tariff,* 1953.
Putnam, Palmer. *Energy in the Future,* 1953.
Rostow, W. W. *The Stages of Economic Growth,* 1960.
Russell, E. John. *World Population and World Food Supplies,* 1955.
Sharp, W. R. *International Technical Assistance,* 1952.
Shimm, M. G., ed. *Population Control: The Imminent World Crisis,* 1961.
Singh, Baljit. *Federal Finance and Underdeveloped Economy,* 1952.
Spengler, J. S., ed. *National Resources and Economic Growth,* 1961.
Staley, Eugene. *The Future of Underdeveloped Countries,* 1954.
Thompson, Warren S. *Population Problems,* 1953.
Viner, Jacob. *International Trade and Economic Development,* 1952.
Wiggins, J. W., and Helmut Schoek, eds. *Foreign Aid Re-examined: A Critical Appraisal,* 1958.
Williamson, H. F., and J. A. Buttrick, eds. *Economic Development: Principles and Patterns,* 1954.
Woytinsky, W. S., and E. S. Woytinsky. *World Population and Production,* 1953.
Zimmermann, E. W. *World Resources and Industries,* 1951.

27—Psychological Forces and Propaganda

Allport, G. W. *The Nature of Prejudice,* 1954.
Buchanan, William, and Hadley Cantril. *How Nations See Each Other,* 1953.
Cantril, Hadley, ed. *Tensions That Cause Wars,* 1950.

Claude, I. L., Jr. *National Minorities: An International Problem,* 1955.

Deutsch, K. W. *Nationalism and Social Communication,* 1953.

Dovring, Karin. *Road of Propaganda: The Semantics of Biased Communication,* 1959.

Dunn, F. S. *War and the Minds of Men,* 1950.

Holt, R. T. *Radio Free Europe,* 1958.

Irion, F. C. *Public Opinion and Propaganda,* 1950.

Janis, I. L. *Air War and Emotional Stress,* 1951.

Klineberg, Otto. *Social Psychology,* 1954.

————. *Tensions Affecting International Understanding,* 1950.

Kohn, Hans. *Nationalism: Its Meaning and History,* 1955.

Lerner, Daniel, ed. *Propaganda in War and Crisis,* 1951.

Pear, T. H., ed. *Psychological Factors in Peace and War,* 1950.

Sargent, William. *Battle for the Mind,* 1957.

Shafer, B. C. *Nationalism: Myth and Reality,* 1955.

Snyder, L. L. *The Meaning of Nationalism,* 1954.

Stanton, A. H., and S. E. Perry. *Personality and Political Crisis,* 1951.

West, Ranyard. *Conscience and Society,* 1951.

Whitaker, U. G., Jr., ed. *Nationalism and International Progress,* 1960.

————, ed. *Propaganda and International Relations,* 1960.

Znaniecki, Florian. *Modern Nationalities: A Sociological Study,* 1952.

28—Regionalism

Allen, James J. *The European Common Market and the GATT,* 1960.

Canyes, M. S. *The Organization of American States and the United Nations,* 1955.

Florinsky, Michael. *Integrated Europe?* 1955.

Haines, C. G., ed. *European Integration,* 1957.

Kiser, Margaret. *Organization of American States,* 1955.

Lindsay, Kenneth. *European Assemblies: The Experimental Period 1949–1959,* 1960.

McLachlan, Donald. *Atlantic Alliance,* 1952.

Madariaga, Salvador de. *Portrait of Europe,* 1953.

Mason, H. L. *The European Coal and Steel Community,* 1955.

Robertson, A. H. *The Council of Europe,* 1956.

Sannwald, Rolf, and Jacques Stohler. *Economic Integration: Theoretical Assumptions and Consequences of European Unification,* 1959.

Viner, Jacob. *The Customs Union Issue,* 1950.

Warne, J. D. *NATO and Its Prospects,* 1954.

29—Contemporary International Organizations

Alexandrowicz, C. H. *International Economic Organizations,* 1953.

Ascher, C. S. *Program-making in UNESCO, 1946–1951,* 1951.

Asher, R. E., W. M. Kotschnig, and W. A. Brown, Jr. *The United Nations and Economic and Social Cooperation,* 1957.

Beckel, Graham. *Workshops for the World: The Specialized Agencies of the United Nations,* 1954.

Bentwich, Norman, and Andrew Martin. *A Commentary on the Charter of the United Nations,* 1950.

Besterman, Theodore. *UNESCO: Peace in the Minds of Men,* 1951.

Bloomfield, L. P. *Evolution or Revolution: The United Nations and the Problem of Peaceful Territorial Change,* 1957.

Brown, B. H., and J. E. Johnson. *The U.S. and the U.N.,* 1954.

Bryson, Lyman, *et al. Foundations of World Organization: A Political and Cultural Approach,* 1952.

Charmian, C. E. *The Trusteeship System in the United Nations,* 1956.

Chase, E. P. *The United Nations in Action,* 1951.

Cheever, D. S., and H. F. Haviland, Jr. *Organizing for Peace,* 1954.

Chowdhuri, R. N. *International Mandates and Trusteeship Systems,* 1955.

Claude, I. L., Jr. *The United Nations and the Use of Force,* 1961.

Codding, George. *The International Telecommunication Union,* 1952.

Eagleton, Clyde. *International Government,* 1957.

Feller, A. H. *United Nations and World Community,* 1952.

Goodrich, L. M., and A. P. Simons. *The United Nations and the Maintenance of International Peace and Security,* 1955.

Green, J. F. *The United Nations and Human Rights,* 1956.

Hambidge, Gove. *The Story of FAO,* 1955.

Haviland, H. F., Jr. *The Political Role of the General Assembly,* 1951.

Hill, Norman. *International Organization,* 1952.

Hogan, W. N. *International Conflict and Collective Security,* 1955.

Hovet, Thomas, Jr. *Bloc Politics in the United Nations,* 1960.

Jiménez de Arechaga, Eduardo, Jr. *Voting and the Handling of Disputes in Security Council,* 1951.

Keeny, S. M. *Half the World's Children,* 1957.

Leonard, L. L. *International Organization,* 1951.

McClelland, C. A. *The United Nations: The Continuing Debate,* 1960.

MacLaurin, John. *The United Nations and Power Politics,* 1951.

Mangone, G. J. *The Idea and Practice of World Government,* 1951.

———. *A Short History of International Organization,* 1954.

Martin, Andrew. *Collective Security: A Progress Report,* 1952.

Mortimer, Molly. *Trusteeship in Practice,* 1951.

Northrop, F. S. C. *The Taming of the Nations,* 1953.

Potter, P. B. *An Introduction to the Study of International Organization,* 1951.

Riggs, R. E. *Politics in the United Nations: A Study of United States Influence in the General Assembly,* 1958.

Ross, Alf. *The Constitution of the United Nations,* 1950.

Sayre, W. S. *The United Nations Secretariat,* 1950.

Schwebel, S. M. *The Secretary-General of the United Nations,* 1952.

Sohn, L. B., ed. *Basic Documents of the United Nations,* 1956.

Taylor, A. M. *Indonesian Independence and the United Nations,* 1960.

Tew, Brian. *International Monetary Cooperation, 1945–52,* 1952.

Vandenbosch, Amry, and W. N. Hogan. *The United Nations: Background, Organization, Functions, Activities,* 1952.

Watkins, J. T., and J. W. Robinson, eds. *General International Organization,* 1956.

Watts, J. O. *The United Nations: Planned Tyranny,* 1955.

White, Lyman. *International Non-governmental Organizations: Their Purposes, Methods, and Accomplishments,* 1951.

Wightman, David. *Economic Co-operation in Europe,* 1956.

Wilcox, F. O., and C. M. Marcy. *Proposals for Changes in the United Nations,* 1956.

INDEX

In this Index the numerals in bold-face type designate detailed discussions. Where the subject is a country, the discussion generally includes some or all of the following matters: number and traits of the population, territorial extent, natural resources, technology, foreign trade, governmental structure, and foreign policy. The other numerals designate shorter discussions or brief references.